# Secrets of
# Software Quality

## Other McGraw-Hill Books of Interest

# Secrets of Software Quality

### 40 Innovations from IBM

**Craig Kaplan**

**Ralph Clark**

**Victor Tang**

**McGraw-Hill, Inc.**

New York   San Francisco   Washington, D.C.   Auckland   Bogotá
Caracas   Lisbon   London   Madrid   Mexico City   Milan
Montreal   New Delhi   San Juan   Singapore
Sydney   Tokyo   Toronto

**Library of Congress Cataloging-in-Publication Data**

Kaplan, Craig.
   Secrets of software quality : 40 innovations from IBM / by
Craig Kaplan, Ralph Clark, Victor Tang.
      p.    cm.
   Includes index.
   ISBN 0-07-911795-3
   1. Computer software—Quality control.  I. Clark, Ralph.
II. Tang, Victor.  III. Title.
QA76.76.Q35K36  1994
005.1'068'5—dc20                      94-10476
                                         CIP

1 2 3 4 5 6 7 8 9 0  DOC/DOC  9 0 9 8 7 6 5 4

ISBN 0-07-911795-3

*The sponsoring editor for this book was Marjorie Spencer, the editing supervisor was Ruth W. Mannino, and the production supervisor was Pamela Pelton. It was set in Century Schoolbook by McGraw-Hill's Professional Book Group composition unit.*

*Printed and bound by R. R. Donnelley & Sons Company.*

*To the highly innovative people at IBM Santa Teresa, whose efforts to improve quality made this book possible.*

# Contents

# Preface

This book contains 40 innovations that helped one of IBM's software development labs achieve unprecedented improvement in the quality of its software and development processes. When we began our quality improvement journey in 1989, our lab was the largest software development site in the world. In fact, our single lab produced more revenue than all but one independent software company. Our products were of high quality and already had fewer defects than the industry average. Yet, after implementing the innovations described in this book, the average number of defects in our key products dropped 46%. At the same time, service costs dropped 20%, revenue per employee rose 58%, and customer satisfaction increased 14%. More impressively, these improvements occurred at a time when IBM as a whole was suffering losses.

Finally, as we go to press, it has just been announced that our lab has been awarded the gold medal for excellence—IBM's highest and most prestigious quality award. The award, which is modeled after the Malcolm Baldrige National Quality Award, and which uses Baldrige examiners, has three levels of achievement: bronze, silver, and gold. Every year many labs enter the competition, but only a fraction make it even to the bronze level of achievement. Our lab is the first within IBM to have worked its way up through bronze and silver to reach the gold medal.

We believe that our lab's positive results are largely the result of technical and management innovation. The 40 innovations contained in this book represent a small fraction of the many efforts by members of our laboratory to improve the quality of our software products and development processes. We have tried to include the lab's most effective innovations as well as some that proved less successful, but that were important for the lessons they taught us.

Most of our innovations are well-suited to small organizations since they were developed originally by small teams of programmers. Our primary goal has been to make it easy for others to understand and apply the innovations to their own organizations. For each innovation, we have included implementation advice as well as many figures and tables. The annotated Selected Readings at the end of the chapters point to sources of additional information.

Throughout, we treat all our topics in an action-oriented manner. For example, we show how to tailor the sometimes obscure quality criteria of the

Malcolm Baldrige National Quality Award template and ISO 9000 to the field of software development. Although the authors have Baldrige Award–winning expertise, our focus is not on how to win awards but on how to put these criteria to work in an organization.

The content and organization of the book reflect our belief that quality improves most rapidly when technological innovation is tightly coupled with innovations in process and in leadership. Together, technology, process, and leadership form an iron triangle that spearheads rapid quality improvement. The iron triangle approach has led us to include three types of innovations aimed at improving technology, processes, and leadership.

Software developers may want to concentrate first on the technology and process innovations—especially those occurring later in the book. There we describe new technologies such as the computer-supported team work spaces that have revolutionized the way we develop software and hold meetings.

Managers, CIOs, and students of Total Quality Management may find the leadership sections most interesting. There we tell the story of our lab's 4-year quality transformation and of the management inventions that made it possible. Some of these innovations, such as the Excellence Council which measured every group in the lab by the Baldrige criteria, were immensely controversial, yet played a critical role in transforming the lab's culture.

We encourage all readers to read the sections outside their normal areas of expertise for context. We also recommend reading the introduction first. It provides a brief overview not only of the 40 innovations but also of a four-stage quality maturity framework that describes when each innovation is most likely to be useful.

The last chapter provides specific advice, and a systematic approach, that organizations can use to identify a set of innovations that matches their needs. The appendix and computer disk offer three quick and easy ways to perform a Baldrige-style assessment of your software organization.

Finally, we feel this book is unique in an area that is flooded with the advice of quality gurus and academic theories. We have consulted with the best minds we could find at the business schools of Harvard, MIT, Stanford, and others, yet this book remains grounded firmly in reality. All the techniques that we describe have been used or prototyped at IBM's largest software lab. There are lots of quality gurus out there who will give you advice. But they usually don't have to live with the results. We have had to live with our failures as well as our successes.

We believe that managers, software professionals, executives, and students will find our experiences helpful. We hope they will continue to innovate where we left off.

*Craig Kaplan*
*Ralph Clark*
*Victor Tang*

# Acknowledgments

A book, like quality improvement itself, is a team effort. The collaboration of the authors is really only the tip of a pyramid that is built on many people's knowledge and dedicated efforts.

Tom Furey heads the list of people to whom we owe a debt of gratitude. When Tom came to IBM Santa Teresa in 1989 from Baldrige Award–winning IBM Rochester, he brought with him a vision of the World Class laboratory that IBM Santa Teresa could become. Through ceaseless efforts to communicate that vision, through one-on-one coaching sessions, and through staunch support of innovation and quality improvement efforts, Tom transformed the consciousness of the lab. He was not only the driving force behind Santa Teresa's quality transformation but also the inventor of many of the leadership innovations described in this book. We thank Tom for his visionary leadership and for his deep commitment to improving software quality through innovation.

We would also like to thank the general managers who continued to support quality improvement efforts after Tom Furey left Santa Teresa, Steve Mills and Chris Arnold.

While committed leadership from the General Manager's office was essential, ultimately it was the creativity and efforts of hundreds of individuals at all levels that got results. It is impossible here to acknowledge everyone who contributed by name, but we would like to thank the following individuals who were generous with their time and participated in interviews or supplied data to help document the innovations described in this book. The size of this list reflects the penetration of quality to every part of the lab, and the cross-functional effort necessary to achieve results.

Matt Anderson
Jim Archer
John Artim
Tom Ballenger
John Bergren
Sam Bhambani
Inderpal Bhandari
Larry Bjork
Jim Boyle
Nancee Branham
Brenda Brown
Bill Burr
Chris Byrne
Harry Campbell
Su-Jin Chan
Ram Chillarege
Ferd Choss
Cathy Christensen
Rich Clark
Millie Clarke
Deborah Cottingham
Gerry Crane
Pat Cronin
Jim D'anjou
Tho Dao
Mike Darnell
Gary Davidson
Ken Delavigne
Angela Di Giacomo
Michael Dockter
Keith Eckhardt
Frank Eldredge
Mike Enescu
Larry England
Irene Faivre
David Fallside
Justine Fenwick
Art Ferdinand
Mark Fischinger
Phil Foster
Brenda Fox
Marian Francisco
Jim Freeman
Julie Furey
Tom Guinane
Gene Haberman

Pete Hamm
Betty Harding
Gretchen Hargis
Marcia Hartrum
Bryce Hawkins
Lauri Henzlik
Madeleine Holland
Jeff Horton
Armen Hovanessian
John Hurd
Paul Hutchings
Barbara Isa
Susan Jamison
Steve Kauffman
Sue Keenan
Joan Keller
Andy Kendzie
Brian King
Kelly Kjelstrom
Marlin Knight
Bob Lara
Ed Lassettre
Jeff Lee
Herb Leeds
Cleo Lepori-Costello
Craig Lewis
Bob Lo
Peter Lue
Duvan Luong
Peter Mandel
Armine Matensian
Debbie Mayhew
Claire McFeely
Cherri McKinny
Vidmar
Betty McMicken
Barb McLane
Rosanne Mehelas
Pete Musitano
Mark Neiman
Arleen Niblett
Barb Nyby
Denis Orton
Mary Paquet
Michael Pauser
Pete Peterson

Mary Popp
Nancy Prince
Terry Ramirez
Doug Reed
Mike Rhoads
Steve Richer
John Robertson
Ben Rodgers
Rene Ruiz
Charles Sanders
Marlene Santilli
Joan Schwalbe
Larry Shapiro
Tom Sharkey
Shi-In Shirley
Elissa Smilowitz
Marilyn Smith
Rick Spohn
Herb Strandberg
Will Sutter
Craig Sutton
John Tauchi
Stan Taylor
Betty Thana
Terri Tonge
Helen Trollman
Dave Vandeveer
Dan Wardman
Evan Watkins
Val Watson
Colleen Welch
Tina Woodward
Lucy Worthington
Gerri Young
Marty Zwilling

A number of authors and organizations have been very generous in allowing us to reproduce figures and tables from their work. We would like to thank and acknowledge The IBM Corporation, McGraw-Hill, Oxford University Press, the National Institute of Standards and Technology, and the IEEE society. Special thanks are due to Roy Bauer at Competitive Dominance Strategies for allowing us to use his Baldrige Score Card methodology.

We would also like to thank those people outside of IBM who talked with us and provided useful perspectives on quality improvement, innovation, or organizational transformation. We appreciate the time and perspective contributed by John Anderson, Teresa Amable, Victor Basili, John Carroll, Tom Davenport, Pat Guinan, John J. Kao, Dorothy Leonard-Barton, Linda Levine, James March, Terrence McGillen, Vaughan Merlyn, Julia Mulanny, Nintin Nohria, Richard Nolan, Tim Olson, Bill Pollack, Roger Pressman, Michael Ray, Dirk Ruiz, Jay Russo, Herbert Simon, John Sterman, Howard Stevenson, and Richard Swanborg.

We are indebted to a number of people who helped with the data collection, interviews, reviews, and preparation of the manuscript itself. Jessica Keyes and Walter Utz read drafts of the manuscript and provided many keen insights and suggestions for revisions based on their own experience as authors and technology consultants. Armen Hovanessian, Cleo Lepori-Costello, and Betty McMicken helped conduct and transcribe interviews at Santa Teresa despite hectic schedules. Our secretaries, Renee Cantrell and Ruby Carnan, coordinated meetings and provided administrative support. Marjorie Spencer, Ruth Mannino, and Pam Pelton at McGraw-Hill did a terrific job turning our manuscript into a finished book. Our sincere thanks to all of you.

The teamwork on this book spanned both geographies and disciplines. In New York, we would like to thank our dynamic editing guru, Jeanne Glasser, for guiding us through the publishing maze and always going the extra mile. In Walnut Creek, California, we send kudos to Mitch Forcier, our object-oriented programming wizard without whose efforts there would be no disk at the back of this book.

Finally we thank our families and friends for their support, patience, understanding through the ups and downs of the writing process.

# 1

# Introduction

The most important thing about a quality improvement program is that it works. Commitment is a critical success factor. So is understanding why other quality improvement programs have failed. Next you need a framework that serves as a map for the quality improvement journey. You also need some sort of assessment tool to act as compass, telling you where you are on the map and whether you are heading in the right direction. Finally, a set of proven innovations indexed to the framework can help you make rapid progress immediately.

In this introduction, we provide an overview of each of these topics, beginning with some quality results that show what 40 innovations have done for one of IBM's largest software development labs.

## Quality Results at the World's Largest Software Lab

When our lab embarked on its journey of quality improvement in 1989, it broke new ground. Like many software companies, we had read Deming, Crosby, Juran, and a host of quality gurus who seemed to know a lot about manufacturing but not much about software.

Gurus who did know about software development usually concentrated on one piece of it. For example, we heard that software quality was just a matter of the right metrics, or that it was all about process improvement, or that it was a simple matter of reengineering. We tried all those things. Each had some merit, but none was sufficient on its own.

What we wanted was a quality program that would reduce defects, cut service costs, increase customer satisfaction, and increase productivity and revenue. We weren't able to find such a program, so we experimented and invented, creating our own program as we went along. Figure 1.1 offers proof that this experimentation and innovation paid off.

Figure 1.1$a$ shows the average defect levels for the six key database and language products that make up a very large percentage of our lab's revenue. Defect levels declined 46 percent over the course of our quality improvement

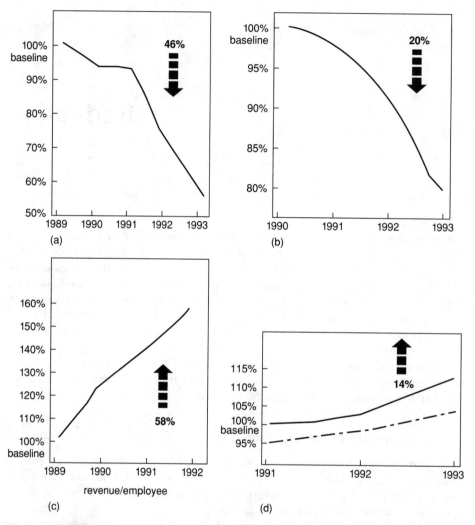

**Figure 1.1**  Quality results at IBM's largest software lab. (*a*) Field defects. (*b*) Service costs. (*c*) Productivity. (*d*) Customer satisfaction with our lab's products (solid curve) versus satisfaction with competitors' key (broken line) products.

efforts. The improvements came more rapidly as our quality efforts moved into high gear.

Figure 1.1*b* shows that our lab's service costs have decreased every year since the lab took responsibility for service in 1990. The decreasing pattern mirrors the dropping defect rates. Overall service costs dropped 20 percent, saving the lab tens of millions of dollars.

Figure 1.1*c* shows how productivity, measured as revenue per employee, has increased steadily since the start of our quality improvement journey. The process and technology innovations described in this book helped fuel the overall 58 percent improvement.

Most importantly, Fig. 1.1*d* shows that as the results of our quality improvement efforts have begun to reach customers, customer satisfaction has increased 14 percent in less than 3 years. Significantly, our customer satisfaction levels are higher than those of our competitors, and we are widening our lead.

Positive trends similar to those shown in Fig. 1.1 can be found in every aspect of our business and are summarized by our steadily increasing score on the Malcolm Baldrige National Quality Award criteria. The Baldrige criteria constitute a measure of an organization's overall level of quality and can be used to assess quality progress. The criteria are scored on a 1000-point scale with world-class organizations and Baldrige award winners typically scoring in the 750 to 850 range.

Figure 1.2 shows the lab's performance as measured by a series of external assessments using the Baldrige criteria. Our score in 1993 is close to that of IBM Rochester when that lab won the Malcolm Baldrige National Quality Award in 1990.

## Getting Committed

The number one reason why quality programs fail is a lack of commitment. Executives are fond of saying, "It's not enough to talk the talk, you've got to walk the walk." This means that if you really want to improve quality, you must commit for the long haul.

As Fig. 1.1 shows, significant improvements in defect levels, service costs, and customer satisfaction did not show until 1992—which was 3 years into our quality program. Worse yet, during the first 2 years, managers and developers at the lab openly stated that our quality improvement goals were unrealistic. Many more secretly hoped the whole quality program would go away. In fact, had the technical and managerial leaders of the quality improvement

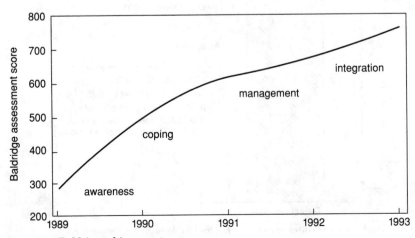

**Figure 1.2**  Baldrige achievement.

efforts thrown in the towel at year 2, or even year 3, the program would have done more harm than good. Quality improvement would have been viewed as just one more fad. Nothing would have been accomplished, and everyone would have been demoralized.

However, the leaders at the lab realized that even though our quality levels were above the industry average, we were still spending 60 to 80 cents of every development dollar on software maintenance and rework of existing code. That left only 20 to 40 cents free to develop new applications.

Unless we reduced these maintenance and rework costs by producing even higher-quality code, improving our development processes, and using more productive tools, we would soon be trailing more innovative competitors instead of leading them. Thus, despite the hype about Baldrige, ISO 9000, "continuous improvement," and "world class" organizations, the sobering realization that quality improvement is a matter of economic survival was at the core of our quality improvement efforts.

Without a clear understanding of the economic implications of quality improvement, it seems unlikely that the leaders would have stayed the course during the first turbulent years of the program. Therefore it is worth considering briefly some of the arguments that strengthened our commitment.

Figure 1.3 presents data from a case study at IBM's Rochester site. A total of 7053 hours was spent inspecting 200,000 lines of code with the result that 3112 potential defects were prevented. Assuming a programmer cost of $40 per hour, the total cost for preventing 3112 defects was $282,120, or roughly $91 per defect.

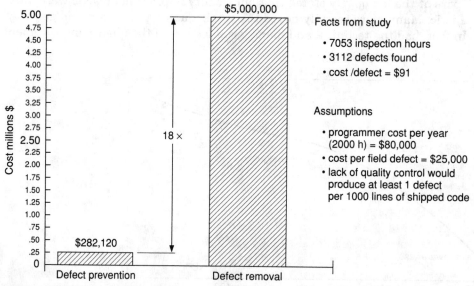

**Figure 1.3**  IBM Rochester case study: 200,000 lines of code. (*L. L. Cradduck, Software Inspections Metrics; IBM*)

Compare these numbers to the cost of defect removal once the product has been shipped to the customer. Suppose that there had been no inspections, but programmers had been extra careful and only one defect per 1000 lines of code escaped into the shipped product. That would mean 200 defects would still have to be fixed in the field. At an estimated cost of $25,000 per field fix, the cost would be $5 million, or approximately 18 times more expensive than the total cost of the defect prevention effort.

The same logic that applies to code defects applies even more strongly to defects in design or in customer requirements. Data from companies outside of IBM (e.g., see Weekley and Markus, 1992) suggest that $1 invested in quality improvement at the design or requirements stage should yield $30 to $50 in cost savings down the road. These numbers make sense when you realize that failing to code the right product features (due to a glitch in the design or in the customer requirements gathering process) can result in a loss of sales or in customer defections to competitive products.

Economic arguments like these convinced us that we needed a quality improvement program and that it couldn't just address code defects. We wanted something that addressed the design and requirements stages as well. Most important, we wanted something that improved quality in the eyes of our customers. It was not good enough to have higher-quality products and more efficient processes if these things did not translate into higher customer satisfaction and increased revenue.

Apparently our lab is not alone in recognizing the importance of software quality improvement. In a 1993 survey of 53 software companies conducted for the American Electronics Association (see Selected Readings), product quality was rated as the most important competitive success factor in the software industry. Interestingly, 74 percent of the survey participants rated product quality as one of their three most important competitive success factors, yet only 8 percent reported implementing a total quality management (TQM) program throughout their company. Perhaps, like us, they saw the problem but no clear solution path.

## Why Other Quality Approaches Fail

Once we knew what we wanted, we had to chart a course to get there. Many of the existing approaches to quality improvement assumed a manufacturing environment. Yet, despite progress with computer-aided software engineering (CASE) tools and reports of "software factories," software development in most companies does *not* happen on an assembly line. In software, the hard part is not producing thousands of units that all look alike. The hard part is getting just one unit that works perfectly. For this reason, many of the technological innovations in this book are different from those you might find in a generic book on quality improvement.

Even so, we recognized that technology alone would not get us where we wanted to go. As a developer of CASE tools, we are familiar with both the strengths and the limitations of CASE. We had also invested hundreds of thousands of dollars in process modeling, prototyping, and reengineering tools from a variety of vendors. Some tools worked better than others, but when used alone, none met our overall quality improvement objectives.

Process improvement was a major part of what was missing. The best tools in the world are only as effective as your development process allows them to be. For example, a high-technology on-line survey tool is useless without a process for distributing the information to the right people at the right times during product development.

Conversely, understanding the development process provides a basis for deciding which tools should have maximum impact on quality. For example, knowing that a process bottleneck is in the requirements gathering stage rather than in the Test department might lead to investment in rapid proto-typing technology (so as to get early customer feedback on prototypes) rather than investment in automated test tools.

Ultimately, however, process and technology improvements must be supported by leadership. We say leadership, and not management, because making resources available to buy new tools and supporting process improvement methodologies are only part of the story. Quality leadership happens at all levels of the organization and requires a personal commitment to quality. It means being willing to take a stand for quality, even if a schedule slips, a budget doesn't balance, or accepted practice gets overturned.

At the senior level, leadership means being willing to take on the task of cultural transformation. It means making sure that quality consciousness gets embedded in everyone's thoughts and in the day-to-day work environment. The entire organization needs to be thinking constantly of how to improve processes and the quality of products. If people aren't sick to death of hearing about quality, there is not enough communication happening and something's wrong with your quality leadership.

Only when we began to focus on all three of these areas—technology, process, and leadership—did we begin to make sustainable quality progress. We call this threefold focus the *iron triangle* because each corner of the triad supports the other two, as illustrated in Fig. 1.4. You might think of the iron triangle as a spearhead for penetrating business as usual and introducing the ingredients for sustainable quality improvement to the organization.

## A Map and Compass for the Quality Improvement Journey

Quality improvement is like a journey. You need a map of where you are going, and you need a compass to tell you where you are at any given time.

It seems as though everyone is peddling a quality system. We've seen 15 points, seven stages of growth, and five stages of awareness. And now, here we are, about to introduce our four stages of quality maturity. Is our new four-stage quality map really necessary?

We think so. First, understand that the proliferation of systems and models reflects a basic human need to know where one is going. Without a map of

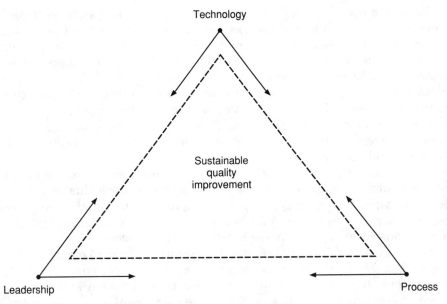

**Figure 1.4**  The iron triangle.

some kind, it is easy to get discouraged and wander in the wilderness instead of making consistent progress.

Just as there are topographic maps, demographic maps, maps for airline pilots, and maps for hikers, so, too, there are many quality maps—each emphasizing a different aspect of the terrain. We do not claim that our four-stage map is the best map for all purposes, but we believe that it is an excellent guide for organizations interested in a consistent and sustainable strategy for creating quality software.

The primary purpose of our four stages of quality maturity is to specify *when* particular innovations are most likely to be helpful. This function alone is enough to distinguish our map from others which tell you where to go, but which give no useful advice about how to get there. For this book in particular, such a map is needed because blind application of the innovations described here is as likely to hurt as it is to help your quality efforts. A recent joint study by the American Society for Quality Control (ASQC) and the consulting firm of Ernst & Young (1992) confirmed what we had already learned by hard experience: Pushing otherwise useful quality activities at the wrong time impedes your quality progress. Timing is key.

A second feature of our four stages is that they reflect the *overall* quality maturity of the organization, including such areas as leadership, operational results, and customer satisfaction, not just the maturity of software development *processes*. This is a key distinction between our framework and the popular five-stage maturity model of the Software Engineering Institute (SEI) which focuses exclusively on process improvement.

We have used the SEI model at IBM and feel it is excellent as far as it goes. However, any approach that focuses exclusively on process improvement has inherent limitations. Recent seminars at SEI on total quality management (TQM) suggest that SEI also recognizes the need for a more comprehensive approach to quality improvement.

In our view, an organization cannot succeed in producing world-class software unless the technology, the processes, and the leadership supporting software development are world-class, too. This view requires a comprehensive quality improvement framework tied to a comprehensive assessment tool such as the Baldrige template.

We use the Baldrige criteria as a compass to tell us where we are and in what directions we need to improve. Chapter 2 describes this use of the Baldrige criteria as a quality compass in more detail. Together with the Appendix, it provides three quick ways to estimate your organization's Baldrige score—even if you've never heard of Baldrige before.

As far as we know, ours is the only framework to link a comprehensive assessment tool (e.g., Baldrige) to stages of an organization's overall quality maturity and then to specific quality innovations for each stage. These unique linkages are what makes our four-stage map useful.

Figure 1.5 illustrates the four stages of quality maturity: *awareness, coping, management,* and *integration.* The *y* axis of Fig. 1.5 expresses the level of quality that can be attained within each stage, using the 1000-point Baldrige scale. Thus, an organization scoring 500 points or less on the Baldrige criteria is considered to be in the awareness stage. Scores between 500 and 625 correspond to the coping stage. Scores from 625 to 750 indicate the management stage, while organizations scoring above 750 are considered to be in the integration stage.

Conceptually, these scores reflect the capacity of an organization's technology, processes, and leadership to produce high-quality products and services. As an organization begins to reach the quality capability limits of a stage, the new technologies, process improvements, and leadership innovations of the next stage must be introduced. The words inside the rectangles of Fig. 1.5 describe the key technology, process, and leadership objectives for each stage.

## Forty Innovations

It's nice to have a quality road map and a compass that tells you where you are, but the really tough problem is how to make progress from stage to stage. When we began our journey in 1989, none of us could solve this problem. We had to experiment and innovate, figuring things out as we went along.

Now, in retrospect, we have been able to assemble 40 of the most important innovations that helped us progress from stage to stage. We call them "innovations" because they were new ideas to us when we implemented them. Some of the innovations—especially ones our lab adapted instead of invented (e.g., joint application design or clean-room techniques)—may be familiar to

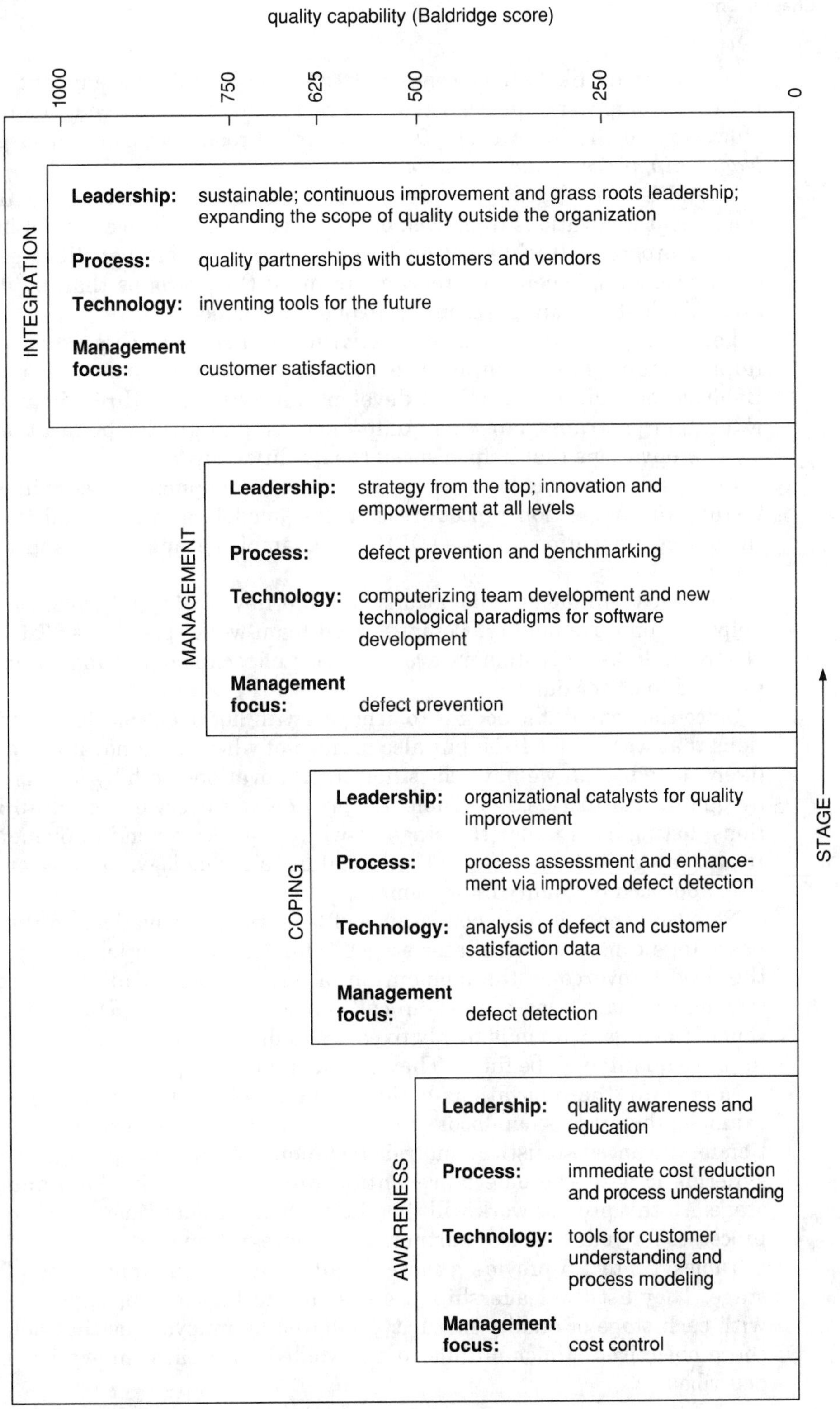

quality capability (Baldridge score)

1000    750   625   500       250        0

INTEGRATION

**Leadership:** sustainable; continuous improvement and grass roots leadership; expanding the scope of quality outside the organization

**Process:** quality partnerships with customers and vendors

**Technology:** inventing tools for the future

**Management focus:** customer satisfaction

MANAGEMENT

**Leadership:** strategy from the top; innovation and empowerment at all levels

**Process:** defect prevention and benchmarking

**Technology:** computerizing team development and new technological paradigms for software development

**Management focus:** defect prevention

COPING

**Leadership:** organizational catalysts for quality improvement

**Process:** process assessment and enhancement via improved defect detection

**Technology:** analysis of defect and customer satisfaction data

**Management focus:** defect detection

AWARENESS

**Leadership:** quality awareness and education

**Process:** immediate cost reduction and process understanding

**Technology:** tools for customer understanding and process modeling

**Management focus:** cost control

STAGE

**Figure 1.5** Four stages of quality maturity.

9

you. Others are likely to be completely new—especially those invented at our lab (e.g., computer-supported team work spaces, or the Excellence Council). However, all the innovations fall into three broad classes or "food groups": *leadership, process,* and *technology.*

The idea of food groups captures our belief that it is important that you implement innovations from each of the three categories to ensure a balanced quality program. It's like eating a balanced meal. More benefit is generally obtained by implementing programs from all three groups than by devoting an equivalent amount of resources to one area alone.

Leadership innovations include activities that serve as catalysts for quality improvement. For example, the Excellence Council, a formal review of Baldrige presentations, helped develop quality leaders throughout the lab. Education programs, lab-wide quality events, and quality publications were other innovations that helped speed the quality transformation.

Process innovations focus on changing the development process itself. New testing and inspection procedures, process modeling efforts, and the use of the defect prevention process (DPP) are examples of innovations in this food group.

Finally, technology innovations include new tools and inventions that helped to improve quality. Computerized team work spaces, CASE tools, and electronic links to customers are examples of technological innovations that have led to better quality.

Since the goal of this book is to arm you with not only knowledge of innovations that worked for IBM, but also an idea of when the innovations are most likely to be useful, we have classified the innovations both by food group and by quality maturity stage. Table 1.1 provides an overview of all 40 innovations, listing each under the stage in which we recommend implementation. It also categorizes each innovation as taking a technology, process, or leadership approach to quality improvement.

Note that there is a preponderance of leadership innovations in the awareness stage compared with later stages. This emphasis on leadership reflects the need to overcome the momentum of business as usual with a series of techniques that sound a wake-up call to the organization. Unless the attention of the organization is firmly fixed on quality, any subsequent attempts to improve quality will be futile. They would simply be ignored.

In general, the innovations build on one another and are synergistic. For example, the process handbooks in the awareness stage can serve as a foundation for advanced statistical analysis techniques in the coping stage, which are synergistic with the defect prevention process efforts in the management stage. All this process work will then help when it comes time to define quality processes for your business partners in the integration stage.

Tables 1.2 to 1.5 provide a more detailed view of the innovations for each stage. They list the leadership, process, and technology objectives associated with each stage of quality maturity, followed by innovations that help attain these objectives. Major pitfalls to be avoided with each innovation are also described.

**TABLE 1.1    Forty Innovations**

| Food group | Awareness stage<br>Baldrige<500 | Coping stage<br>Baldrige 501–624 | Management stage<br>Baldrige 625–750 | Integration stage<br>Baldrige 751–1000 |
|---|---|---|---|---|
| Leadership | Departmental strategy<br>Excellence Council<br>Quality publications<br>Education/seminars<br>Leadership Institute | Center for Software Excellence<br>Management council system | Strategic focus<br>Empowerment<br>Quality Week | Continuous improvement reviews<br>Work Force 2000<br>Quality exchanges and briefings |
| Process | Extended unit test<br>Programming development handbooks | ISO 9000<br>Rigorous code inspection and design reviews<br>Early test involvement<br>Combined line-item and function tests | Competitive product understanding<br>Benchmarking processes<br>Defect prevention process (DPP) | Quality partnerships with customers<br>Business partner quality process |
| Technology | Satisfaction surveys<br>Joint application design (JAD) methodology<br>Process modeling tools and methods | Error-prone module analysis<br>High-risk module analysis<br>Customer survey data linkage analysis | Object-oriented design<br>Computerized team work spaces<br>Electronic meetings<br>On-line code reviews<br>LAN library control system<br>Rapid prototyping<br>Clean Room techniques | Performance mining<br>Orthogonal defect classification (ODC)<br>Quality return on investment |

In general, a quality strategy works best if the leadership, process, and technology innovations are in balance. A program that is overly skewed to one at the expense of the others can produce dysfunctional results. For example, too much leadership can result in a dictatorial group. Too much process emphasis can lead to bureaucracy. Too much technology can lead to technical virtuosity without a consistent direction.

While it is possible to implement individual programs or techniques with favorable results, our experience has been that the overall quality capability of the organization improves most substantially when the innovations are part of a coherent quality management strategy. Without such a strategy it is very difficult to achieve the consistent results needed to progress to the next level of quality maturity. We refer readers to Chap. 23 for detailed advice on how to assemble a balanced set of innovations that match specific organizational needs.

## How to Use This Book

How you read this book depends upon your goals and interests. If you want the complete picture of how a quality program evolves in a software lab, you could read the chapters in sequential order. You might want to read just the leadership, process, or technology sections, or about all the innovations in a single stage—presumably to help your organization move from that stage to

**TABLE 1.2    Awareness Stage Innovations**

| Food group | Objective | Innovative approach | Implementation pitfalls |
|---|---|---|---|
| Leadership | Get management buy-in to quality. | Periodic measurement by the Excellence Council. | Wavering leadership on push-back. |
| | Foster department-level understanding. | Departments create vision/ mission/goals in their department quality strategy. | Lack of overall organizational strategy. |
| | Increase overall knowledge and skills. | Education and guest speakers in advanced education seminars. | Low quality, lack of relevancy. |
| | Remove organizational/ cultural inhibitors. | Intensive workshops as part of a Leadership Institute. | No follow-up; no executive leadership. |
| | Provide visible, persistent communication. | Publicize success stories and share information in quality publications. | Propaganda without useful content. |
| Process | Develop software process that is consistent and repeatable. | Document development process in programming development handbooks. | Rigid, mindless rule-following. |
| | Foster teamwork between developers and testers. | Create process linkages between developers and testers and extend unit test in development. | Failure to include testers, planners, etc. |
| | Eliminate errors found in test that result in expensive rework. | | Insisting on radical process redesign. Finger-pointing, "Who needs it?" attitudes. |
| Technology | Use software quality metrics; gain a complete and accurate view of internal capabilities and of customers. | External satisfaction surveys. Internal satisfaction surveys. | Oversurveying. Not acting on survey information. |
| | Ensure process/quality ownership. | Joint application design (JAD). | Wrong people; poor preparation. |
| | Eliminate process failures that cause delays, cost overruns, and customer complaints. | Process modeling. | Ad hoc modeling, unclear objectives. Hard-to-use tools. |

the next. Finally, because each innovation is described according to a modular template, it is possible to read individual chapters—or even single innovations within a chapter—and still gain useful information.

Table 1.6 lists some of the common interests readers may have and the chapters that discuss these interests most fully.

Finally, we have tried to ensure that this book (and the free software) is as error-free as possible. However, our experience with software quality has taught us that you rarely get a project of this size perfect the first time. In the spirit of continuous improvement, we would very much appreciate any

**TABLE 1.3    Coping Stage Innovations**

| Food group | Objective | Innovative approach | Implementation pitfalls |
|---|---|---|---|
| Leadership | Get line organization to take quality responsibility; promote organizational learning. | Create a group to act as a quality improvement catalyst and experience factory—the Center for Software Excellence (CSE). | Failure to evolve CSE. Lack of preparation for push-back. |
|  | Get powerful informal "shadow" organization that has bought into quality. | Tap into informal organization via a management council system. | Wrong people staffing CSE. NATO—no action, talk only. |
| Process | Meet ISO 9000 requirements and use Baldridge. | Do both: Baldrige: Tell me. ISO 9000 Strategy: Show me. | Excluding one for the other; ignoring synergism. |
|  | Promote design and code inspections. | Reinstate rigorous design reviews and code inspections. | Wavering on push-back, poor preparation, no follow-up or communications. |
|  | Reduce cycle times; improve quality. | Use train method as part of early test involvement. | Giving up; focus on failures. |
|  | Improve testing; increase effectiveness. | Integrate development and test in a combined line-item and functional test (CLIFT) program. | Failure to provide tools and education; no postmortems, no learning from mistakes. |
| Technology | Reduce errors in the field. | Error-prone module analysis statistically identifies problem code modules. | Failure to act on analysis; belief this is more bureaucracy. |
|  | Predict and prevent error-prone code. | Determine "fingerprint" of error-prone code early via high-risk module analysis. | Failure of data collection mechanism; failure to act on information. |
|  | Ensure we can answer: "Will our efforts improve customer satisfaction?" | Linking customer satisfaction to investment via data linkage analysis. | Using naive statistical analyses. |

comments or corrections from our readers. While we cannot guarantee that we can respond to every such letter, we do promise to read each letter personally and to incorporate revisions in future editions of the book as appropriate. Please send any comments to the authors, care of Craig Kaplan, I.Q. Company, P.O. Box 554, Santa Cruz, CA 95061-0554. Thank you very much!

**TABLE 1.4    Management Stage Innovations**

| Food group | Objective | Innovative approach | Implementation pitfalls |
|---|---|---|---|
| Leadership | Provide strategic focus and integration with quality. | Large-scale strategic planning, education, and tools; Baldrige assessment of planning groups and strategic focus initiatives. | Failure to take a business perspective. Not shifting from production quality to strategic quality. |
| | Generate innovations and breakthroughs. | Emphasize and reward empowerment. | Yo-Yo management style; settling for incremental progress. |
| | Improve morale, achieve deep quality deployment, encourage bottoms-up activity. | Showcase innovations, tools, teams, and progress in a grass roots Quality Week. | Not making it fun; low relevancy, anemic content, less than total participation. |
| Process | Shift from defect detection to defect prevention. | Root cause analysis as part of the defect prevention process. | Expecting immediate results, failure to implement recommended actions. |
| | Ensure we can answer: "Are our processes world-class?" | Process benchmarking. | No benchmarking plan and preparation. Limiting benchmarking to one industry. |
| | Ensure we can answer: "Are our products competitive?" | Competitive analysis. | Failure to identify right market segments. Unactionable analyses. |
| Technology | Improve meeting productivity. | Computerized team work spaces. | Skepticism, funding issues. |
| | Eliminate problems in participation, productivity, prioritization. | Electronic meetings (TeamFocus®). | Unskilled moderator, poor session preparation. |
| | Eliminate unproductive code reviews. | Revufile technology enabling online reviews. | No cross-functional participation. |
| | Reduce coordination problems with team code development. | LAN library control systems. | Impatience, lack of training and education. |
| | Reuse code. | Object-oriented programming and design. | Learning curve. |
| | Fast "proof of concept." | Rapid prototyping. | Appropriate tool selection. |
| | Improve on the waterfall process. | CleanRoom techniques. | Lack of education, insistence on "whole hog" deployment. |

**TABLE 1.5  Integration Stage Innovations**

| Food group | Objective | Innovative approach | Implementation pitfalls |
|---|---|---|---|
| Leadership | Sustain quality improvement momentum after transformation. | Streamline and include ISO 9000 in continuous improvement reviews. | Settling for results achieved or signaling that the journey is over. |
|  | Find out "What you don't know you don't know." | Quality exchanges and briefings ongoing with other companies. | Fear of sharing, getting arrogant. Failing to seek the best exchange partners. |
|  | Strengthen linkages to the community. | Long-term involvement looking to Work Force 2000. | Making it a public relations function; not focusing on actions that provide value. |
| Process | Further reduce defects and improve customer satisfaction. | Quality partnerships with customers (throughout product life cycle). | Arbitrary customer selection. Mindless attention to only participating customers' input. |
|  | Improve supplier quality processes. | Quality partnerships with vendors and related process initiatives. | Overwhelming partners with bureaucracy. "You're not OK, I'm OK" syndrome. |
| Technology | Find better ways to predict trouble spots in software development process. | Determine trouble spots by using error classification method: orthogonal defect control. | Failing to invest in data-collection infrastructure. Lack of adequate training. |
|  | Improve run-time performance of code. | Use computer-supported team work space for performance mining. | Introducing new defects while correcting old ones. |
|  | Find out where to invest quality dollars. | Record cost of quality activities and develop metrics to estimate Quality ROI. | Mindless use of metrics. Failure to improve metrics. |

**TABLE 1.6  Recommended Chapters Based on Reader's Interest**

| Reader's interests | Recommended chapters |
|---|---|
| Advanced technical and process innovations | 11, 12, 15–18, 22 |
| Baldrige and ISO 9000 | 2, 4, 10, Appendix |
| Leadership innovations only | 4, 5, 9, 14, 20 |
| Process innovations only | 6, 10, 11, 15, 21 |
| Technology innovations only | 7, 12, 16–18, 22 |
| Case study of TQM at a software lab with details of implementation | All chapters in sequential order, especially Chap. 9 |
| Overview of TQM at a software lab | 3, 4, 8, 9, 13, 14, 19, 20 |
| Assembling your own TQM program | 2, 23, Appendix, various |
| Cultural transformation | 2–5, 8, 9, 13, 14, 19 |

## Selected Readings

Arthur, L. J. (1993) *Improving Software Quality: An Insider's Guide to TQM.* New York: Wiley. *A current look at some standard TQM methods applied to software.*

Bauer, R., Collar, E., and Tang, V. (1992) *The Silverlake Project: Transformation at IBM.* New York: Oxford University Press. *The inside story of how IBM Rochester developed the AS/400 computer system and software.*

Ciampa, D. (1992) *Total Quality.* Reading, MA: Addison-Wesley. *A management consultant's view of how to implement TQM—some good ideas.*

Crosby, P. B. (1979) *Quality Is Free.* New York: McGraw-Hill. *A classic book advocating quality improvement programs by one of America's leading quality gurus.*

Deming, W. E. (1986) *Out of the Crisis.* Cambridge, MA: MIT Center for Advanced Engineering Study. *This 600 + page book contains the thoughts of one of America's leading quality gurus, but it can be tough reading.*

Dobyns, L., and Crawford-Mason, C. (1991) *Quality or Else.* Boston: Houghton Mifflin. *An easy-to-read introduction to the basic tenets of the quality movement.*

Ernst & Young and the ASQC (1992) *Best Practices Report: An Analysis of Management Practices that Impact Performance.* Available from ASQC: 1-800-248-1946. *A good survey of the effects of popular business practices (e.g., benchmarking), together with recommendations of when various practices are likely to be useful.*

Fairley, R. E. (1985) *Software Engineering Concepts.* New York: McGraw-Hill. *An excellent introduction to software engineering with a first-class set of references.*

Ferdinand, A. E. (1993) *Systems, Software, and Quality Engineering: Applying Defect Behavior Theory to Programming. A seminal book that brings the power and mathematical rigor of statistical mechanics to bear on the behavior of software systems.*

Humphrey, W. S. (1988) "Characterizing the Software Process: A Maturity Framework." *IEEE Software,* 5(3):73–79. *The short version of Humphrey's process maturity model.*

Humphrey, W. S. (1990) *Managing the Software Process.* New York: Addison-Wesley. *The long version of Humphrey's process maturity model with many other management gems besides.*

Jones, C. (1991) *Applied Software Measurement: Assuring Productivity and Quality.* New York: McGraw-Hill. *A hefty volume filled with useful information on software metrics.*

Juran, J. M. (1988) *Juran on Planning for Quality.* New York: MacMillan. *A popular volume by one of the leading quality improvement gurus.*

*1993 Survey of Quality and Productivity Programs in the Software Industry* (Contact Pittiglio Rabin Todd & McGrath in Mountain View, CA, or the American Electronics Association for more information.) *The survey assesses the product development strategies employed by companies and the state of their quality and productivity programs.*

Nolan, R. (1973) "Managing the Computer Resource: A Stage Hypothesis." *Communications of the ACM,* 16(7):392–405. *Describes a four-stage model of how computer resource use changes over time.*

Paulk, M. C., Curtis, B., and Chrissis, M. B. (1991) *Capability Maturity Model for Software,* CMU/SEI-91-TR-24. Pittsburgh, PA: Carnegie Mellon University.

Pressman, R. S. (1988) *Making Software Engineering Happen,* Englewood Cliffs, NJ: Prentice-Hall. *An excellent book about how to apply software engineering techniques in the real world.*

Pressman, R. S. (1993) *A Manager's Guide to Software Engineering.* New York: McGraw-Hill. *A single volume that addresses most of the issues managers need to concern themselves with when implementing software engineering techniques—by a top-notch authority.*

Schulmeyer, G. G. (1990) *Zero Defect Software.* New York: McGraw-Hill. *Popular book describes application of Shingo's inspection principles for Japanese manufacturing to error detection and elimination in software.*

Walton, M. (1986) *The Deming Management Method.* New York: Putnam. *A short theoretical book that summarizes Deming's ideas in a readable fashion.*

Weekley, H. G., and Markus, M. (1992) "Quality Management: The Secret to High Productivity," in J. Keyes, ed., *Software Engineering Productivity Handbook.* New York: McGraw-Hill. *The handbook itself is worth a look; it contains a large number of short and informative chapters on a wide variety of topics relevant to software engineering, productivity, and quality.*

# 2

# Assessing an Organization's Stage of Quality Maturity

## Why Assessments?

The four stages of quality (described in Chap. 1) constitute a road map for quality improvement, but such a map is useless without knowledge of where you are and how to orient yourself. A quality assessment provides the compass to go along with the map. At a minimum, a quality assessment will tell you which stage of quality maturity you're in. If you choose to perform a detailed quality assessment, you will learn far more, including which specific areas you need to target for improvement.

Unfortunately, quality assessments have gotten a bad rap. Software professionals will routinely use debuggers that count and detect bugs in programs, but many balk at the idea of doing ISO 9000 or Baldrige. It just seems like more bureaucracy. Yet these tools were designed to debug organizations. Properly used, a measurement template can highlight the need for improved technology, improved processes, or leadership innovation.

Even relatively small groups can benefit from an understanding of the Baldrige principles. For example, Baldrige's focus on customer satisfaction applies whether you deal with external customers or internal customers. Developers might view the Test department as their customers and might use the Baldrige criteria to evaluate the performance of Development as if Development were an independent business.

The insights from these kinds of exercises sometimes lead to innovation and improvement. For example, the combined line-item and functional test (CLIFT) methodology described in Chap. 11 stemmed from a recognition that Development needed to work more closely with its customers in Test.

If nothing else, learning about the measurement templates gives software professionals more ammunition to use in the funding battles for their projects. Having measurements on your side is one of the most powerful ways to argue for change and for the resources needed to accomplish it.

There are many measurement tools available. Some, such as function point analysis (Jones, 1991) or the SEI process maturity index (Humphrey, 1990), are specific to the software industry. Others, such as criteria for the Deming Prize, the European Quality Award, ISO 9000, or the Malcolm Baldrige National Quality Award, are applicable to a wide variety of businesses.

Still others may be unique to a particular organization or company. For example, our lab conducts a wide range of different types of assessments as indicated in Table 2.1.

Having so many options available can be confusing. Fortunately, deciding *which* measurement template to use is probably less important than deciding to use *something* to measure your quality progress rigorously.

What you're after is an assessment tool that you can use as a yardstick—something that will measure where you are today and tell you if you are heading in the right direction. It should also give you some idea of where to focus your efforts to make maximum quality gains.

If you already know that process is your problem, something like the SEI process maturity model or ISO 9000 can start you off on the right track. But for a broader view of quality, you may want to consider the Malcolm Baldrige National Quality Award criteria.

There is no rule (except perhaps the law of limited resources) that says you have to use only one yardstick. We have used several, including IS0 9000 and SEI and the others listed in Table 2.1. Still, the main driver of our quality system has been the Baldrige template.

**TABLE 2.1   Sample Assessments: Quality Assessment Information by Type**

| Type | Method | Purpose | Auditor | Frequency |
|---|---|---|---|---|
| Systems and practices | Internal audits | Corporate compliance | Internal auditors | Annually |
| | External audits | Standards compliance | External auditors | Annually |
| | Supplier audits | Ensure supplier security | Internal auditors | Continuous |
| MDQ | Written application | Continual improvement | Quality Council | Annually |
| ISO | External audits | ISO 9000 compliance | External ISO auditors | Annually |
| Processes | C.I. 101 assessments | Process improvement | Internal auditors | Annually |
| | Maturity evaluation | Process improvement | Process owners | Semiannually |
| | Excellence councils | Process improvement | Executives, key leaders | Semiannually |
| Products | C.I. 105 assessments | Product improvement | Product-quality assessors | Phases, announce |
| | Quality plans | Product improvement | Quality plan reviewers | Phase I, announce |
| | Measurement evaluation | Product improvement | Quality management reviews/quality operational reviews | Monthly |
| | Product test | Defect elimination | Project test teams | Product cycle |
| | Quality certification | Executive approval | Executives and project team | Announce, release |
| Customer satisfaction | Customer survey 90-day callback | Satisfaction improvement | Planners and management | Quarterly |
| | | Satisfaction improvement | Service development | Per license sold |

## Why Baldrige?

The first point in Baldrige's favor is that it seems to work. At IBM, we found an empirical correlation between use of the Baldrige template and business success. All IBM's major business organizations must do annual quality assessments, using the Baldrige criteria. IBM's management presents medals to those divisions that score within predetermined ranges. As of this writing, the medal-winning divisions outperformed IBM at large in customer satisfaction, employee morale, market share, revenue, and profits.

Outside of IBM, past Baldrige winners such as San Jose-based Solectron Corp. (1991) and GM's Cadillac division (1990) reported sales increases following their quality efforts.

According to the General Accounting Office (GAO), the 20 top-scoring Baldrige companies in 1988 and 1989 reported similar results. For these 20, on average, the market share increased 13.7 percent, sales per employee rose 8.6 percent, profits grew by 0.4 percent, customer satisfaction rose 4 percent, and customer complaints fell 12 percent. In addition, reliability, on-time delivery, order processing, inventory turnover rates, time to develop new products, and product defect rates all improved.

These results were summarized in a 1991 article in the *Harvard Business Review,* and they are reproduced in Table 2.2. The *Harvard Business Review* article says: "Using a detailed survey and extensive follow-up interviews, the GAO concluded that there was a cause-and-effect relationship between total quality management practices embodied in the Baldrige criteria and corporate performance measured by employee relations, productivity, customer satisfaction, or profitability."

But for the record, you can win the Baldrige and still go bankrupt. Wallace Corp., an oil field equipment distributor that won the Baldrige in 1990, declared bankruptcy in 1992. Interestingly, *Electronic Business* magazine quoted the CEO as saying: "We believed in the Baldrige then and we believe in it now...we'd have been in reorganization long ago if it hadn't been for our TQM efforts." (The article suggests that a slump in the oil business and a bank failure—not the use of the Baldrige criteria—were the causes of the bankruptcy.) Overall, we feel that Baldrige has the best track record of the various quality assessment techniques, but it's not a silver bullet.

Having said that, there are a couple of other reasons why Baldrige is a good choice. First, Baldrige is comprehensive. It is natural to associate quality with fewer defects in the final product or service that is delivered to the customer. However, quality improves most with a comprehensive effort that touches all aspects of the organization.

The seven categories of the 1993 Baldrige application cover leadership, information and analysis, strategic quality planning, human resource development and management, management of process quality, quality and operational results, and customer focus and satisfaction.

While Baldrige is not perfect, as assessment tools go, its coverage is pretty complete. And the tool is general enough to be applied to manufacturing as well as service companies, and to small as well as large companies.

**TABLE 2.2   Selected Results from the GAO Study**

| Performance indicator | Number of responding companies | Direction of indicator | | | Average annual improvement, % |
|---|---|---|---|---|---|
| | | Positive) (favorable) | Negative (unfavorable) | No change | |
| **Employee-related indicators** | | | | | |
| Employee satisfaction | 9 | 8 | 1 | 0 | 1.4 |
| Attendance | 11 | 8 | 0 | 3 | 0.1 |
| Turnover | 11 | 7 | 3 | 1 | 6.0 |
| Safety/health | 14 | 11 | 3 | 0 | 1.5 |
| Suggestions received | 7 | 5 | 2 | 0 | 16.6 |
| Total | 18* | 39 | 9 | 4 | |
| **Operating indicators** | | | | | |
| Reliability | 12 | 12 | 0 | 0 | 11.3 |
| On-time delivery | 9 | 8 | 1 | 0 | 4.7 |
| Order-processing time | 6 | 6 | 0 | 0 | 12.0 |
| Errors or defects | 8 | 7 | 0 | 1 | 10.3 |
| Product lead time | 7 | 6 | 0 | 1 | 5.8 |
| Inventory turnover | 9 | 6 | 1 | 2 | 7.2 |
| Costs of quality | 5 | 5 | 0 | 0 | 9.0 |
| Cost savings | 9 | 9 | 0 | 0 | NA† |
| Total | 20* | 59 | 2 | 4 | |
| **Customer satisfaction indicators** | | | | | |
| Overall customer satisfaction | 14 | 12 | 0 | 2 | 2.5 |
| Customer complaints | 6 | 5 | 1 | 0 | 11.6 |
| Customer retention | 10 | 4 | 2 | 4 | 1.0 |
| Total | 17* | 21 | 3 | 6 | |
| **Financial performance indicators** | | | | | |
| Market share | 11 | 9 | 2 | 0 | 13.7 |
| Sales per employee‡ | 12 | 12 | 0 | 0 | 8.6 |
| Return on assets | 9 | 7 | 2 | 0 | 1.3 |
| Return on sales | 8 | 6 | 2 | 0 | 0.4 |
| Total | 15* | 34 | 6 | 0 | |

*Indicates the total number of companies providing data and not the total number of responses for all performance indicators.

†NA = not available.

‡Unadjusted for inflation.

SOURCE: GAO's analysis of company-provided data. To order a copy of the GAO's report free of charge, call (202) 512-6000 and ask for GAO NSIAD 91-190.

Second, Baldrige has become something of an industry standard. It has been adopted by the National Institute of Standards and Technology (NIST) in the U.S. government, and it has been refined by some of the best minds in industry, government, and academia.

Baldrige has been adopted both by industry giants including Motorola, Xerox, IBM, Federal Express, and AT&T and by smaller companies such as Granite Rock construction, a firm with about 400 employees. To the extent that your organization interacts with other Baldrige practitioners, it helps to share the Baldrige quality vocabulary.

The fact that Baldrige is general enough to apply to businesses other than software makes it especially appealing to large corporations with a variety of businesses, and to companies who deal with suppliers and customers in other industry segments.

## A Quick Overview of Baldrige

If you are already familiar with the 1994 Malcolm Baldrige National Quality Award criteria, you may want to skip ahead to our description of three quick and easy assessment techniques. Here we provide a quick tutorial on basic Baldrige.

The Malcolm Baldrige National Quality Award (Baldrige for short) was established in 1987 for the purpose of recognizing "U.S. companies that excel in quality management and quality achievement." The award criteria consist of seven categories, each of which is worth a certain number of points. A perfect score on all categories would yield 1000 points, and organizations scoring between 875 and 1000 are considered "world-class," or among the best anywhere.

The seven categories exist in a framework that has four basic elements: *driver, system, measures of progress,* and *goal.* Figure 2.1, reproduced from the award criteria (see Suggested Readings), shows the relationships between these four elements.

The *driver* is senior executive leadership—the leaders who must create the values and goals of the organization and who guide pursuit of the goals. The *system* consists of all the processes that the organization uses for meeting its goals. *Measures of progress* provide the yardsticks to gauge whether the organization is moving toward its goals. Finally, the *goal* states what the organization wants to achieve, e.g., deliver ever-improving value to customers.

The advantage of the Baldrige view of quality is that it recognizes the interdependency of various parts of the organization. You can use Baldrige to assess the maturity of the whole organization and then zoom in on specific areas that need attention. This "zooming in" is accomplished by the scoring process.

Table 2.3 shows the categories and point values used by the 1994 Baldrige criteria. The point values for the categories tend to change from year to year, as the award criteria are fine-tuned, but the areas covered and the heavy weighting of customer satisfaction have remained relatively constant.

For each category, there are more detailed "items" that an organization must address in order to score points. For example, leadership (category 1) has three items: 1.1 senior executive leadership, 1.2 management for quality, and 1.3 public responsibility and corporate citizenship. There are 28 items in all in the 1994 Baldrige criteria.

Zooming in even further, we see that each item has several areas to address. For example, areas under item 1.1 include involvement and visibility, customer focus and quality values, communication and reinforcement, and evaluation and improvement.

Considering each of the categories, items, and areas to address forces you to think about how your organization performs on hundreds of quality-related

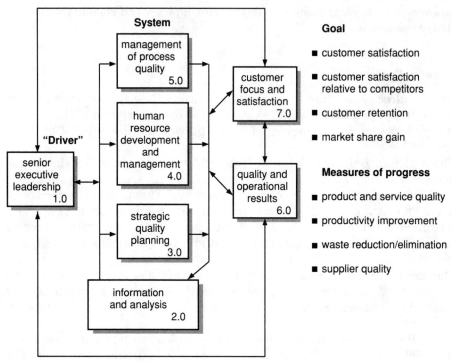

**Figure 2.1**  Baldrige award criteria framework; dynamic relationships. (*U.S. Department of Commerce, NIST*)

**TABLE 2.3   1994 Baldrige Categories and Point Values**

| Category | Point value |
|---|---|
| 1. Leadership | 95 |
| 2. Information and analysis | 75 |
| 3. Strategic quality planning | 60 |
| 4. Human resource development and management | 150 |
| 5. Management of process quality | 140 |
| 6. Quality and operational results | 180 |
| 7. Customer focus and satisfaction | 300 |
| Total | 1000 |

points. By considering your category and item scores—together with the criteria in the areas to address under each item—you can use Baldrige to pinpoint the areas where your organization needs the most work.

Equally important, Baldrige forces you to think about your product or service from a customer's perspective and to think about your whole business in a systematic, organic way. Therefore, as your overall score and scores on individual Baldrige categories improve, you should be making progress toward increased customer satisfaction—not just toward reductions in the defect rate.

## Three Quick and Easy Baldrige Assessments

Baldrige assessments come in a variety of shapes and sizes. You can score yourself (a self-assessment) or have outsiders score you (an external assessment). You can address the quality criteria by writing a 70+-page quality document (required for formal application for the Malcolm Baldrige National Quality Award), or you can put together a presentation following the criteria for internal purposes (standard practice at IBM). The document or presentation can be prepared by a single individual or by a team of researchers, writers, and presenters. The assessment can cover a small department of 10 or a company of thousands.

Books have been written about how to meet the criteria (see Suggested Readings), and consultants make a living advising companies on how to perform assessments. But you don't need to perform a detailed assessment to get a rough idea of your organization's level of quality maturity. For starters, we recommend choosing one of the three quick and easy assessment methods detailed in the Appendix.

The first method is our paper-and-pencil quality maturity quiz. Because Baldrige is meant to be used by a wide variety of companies, the official criteria are worded in very general terms. When you read the criteria for the first time, it's often very difficult to see how they relate to the software business. In our paper-and-pencil quiz, we have translated the 28 items of the 1994 Baldrige criteria into questions that make more sense to software organizations. You score each question on a simple scale from 1 to 5. From the total quiz score, you can estimate what your Baldrige score would be.

The second method is a computerized version of the first. If you have a personal computer (PC) running the Windows operating system, you can use the disk supplied with this book to take the quiz on-line. The advantage of this method is that the computer does all the scoring for you. The program displays a summary of score results that can be broken down to finer and finer levels of detail. Thus you can zoom in on trouble spots. The program also lets you save and retrieve quiz results and change your answers to any of the questions without having to retake the entire quiz.

The final method was developed by Roy Bauer of Competitive Dominance Strategies in Rochester, MN. Bauer has served as a Baldrige examiner himself and helped IBM's Rochester site win the Malcolm Baldrige National Quality Award in 1990. Bauer's method uses quick-scoring cards for each of the seven Baldrige categories. The cards can cut down the time for performing a Baldrige assessment considerably. However, because the cards use the language of the actual criteria, this method may be best for those with some familiarity with Baldrige.

For those interested in performing more detailed team assessments using the Baldrige criteria, we recommend reading about the Excellence Council—an innovation for incorporating Baldrige into periodic quality reviews—in Chap. 4. Serious readers will also want to order copies of the award criteria from the American Society for Quality Control.

## Finding Your Organization's Stage of Quality Maturity

Once you have obtained an estimate of your Baldrige score, the next step is to determine your organization's stage of quality maturity. Because Baldrige covers all aspects of the organization, including support functions, it is important to remember that the Baldrige score will estimate your *overall* quality maturity. It may be, e.g., that your software development process is of a higher or lower quality maturity than your overall organization. However, since the quality of your products ultimately depends on the entire organization, and since the innovations in this book are indexed to *overall* quality maturity, knowing your overall stage is valuable information.

Table 2.4 identifies your stage of quality maturity based on your estimated Baldrige score.

The first thing to notice about this mapping of Baldrige to the maturity stages is that the four stages cover only about 250 points—from 500 to 750. This fact stems from the heavy weight given in Baldrige to results (180 points) and customer satisfaction (300 points). These bottom-line indicators change as your quality maturity increases, but they generally lag behind process improvements, leadership actions, and other activities which are given less weight in Baldrige scoring.

The net result is that you can move through the first two stages simply by improving your quality processes and focusing on the approach and deployment of quality improvement activities. But you cannot make the jump to the management and integration stages until results begin to manifest from the quality activities. And results take time—at least one development cycle—to appear.

We have geared the score ranges of our four stages of maturity to provide milestones along the most difficult part of the quality journey—the lag period between quality deployment and the manifestation of results from the deployment.

The score boundaries between different stages are approximate. They reflect our experience, but the specific numbers may not hold for your organi-

**TABLE 2.4   Determining Your Maturity Stage by Using the Baldrige Score**

| Baldrige score | Quality maturity stage |
| --- | --- |
| <501 | Awareness |
| 501–625 | Coping |
| 626–750 | Management |
| 751–1000 | Integration |

zation. You might also want to consider that different areas in an organization typically mature at different rates.

For example, a score of 500 on Baldrige does not necessarily mean that an organization has gotten 50 percent of the available points for each Baldrige category. In fact, certain areas such as "leadership" are likely to score higher than 50 percent, and others such as "results" are likely to score less. Again, this pattern reflects the fact that some categories of Baldrige are leading indicators, while others are followers. Table 2.5 gives a detailed breakdown of how an organization might score at different stages. The breakdown is based on our own quality assessments and our experience with leading and trailing indicators.

Figure 2.2 presents another view of leading and trailing business indicators published in *Harvard Business Review* in 1991. As you can see, the author's illustrative charts are generally in agreement with our experience. Leadership comes first, results come last. That is what makes quality improvement such a challenge.

Finally, in addition to Baldrige scoring which provides a quantitative mechanism for determining an organization's quality maturity, the Baldrige criteria can be used qualitatively. Tables 2.6 to 2.9 describe qualitative Baldrige indicators that we have used to cross-validate the maturity stage predicted by numerical Baldrige scores.

**TABLE 2.5   Maximum Percentage of Points likely to be Scored in Each Maturity Stage**

| Category | Awareness | Coping | Management | Integration |
|---|---|---|---|---|
| 1.0 Leadership | 75 | 90 | 95 | 100 |
| 2.0 Information analysis | 60 | 80 | 85 | 100 |
| 3.0 Quality planning | 40 | 75 | 80 | 100 |
| 4.0 Human resources | 45 | 50 | 70 | 100 |
| 5.0 Process management | 60 | 80 | 90 | 100 |
| 6.0 Quality results | 40 | 45 | 60 | 100 |
| 7.0 Customer satisfaction | 45 | 55 | 70 | 100 |

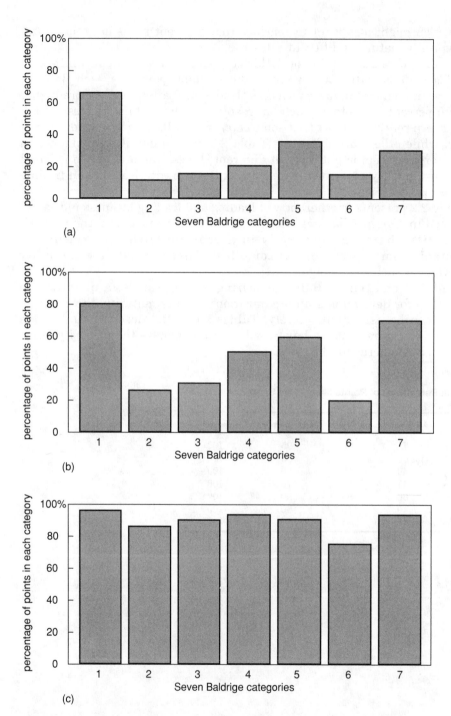

**Figure 2.2** Mapping progress through the Baldrige. (a) Low scorers (awareness/coping). (b) Medium scorers (coping/management). (c) High scorers (management/integration). These charts are illustrative only and are derived from discussions with Baldrige judges, senior examiners, and examiners. The charts depict general trends of how companies progress through the Baldrige criteria over time. *(From Harvard Business Review, 1991)*

**TABLE 2.6   Qualitative Indicators for the Awareness Stage**

| Baldrige area | Indicators |
|---|---|
| 1.0 Leadership | Skeptical "let's try it" attitude<br>Uneven throughout the organization |
| 2.0 Information and analysis | Lack of data<br>Few defined quality measurements<br>External customer and/or supplier indicators undefined or lack data |
| 3.0 Strategic quality planning | Ad hoc, unsystematic<br>No closed-loop process<br>Process unable to continuously improve |
| 4.0 Human resource development and management | Lack of quality education<br>Few voluntary participants in quality activities |
| 5.0 Management of process quality | Little or no focus on quality of processes<br>Processes are not closed-loop<br>Processes unable to continuously improve |
| 6.0 Quality and operational results | Lack of data on quality levels<br>Lack of trend and competitor data<br>No impact of quality efforts on operational results |
| 7.0 Customer focus and satisfaction | Lack of systematic customer satisfaction measurements and data<br>Lack of comparison data with competitors |

**TABLE 2.7   Qualitative Indicators for the Coping Stage**

| Baldrige area | Indicators |
|---|---|
| 1.0 Leadership | Senior leaders committed<br>First-line management unsure |
| 2.0 Information and analysis | Some data collected<br>Beginning to define quality measurements<br>External customer and/or supplier indicators defined but no data |
| 3.0 Strategic quality planning | Overall quality strategy/plan in place<br>Some departmental strategies/plans in place<br>Working to define repeatable strategic planning process |
| 4.0 Human resource development and management | Quality education courses available<br>Morale low, but participation in quality activities increasing |
| 5.0 Management of process quality | Initial efforts to understand and document processes<br>Focus on easy-to-fix process elements<br>Defect detection and test emphasis<br>Little or no focus on supplier processes |
| 6.0 Quality and operational results | Beginning to get data on quality levels<br>Lack of trend and competitor data<br>Little or no impact of quality efforts on operational results |
| 7.0 Customer focus and satisfaction | Developed systematic customer satisfaction measurementsLack of comparison data with competitors |

**TABLE 2.8    Qualitative Indicators for the Management Stage**

| Baldrige area | Indicators |
|---|---|
| 1.0 Leadership | Commitment consistent at all levels of management |
| 2.0 Information and analysis | In-process quality measurements defined<br>Internal/external data collected<br>Some data analyzed; attempts to improve data analysis techniques |
| 3.0 Strategic quality planning | Strategic planning process defined<br>All departmental strategies/plans in place<br>Working to improve strategic planning process<br>Strong and widely used in-process measurements |
| 4.0 Human resource development and management | All employees have quality education<br>All employees have some participation in quality activities<br>Team-oriented measurement and rewards |
| 5.0 Management of process quality | Processes well understood<br>Critical processes documented<br>Focus on defect prevention<br>Some focus on supplier quality<br>Strong cross-functional teams widely deployed<br>Broad-scale process reengineering<br>New technology to support all processes |
| 6.0 Quality and operational results | Good data on product quality levels<br>Some trend and competitor data<br>First tentative signs of positive quality impact on operational results |
| 7.0 Customer focus and satisfaction | Good data on customer satisfaction<br>Beginning to gather data on customer satisfaction with competitors' products |

**TABLE 2.9   Qualitative Indicators for the Integration Stage**

| Baldrige area | Indicators |
|---|---|
| 1.0  Leadership | Everyone in the organization is a quality leader |
| 2.0  Information and analysis | Trend data collected and available<br>Data on competitors collected<br>Data analyzed and used to drive process improvements on a regular basis |
| 3.0  Strategic quality planning | Strategic planning process accepted<br>Closed-loop improvement process in place<br>Strategy is focused on customer |
| 4.0  Human resource development and management | Ongoing quality education<br>Participation in quality activities is business as usual<br>Measurements and incentives for team performance well established |
| 5.0  Management of process quality | Processes documented<br>Processes have continuous improvement built in<br>Focus on customer, business partners, and supplier quality<br>Benchmarking widely practiced |
| 6.0  Quality and operational results | Trend data on product quality<br>Trend and competitor data<br>Quality impact on operational results linked to approach and deployment |
| 7.0  Customer focus and satisfaction | Trend data on customer satisfaction<br>Trend data on customer satisfaction with competitive products<br>Customer satisfaction strongly linked to all functions of the business |

## Selected Readings

Brown, M. G. (1991) *Baldrige Award Winning Quality: How to Interpret the Malcolm Baldrige Award Criteria.* Milwaukee, WI: ASQC Quality Press. *A step-by-step interpretation of what Baldrige examiners are looking for in each area of the Malcolm Baldrige criteria.*

Cortada, J. W. (1993) *TQM for Sales and Marketing Management.* New York: McGraw-Hill. *A very clear, general discussion of TQM with some useful Baldrige-specific information.*

Garvin, D. A. (1991) "How the Baldrige Award Really Works." *Harvard Business Review,* 69(6): 80–93. *A good overview of Baldrige and the rationale behind it.*

Garvin, D. A., et al. (1992) "Does the Baldrige Award Really Work?" *Harvard Business Review,* 70(1): 126–147. *Garvin referees while a variety of quality gurus provide their perspectives on Baldrige; some like it, others hate it.*

Humphrey, W. S. (1990) *Managing the Software Process.* New York: Addison-Wesley. *The long version of Humphrey's process maturity model with many other management gems besides.*

Jones, C. (1991) *Applied Software Measurement: Assuring Productivity and Quality.* New York: McGraw-Hill. *A hefty volume filled with useful information on software metrics.*

*The 1994 Award Criteria.* Order from the American Society for Quality Control (800-248-1946), or call the National Institute of Standards and Technology for a free copy (301-975-2036).

Olson, T. G., Humphrey, W. S., and Kitson, D. H. (1989) *Conducting SEI-Assisted Software Process Assessments.* Software Engineering Institute, Pittsburgh, PA, CMU/SEI-89-TR-7, DTIC number ADA219065.

Steeples, M. M. (1993) *The Corporate Guide to the Malcolm Baldrige National Quality Award,* rev. ed. Milwaukee, WI: ASQC Quality Press. *Another of the guides seeking to help companies apply for the Baldrige award.*

# 3

# Stage 1: Awareness

## Are You in the Awareness Stage?

You know you are in the awareness stage when most of the organization ignores quality issues altogether. Those who are aware of quality tend to view it as management's latest kick. *Malcolm Baldrige* and *ISO 9000* are viewed as buzzwords.

When we were in the awareness stage, we were scoring below 500 on the Baldrige assessment. Table 3.1 shows specific indicators that we saw in each

**TABLE 3.1   Baldrige Indicators of the Awareness Stage**

| Baldrige area | Indicators |
|---|---|
| 1.0 Leadership | Skeptical "let's try it" attitude<br>Uneven throughout the organization |
| 2.0 Information and analysis | Lack of data<br>Few defined quality measurements<br>External customer and/or supplier indicators undefined or lack data |
| 3.0 Strategic quality planning | Ad hoc, unsystematic<br>No closed-loop process<br>Process unable to continuously improve |
| 4.0 Human resource development and management | Lack of quality education<br>Few voluntary participants in quality activities |
| 5.0 Management of process quality | Little or no focus on quality of processes<br>Processes are not closed-loop type<br>Processes unable to continuously improve |
| 6.0 Quality and operational results | Lack of data on quality levels<br>Lack of trend and competitor data<br>No impact of quality efforts on operational results |
| 7.0 Customer focus and satisfaction | Lack of systematic customer satisfaction measurements and data<br>Lack of comparison data with competitors |

of the seven areas covered by Baldrige. An organization exhibiting most of or all these signs is probably in the awareness stage.

## Objectives for the Awareness Stage

The cost of poor quality is like a fire smoldering and going unnoticed. An organization's top priority must be to get the fire under control, and the first step is to sound the alarm.

Since most people in the organization will be going about their business as usual, it is the leader's job to increase awareness of the quality crisis via communication and education. There is a saying (that has been validated by psychological research): "I hear, I forget. I see, I remember. I do, I understand." The leader should strive to increase quality awareness via hands-on activities wherever possible.

The process goals in the awareness stage are to make immediate progress toward cost reduction. The first step here must be process understanding and documentation. Unless the processes are understood, no systematic improvement is possible and changes will tend to be random and ad hoc, some helping and others hurting.

Finally, the technology objective is to support the process understanding efforts and to ensure that the customer is included early on in the quality efforts.

In terms of the Baldrige criteria, Fig. 3.1 lists the most critical focus items for the awareness stage. Note that they reflect a concern with leadership, values, education, assessment, and fostering an awareness of customers. Each of these areas is essential to getting your quality improvement efforts off the ground.

## Overview of Awareness Stage Innovations

The central challenge in the awareness stage is one of cultural transformation. How do you focus attention on quality and take the first steps toward creating an organization where quality improvement is second nature?

Table 3.2 offers 10 innovative approaches to taking these first steps. Leadership innovations such as the *Excellence Council* and *departmental quality strategies* are aimed at raising the awareness and getting the

---

1.1 Senior executive leadership  *Get the personal commitment and involvement from the leader of the organization.*

1.2 Management for quality *Begin integrating quality values into day-to-day management and leadership*

4.3 Employee education and training  *Make quality education ubiquitous.*

5.5 Quality assessment  *Find out what your current levels of quality are, and chart where you want to go.*

7.4 Customer satisfaction determination  *Who are your customers, and how will you determine what they want?*

---

**Figure 3.1**  Baldrige items for improvement in the awareness stage.

**TABLE 3.2    Awareness Stage Innovations**

| Food group | Objective | Innovative approach | Implementation pitfalls |
|---|---|---|---|
| Leadership | Get management buy-in to quality. | Periodic measurement by the *Excellence Council.* | Wavering leadership on push-back. |
| | Foster department-level understanding. | Departments create vision/ mission/goals in their department quality strategy. | Lack of overall organizational strategy. |
| | Increase overall knowledge and skills. | Education and guest speakers in *advanced education seminars.* | Low quality, lack of relevancy. No follow-up; no executive leadership. |
| | Remove organizational/ cultural inhibitors. | Intensive workshops as part of a *Leadership Institute.* | |
| | Provide visible, persistent communication. | Publicize success stories and share information in quality publications. | Propaganda without useful content. |
| Process | Develop software process that is consistent and repeatable. | Document development process in *programming development handbooks.* | Rigid, mindless rule-following. Failure to include testers, planners, etc. |
| | Foster teamwork between developers and testers. | Create process linkages between developers and testers and *extend unit test in development.* | Insisting on radical process redesign. |
| | Eliminate errors found in test that result in expensive rework. | | Finger-pointing, "Who needs it?" attitudes. |
| Technology | Use software quality metrics; gain a complete and accurate view of internal capabilities and of customers. | *External satisfaction surveys. Internal satisfaction surveys.* | Oversurveying. Not acting on survey information. |
| | Ensure process/quality ownership. | *Joint application design (JAD).* | Wrong people; poor preparation. |
| | Eliminate process failures that cause delays, cost overruns, and customer complaints. | *Process modeling.* | Ad hoc modeling, unclear objectives. Hard-to-use tools. |

endorsement of all levels of the organization. *Advanced education seminars,* the *Leadership Institute,* and *quality publications* educate and equip the organization with the knowledge needed for action.

Process innovations focus on process documentation and test. The idea is to document the current process as a precursor to process improvement. And it is just as important to produce immediate results which encourage participants. Because Test is the easiest place to see immediate quality results, that's where we start, even though improved testing efforts will be supplemented by preventive efforts at later stages.

Technological innovations emphasize surveys and tools to support the understanding of customers and the development process. For example, *satisfaction surveys* provide a baseline for measuring quality improvement. *Joint application design sessions* and *process modeling methods and tools* offer ways to help groups of developers understand and improve their processes.

Chapters 4 to 7 describe each of these leadership, process, and technological innovations in more detail. Don't be surprised if some of these innovations seem low-technology or well known. At the awareness stage, radical change may not be feasible. What these innovations offer is a way to jump-start a quality program and to accelerate the organization to the next stage of quality maturity.

## Obstacles and Pitfalls

Without a doubt, the biggest obstacle you will encounter in the awareness stage is the resistance to change. Our initial attempts to deploy quality improvement efforts were greeted with something like this: "We've seen this before. A few years ago there was Excellence Plus, and before that there was PRIDE, and before that there was some other program. This, too, shall pass."

Unfortunately, this response is perfectly rational given the history of most large companies. IBM's own history is littered with the wreckage of aborted quality programs. Each time a program fails, the easy response is to just try something different. But good technical people tend to have long memories. After two or three aborted attempts at quality improvement, even the most open-minded professional turns a bit cynical.

The biggest pitfall for a manager or software professional is to believe that there is an easy way to tackle the quality problem. The typical cycle for organizations seeking a quick fix to quality goes like this:

1. Management recognizes there is a quality problem.
2. Management tries the path of least resistance, which is to send people to seminars on CleanRooms, reengineering, reverse engineering, code reuse, and CASE tools.
3. The technical people come back fired up.
4. Money is spent on technology consultants and tools.
5. The new technology is implemented.
6. Sustainable results fail to appear. Quality is not just a matter of technology.
7. Managers try process improvements next. These tend to be more disruptive, but are recommended by all the quality experts.
8. Sustainable results still fail to materialize because quality is not just a matter of process.
9. Managers get transferred or promoted; new managers come in.
10. Go to step 1—but increase the resistance factor because the technical people are now jaded about quality improvement programs.

The more difficult but more effective approach is the way of the quality fanatic. To all appearances, it is the path of most resistance. From day one it looks like a big headache. It starts with the assumption that process and technological improvements will stick, but only if these changes are preceded or accompanied by a change in culture. When software developers are primarily concerned with quality, when they see quality issues wherever they look, then they will naturally use whatever tools are most appropriate to achieve the highest levels of quality possible. Instead of quality being seen as a disruption of "real work," quality will be seen as part of the real work.

Bringing about this change in thinking is much harder than implementing a new tool or process. But it is far more powerful. That's why cultural transformation became a high priority in our quality improvement activities.

Unfortunately, even recognizing the need for cultural transformation does not guarantee success. There are plenty of opportunities for mistakes in the implementation of such a program. Figure 3.2 lists 10 leadership pitfalls we made. Most of these could have been corrected from the start in the awareness stage. The good news is that none of these proved fatal, once corrected.

## Signs of Progress

If you are making progress in the awareness stage, you should be able to see it reflected in an increasing Baldrige assessment score. (Pay special attention to the areas described in Fig. 3.1.) But there are other indications as well.

Ironically, if people are complaining, that may be one of the best indications that a cultural transformation is under way. Radical quality improvement requires visionaries who are not afraid of a certain amount of creative destruction. Visionaries are not uncomfortable with the label *unreasonable*. A visionary thinks: "If being reasonable got us into this quality mess, then maybe it is time to be a little unreasonable."

One could argue that in the awareness stage perception is more important than reality. The reality is that not much will change right away, despite your best leadership efforts. This reflects the fact that in most organizations there is a tremendous amount of cultural inertia. Trying to budge our organi-

---

1. Failure to focus on culture transformation
2. Failure to focus on an external view of quality (e.g., customer satisfaction, market share, competitiveness)
3. Sending mixed signals on top management's commitment to quality
4. Telling people it is an easy and quick fix
5. Not having milestones to show people that they are making progress
6. Telling people that *they* are the problem instead of realizing that *we* have a quality problem
7. Failing to address process issues
8. Doing it with bureaucracy instead of common sense
9. Letting nonperformers get away with it
10. Failure to identify the real leaders in the informal "shadow" organization, as opposed to the managers listed on the organizational chart.

**Figure 3.2**  Ten leadership pitfalls to avoid from the start.

zation even an inch on quality required an inordinate amount of sweating, huffing, and puffing.

That is why pointing to reality, i.e., changes in results, is probably not the most effective way to win converts to the good fight early on. Instead, invest in quality education, change the measurement and recognition system, spend your own time in quality-related activities, and take a tough stand on quality. Send the message in every highly visible way you can that you are *serious* about quality. All these activities help create the perception that quality is improving. And in all fairness, these things are all necessary precursors to change.

Early converts are your indication that something is working. When the first converts join up and begin to have successes, it is especially important to publicize and promote the success stories. These are the fragile buds which herald the blooming field to come. Unless they are nurtured, your quality garden can wither with the first harsh blast of criticism.

On the other hand, there is one sure sign that something is wrong. Negative reactions are fine, but lack of reaction is not. If people are ignoring your quality activities, then you need to step up the communication and leadership activities.

Finally, perhaps the best way to convey a feeling of the challenges of the awareness stage is to describe what we saw happening at our lab. Although we will present a management view, it should be useful to managers, software professionals, and students of software engineering or TQM.

## Our Lab in the Awareness Stage

Before we began the quality journey in 1989, our approach to quality was pretty typical for the software industry. For years, quality, as measured by defect levels, remained fairly constant while the cost of fixing defects and maintaining code continued to grow. Our quality levels were well above the industry averages according to external reports (e.g., Jones, 1991), so we weren't too worried.

To most lab employees, quality meant quality assurance—just another step in the approval process necessary to get a product out the door. The Quality Assurance department itself was a small group, buried in the lab's reporting structure. The group had little power and was perceived as a roadblock by the product developers who needed what they thought of as rubber stamp approval from Quality Assurance.

All that changed with the arrival of Tom Furey, our new lab general manager (GM), who recognized quality as an important differentiator that provided competitive advantage. He had a track record of transforming businesses into winners, having done so in IBM Rochester with the AS/400, leading that lab to a Baldrige award.

One of his first actions was to transform the Quality Assurance group into the Center for Software Excellence (CSE), an innovation described in Chap. 9. The CSE reported directly to the GM—a visible sign of commitment to quality.

The mission of the new group was to act as a catalyst and sponsor of quality activities throughout the lab. Its members served as consultants, teachers, cheerleaders, and documenters.

The new group redefined quality. Suddenly quality encompassed more than just defects. It included process improvement, customer satisfaction, time to market, and a culture committed to continuous improvement. These quality values led to quality education, process assessments, surveys of customers, and the selection of the Baldrige criteria to act as our quality compass.

From 1989 to 1990, the lab slogged its way through the awareness stage. The Malcolm Baldrige template was promoted throughout the lab as an assessment tool, and some leading-edge departments began calculating their Baldrige scores. Nevertheless, the majority of the employees remained unconvinced that the energy being directed to quality was really worthwhile.

For example, one of our database products essentially ignored the quality program until the GM began to systematically replace the management team. In most cases, such drastic measures were not necessary, but it took consistent and persistent communication before the lab realized that the focus on quality was here to stay.

The first sign of any positive action, besides the industrial-strength quality communication and education programs that were going on, was that people began to become more aware of their development processes. We had documented the lab's standard process in a series of booklets which were stacked, free for the taking in the library.

Previously, new employees might pick up a few copies, but for the most part the booklets just gathered dust. We knew something was happening when the booklets began disappearing rapidly from the shelves.

The booklets outlined our adaptation of the well-known waterfall process, shown in Fig. 3.3. The waterfall process gets its name from the fact that it consists of a series of stages. As work is completed in one stage, that work cascades down to the next stage where it is further refined or transformed. Because it is a serial process, the total development time is the sum of the times to complete each stage. Under the pressure of meeting deadlines, often corners had been cut on anything that might lengthen a given stage, such as extra quality inspections. As the focus on quality intensified, one of the first signs of progress was that fewer corners were cut.

The process begins with the planning and gathering of customer requirements. Next senior programmers sit down to design the specifications of the product or new release. These specifications are often expressed in terms of a laundry list of different functions or line items.

Once the specifications are written, they are passed to developers who do the coding. Typically the coding is done one line item at a time, and then all the line items are integrated into a body of code which is passed to the test department.

Testers test the code by itself (unit test), together with the rest of the product (component test), and in a simulated customer computing environment

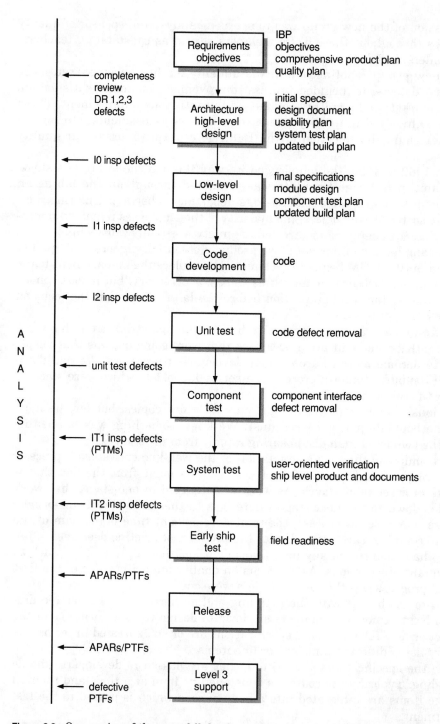

**Figure 3.3** Our version of the waterfall development process. Analysis is of defects from each step. (*Courtesy of IBM*)

(customer, or system test). After testing is complete, any errors are fixed by development and the product is shipped to the customers.

Service support is traditionally not considered part of the waterfall process, but here's how service worked: As problems came in from the field, they were ranked for severity and the source of the problem. For example, severity 1 meant the problem had to be fixed immediately—in a matter of hours. APARs (authorized programming analysis requests) meant that there was a bug in the code that needed to be fixed; UPARs (user programming analysis requests) meant that the code was technically ok, but for some reason (perhaps a usability or documentation glitch) the user still had a problem.

Problems from the field were filtered through IBM's service support staff, which had three levels. Simple questions and inquiries got handled by level 1 staff. Level 1 was expert at human relations. Level 2 could handle most commonly asked questions and problems with the product. Finally, level 3 consisted of the actual product developers.

In the waterfall process, traditionally the place to improve quality was in Test. Test, by definition, had the responsibility of making sure that high-quality code got shipped to the customer. Moreover, the Test department was the organization best equipped to do something immediately about quality.

So in the awareness stage, the few leading-edge groups that were concerned with quality tended to be the Test groups. Everyone else assumed that the obsession with quality would pass.

In late 1990, as we stepped up our quality efforts, morale began to drop, as measured by our annual opinion survey. Even more disheartening were the measures of employee endorsement of our market-driven quality (MDQ) efforts.

At IBM, where the top executives in the company take morale very seriously, these numbers began to put the heat on our general manager (GM). On top of this, we recognized that we were reaching the limits of the quality awareness stage. A few test groups had improved their processes, but little else concrete seemed to be changing. Despite the education and consciousness raising, there remained a resistant core of managers and employees who hoped that the obsession with quality was a passing phase. Some of these core resistors did not buy in to quality until we had concrete results, several years later.

## Suggested Readings

Boehm, B. W. (1981) "An Experiment in Small-Scale Software Engineering," *IEEE Transactions Software Engineering*, SE-7(5): 482–493. *This paper describes and discusses the application of large-scale software engineering techniques to small software projects.*

Boehm, B. W. (1981) *Software Engineering Economics*. Englewood Cliffs, NJ: Prentice-Hall. *An oft-cited work that describes many of the critical issues in software development including quality, costs, and productivity.*

Brooks, F. (1975) *The Mythical Man-Month*. Reading, MA: Addison-Wesley. *It has been called "the sole true classic in the field of software engineering," and it is a gold mine of software management advice.*

Glass, R. L. (1991) *Software Conflict: Essays on the Art and Science of Software Engineering.* Englewood Cliffs, NJ: Prentice-Hall/Yourdon Press. *A fun introduction (via short essays) to many of the issues involved in software engineering.*

Hauser, J. R., and Clausing, D. (1988) "The House of Quality." *Harvard Business Review,* May/June, pp. 63–73. *A good overview of how to introduce customer input into the design process by using the quality functional deployment (QFD) methodology.*

Humphrey, W. S. (1987) *Managing for Innovation: Leading Technical People.* Englewood Cliffs, NJ: Prentice-Hall. *An informationally rich distillation of software management experience at IBM.*

Jones, C. (1991) *Applied Software Measurement: Assuring Productivity and Quality.* New York: McGraw-Hill.

Kidder, T. (1981) *The Soul of a New Machine.* New York: Atlantic Monthly Press. *This Pulitzer Prize–winning story provides a good sense of the organizational complexities involved in developing a new computing (hardware and software) system.*

Patterson, M. L. (1993) *Accelerating Innovation: Improving the Process of Product Development.* New York: Van Nostrand Reinhold. *Only 159 pages long, but this book is rich in management insight on the subject of innovation.*

Peters, T. J., and Austin, N. (1985) *A Passion for Excellence.* New York: Random House. *The successful follow-on to* In Search of Excellence.

Peters, T. J., and Waterman, R. H. (1982) *In Search of Excellence.* New York: Harper & Row. *The popular book that (arguably) did more than any other to raise quality awareness in the United States.*

Taguchi, G., and Clausing, D. (1990) "Robust Quality," *Harvard Business Review,* Jan./Feb., pp. 65–75. *A good overview of how to improve overall product quality through robust design and tighter specifications for component parts.*

Utz, W. J. (1992) *Software Technology Transitions: Making the Transition to Software Engineering.* Englewood Cliffs, NJ: Prentice-Hall. *A technical look at many of the issues faced by software companies trying to shift from software development to software engineering.*

# 4

# Starting a Cultural Transformation

This chapter focuses on innovations that promote awareness of quality issues within the organization. The Excellence Council and departmental strategies raise awareness and act as catalysts in the cultural transformation that is necessary to ensure sustainable quality improvement.

At a sitewide level, the Excellence Council provides a means of educating everyone about quality improvement via periodic quality assessments. It is a completely new approach, invented at IBM, for jump-starting a cultural transformation. Among the innovations in this book, it is unusual in that it was developed to apply to a large organization or company. Strictly speaking, it is an innovation for senior managers, CIOs, and CEOs. However, its principles can be applied in smaller groups, and it is fascinating as a case study of how TQM was implemented at IBM. Although this innovation spanned three of the four stages of maturity, we classify it as an awareness stage innovation because that is where the implementation is most crucial.

At the department or small group level, departmental strategies help translate the organization's general quality goals into specific visions, missions, and objectives for smaller departments. Together with the Excellence Council, departmental strategies launched our quality journey.

Table 4.1 summarizes these innovations, the objectives they help accomplish, and the major pitfalls we encountered while implementing them.

**TABLE 4.1   Stage: Awareness / Food Group: Leadership / Theme: Promote Quality Awareness**

| Objective | Innovative approach | Implementation pitfalls |
|---|---|---|
| Gain management buy-in | Excellence Councils<br>  Baldrige template<br>  Managers' design strategy | Wavering leadership<br>  on push-back |
| Increase department- | Departmental Quality Strategy<br>Bottoms-up creation of<br>  vision/mission/goals | Lack of overall organ-<br>  zational strategy |

## Innovation 1 (Leadership): The Excellence Council

Because the Excellence Council is one of the most crucial but least understood of all the quality innovations in this book, some historical context and an overview is in order.

Cultural change and "buy-in" are the Achilles heel of transformational change and business reengineering. For organizations with more than 500 employees, the challenge is to orchestrate the change and buy-in of more than 20 "influencers" and then accelerate the education and deployment among the remaining managers and employees. This challenge can take years, or can doom the change efforts altogether.

In 1989, Tom Furey, a new General Manager, arrived with visionary ideas about software quality. Fresh off a highly successful tour of duty as the Laboratory Director at IBM Rochester, where he had led a team of 3000 planners, programmers, engineers, and technologists through the highly successful development and launch of the IBM AS/400 minicomputer family, he was intent on transferring some of the lessons learned to the world of mainframe software development.

He spent most of his first 6 months listening to managers and employees in dozens of roundtable discussions, where employees and managers could openly share their ideas, insights, and (sometimes) complaints.

With this input, he performed a situational analysis of the challenges involved in trying to transform IBM's largest software development site. Unlike IBM Rochester, which built and controlled the entire AS/400 system, this new West Coast lab was only a software provider for the mainframe products organization based in Poughkeepsie, NY, and usually was a second-order interface to IBM's worldwide customer base. This problem was further aggravated by the fact that software service support was provided by a worldwide marketing service organization which billed our lab for its services. Finally, like IBM Rochester, the members of the lab frequently attended user group meetings designed around the lab's specialized products, with the result that interactions became increasingly focused on technical details and long-range IS-dominated grand strategies.

These insular dynamics—little opportunity for direct contact with customers or for getting a balanced view of the marketplace—had the potential to create large obstacles for a market- and customer-driven total quality management system. Yet such a system was exactly what Furey hoped to introduce into the software world.

Since mainframe software cycles were woefully long to begin with (sometimes 48 to 60 months), he needed an accelerated program to step up the change cycle and facilitate buy-in.

At the time of his arrival, Furey had just completed a review of IBM Rochester's Malcolm Baldrige National Quality Award application. He was impressed by how well the document tied together all the elements of the system that the Rochester team had installed to focus on their customers, suppliers, human resources, and processes—including continuous improvement and leadership processes. And although IBM Rochester would have to wait until 1990 to win the prestigious Baldrige award, Furey and everyone associated with the Rochester efforts learned an enormous amount about closed-loop total quality management from the 1989 efforts.

From this background arose the innovative idea to transform the West Coast laboratory. Furey reasoned that if he could get all his senior managers to learn and internalize the total quality management approach, as exemplified in a Baldrige application, he could reduce some of the natural resistance to change. Then, if he could reach down into the organization to make middle-level managers responsible for the day-to-day plans for change, he could eliminate one of the greatest stumbling blocks in large organizations—the impenetrability of the middle management layer.

Since total quality management requires constant learning and continuous improvement of all organizational systems and processes, Furey realized he would need a large number of "converts" and potential coaches to succeed.

To accomplish these goals, he conceived the idea of a forum where all functional managers would be required to fill out the Baldrige application for their functions quarterly, and review it with a committee that would score their efforts and provide feedback in the form of a list of strengths and weaknesses.

By including the senior managers that the functional leaders reported to as part of the judging team, two goals were accomplished. First, the senior managers learned about Baldrige. Second, they were motivated to help their functional managers with coaching.

To ensure that the judging didn't become political or incestuous, a second panel of outside judges from various IBM headquarters organizations, and from Silicon Valley firms, participated as well. The scores were compiled by adding the scores of the outside judges to the scores of the judges from the lab. This process provided a valuable outside perspective of strengths and weaknesses from a group that had no biases and that, in most cases, didn't understand the products, the customer environments, or the mountain of acronyms that support the mystique of software.

To help facilitate the transfer of knowledge across functional boundaries, Furey acted as coach to the functional managers. Given the tremendous visibility they would have in presenting their case to the judges, everyone was eager and willing to seek help and coaching. The old syndromes of "not invented here" and "what could I possibly learn from a nontechnical functional area" quickly faded into the background.

The idea for the forum had merit, but there were also many downsides. People had to prepare for the quarterly presentations while also doing more with less resources, and while trying to implement stretch quality goals that called for improvement of quality by a factor of 10 within the next 2 years.

There was more than ample room for resentment and resistance, so the challenge was to portray this forum as a vehicle to help the laboratory on its quality journey. Specifically, the challenge was to portray the forum as part of the education and continuous improvement process, and not as a quality process itself. Because Baldrige focuses on total quality management with continuous improvement to achieve world class status, Furey named the forum the Excellence Council. The name reflected the idea that excellence was required in developing and internalizing the total quality management principles that would result in world class software processes and management systems. But just as important was the idea that excellence was required in tomorrow's leaders who would embrace TQM as part of their management credo.

### The objective

Once a manager is convinced that quality is a top priority, the single greatest challenge is to get the attention and then the buy-in of other levels of management and the technical staff. Once you've got their attention, the trick is to keep it focused on quality long enough for quality to become a habit, engrained in the culture.

### An innovative approach

The Excellence Council concept is simple: create a formal mechanism for periodic review of the quality improvement activities within the organization. But implementing the reviews so that everyone in the organization takes them seriously and focuses on quality can be incredibly difficult.

At our lab, the Excellence Council evolved in three distinct phases over time. As our quality maturity increased, the implementation of the Excellence Council changed to spur the organization toward higher levels of quality.

The leftmost column of Table 4.2 shows the Excellence Council as it was first implemented when the lab was at the awareness stage of quality maturity. At each of the next three stages of maturity, the implementation of the Excellence Council changed, although its role as catalyst for change remained constant. Finally, as we neared the integration stage, the Excellence Council was no longer needed and was replaced with continuous improvement reviews, described in Chap. 20. However, without some sort of periodic review like the Excellence Council, it is unlikely that the lab would have persisted in its quality efforts long enough to reach the integration stage, and the gold medal award for quality excellence which we received late in 1993.

### Phase I

The goal of the initial Excellence Councils was to get senior management and the functional managers (middle management and product owners) educated and focused on quality issues. The education was accomplished by stipulating that all the presentations to the council would follow the Malcolm Baldrige guidelines. This meant that both those sitting on the council—the judges—and those presenting to the council—the presenters—had to be well versed in the Malcolm Baldrige quality criteria.

**TABLE 4.2    Evolution of the Excellence Council**

|  | Phase I: Awareness | Phase II: Coping | Phase III: Management |
|---|---|---|---|
| Focus | First three levels of management buy-in to approach | Management buy-in to deployment | Technical community buy-in innovation and teamwork results |
| Template | 1990 standard Baldrige template | 1990–1991 Baldrige; innovation questions | 1991–1992 Baldrige; innovation questions |
| Format | Formal $\frac{1}{2}$-h presentations | Presentations televised for customers. Site presentations added | 2-h presentations televised throughout lab |
| Presenters | Functional managers | Functional managers (one team presentation) | Cross-functional teams for each product area |
| Assessors | Senior management IBM executives External Baldrige examiners | Senior management IBM executives External Baldrige examiners | Senior technical professionals added as assessors |
| Coach | General Manager | General Manager | Functional managers General Manager = head coach |
| Recognition | Super Bowl tickets to top presenters | $100,000 to top functional area | Variable pay based on performance of all teams |
| Achievement measure | Baldrige score | Baldrige score Corporate bronze-level MDQ award | Baldrige score Corporate silver-level MDQ award |
| Dates | April 1990 July 1990 | October 1990 March 1991 | December 1991 |

Focus was achieved via the formal, almost ritualistic, format of the presentations which was modeled on the formal management review councils held by top executives of IBM in 1989. It was observed that just before a management review council, there was typically a flurry of activity as managers rushed to resolve issues so that they could present a coherent story to their superiors. Thus, while the councils seemed to be simply a review process on the surface, in reality they were a powerful catalyst for change and quick action.

Endorsement of the Excellence Council concept by senior managers was secured by requiring them to participate as judges on the council, along with IBM executives from outside the lab, external Baldrige examiners, and executives from other companies. The commitment of middle managers was secured by requiring them to present to this prestigious panel of judges. Each presentation was scored according to the Malcolm Baldrige criteria, and awards were presented to the top presenters.

But more than the pressure of preparing for judgment was needed. The middle managers also had to learn about Baldrige and about assembling, implementing, and presenting a workable quality strategy.

To this end, the GM switched roles from critic to coach. During the months preceding each Excellence Council, he held a seemingly endless series of one-on-one coaching sessions with each presenter. During these sessions, the GM pointed out the strengths and weaknesses of each presentation and shared his perspective on quality as head of the lab.

Besides direct access to and support from the GM, presenters had access to Baldrige education and to quality experts within the site.

All this effort culminated in two Excellence Councils in 1990, one in April and one in July. The councils focused on the site's approach to quality improvement, and this resulted in detailed feedback highlighting the areas that needed greater focus on quality. Without exception, presentations scored better in the second Excellence Council than in the first. Progress was being made at the same time as middle managers were getting more sophisticated in their ability to perform Baldrige-style quality assessments.

## Phase II

As a mechanism for seizing the attention of upper levels of management at the lab, the first phase of the Excellence Council was a tremendous success. Having senior managers act as judges for the Baldrige presentations of the functional managers ensured that senior and middle management was thoroughly steeped in Baldrige. But the Excellence Council had an almost elitist aura to it.

The fact that the best presenters got tickets to the 1990 Super Bowl, and that the presentations were cloistered in a plush conference room, probably exacerbated this aura.

However, it is impossible to have a quality transformation if the only people who believe in quality are an elite few. Sooner or later the sparks that were kindled with the elite group must set the entire organization ablaze with quality fever. Thus it was inevitable that the format of the Excellence Council would change. The trick was to change it at the right speed and in the right direction.

The second column of Table 4.2 shows how the Excellence Council changed from the awareness stage to the coping stage. The first row in the matrix indicates that the focus shifted from management buy-in to approach, to management buy-in to deployment. This was a subtle change in what the judges began to look for when they scored the presentations.

Whereas in the phase I Excellence Councils presenters were complimented if they showed plans to address quality concerns, in the phase II Excellence Councils plans were no longer enough. The judges were looking for evidence that the plans actually had been implemented in the functional organizations. Woe to the presenter who tried to dazzle the judges with fancy double-talk about quality. If the plans weren't implemented, the glitz just wouldn't cut it.

A second change was more obvious. The 1990 and 1991 Baldrige examination criteria did not address the subject of innovation. Yet, it was clear that we were not going to be able to meet our quality improvement goals without significant innovation. So we augmented the Baldrige criteria by adding some questions on innovation to Baldrige category 5 (quality assurance of products and services). This change signaled that innovation was to become a key focus for the future.

A third change was to televise the Excellence Council proceedings for customers and other interested parties who could not fit in the presentation room itself (which was filled by the 13 judges). This also pilot-tested the logistics of televising the Excellence Council. If it were successful, the next step would be to broadcast to the entire lab.

The presenters remained unchanged from phase I except that we experimented with our first team presentation. The planning organization was on the leading edge in using a team of presenters instead of a single manager.

Finally, the recognition system changed, too. Instead of Super Bowl tickets given to a single individual, we had a $100,000 cash award to be distributed among the members of the winning functional organization. This caught the imagination of the lab. Suddenly, the Excellence Council affected everyone, not just the presenters.

## Phase III

The buzzwords for phase III of the Excellence Council were *accelerated innovation* and *teamwork*. Innovation is necessary because it is impossible to make quantum improvements in the quality levels of products by just doing the same process with more rigor. Instead, the process must be changed, and new technologies must be invented that boost productivity and quality.

But innovation won't result in higher quality unless the organization simultaneously makes breakthroughs in teamwork. For example, redesigning the development process won't work unless all the departments involved can work together and are willing to assume new roles. Other innovations will remain limited in scope and effectiveness if there is no way to extend them beyond departmental boundaries.

This increasing emphasis on innovation and teamwork meant that the technical community had to play a much larger role in the Excellence Councils. In earlier phases of the Excellence Council (see Table 4.2, columns 1 and 2), the presenters and judges had been composed exclusively of managers. This had been necessary to secure management buy-in, but it had unfortunate side effects. By 1990, there was already a perception by many at the lab that the Excellence Council was a "beauty contest" where managers vied with each other to see who could present the most colorful overhead transparencies. Thus, the Excellence Council was seen both as a managers-only event and as an event which fostered competition rather than teamwork.

The trick was to evolve a new version of the Excellence Council that addressed these perceptions, fostered technical innovation, and emphasized teamwork. The third column of Table 4.2 shows how the Excellence Council looked in phase III.

The row labeled "Focus" shows how the focus of the Excellence Councils evolved from obtaining management buy-in to a quality approach, to getting management buy-in to deployment of quality activities, to getting the technical buy-in to results in the form of new innovations and increased teamwork.

Phase III still required presenters to follow the Malcolm Baldrige template, ensuring that both presenters and assessors continued to internalize the Baldrige concept of quality improvement. However, the presentations were lengthened to 2 hours to allow for more detail. This longer presentation format, together with an increased focus on results and the fact that the presentations were being televised throughout the lab, put a spotlight on innovation.

More important, the presentations were no longer prepared by a single functional manager and her or his people. Instead, cross-functional teams worked on each presentation. One representative would make the presentation for each cross-functional team. The teams were composed of both managers and nonmanagers from all the major functional areas at the lab. Table 4.3 shows the composition of the various cross-functional teams.

Adding senior technical leaders to the blue-ribbon panel of assessors (judges) was a way to involve the leaders of the technical community. It also meant that fast-talking managers were less able to finesse technical issues in their presentations. If an approach to quality improvement was technically unsound, the technical judges would call the presenter on it. The functional managers remained involved as coaches to the cross-functional teams. The GM played the role of head coach or "coach of the coaches." Figure 4.1 summarizes these changes in a single picture.

The last change, which was introduced in 1992, was to reward everyone at the lab with a variable pay bonus based not on the performance of a single presenter, but on the scores of *all* the cross-functional teams. This created an environment which maximized cooperation between teams. Thus, the third phase of the Excellence Council engendered an "all for one and one for all" mind-set which help innovations spread and reinforced the idea that quality improvement required team effort.

Because the team presentations reflected an improvement in the level of quality—our lab surpassed a Baldrige score of 625 and was awarded a silver-level quality award by IBM Corporate Headquarters—the employees at the lab also received a variable pay incentive linked to quality improvement.

**TABLE 4.3   Excellence Council Cross-Team Plan**

| Product | Human Resources | Center for Software Excellence | Information Development | Information Systems | Legal | Marketing and Service | Planning | Pricing | Site Operations |
|---|---|---|---|---|---|---|---|---|---|
| Cross-team 1 | x | x | x | x | x | x | x | x | x |
| Cross-team 2 | x | x | x | x | x | x | x | x | x |
| Cross-team 3 | x | x | x | x | x | x | x | x | x |
| Cross-team 4 | x | x | x | x | x | x | x | x | x |
| Cross-team 5 | x | x | x | x | x | x | x | x | x |
| Cross-team 6 | x | x | x | x | x | x | x | x | x |
| Site team | x | x | x | x | x | x | x | x | x |

Note: Malcolm Baldrige template was used. Teams were composed of managers and technical leaders. Functional managers acted as team coaches. Judging included internal and external judges.

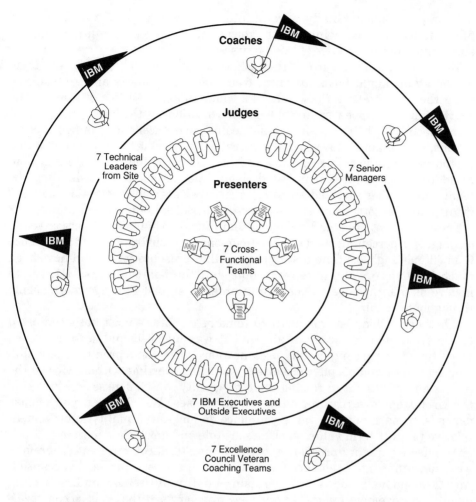

**Figure 4.1** Excellence Council phase III format. Presenters: seven cross-functional teams. Judges: seven technical leaders from site, seven IBM executives and outside executives, and seven senior managers. Coaches: seven Excellence Council veteran teams. (*Courtesy of IBM*)

## Costs, benefits, and risks

The Excellence Council is expensive to implement primarily because it is time-intensive. Because its purpose is to educate and create a passionate focus on quality, the program requires a substantial time commitment from everyone involved.

For example, the GM devoted approximately 20 percent of his calendar just for coaching activities during the months preceding each Excellence Council. The senior and middle managers devoted similar amounts of time, learning the Baldrige criteria and managing the data-gathering activities in their functions that would support their Excellence Council presentations. Technical people had to interrupt their normal work to gather data and to help prepare charts. Finally, several internal quality experts were kept busy full time for months, helping with education, offering presentation support, and managing the logistics of the 2-day sessions.

To give a sense of the size of the task, consider that each of the seven team presentations might have anywhere from 100 to 200 charts and graphs, covering the Baldrige criteria. Figure 4.2 contains sample titles of some of the charts that have appeared in Baldrige presentations at the lab.

In phase III, when cross-functional teams gave Excellence Council presentations, each team had seven Baldrige category "owners" who invested 2 to 3 person-months apiece researching and preparing for the team presentation. In addition, a team leader invested about 4 person-months coordinating the team. The coaches invested about a person-week's worth of valuable management time. The total came to 2 to 3 person-years per team presentation.

The overall cost (we had seven presentations) was about 18 person-years, or roughly 1 percent of the lab's total personnel resources for each Excellence Council meeting. The time cost to put together presentations could have been much lower by involving fewer people, but the point of phase III was to involve as many people as possible in order to spread Baldrige more deeply throughout the lab.

Whether all this cost was justified remains one of the most hotly contested topics at the lab. Some maintain that it was unconscionable to devote so much time to preparing quality presentations when some products were slipping schedules and people were already working overtime. Others viewed the cost as an investment in raising the lab's quality consciousness and in taking the first step toward improving our processes. Which camp you choose depends primarily on the value you place on long-term quality improvement relative to short-term values such as schedule and immediate morale.

An effective quality program requires a long-term commitment. Therefore, we believe that the Excellence Council is worth the cost, primarily because it was tremendously successful at raising quality awareness and catalyzing quality improvement efforts. In our view, the very fact that it is so controversial—that you can ask any employee and get a strong opinion one way or another—is proof of its success. As one manager put it, the worst thing that can happen to your quality program is to have it ignored.

The benefits of the Excellence Councils have included

1. Helping people to internalize the Baldrige criteria and attain a quality-focused mind-set. This mind-set included a focus on customer satisfaction and supplier quality, employee empowerment and skills development, use of benchmarking, a focus on continuous process improvement, an awareness of process linkages, and a concern with defect elimination which ultimately drives cost reductions and organizational efficiency.

2. Heightening awareness of the need for innovation related to quality improvement.

3. Facilitating the sharing of ideas and innovations across functional boundaries. Engendering a spirit of teamwork.

**Figure 4.2** Sample titles of charts from Baldrige presentations. (*Courtesy of IBM*)

Sources and Uses of Customer-Related Data.

Sources and Uses of Product and Service Quality Data.

Sources and Uses of Internal Operations and Performance Data.

Sources and Uses of Supplier Performance Data.

Business and Quality Processes.

Data Analysis Techniques.

Strategic Planning Process.

Product Maturity Curve.

Investment Actuals and Goals, by Platform.

Key Quality Objectives and Related Actuals/Goals, 1990–1997.

Summary of Resource Commitments, 1993.

Human Resource Processes, Measures, and Plans, by HR Initiative.

Employee Empowerment, Responsibility, and Innovation Requirements and Goals.

Buy-In Index and Participation Index by Employee Category, 1989–1993.

Empowerment Index by Employee Category, 1989–1993.

Employee Productivity ($M/employee), 1990–1993.

Employee Innovation and Technical Vitality Measures, 1989–1993.

Employees Achieving Author Recognition Plateaus, 1989–1993.

Determination of Required Skills.

% Employees Receiving Quality and Related Education, 1989–1993.

Average # of Quality and Related Education Hours per Employee, 1989–1993.

Recognition/Award Programs Reinforcing Quality Values, 1993.

Team and Individual Awards.

# of Individual and Team Awards by Employee Category, 1989–1993.

Attrition Trends (% of Employees).

Employee Well-Being Measures by Employee Category, 1989–1993.

Empowerment and Team Indices.

Department Quality.

Process Model.

Software Development Process.

Design Process for Customer Requirements.

Examples of Formal Methodologies We Use to Strengthen the Linkage Between Customer

Requirements and Design Characteristics.

Process Design Process.

Programming Process Reviews and Measurements for Software Products/Services.

Key Processes.

Process-Management Process.

Process Design Evolution.

Defect Prevention Process.

Five-Step Template for Process Improvement.

Process for Research and Use of Alternative Technologies.

New Processes and Technologies.

Key Business Process and Measures.

Supplier-Relationship Process.

Supplier Quality Requirements by Type.

Quality Assessment Information by Type.

Quality Assessment Information by Development Phase.

Industry Awards and Recognition, 1992–1993.

Database and Language Products' Customer-Based CUPRIMDSO Prioritization, 1993.

TVUAs for Database Products, 1989–1993.

TVUAs for Language Products, 1989–1993.

DB2 Product Defects, First Year after GA.

IMS Product Defects, First Year after GA.

QMF Product Defects, First Year after GA.

FORTRAN Product Defects, First Year after GA.

COBOL Product Defects, First Year after GA.

PL/1 Product Defects, First Year after GA.

TVUAs per Function Point.

Product PEs, 1989–1993.

Total Problems/Year for All Key Products.

Total Problems/Year, by Product.

U.S. Problem Comparisons, 1992.

Fix Cycle Time Trends.

Service Callback Responsiveness Trends.

Service Callback Responsiveness Comparisons.

Data Systems Workload Transaction Rate on Top Processors at Release.

Database Transactions Performance Comparisons.

DB2 Performance—Competitive Benchmark

*(Continued)*

| | |
|---|---|
| Batch Query Performance—Competitive Benchmarks. | Publication, Early and Late In-Process Assessments. |
| COBOL Performance Comparisons. | Operational Indicators and Associated Key Internal Measurements. |
| VS FORTRAN Performance. | |
| Total Documentation APARs across Key Products. | Revenue, 1992 Industry Comparison. |
| | Gross Margin, 1992 Industry Comparison. |

**Figure 4.2**  *(Continued)*

4. Educating the lab (via televised proceedings) and new employees (via videotapes of the proceedings) about the function and quality activities of their own and other areas.

5. Gaining widespread participation in quality efforts, including the participation of the technical community which is the source of most innovation. In fact, quality participation has increased from year to year since 1989, primarily as a result of the Excellence Councils.

6. Providing feedback in the form of hundreds of specific "strengths" and "improvement suggestions" from the internal and external judges.

7. Demonstrating a continued commitment to quality to the lab as well as to our customers who viewed the proceedings. (Note that we recommend bringing in customers to view the proceedings only after you have had experience with a couple of Excellence Councils and you can identify what the value for customers will be.)

8. Reinforcing the commitment to quality among middle managers by asking them to assume the role of coach for their teams. This step is important in embedding quality in the culture, since teaching or coaching is one of the best ways to master a discipline.

9. The development of new in-process measurements and the development of and experimentation with many of the other innovations described in later chapters of this book.

Many of these benefits did not come immediately. Instead the Excellence Council served as a catalyst whose effect was to continually shape the way that the lab views quality. But one immediate benefit was that the Excellence Council forced management to apply Baldrige criteria rigorously to its operations. Managers needed data for their presentations, or they would look silly in front of their peers, their bosses, and CEOs from other companies. So the managers were going to get those data, and they were going to invest a lot of time doing so.

But once the presentation was over, those data didn't just disappear. Neither did the learning that occurred amid the rushing around madly to get the presentation together. Smart managers realized that they might as well use those data to make process improvements and manage quality. Besides, another Excellence Council was just around the corner, and this time they would need to show not only deployment, but also results.

Quarter by quarter, the Excellence Council reached more and more people until almost everyone in the lab had been involved either directly or indirectly. By the time we reached the management stage of quality maturity, the culture had changed, and the results of that change were finally materializing in concrete ways.

Having said that, we acknowledge that there are a number of risks associated with the Excellence Council. First, the program can succeed only with the firm and unwavering commitment of the senior executive of the organization. Without this commitment, managers who are not convinced will find ways not to participate. After all, if the managers all already saw the value of the Excellence Council, it wouldn't be necessary, right? Yet without full participation, the program cannot succeed. Unlike many of the other innovations in this book, there is no "pilot" option with the Excellence Council. The senior executive has to make up his or her mind to do it all the way, or not to do it at all.

Second, there will be push-back and a drop in morale as the various departments begin to feel the bite of having to stop what they are doing to "gather data for another fancy management presentation." For example, in a laboratory-wide survey, comments like the following were typical:

"I think the Excellence Council is a waste of valuable time and money."

"The Excellence Council is of very little real value. If a vote were held..., it would be voted down."

"Gets the awards and recognition from above, but it doesn't affect the day-to-day business as much as it should."

"Lots of overhead for no benefit."

This seems like harsh criticism, yet the Excellence Council was so effective at raising awareness that companies outside of IBM began adopting it. Perhaps a more objective evaluation comes from a billion-dollar-plus Silicon Valley company that adapted the Excellence Council concept. Here's what one vice president and general manager had to say:

The excellence council/Baldrige team has been probably one of the most beneficial, probably one of the most significant engines in driving our business unit's culture change. It has been far more successful than I had anticipated when we first kicked off in June of 1991. I think that the excellence council/Baldrige team is a process that really embodies and demonstrates the power of involvement, continuous improvement, teamwork, and data-based activity.

Our own view is that if senior management holds its ground, all the first-line managers and technical staff will eventually get exposed to the new quality focus, which in turn will become an ingrained part of the culture.

## Synergy

The Excellence Council is synergistic with most quality education and assessment activities. It might be seen as a catalyst that drives these activities. For example, training in the Baldrige, ISO 9000, or some other assessment methodology is complementary to the Excellence Council.

## Prerequisites

The chief prerequisite is commitment from the senior executive in the organization. Without this commitment, the Excellence Council has little chance of success. There are no other innovations that are prerequisites for the Excellence Council.

## Implementation advice

In discussions of what works and what doesn't, practitioners all agree that the value of the Excellence Council lies in the process of actually doing the self-assessment to prepare for the presentations—not in the presentations themselves. One of our colleagues put it this way: "If you could do all the work for the Excellence Council and then cancel it without getting anybody upset, you'd have gotten all the benefit out of the concept. The problem is, people would get upset if you canceled it."

In all likelihood, people will get upset anyway. One difficulty we encountered early on was the perception that the Excellence Council was a sort of beauty contest for middle management. In retrospect, we could have minimized this perception by emphasizing the value of doing the self-assessments as opposed to rewarding slick presentations.

Unfortunately, we awarded Super Bowl tickets to the manager whose presentation attained the highest Baldrige score. While this may have motivated the presenters, it did little to help communicate the overall purpose of the Excellence Council to the organization. With the benefit of hindsight, we would recommend that awards be more team-based right from the start.

A related pitfall is the failure to communicate the results and feedback to *all* the organization. Management needs to avoid sending a signal that says only the presenters get the benefit of visibility, coaching, and feedback. The presenters are representatives of their respective organizations and should be treated as such.

It should be clear from our evolutionary experience with the Excellence Council that this innovation is flexible. In fact, the Excellence Council has been adopted by half a dozen other IBM sites and other companies, and it seems always to be evolving.

For example, IBM's Services Sector division allows each of its suborganizations to determine what form of review would be most helpful. Some suborganizations request a less formal review that allows for more interchange of comments and clarifications.

Higher in IBM's hierarchy, senior executives have increased the breadth of the Excellence Council concept to include presentations that span several IBM development sites.

Outside of IBM, one general manager has taken the Excellence Council one step further. Rather than scoring all presentations strictly as a Baldrige examiner would, a weighted scoring scheme was developed. "We change the scoring depending upon which team is presenting," the GM says. "For example, if a marketing team is presenting, we give more relative weight to the customer satisfaction section of Baldrige than we would for a manufacturing team."

However, despite its flexibility, there are three essential elements of a successful Excellence Council.

First, you must have senior executive commitment. We were fortunate in this respect. The GM actively shaped the format of the Excellence Councils and devoted many hours to one-on-one coaching sessions with the individual presenters, before they made their formal presentations. Having the GM behind the program went a long way toward overcoming the inevitable complaints and push-back that characterize an organization trying to overcome inertia and change its culture to be more quality-oriented.

Most important, the GM became a coach for success, not a critic. The judges played the role of critic, which allowed the leader to be a catalyst for improvement instead of a threat.

The second critical factor is a measurement tool that doubles as a template for the Excellence Council presentations. A good measurement tool challenges the processes you are using and helps you imagine the kind of processes you would like to have. It's a vision tool.

We used Baldrige as our vision tool (see Chap. 2), because it seemed to provide the most comprehensive coverage of quality issues. All the presentations followed the Baldrige criteria, listing activities that demonstrated progress in each of the Baldrige categories.

The fact that Baldrige is well known and accepted made it easier to find judges from outside IBM who were willing to join the council and score presentations as Baldrige examiners would.

Something we learned in this respect was the importance of reporting the assessment scores of both internal and external judges. As Fig. 4.3 shows, judges from inside and outside the organization may not agree in their Baldrige scoring. In our case, the internal judges were harsher in their assessment at first than the external judges. However, over time as the internal judges became more familiar with Baldrige criteria and as the external judges became more familiar with the operations of a software business, the scores began to converge. Without the "sanity check" of external judges, we would have had no way of measuring how well we were learning to apply the Baldrige template. With them, we could use the discrepancy between internal and external scores as a measure of our learning and as an indicator of progress.

The third key ingredient is a motivating ritual. We used periodic formal reviews with distinguished external and internal judges to motivate the presenters.

Once you have an approach that incorporates these three critical success factors, you will need to answer these questions: Who judges the presentations? Who presents? Do we have awards? How frequent should the reviews be?

How you answer these questions will probably depend on your organization's level of quality maturity and your specific needs and objectives.

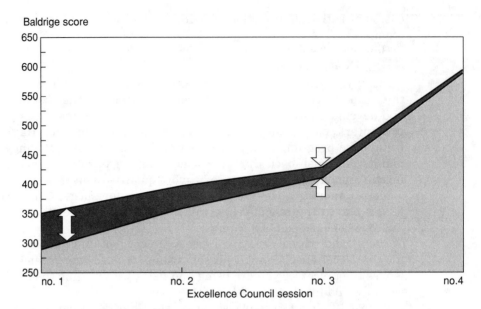

**Figure 4.3** Internal and external judging of the Excellence Council. Top line = external judge scores. Bottom line = internal judge scores. The scores for internal and external judges converged over time. (*Courtesy of IBM*)

As a default approach for an organization in the awareness stage, we recommend having middle management make the presentations and senior management judge them. However, awards must be handled carefully, and the value of the preparation in terms of education and quality focus should be clearly articulated. If cross-functional teamwork is already accepted practice in your organization, you may want to modify these suggestions along the lines suggested in phase III.

Figures 4.4 and 4.5 summarize our implementation advice for phase I and II of the Excellence Council, respectively. There are some additional considerations for phase III where cross-functional teams are involved.

Executive commitment and support continue to be key factors in the success of the third phase of the Excellence Councils. However, the fact that teams were involved, and that the team members were removed by several layers of management from the General Manager, meant that phase III was a test of how well middle management had internalized the knowledge and quality values expressed by the Baldrige template. (In small organizations, these concerns are not as likely to be so pronounced.) In addition, teamwork issues that need skillful handling inevitably crop up.

For example, it was important to make sure that nondeveloper team members were included in all the team decisions. Since the team leaders tended to be product developers, this required pointing out to the team leaders that (1) products could not get out the door without the help of the support organizations and (2) the support team members had access to critical information for the Baldrige presentations.

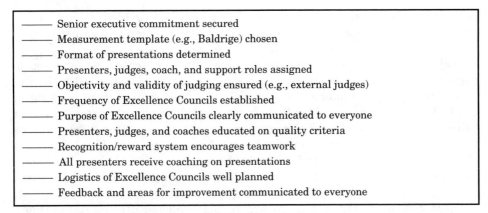

**Figure 4.4**  Excellence Council phase I checklist.

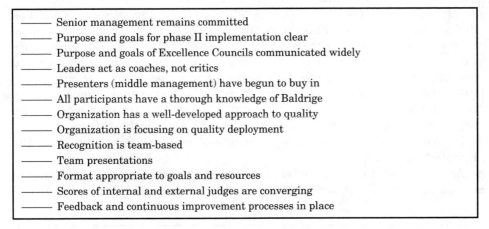

**Figure 4.5**  Excellence Council phase II implementation checklist.

A related challenge was getting the teams to cooperate, not compete. Because competition was reinforced in earlier phases of the Excellence Council by giving cash prizes to the best presentation, this was a tough mindset to break. But in phase III, no one could "win" (i.e., get the highest variable pay bonus) unless all the teams improved their Baldrige scores. So sharing information became a prerequisite for success.

Televised proceedings added another level of complexity to the logistics of the Excellence Council, but they also added value in that the entire lab could see the presentations. We hired a vendor (production company) to videotape the proceedings. A shoestring budget alternative is to videotape the Excellence Council yourself and then make copies of the tape available for viewing.

Probably the toughest part of the entire Excellence Council implementation was trying to get teams to see the value as clearly as they could see the cost. Typically team members were much more resistant to the idea of participating on an Excellence Council team ("I can't do this, I've got real work to do!")

before they started than after they had finished. The problem is that you've got an unknown, intangible thing called *quality* competing against a well-known, and very concrete, thing called *product schedule*.

Asking for volunteers doesn't always work. In those cases, we resorted to various forms of persuasion (stopping short of bamboo slivers under the fingernails). It wasn't comfortable, and without senior management backing, it would have been impossible. But uncomfortable moments are when your belief in quality is tested. Either you see quality as a matter of survival, or you don't. If it's a matter of survival, you let people know it. If not, then you shouldn't be messing around with the Excellence Council, because it is a tremendous drain on resources that could be going into product development or whatever it is that you think is more important.

There are some issues with regard to the Baldrige presentations themselves that are worth mentioning. For one thing, as your Baldrige score increases, it becomes harder and harder to get additional points. To get more points, you need more and more and more detailed information which can be difficult to communicate in a timed presentation. This difficulty is one reason why the time allowed for presentations was increased as the Excellence Council evolved through its phases. It is also one of the reasons why a written document is the type of Baldrige assessment required by the national examiners and by our own corporate examiners (for silver-level or higher awards). A written document provides the detail needed to determine whether an organization deserves those extra five points for a particular category.

Figure 4.6 summarizes some implementation steps for phase III of the Excellence Council.

As a final word of advice, don't embark on the Excellence Council concept unless you are willing to follow through all the way. As a long-term invest-

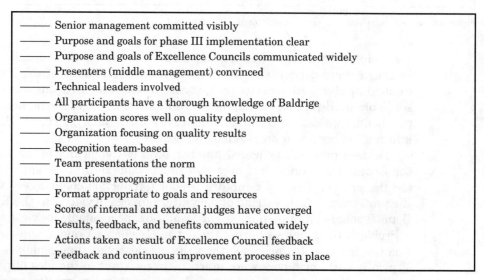

—— Senior management committed visibly
—— Purpose and goals for phase III implementation clear
—— Purpose and goals of Excellence Councils communicated widely
—— Presenters (middle management) convinced
—— Technical leaders involved
—— All participants have a thorough knowledge of Baldrige
—— Organization scores well on quality deployment
—— Organization focusing on quality results
—— Recognition team-based
—— Team presentations the norm
—— Innovations recognized and publicized
—— Format appropriate to goals and resources
—— Scores of internal and external judges have converged
—— Results, feedback, and benefits communicated widely
—— Actions taken as result of Excellence Council feedback
—— Feedback and continuous improvement processes in place

**Figure 4.6**  The Excellence Council phase III implementation checklist.

ment in cultural change, it can be an extremely valuable catalyst. It can also serve to maintain the organization's quality momentum. The prospect of the next Excellence Council means that the organization can never forget about quality, even if it has just completed a successful quality review.

But changing a culture is hard work and requires long-term commitment. Without follow-through, the Excellence Council can easily become a fad instead of a powerful management tool. If it does become a fad, it damages management's credibility and ultimately hurts the cause of quality more than if you did nothing at all.

## Innovation 2 (Leadership): Departmental Quality Strategies

### The objective

While global frameworks and approaches such as the four stages of maturity and the Excellence Council provide a sense of direction for the organization as a whole, individual departments within the organization also need to understand their roles in the overall quality effort. Without such an understanding, quality improvement activities can degenerate into a hodgepodge of quick fixes that do not really advance the organization's quality maturity. The four stages are good as a rough map, but they cannot anticipate the unique concerns of specific departments.

### An innovative approach

Our approach was to let each of the individual departments try to come up with a statement of its vision, mission, and goals which would fit into the overall quality strategy of the organization. The idea was that a bottom-up approach would increase commitment to the quality efforts. Besides, no one knew the concerns of the departments better than the departments themselves.

Ideally, members of a department would meet for 2 days. One day would be spent covering the organization's overall quality strategy and the basics of Baldrige. The other day would be spent arriving at vision, mission, and goals statements for the department that tied in with the organization's overall quality strategy.

In reality, the development of departmental strategies is not so clear-cut. For one thing, the organization's larger strategy is shaped by the departmental strategies at the same time as the departmental strategies are molded by the organization's strategy.

And we've had more than our share of mission statements that were hammered out in off-site meetings and which no one could remember 2 weeks later. Strategy development is not an easy task. Perhaps the best advice we can offer is to simplify.

After you take all the research and various perspectives into account, ask yourself: What is the essence of this strategy? How could I say it in simple, memorable terms?

For example, our lab had an overall goal of 10-fold quality improvement, and there was talk of increasing this to 100-fold improvement. The genius of these goals was that they were easy to remember and outrageous. They caught the attention of the lab. Everybody argued over exactly how to count improvement, and the goals were seen universally as overly optimistic, but nobody had trouble remembering what they were. Those goals served to spur development in a positive direction.

### Costs, benefits, and risks

Theoretically, the resource cost is about 20 person-days of effort, or the time it takes a department of 10 to meet for 2 days. Our experience has been that such meetings tend to run longer than 1 day—especially if you have a group prone to heated discussion.

The benefits include heightened awareness of the organization's quality efforts, commitment at the department level, and better coordination between the quality efforts of various levels of the organization.

The main risk is that the strategy meetings could end up being a waste of time if there are no follow-on activities or if the vision, mission, and goals don't seem very meaningful. It is easy for this sort of meeting to turn into an argument session, and for the vision, mission, and goals statements to be convoluted expressions assembled from everyone's favorite words, but which no one can remember once the meeting is over.

### Synergy

Departmental quality strategies are synergistic with the self-assessment activities and other awareness-heightening activities characteristic of the awareness stage.

### Prerequisites

It does not make much sense to hold departmental quality strategy meetings unless the organization already has a clear idea of its overall quality strategy. The exception to this rule would be cases where the department is trying to pilot certain quality improvement activities. In this case, development of a departmental strategy might be used as a way demonstrate to upper management the advantages of a certain approach to quality improvement.

### Implementation advice

In retrospect, the departmental quality strategy meetings were a qualified success. They succeeded in their primary function as a way to get the attention of departments focused on quality. However, because we were unclear as to our organization's overall quality strategy—we lacked the four-stage road map because we had not invented it yet—the departmental strategies did not really result in the coordinated quality actions we had hoped for.

With regard to vision, mission, and goals statements, we used the following guidelines:

A vision should be a succinct statement that paints a picture of where the department is headed or what it will look like when it has arrived. For example, our lab's vision is to become a world-class software laboratory. (Depending on your point of view, this vision is either vague—because it leaves *world class* to the imagination—or politically brilliant—because everyone can agree that being world-class is a good thing.)

A mission statement presents what the organization does, to whom, and for what purpose. Specifically, there are no quantified results statements in a mission statement. Part of our mission statement is to "develop and support software technologies that empower customers to create, manage, and utilize information assets."

Finally, goals can be translated to objectives which are concrete statements of a desired result, e.g., win the Malcolm Baldrige Award in 1994 or achieve tenfold quality improvement in 1992.

Figure 4.7 shows the overall vision, mission, and goals for our lab in 1993.

Reactions to time spent learning about market-driven quality and then creating departmental vision, mission, and goals statements were mixed. Feedback from the departments ranged from "very useful" to "a complete waste of time." Here are some representative comments from a survey we conducted that covered every department and 25 percent of the lab's population:

> "We are still evolving our [quality] strategy. But it has been very useful to us, to help determine how, as a services organization, we can create value for the lab and have goals that help fulfill our customers' needs."

> "I think it brought up some good issues of what department members thought was important to solve quality problems. However, we had a hard time coming up with consensus as to what items to work on, because everyone thought that the `hard' items would take too much time away from already committed development items."

---

**Vision:** To become the world-class leader in software technology

**Mission**

- To build customer partnerships that create complete satisfaction
- To develop, market, and support software technologies that empower customers to gain strategic advantage by productively creating, managing, and utilizing information assets
- To exceed expectations and delight our customers by demonstrating leadership in software quality, value, and integration

**Goals**

- Differentiate our laboratory offerings through world-class quality
- Empower and nurture people to create a market-driven laboratory
- Sharpen our focus on reducing time to market

**Figure 4.7**  Sample vision, mission, and goals statement.

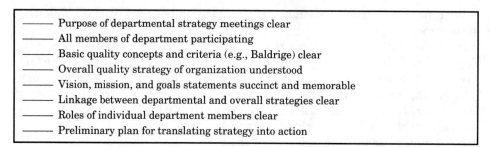

——— Purpose of departmental strategy meetings clear
——— All members of department participating
——— Basic quality concepts and criteria (e.g., Baldrige) clear
——— Overall quality strategy of organization understood
——— Vision, mission, and goals statements succinct and memorable
——— Linkage between departmental and overall strategies clear
——— Roles of individual department members clear
——— Preliminary plan for translating strategy into action

**Figure 4.8**   Departmental quality strategy checklist.

"It would be ok if it were the only tool we used; tends to get lost in the crowd since we have so many other organizational tools and techniques. 'Vision' and 'mission' now have humorous overtones."

"Helps sharpen your processes. Gives you a consciousness-raising perspective."

"Must be emphasized more in the day-to-day job to be effective."

Taken together, these comments touch on the major implementation issues: gaining consensus, creating vision statements that are meaningful as opposed to humorous, and following up with day-to-day implementation actions.

To the extent that these issues are addressed, you will get more value out of the departmental quality strategy concept. However, keep in mind that probably the most important function of such meetings is to get people to focus on quality in a participative way. And that, after all, is the main goal in the awareness stage.

Figure 4.8 summarizes the key points for successful implementation of MDQ departmental strategies.

## Suggested Readings

Beer, M., Eisenstat, R. A., and Spector, B. (1990) "Why Change Programs Don't Produce Change." *Harvard Business Review,* November/December, pp. 158–166. *Read for a view of why change from the top doesn't always work and how you can change things from the periphery of an organization.*

Born, D. (1992) *Adapting IBM's Excellence Councils: Culture Change Using the Malcolm Baldrige National Quality Award.* Presentation available from the Council for Continuous Improvement, San Jose, CA.

Covey, S. (1988) *The Seven Habits of Highly Effective People.* New York: Fireside. *Provides some guidance on creating effective vision, mission, and goals statements. See pp. 139–143.*

Ross, N. (1990) "Using Metrics in Quality Management." *IEEE Software,* 7(4): 80–82, July.

Schultz, H. P. (1988) *Software Management Metrics,* Bedford, MA: Mitre, ESD-TR-88-001, May. *May be of interest to presenters trying to incorporate more measurements into their presentations.*

Wall, S. J., and Zeynel, S. C. (1991) "The Senior Manager's Role in Quality Improvement." *Quality Progress,* January, pp. 66–68. *Worth reading, especially for organizations contemplating top-down change.*

# 5

# Quality Education and Leadership

This chapter describes leadership innovations aimed primarily at raising the organization's knowledge of quality improvement via quality education, leadership workshops, and quality publications. Table 5.1 summarizes each of these leadership innovations, the objectives they helped achieve, and the major pitfalls we encountered during implementation.

The educational seminar series can provide a special kind of knowledge that is critical early in an organization's quality efforts—the knowledge that a quality transformation can occur. For example, we still remember a presentation by Bill Smith, VP of Motorola, at the earliest stage of our quality improvement efforts. What we needed more than concrete techniques was assurance that radical quality improvements could be made. As a speaker in our seminar series, Smith showed us that Motorola had traveled the quality path before and won.

The Leadership Institute focuses on a different kind of knowledge—knowledge of self. In an intensive workshop setting, software professionals begin to assess their own potential for leading the quality improvement efforts in their groups.

Finally, quality publications deal with the spread and capture of knowledge. The publications not only communicate the latest breakthroughs to all parts of the lab, but also document innovations so that they will not be lost when people change job assignments.

**TABLE 5.1    Stage: Awareness / Food Group: Leadership / Theme: Elevate Knowledge Level**

| Objective | Innovative approach | Implementation pitfalls |
|---|---|---|
| Increase level of overall knowledge and skill | *Educational seminar series:* seminars with guest speakers | Low quality, lack of relevancy |
| Remove organizational and cultural inhibitors | *Leadership Institute:* intensive workshop on leadership | No follow-up; no executive leadership |
| Provide visible, persistent communications | *Quality publications:* publish periodicals on quality | Propaganda and management exhortation without *useful* content |

Together, these three innovations converge to increase the organization's overall quality knowledge and effectiveness.

## Innovation 3 (Leadership): Seminar Series

### The objective

While innovations such as the Excellence Council can produce the intense flash of heat necessary to ignite an organization's quality efforts, educational programs are the fuel that sustain such efforts—especially during the early stage of awareness. Moreover, investing in education is like putting money in the bank. The earlier you invest, the longer the results can compound.

The educational challenge can be broken down into two components. On one hand, you need pragmatic training courses that provide software developers with tools that they can use right away. These courses not only heighten quality awareness but also give folks the tools to make immediate progress in well-defined areas. Education about many of the innovations described in

Continuous Improvement
Creating World Class Capabilities (I and II)
Quality Mini-assessment Workshop
Rochester Quality Showcase '92
IBM's Market-Driven Quality Strategy
Cleanroom Software Engineering (Overview)
Overview of the Baldrige Award
Quality Improvement Process Workshop
Fix the Process—Application Development
Malcolm Baldrige Examiner Assessment Training
A Practical Approach to Process Workshop
ISO 9000 Seminar
Key Elements in Total Quality Management—Processes
Benchmarking Skills—A Strategic Approach
Integration of ISO 9000 and Baldrige Concepts
Total Product Assurance
The Quest for Excellence (I to IV)
Quality Management Approaches to the Malcolm Baldrige Award
Leadership and Technology in Transforming Organizations
Implementing Change
Fostering Empowerment in the Workplace
Process Analysis Techniques
Software Development Quality Symposium
Working in a Team Environment
Managing in a Team Environment
DPP—Defect Prevention Process
ODC—Orthogonal Defect Classification
Market-Driven Quality Process Management Awareness

**Figure 5.1** Sample of quality-related courses taught at IBM.

this book would fall under that category. And IBM, like most large companies, has an extensive set of course offerings to address this challenge. Figure 5.1 shows a small sample of some of our quality-related course and seminar offerings.

Courses similar to these, and many others, are available from IBM's spinoff education company (Skill Dynamics), the American Society for Quality Control (ASQC), the I.Q. Company, and many other sources. We list some sources for this kind of education in Suggested Readings. Large organizations might also conduct specific training courses in-house. For example, our basic one-day seminar covers an introduction to and history of the Baldrige Award, detailed exploration of the Baldrige criteria including examples from other companies, and case studies. Students play the role of Baldrige examiners, actually scoring the case studies and justifying the scores.

Because most companies are aware of the need for training in the form of courses and seminars, we will not discuss it in depth here. But there is another, much more subtle educational need, one that often goes unaddressed. This is the need to keep a steady flow of new ideas coming into the company so that the software developers remain technically vital and creative.

Most companies give lip service to this sort of education, and perhaps they send their employees off to an occasional conference or seminar for "technical enrichment," but this is neither an efficient nor a sufficient means for fostering creativity and innovation.

Psychological research suggests that one of the most important factors in creativity is keeping people bathed in a steady stream of new ideas. There is no way to predict accurately exactly which idea will lead to the next technological breakthrough. But the continuous stream idea appears to pay off as a long-term strategy. Libraries, on-line information services, and conversations with colleagues are standard ways of gaining exposure to new ideas, but in the early 1980s we felt these were not enough.

## An innovative approach

In 1984, we launched the *educational seminar series*. The concept was to bring in exciting speakers who were at the forefront of science, technology, or industry and to allow them to share their enthusiasm and knowledge. The speakers did not have to be in the information technology business per se, but their ideas had to be in some way relevant. Above all, they had to be interesting, since attendance at the seminars, which were held in the cafeteria, was completely voluntary.

From a humble beginning of three seminars in 1984, over 200 seminars have been given and over 30,000 people have attended them. On average, our lab holds 25 seminars a year compared with other companies with similar programs that may offer 9 to 12 seminars a year.

Speakers come from IBM (worldwide), IBM customers, industry, universities, and government, and they speak on a diverse set of topics. For example, Scott Carpenter described what it's like to be an astronaut, John McCarthy told us about artificial intelligence, Jaron Lanier explained virtual reality, Ted Nelson expounded upon the virtues of hypertext, and Bill Smith told us about Six Sigma and the quality efforts at Motorola.

We have heard from astronomers, creativity researchers, bank executives, heads of IBM forecasting and research, CEOs of computer firms, fractal researchers, earthquake researchers, computer animation experts, software technologists, futurists, and many other creative individuals.

People come because the speakers are interesting, and there is anecdotal evidence that when creative people hear other creative people speak, good things result. For example, the inventor of one of our most successful innovations, a computer-supported collaborative work environment, said that he got several of his key ideas from a speaker at one of the educational seminar series.

## Costs, benefits, and risks

The costs of the program can be quite low. For example, an analysis of costs for our 1990 program showed a cost of approximately $2.50 per attendee. With few exceptions, outside speakers are offered an honorarium that has ranged from $200 to $500, and a large number of outside speakers take no fee. The key here is to have a skilled negotiator in charge of arranging the speakers.

Because of the volume of speakers in each year, we have one person whose primary job is to arrange for the speakers and run the logistics of the program. However, for smaller organizations, it is possible to set up a program on a shoestring budget, using volunteer time if a group of people are motivated to make the program happen. One way to keep the costs down is simply to turn away speakers who request fees greater than $1000. It is amazing how many speakers will come for a modest honorarium, provided they are contacted well in advance and provided you are persistent.

Benefits are difficult to quantify, but the following comments from a random survey are fairly typical of the lab's perceptions:

"Good topics. Good presenters. I don't feel that I can attend as many as I would like since it is 'away from the desk' where all this work lies. I'd like to not feel guilty when attending them."

"Great way to hear from the outside world. Many interesting topics."

"Absolutely the best thing going....A breath of fresh air. Allows one to think on new and provocative ideas."

"They are fun, but don't really add to the quality of products produced."

"Depends on the seminar. Oftentimes making the time to attend the seminars is difficult. Personally, I would like to see more of them videotaped with a package of the foils [copies of overhead transparencies] attached so that I could view these when I had time."

"Love 'em."

In our own view, the benefits probably fall into two general classes. Most important is the exposure to new ideas which can lead to innovation in the organization. But also important is the sense of excitement and reward that having a famous speaker come to the lab brings. It reinforces the self-esteem of the lab to have the top speakers in leading-edge areas talk with us.

The primary risk is that you can alienate both speakers and your audience if the program is not executed well. Also if there is only one coordinator for the program, with no backup, you may have a problem.

## Synergy

If there is a particular program that is being launched, sometimes the seminar series can be a good way to kick off the program. For example, Motorola's vice president of quality came to speak at a time when we were just beginning to kick off our own quality transformation efforts.

## Prerequisites

One prerequisite for the program is a meeting room large enough to hold the expected audience. Another is finding an individual or group who are really excited about the project. A third prerequisite is to make sure that the managers in the organization recognize the benefit of the program and are willing to let their people attend on a voluntary basis.

## Implementation advice

The success of the seminar series depends primarily on the quality of the speakers. Since most organizations cannot afford to pay top dollar, you have to substitute creativity and persistence for money in attracting these speakers. Secondary factors include logistics support, publicity, and follow-up. Over the years we have developed a seven-step process which other organizations might use as a model for their programs. Figure 5.2 lists the seven steps. They are explained in more detail below.

**Research.** The foundation for getting good speakers is good research. You need to do lots of reading, to get input from other people in your organization, to keep track of talks going on in other organizations, and most importantly

---

——— Research and environmental scanning for good speakers
——— Obtain speaker; schedule checkpoints
——— Logistical support for the speaker
——— Leverage speaker's presence for multiple activities
——— Publicity
——— Host duties when speaker arrives
——— Follow-up

**Figure 5.2** Seminar series implementation checklist.

to build a network of contacts that can help you find speakers. Informal evaluation forms, passed out at the end of seminars, can help focus your research on the subjects most interesting and valuable to your audience.

**Getting the speaker.**   Everyone probably has an individual style when it comes to approaching and asking someone to speak, but there are a few basic rules that have worked for us. First, everyone is approachable. Never be stopped by the position or fame of a person. You will know only from the attempt whether or not you will be successful. And often, when the person you want cannot do it, that person will point you to someone who can.

Second, always treat the people you are approaching with extreme respect. Make them understand that they are the important ones. They are doing you a favor.

Try to work well in advance of the talk. Three months' warning gives the speaker the best opportunity to come at a convenient time. Suggest a time for the talk, but always try to have alternatives and never give up the opportunity to have a speaker at the speaker's convenience. For example, one approach that works well is to look for a business trip that can be combined with the talk.

Third, don't give up! You will always lose a few speakers, but you will gain many more. We have had speakers that we communicated with for 2 to 3 years before we got them here. Some speakers say yes the first time, but most require some negotiation on subject matter, focus, fees, expenses, and schedule.

Fourth, follow up. If the first response is a "soft" no, keep in contact with the speaker on a regular basis. We recontact resistant speakers every 6 months or so.

When you do reach an agreement, close with a letter to an outside speaker or with a note (if the speaker is from your own company). Set checkpoints for receipt of the abstract material needed for publicity announcements. Set checkpoints for getting back to the speaker one month prior to the talk. Then periodically check on how things are going, and try to have lunch with the speaker before the talk. Offer to help in any way with logistics (e.g., hotel reservations and directions to your company).

**In-house support.**   Make certain that all aspects of each talk are clearly understood by the support people—the people who set up the chairs, the audiovisual people, and so on.

**Try to leverage the speaker's presence.**   Depending upon who the speaker is and the topic to be covered, try to schedule the speaker into other activities where possible. For example, set up meetings with managers or technical experts in the same area. See if the speaker would be interested in teaching a half-day class in addition to the talk. In general, the strategy is to make the most of the speaker's visit.

**Publicity.**   Work with communications people in your organization to get the word out. Or, if you are a small group, make sure you have a way to let everyone know what's happening.

We try to ensure that an announcement is up at least 7 calendar days prior to the talk. E-mail to key managers who you know will get the word out is also a good method of publicity.

By inviting associates from other companies to hear a talk hosted at your organization, you can build a reciprocal relationship that would allow people to have the benefit of attending many seminars while only hosting a fraction of these. So don't forget to include external publicity if appropriate.

We found that non-IBMers typically represented 10 to 15 percent of the audience attending a given talk.

**Seminar day activities.**   Be there to personally greet the speaker when she or he arrives at the reception area. Be prepared to spend time with the speaker before the talk unless other meeting arrangements have been made.

Usually the speaker will bring material (overhead projection foils, 35-mm copies) for the talk. If possible, ask to make copies before the talk so that they can be made available to interested seminar attendees at the time of the talk.

When possible, videotape the talk and make the tape available for checkout for those who cannot attend the seminar.

Review the format and logistics of the talk with the speaker and ask how he or she would like to be introduced.

**Follow up.**   Acknowledge the speaker via a letter or a note. In the case of internal speakers, let the speaker's manager know if things went well.

Finally, recognize that there is a learning curve. It took us at least 6 months to gain experience in learning how to contact speakers and convince them to participate in the seminar series. And it took experience with at least a dozen speakers to learn how to approach fee negotiation on a win-win basis. Since this sort of program is often first on the list of potential cut-backs, it is important to collect good feedback on the value of the program from the attendees and to keep the costs low by finding creative ways to attract speakers.

## Innovation 4 (Leadership): The Leadership Institute

### The objective

The Excellence Council helped get managers committed to quality, but we also wanted software professionals to take leadership roles in the quality improvement efforts. After all, they were the leaders who actually produced our products. The challenge was to educate and convert these technical leaders of the lab to a new way of thinking about quality.

### An innovative approach

One vehicle for providing the education and skills that would enable the leaders to guide the rest of the lab through the quality transformation was an invention called the *Leadership Institute*.

We held our first large-scale Leadership Institute in April 1991, following a pilot in 1990. The April 1991 Leadership Institute was held twice, in two 4-day sessions. Two hundred managers and top technical people at the lab attended each session, for a total of 400 attendees, or roughly 25 percent of the lab.

The theme was "Change through Empowerment," and the speakers included organizational change consultants, business school professors, CEOs of leading-edge software companies, and the general manager of our lab. Lecture topics included Transformational Leadership in a Market-Driven Environment, Pathways to Power in Turbulent Times, the New Work Environment, CASE Technology and Object-Based Methods, Software in the 1990s, and the Care and Feeding of Ideas. Complementing the lectures were a series of workshop sessions in which participants got an opportunity to practice the concepts discussed in the lectures. The workshops focused on empowerment, communication, motivators, and personal values.

The speakers were excellent, but most participants felt that the highlight occurred when the general manager took the microphone and answered questions from any employee. He did this after the participants had just been charged up with several hours of pep talk about empowerment and the need to change, so the questions came fast and furiously. The fact that he was willing to face the resistance and address a flurry of objections and concerns head on was probably the most significant event of the 4 days. It sent a clear message that the lab was serious about cultural change even if that change was uncomfortable.

In 1992, the lab repeated the Leadership Institute, this time holding it on site to economize at a time when IBM as a whole was slashing costs. While some felt that having the Institute on site made it too easy for people to go back to their offices and think about their regular work, the response to the second Institute (which was open to all employees) was generally favorable. About 500 people attended the 1992 Leadership Institute.

### Costs, benefits, and risks

The cost for the 1991 Leadership Institute—speakers, renting an off-site convention center, and handling all the details such as food and transportation—ran about $250,000. The greater cost, of course, was the expense of having the 400 top people at the lab off the job for 4 days. That's roughly 6.5 person-years, just for the time spent in the Leadership Institute. Add another person-year for the time required to plan, coordinate, and follow up an event of this size.

Obviously, the cost will vary with the size of the event, whether it is held on site or not, and how it is implemented. The second Leadership Institute was held on site at considerably less out-of-pocket expense.

The main benefit of the Leadership Institute was that it acted as a quality focus supercharger. Brainstorming, empowerment, listening techniques, CASE, innovation—everything was focused on quality. So you came out of there not only having been stimulated and sharpened by a series of experts, but with new quality ideas to apply. Even the workshops were designed around real-world quality problems at the lab, not academic exercises.

According to a detailed survey conducted at the time, participants were most interested in learning more about how to handle resistance to change, in increasing their personal levels of creativity, and in leadership topics. Subjectively, there was a definite glow and enthusiasm about quality for several days following the events. But exactly how this glow translated into concrete actions was more difficult to assess.

In a follow-up survey 2 years after the event, we got comments like the following:

"One of those things that inspire but is easily forgotten."

"I saw no measurable changes in my people who attended."

"It was a good ritual to have to get folks to think about the changes and how they fit into the big world picture. I think we are past it now, at least in the form it has taken this past year."

"Good for helping individuals to understand the vision of the lab."

"Good technique for mass indoctrination, wasn't followed up on. I did not see folks use what they had learned for more than a week."

On the whole, the Leadership Institute seemed effective at raising quality consciousness and getting people focused on quality—its primary mission. However, on average, the 74 respondents to our random lab-wide survey rated the Leadership Institute as only moderately valuable when asked how valuable they thought it was to them or their department in improving quality. The trouble spots seemed to be in the follow-up. Without adequate follow-up you risk wasting a lot of time and money for little concrete results.

A related risk is that the Leadership Institute may raise people's hopes and expectations, only to have these hopes dashed when the participants return to the business-as-usual work environment with their colleagues who did not attend.

Finally, there are always some technical types who view mushy, but important, topics such as psychological resistance, communication, and transformation with suspicion and can be turned off by the whole process. We try to address these risks in our implementation advice below.

## Synergy

The Leadership Institute is highly synergistic with just about any quality innovation or activity that is in the beginning or start-up phase. Think of it as a shot of adrenaline that gets people excited and points out the opportunities for change. This shot is often just what is needed to overcome the inertia and resistance encountered at the beginning of a longer-term quality improvement project.

## Prerequisites

There are no prerequisites for a Leadership Institute, except the desire for the top leader to create a different kind of culture within the organization.

## Implementation advice

Our first recommendation is to plan follow-up activities for after the Leadership Institute is over. For example, departmental strategy meetings would be an ideal follow-up to the Leadership Institute. Better yet, the charge from the Leadership Institute might be channeled into specific quality improvement innovations if the department already has a clear quality focus and direction.

The trick is to be aware that a 4-day seminar on change is going to stir things up, and management has to be ready to pick up the ball when people come out looking for something to improve.

In our case, we had optional half-day empowerment workshops with two of the consultants from the Leadership Institute as a follow-up activity. The problems were twofold. First, empowerment was the subject that people were the least interested in. Second, the workshops were not perceived as directly relevant to quality problems facing the lab.

Without follow-up activities, the Leadership Institute can achieve its primary objective of raising awareness, but most folks will feel like the manager who said, "I saw no measurable change in my people who attended."

It is also helpful to remember that the purpose of the Leadership Institute is to jump-start quality improvement efforts. There is no way that a 4-day seminar is going to solve your quality problems; but it can generate the enthusiasm and focus needed to get your own solutions off to a good start.

There are a few more technical implementation hints that we can pass on as well. We assembled the Leadership Institute from a custom set of speakers, after surveying departments to determine their needs. If members of two departments needed to work together better, we tried to schedule personnel from each department to attend the Leadership Institute at the same time. That way, the intense brainstorming and communication exercises could have the effect of bonding the two departments together.

On the other hand, if intraorganizational connections were needed, we tried to get members of different organizations to mingle together in the workshop teams.

One of the advantages of an off-site meeting is that you really have everyone's attention focused on the Leadership Institute activities. When we held the Leadership Institute in the lab's cafeteria, if people didn't like what they were seeing, they just left and went back to their offices. One could debate whether this was a good thing, but it clearly was not as effective at focusing attention on quality.

Figure 5.3 provides a checklist of some of the issues related to holding a Leadership Institute. The obstacles encountered as you work your way through this list can range from minor (e.g., arranging special meals for peo-

—— Identification of customer needs
—— Plan creation, articulation, revision
—— Vendor selection, partnerships, contracting
—— Facility selection
—— Event scheduling, rescheduling
—— Steering committees formed
—— Event measurement and evaluation
—— Curricula specification
—— Curricula development
—— Implementation
—— Funding
—— Budget control
—— Project management
—— Administration
—— Follow-up activities planned

**Figure 5.3**    Leadership Institute implementation checklist.

ple who are allergic to certain foods) to major (e.g., getting the various organizations in the lab to agree to fund the project out of their budgets).

## Innovation 5 (Leadership): Quality Publications

### The objective

Two challenges are probably greater during the awareness stage than at any other point on the quality journey. The first is to communicate effectively the need to change. The second is to get people to continue changing, even when it is uncomfortable and despite a lack of evidence that any benefits are resulting from the change.

Both challenges require ongoing, consistent communication that reinforces the successes and continually focuses the organization on the ultimate destination of the quality journey.

The Excellence Council and Leadership Institute were ways to jump-start the quality transformation and seize management attention. But what would keep attention on quality? And as the results came in, how could these results be captured and communicated effectively?

### An innovative approach

The solution has to involve regular communication. Lab-wide quality-related publications are one way to accomplish this. Over the course of 4 years, we developed four different quality-related periodicals, two of which are still active. Each had a unique implementation and focus, but all share certain benefits and concerns.

*Reflections* was the first magazine to focus on quality-related issues. It was a glossy, high-budget production of 20 pages or so that was distributed quarterly to all employees and to customers. The purpose of *Reflections* was to keep the lab and customers informed about major lab events like product releases and our quality transformation. It showed the lab at its best, and while this was useful in the sense that it kept everyone up to date on major activities, the fact that customers were reading it as well kept it from getting too technical or controversial.

About a year into our quality journey, the need became evident for something other than *Reflections*. There was a general hankering for something that would come out frequently, that would be easy to read and recycle, and that would contain information that could be used by employees in their day-to-day activities. And so *Connections* was born. (It's a requirement that all our magazines end in "ions.")

*Connections* was a two-page, low-key, jazzy-looking publication full of hints like how to change your phone-mail greeting, how to recycle office paper, and how to get hooked into the lab-wide electronic bulletin boards for quality. *Connections* was distributed monthly to lab employees, and it contained information that was useful at the lab but would be meaningless to outsiders.

As our quality activities increased and as we began to adapt and invent new quality improvement technologies, it became apparent that the lab needed some way to communicate "techie to techie" about specific quality innovations that could be of use to the software development community both at our lab and at other IBM sites. So *Q* magazine was developed by the quality department to fill this niche.

*Q* was an extremely high-quality magazine that described some of the same innovations discussed in this book. The magazine also provided an opportunity for developers to express their quality beliefs and concerns and to exchange information that could help everyone meet the quality improvement goals set by the lab.

*Innovations,* our most recent quality publication, is a no-nonsense, photocopied production that is edited, reproduced, and distributed by one dedicated individual—our technical vitality coordinator—on his own time. It contains articles of all sorts relating to the quality efforts and innovations going on at the lab. Because the magazine is a grass roots effort that sprang up on its own, it is probably the publication of which we are most proud.

It didn't come about as the result of any executive decision. And yet we are not sure that something of this sort would have appeared if the ground had not been prepared by the years of quality transformation work that preceded it. In any case, the hardy little magazine embodies the spirit of a new, lean IBM where innovations are valued for their intellectual content and effectiveness, not for their glossy packaging.

## Costs, benefits, and risks

As suggested above, the cost for a lab-wide magazine can vary from next to nothing (in the case of a volunteer-edited periodical that is produced by a word processor and a photocopy machine) to thousands of dollars per issue (in the case of a high-gloss, four-color magazine with fancy artwork). Which you opt for has a lot to do with your intended purpose. If the magazine is going to be used for external marketing and promotion, then something along the lines of *Reflections* or *Q* might be called for. But for internal use, you can probably dispense with the packaging as long as you have good content.

Each of the magazines at our lab had different benefits. *Reflections* and *Q* could serve both the internal and external communities at the same time, and both magazines were high-class productions that people might keep around for reference.

*Connections* was designed as a read-it-and-recycle type of thing, but it was very functional. It provided information that could be used immediately at low cost.

*Innovations* provided several benefits to the lab at very little cost. First, it promoted technical exchanges of information within the lab, which helped keep the community technically vital. Second, it helped establish a climate of innovation. Its presence sent the message that innovation was something valued and encouraged. Third, *Innovations* profiled successful people who had taken the "technical" side of IBM's dual ladder, and thus it promoted positive role models within the lab.

Here are some of the comments from a random survey asking about the value of the quality publications at the lab:

"In general, I think [*Q* magazine] is a good idea; in specific, I haven't gotten a lot out of it."

"I may be prejudiced, but you gotta have a technical publication at a location like this. It is a sad statement about technical vitality when there is no technical dialog."

"I am biased since my department produced *Q* magazine, but I think it provides a platform for people to speak out for quality. Some people feel very strongly about quality and want others to know their feelings."

"It is only one channel—the quality message needs to be spread using all possible channels."

The risks with any publications are that they can be viewed as "propaganda" in the case of glossies or "unprofessional rags" in the case of the low-budget publications. However, in our experience, these risks have proved minimal, so long as the publications contained useful content.

## Synergy

Glossy publications are synergistic with customer briefings, quality exchanges, and other activities external to the lab. The low-budget, internal-use-only publications are synergistic with the innovations described in them and with leadership innovations designed to foster teamwork and communication.

## Prerequisites

Being clear on the purpose of the magazines and having something useful to say are probably the only prerequisites. In our view, the earlier a publication of the appropriate sort is started, the better, since it helps promote a quality focus.

Depending upon the nature of the publication, legal clearance and approval of the communications department may be necessary.

## Implementation advice

Since *Q* and *Innovations* were similar in their technical content but were implemented differently, we can draw some implementation lessons by contrasting the two.

*Q magazine.*   *Q* magazine was a success in sharing ideas, but it was short-lived. Part of the problem was that *Q* tried to serve two different audiences with two different sets of needs. Internally, the demand was to produce the magazine on a frequent basis, but the fact that the magazine was read externally imposed a demand for a high-quality look.

The process of actually assembling an issue of *Q* began with requesting the articles from various developers in the lab. This was not difficult since there are a huge number of ideas and innovative projects floating around the lab at any one time. However, not everyone is equally skilled at communicating them.

That's where the editing comes in. Ideally, you would have one editor with a clear sense of the audience. But with *Q,* we had multiple editors as well as multiple audiences. This led to some sticky situations. For example, the internal audience wanted a magazine with a simple look that came out frequently. But the external audience demanded a more sophisticated look, which added time and cost to the development cycle. When the external readership was satisfied, the internal audience wasn't. And so we learned the rule of one audience and one primary editor per publication.

*Innovations.*   In contrast, *Innovations* served a single customer—the developers at the lab. The implementation story was different from start to finish.

To begin with, *Innovations* was the brainchild of one individual who happened to be concerned about promoting innovation at the lab. No surveys were done; no committees were consulted. The newsletter was a unilateral decision based on a perceived lack at the lab. In the words of the editor/publisher: "I decided I would do it and then see what happened."

Unlike *Q, Innovations* was a low-cost newsletter. It was done on a simple word processor, printed on recycled paper, and distributed to employees and managers. The publication process was simple. With *Innovations,* one person simply chose a format, learned how to create the thing with a word processor, figured out how to distribute it to everyone at the lab, got input from the legal and communications departments, borrowed articles from other sources, and produced the thing.

The process for getting new articles was equally direct: networking. In the editor's words: "If I see someone that I think is technically on top of things, I ask him: When are you going to write me an article?"

The first section of *Innovations* is devoted to innovative practices of people at the lab. The purpose there is to not only to get innovations adopted and publicized but also to send a message to the lab population that we have a culture that is conducive to innovation. So there is a metamessage that goes along with the publication as well as what is directly communicated in it.

But even this simple approach had its difficulties. Someone complained that we were killing too many trees with yet another publication. We countered by offering to distribute *Innovations* electronically if there was a demand for it. To date, it appears that people would prefer to read and recycle the hard copy.

A final caution: As indicated by one of the survey comments, it would be a mistake to expect any magazine to be the only or primary way of communicating about quality efforts. At our lab, in addition to the magazines, we had computer mailboxes where senior managers would respond to complaints, comments, or questions via E-mail within 24 hours. Computer bulletin boards or forums (as they are called at IBM) were another method of communication that proved effective in an environment where developers were more inclined to send E-mail than pick up the phone.

More important was the face-to-face communication that took place. At roundtable meetings, employees would be invited, a dozen at a time, to meet with their senior managers and share their views in an atmosphere of complete frankness. At "all-hands" meetings, senior managers communicated to the entire organization, addressing common concerns that had been expressed at roundtables. And most important of all were the numerous hallway chats which defy classification but which seem to make an organization run.

Figure 5.4 provides a checklist for starting a quality publication.

---

———— Need for publication clear
———— Purpose of the publication clear
———— Single, primary audience of publication
———— Single, primary champion (editor-in-chief) identified
———— Content and format match purpose and audience
———— Budget exists
———— Distribution channels clear
———— Contributors for future issues lined up
———— Simple production process

**Figure 5.4**  Quality publications implementation checklist.

## Suggested Readings

Brinkerhoff, R. O. (1989) *Evaluating Training Programs in Business and Industry*. San Francisco: Jossey-Bass.

Carnevale, A., Gainer, L., and Schulz, E. (1991) *Training the Technical Workforce*. San Francisco: Jossey-Bass. *A compendium of facts, figures, and case examples drawn from a 30-month research effort to explore the training practices in U.S. employer institutions.*

*Communications of the ACM. The calendar of events in this journal is a good source of information regarding upcoming technical conferences.*

*Innovations* and *Connections* are IBM internal-use-only publications.

McSteen, W., Gottier, B., and Schmick, M. (1990) *Software Engineering Education Directory*. CMU/SEI Technical Report, CMU/SEI-90-TR-4, ADA223740. Pittsburgh, PA: Carnegie Mellon University. *Provides information about software engineering degree programs and courses offered by U.S. universities. (See also: CMU/SEI-91-TR-9 or the most current version of this report.)*

*Q*, 1(1), June 1991, and 2(1), March 1992. Available from Rich Clark, Technical Editor, IBM Santa Teresa, San Jose, CA. *Our lab's glossy quality magazine for external (now discontinued) consumption.*

*Reflections* (past issues) available from Mary Popp, Editor, IBM Santa Teresa, Communications Department, San Jose, CA. *Our lab's glossy magazine (now discontinued) for external communication on general topics.*

Simerly, R. G. (1990) *Planning and Marketing Conferences and Workshops*. San Francisco: Jossey-Bass. *A good resource for anyone planning something along the lines of our Leadership Institute workshop.*

Wiggenhorn, W. (1990) "Motorola U.: When Training Becomes an Education." *Harvard Business Review*, July/August, pp. 71–83. *An interesting account of Motorola's top-down approach to quality (and other types of) training and education.*

## Some sources for quality-related education and training:

| | |
|---|---|
| Skill Dynamics | 1-800-IBM-TEACH |
| ASQC | 1-800-248-1946 |
| I.Q. Company | 1-408-475-4260 |

# 6

# Understanding and Stretching the Development Process

In the awareness stage, a primary goal is to understand your own processes better. The Baldrige assessments described in Chap. 2 are among the best overall ways to accomplish this. But a software development organization will also want to document the way(s) in which products are developed. Once the process is clearly defined, immediate steps can be taken to begin improving the quality.

At our lab these goals were accomplished by developing a set of software development guidelines and by using these guidelines to target the test stage as the place where the most immediate quality improvement results could be realized.

Table 6.1 summarizes the two process innovations described in this chapter. They are aimed at the initial goals of understanding and improving the development process without introducing radical change too early.

Ultimately, the goal is to move from a philosophy of testing quality into a product to a philosophy of designing quality into the product, the processes, and the interfaces with suppliers, customers, and business partners. But you have to start somewhere.

Ideally, you would start by improving the design processes. Pragmatically, however, your organization is likely to be under intense pressure to achieve

**TABLE 6.1  Stage: Awareness / Food Group: Process / Theme: Repeatable Process with Improved Test**

| Objective | Innovative approach | Implementation pitfalls |
|---|---|---|
| Create software development process that is consistent and repeatable. | Programming development handbooks: Document development process. Make consistent with Baldrige and ISO 9000. | Rigid, mindless adherence to rules.<br>Failure to include testers, planners, etc. |
| Improve teamwork between developers and testers. | Extended unit test stage of development. Create process linkages. | Insisting on radical process redesign.<br>"Who needs it?" attitude. |

measurable quality results as quickly as possible. For the products or releases already under development, it is too late to design quality in. You would have needed to read this book 2 years ago for that. So all you can do for these products is to improve Test. For other products, you can and should improve the design, using the techniques described in later chapters. But the first step, before improving anything, is to know where you are and what you are doing.

Different software products may be developed according to different procedures, and the procedures are likely to reside in the heads of the developers instead of being contained in a document. As a result, quality is highly variable.

## Innovation 6 (Process): Programming Development Handbooks

### The objective

Despite the fact that developing software is still very much an art, IBM realized early on that some sort of consistent process was required. Even artists have standard ways of preparing canvases.

Similarly, software developers need a process that supports their creative efforts. Moreover, it is impossible to make consistent progress unless that process is repeatable. We would argue that it is better to do something consistently poorly than to do it haphazardly. Because if you are consistently making the same mistake, it is easy to see what needs to change in order to see improvement. But if you make new mistakes each time because you have no consistent process, there is no systematic way to improve.

So the first thing is to become aware of the consistency in the way that you develop software (if you have not already done so) and then document that consistency in a form that can be communicated easily throughout the organization.

### An innovative approach

Our repeatable process for software development took the form of eight volumes that we call the *programming development handbooks*. The handbooks average about 25 pages apiece and cover the various aspects of developing a software product. Figure 6.1 lists and briefly describes each of the volumes.

The programming development handbooks are guidelines. The closest we got to enforcement was in the mid-1980s when the assurance organization required product managers to state a reason if they chose to use a process other than the standard processes outlined in the guidelines. Since then we have backed off from this requirement. The developers felt it was too much like having Big Brother watching. And they had a point. They are the ones who carry the primary responsibility for developing the code, and the quality assurance organization is supposed to be there to assist them, not oppress them.

1. *Development Process Overview* presents a high-level overview of the development and business processes.

2. *Requirements and Planning* presents information and guidelines for specifying requirements and planning the development and testing of the product.

3. *Programming Specifications* outlines the programming specifications and packaging specifications process.

4. *Programming Logic Specifications* presents information and guidelines for documenting a program design.

5. *Reviews and Inspections* presents information for planning, moderating, preparing for, and participating in reviews and inspections of design and code.

6. *Testing and Installation* describes the process for an installation walk-through as well as the procedures for conducting various tests and using the early support program.

7. *Information Development Overview* outlines the procedure for preparing information (manuals, tutorials, etc.) that will accompany the product.

8. *Quality and Productivity* contains guidelines for creating quality and productivity plans, for tracking quality, and for obtaining a quality certification. It also contains methods for projecting levels of software quality.

**Figure 6.1**  Programming development handbooks.

The primary purpose of the guidelines since then has been to educate new programmers, to comply with quality standards such as ISO 9000, and to serve as a common reference point for quality-related process improvements.

For most products the handbooks are used as a baseline process and development processes are customized to fit their unique needs. When the lab set 10-fold quality improvement goals, most development managers realized that having a documented process was a key step in reaching these goals. As mentioned earlier, increased process rigor, or "doing the same process better," is the easiest and quickest way to get immediate quality improvement.

A final function of the handbooks is to serve as a communication vehicle for the lab. When new corporate guidelines appear, they are incorporated into the handbooks. More recently, some of the well-established software development innovations have also been revised into the guidelines as optional process steps.

## Costs, benefits, and risks

It is difficult for us to estimate the cost of developing the handbooks from scratch, since they have evolved from a number of different IBM programming guides. However, at our lab, we have a single person who owns the handbooks and who is responsible for updating them, distributing them, and gathering feedback for revisions. This activity takes about half of his time.

Other factors affecting costs include the length and format of the handbooks. We chose a low-cost photocopied approach both because it keeps costs down and because it makes the handbooks less intimidating. They are guidelines and as such should not have too formal an appearance. Also, if they are to be useful, you must be willing to revise them constantly, and it is harder and more costly to revise something that has to be specially typeset or bound.

An alternative to printing the handbooks is to make them available on-line. This not only reduces printing costs, but also makes it much easier to revise and update them—a key factor to their success. Currently our lab's handbooks are available both in low-cost paper form and on-line.

Most developers and managers, in a random survey, saw value in the handbooks. Here are some of their comments:

"A good starting point."

"A design process is good to have. I think the handbooks are too restrictive—i.e., you must follow this design/development process."

"Especially good for newcomers to the organization."

"It lists the guidelines—one-stop shopping and get all you need for quality data/process."

"Read it. Understand it. Of course, the handbooks need to be updated to reflect today's need for more efficient processes, different size projects, etc."

"These handbooks are the basis for our development process. Even though we may deviate, we still refer to the base for analysis of our process."

"They help us know when to be proactive with various products."

In our view, the main benefit of the handbooks is that they lend consistency and repeatability to a process. They also makes a process less vulnerable to the variability that is introduced by changes in personnel or scheduling.

For example, a product might be developed with consistently high quality so long as a certain key employee is involved in the process. But should this employee leave the organization, get transferred to another job, or simply take a vacation, the consistency leaves with him/her, injecting variability into the process. In general, the more variability that is introduced, the more quality problems you will have. [This principle underlies the entire field of statistical process control (SPC).] So guidelines can be viewed as a way to reduce unwanted variability in your process.

The flip side of the coin is that a rigidly controlled process will not be adopted by developers voluntarily. No artist likes to be told how to do every little thing—especially when many of the "little things" don't apply. The main risk in developing something like the handbooks is that they will be resented (if enforced) or ignored. The key to minimizing this risk is to make them as useful as possible. Each organization needs to find the fine line between useless, oppressive bureaucracy and helpful advice that leads to more consistent development and higher-quality products.

## Synergy

The programming development handbooks are synergistic with the Baldrige assessments, with process modeling tools and methods, and with ISO 9000. The fact that ISO 9000 requires process documentation anyway makes these handbooks an ideal way to satisfy ISO and gain the other benefits described above.

## Prerequisites

The prerequisite for producing something like the programming development handbooks is a clear understanding of your business and development process. If you do not have that understanding, Baldrige assessments (Chap. 2) and process modeling tools and methods (Chap. 7) can help you arrive at one. If you are starting from scratch, check out the books listed in Suggested Readings for advice.

## Implementation advice

One of the tricky things about creating the handbooks was that we did not have just *one* development process that everyone was using and that was just waiting to be written down. We had a multitude of processes. And somehow we had to extract from all this activity what seemed to be the core elements of most of the successful products.

To know what to include and what to exclude, we began with a set of goals that expressed what we thought the purpose of the handbooks should be. Figure 6.2 lists these goals.

We also defined our audience to include programmers, testers, writers, planners, managers, and anyone with a need to understand programming development practices.

With these goals and our audience defined, it became clear that we would have to address not only the technical side of software development, but also the business, planning, and management sides. By drawing on two existing guidebooks at IBM and on the experience of our own product developers, we arrived at the hybrid model shown in Table 6.2.

The first column of Table 6.2 describes the general activities that we identified as part of the overall process of software development. These general activities can then be mapped to a series of architectural stages (second column) which are of concern to designers, programmers, and testers and to a series of business phases (third column) which are of concern to planners and managers.

The business phases provide a method of using the technical and business activities that take place in developing a product as checkpoints. At the desig-

---

1. To provide a consistent and orderly description of the programming development process
2. To describe existing or, in some cases, desired programming practices
3. To provide the basis for more consistency in the development of programming products
4. To better enable management of the programming development process
5. To enhance communication among all participants in the programming development process

**Figure 6.2** Goals of the programming development handbooks.

**TABLE 6.2    A Hybrid Development Model**

|  | Process stages | |
|---|---|---|
| Activity family | Architectural stage | Phase |
| Requirements | System requirements and design<br>Product requirements and planning | 0 |
| Design | Product-level design | I |
|  | Component-level design<br>Module-level design | II |
| Implementation | Code<br>Unit test | |
|  | | III |
| Test | Functional verification test<br>Product verification test | |
|  | System verification test | |
| Package and validate | Package and release<br>Early support program | IV |
| Availability | General availability | V |

nated checkpoint within each phase, the product is examined and decisions are made about its future.

For example, phase 0 is the initial business proposal (IBP) phase. The checkpoints for planners at this business phase are shown in Fig. 6.3. In general, planners, developers, testers, and information developers (technical writers) will have similar lists of checkpoints associated with each business phase.

In contrast to the phase process which includes business objectives, the architectural stages focus on the technical development and testing of the code itself. When we spoke of the waterfall process of software development (Chap. 3), we were referring to these architectural stages. Figure 6.4 shows the various architectural stages in graphical form.

The boxes marked DR1, DR2, and DR3 refer to *design reviews*—opportunities to catch bugs in the design of the product. The boxes labeled I0, I1, and I2 refer to *code inspections*—opportunities to catch bugs in the coded product

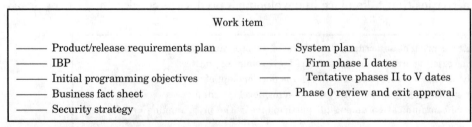

**Figure 6.3**   Planning process checklist for phase 0.

before it is tested. Boxes IT1 and IT2 refer to inspection of the overall test plan and the individual test cases, respectively.

Each box in Fig. 6.4 has clearly defined entry and exit criteria that are documented in the handbooks. There is also a suggested list of activities for accomplishing the task represented by each box.

One critical advantage of having a clearly defined set of stages is that it allows you to focus on which stage offers the greatest potential for immediate quality improvement. When we conducted such an analysis, we realized that we were getting very poor quality out of the unit test stage. As a result, we introduced a new phase—extended unit test—described below.

Figure 6.5 serves as an implementation checklist for some of the steps we went through in developing the handbooks.

## Innovation 7 (Process): Extended Unit Testing

### The objective

The challenge was to get some improvement, any improvement, in the quality of our products as soon as possible. And that meant scrutinizing our current development process for problems and trouble spots.

One thing that is not immediately obvious from the staged description of our development process is that IBM has separate development and test groups for each product. There are good reasons for this separation. For example, it is difficult for the developers of a product to be the most objective testers of same.

However, problems can also arise from this separation. Each group tends to identify with its local mission instead of with the overall goal of getting the product to the customer in the shortest time with the lowest possible defect levels. Often it can seem as if there is an invisible wall separating the Development and Test groups, and sometimes that invisible wall can lead to trouble.

For example, you'll note that our development process (see Fig. 6.4) has a stage called *unit test* that follows right after the final code inspection. Unit test is the stage at which the Development department is supposed to conduct an informal test of its code before passing it on to Test for more formal testing. But because developers don't really think of themselves as testers, this step tends to be executed poorly.

Development would throw its product over the invisible wall to the Test department and wait for Test to find the errors in the functional verification test stage. Then Test would throw the code back over the wall to Development, along with a list of things for Development to fix. The implicit attitude in Development was: "Let's get the code finished as quickly as possible, and Test will find the bugs for us. After all, that's their job, isn't it?"

Unfortunately this attitude is fairly short-sighted. It overlooks the fact that Development ultimately has to fix all the errors that Test uncovers. Development buys a little time while Test is busy trying to find all the bugs,

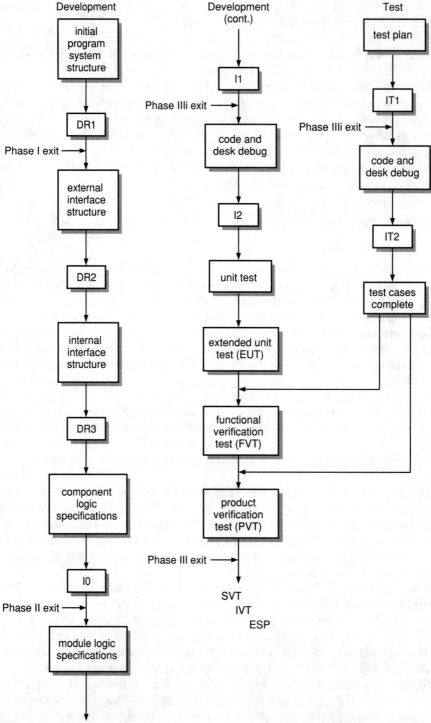

**Figure 6.4**  Architectural stages for software development. (*Courtesy of IBM Santa Teresa*)

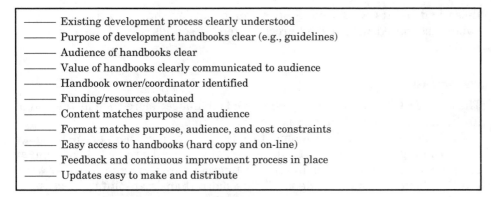

——— Existing development process clearly understood
——— Purpose of development handbooks clear (e.g., guidelines)
——— Audience of handbooks clear
——— Value of handbooks clearly communicated to audience
——— Handbook owner/coordinator identified
——— Funding/resources obtained
——— Content matches purpose and audience
——— Format matches purpose, audience, and cost constraints
——— Easy access to handbooks (hard copy and on-line)
——— Feedback and continuous improvement process in place
——— Updates easy to make and distribute

**Figure 6.5**   Implementation checklist for handbooks.

but it ultimately costs developers more time to try to understand the errors that Test found and fix them than it would have cost to fix the bugs in the first place. And, of course, the product organization as a whole loses because Test is consuming valuable time and resources trying to locate all the bugs that Development left in.

The net result of a "throw it over the wall" attitude is that Development spends more time fixing bugs and Test spends more time trying to catch bugs. Moreover, the overall number of defects is higher because the burden of detection is solely on Test, and the cycle time is much longer because this throw-it-over-the-wall procedure tends to repeat itself several times before all the bugs are caught.

### An innovative approach

Conceptually, the solution was simple: Development needed to do a better job of testing before passing the product on to Test. This would allow Test to do what it does best: find bugs that developers could not think of themselves because of the perspective problem. *Extended unit test* (EUT) is simply the formal mechanism to ensure that Development does its best job at defect detection before passing the code on to Test.

One could argue that there was no need for a new stage named extended unit test. After all, we already had something called *unit test*. And quite frankly, EUT does fall into the category of doing the same process but with more rigor. However, we gave EUT a new name, and we made it a separate process step, for two important reasons.

First, not all products are likely to need the more rigorous testing called for in EUT. In particular, very small projects or those that already are performing rigorous unit tests could probably skip this additional step with no ill effects.

Second, simply pointing out that developers should conduct unit testing more rigorously was unlikely to be effective. Psychologically, unit testing had already become associated with a certain way of doing things. And to break those bad habits would have been much harder than creating new good habits associated with a new process step. It sounds sort of sneaky, but it worked.

## Costs, benefits, and risks

The cost of EUT is that Development needs to budget more time at the end of its coding stage to perform more extensive testing.

The benefits are that Development saves time because there are fewer bugs to fix coming back from Test. Moreover, the overall product development cycle decreases because it is inefficient to cycle code back and forth between the Development and Test departments more than is absolutely necessary. Quality increases because developers are more focused on quality as they become more involved in testing activities. Finally, relations between Test and Development improve since both groups are focusing on improving the overall quality of the product and on helping each other by sharing their respective areas of expertise.

The risk is that developers can perceive EUT as added work—one more step in a development process that already is too long. The key to avoiding this pitfall is to clearly explain how the process step saves time and effort in the long run and how it benefits the product as a whole.

## Synergy

EUT is synergistic with other testing programs such as early test involvement and rigorous reviews and inspections (see Chap. 11).

## Prerequisites

There are no prerequisites for implementing an EUT program, although the program assumes that there is a division of the development and test functions in your organization. If no such division exists, you may want to ask the question, How do we get the external perspective on the code that Development lacks because it is so close to the product? Documenting your development process in a form similar to the program development handbooks (see above) can be useful in defining the stage at which EUT should take place.

## Implementation advice

Perhaps the best advice about implementing extended unit testing comes from the developers themselves. Here's what a random sample of users had to say:

> "Make sure that extended unit test will really run into some complicated testing situation. [Don't allow it to become] just another excuse for delaying code and formal unit testing."

"When Test is involved and the EUT is planned and followed, it works well as part of an effective entry criteria into formal test (FVT). This is a tactical solution to two problems: (1) Unit test is informal, treated like an art, and applied inconsistently. (2) I1 and I2 reviews are not effective enough."

"Allows Test to get an early run at their test cases."

"It was a key factor in the improvement of the quality of our product."

"It will shorten the FVT [formal testing] time."

What follows is our description of the EUT process in our lab. Our advice would be to adapt these steps to fit your own development process, if appropriate.

The first step is to be clear about what you hope to accomplish. At our lab, the objectives of the EUT program are to verify that

1. New function and modified code for line items (i.e., planned function) and/or components individually unit-tested work together when integrated into the product.

2. The code is stable enough for Development to deliver it to Test for formal tests.

The Development manager is responsible for the EUT plan, execution of test cases, and tracking and control of the test. This manager may delegate part of the responsibilities to the EUT coordinators in Development and Test. The EUT coordinator in Development works with her or his counterpart in Test to plan and implement the test successfully.

The process we used for conducting EUT is as follows:

1. *Test case selection.*   The EUT coordinator in Test, with the cooperation of other members of Test, makes a tentative list of test cases to be used in the EUT. These test cases are selected from the test cases which Test has planned to use in its functional verification test (FVT). Up to 10 percent of the FVT cases are selected, reviewed with the EUT coordinator in Development, and substituted or modified as necessary. The idea is to get a representative sample of the test cases that Test will later use to test the code; but the sample is not intended to be exhaustive or too complex.

2. *Building an EUT driver.*   Development builds a EUT "driver" (i.e., a hunk of code ready for test), using a local driver-building tool. This allows for better code control.

3. *Creation of test environment.*   The EUT coordinator in Test, with the cooperation of other members of Test, creates the test environment necessary for Development to execute the selected EUT cases. The environment includes things like a test machine, the driver, and test cases with data that can be executed as batch jobs.

4. *Execution of test cases.* Development runs the EUT cases and records any problems that arise. Then these problems are fixed, and the cases are integrated into the EUT driver.

5. *Tracking, reporting, and control.* The EUT coordinator in Development tracks and reports the status of the EUT daily. The report is sent to the Development manager, the Test manager, and the EUT coordinator in Test. It is also posted in the development area so that the developers are aware of how things are proceeding. This fosters a quality focus on the part of all the developers—not just those directly coordinating the EUT. Any problems inhibiting EUT progress are analyzed and solved.

As with all the stages in the development process, you should have clearly defined entry and exit criteria. Our entry criteria are as follows:

1. Unit test has been completed successfully.

2. EUT cases are agreed upon by Development and Test.

3. New function and modified code have been successfully integrated and installed in the EUT driver.

4. The EUT environment has been properly set up.

The exit criteria for the EUT stage are as follows:

1. All EUT cases have successfully executed.

2. New function and modified code have been successfully integrated and installed.

3. All the problems uncovered during EUT have been fixed.

4. The total number of problems resulting from EUT does not exceed the number agreed to by Development and Test (e.g., five).

5. The Development manager and the Test manager agree that the code is stable enough for Test to begin formal tests.

Large organizations with more than one test department may want to pilot-test EUT with one product. Once the program has been tailored to your organization, it can be replicated in other test groups. Also results from the pilot program will make it easier to sell the idea to development groups which may resist change.

Small organizations may not even have separate test and development departments. However, it should still be possible to have separate individuals develop and test the product. The same principles that apply to departments apply to individuals. To wit: the person who develops the products should conduct testing as part of the development process before passing the code on to an outsider for assessment.

A final word about EUT. The concept seems extremely simple, and many organizations may feel that they already do something like it on an informal basis. In fact, this was much the attitude of our developers when the program

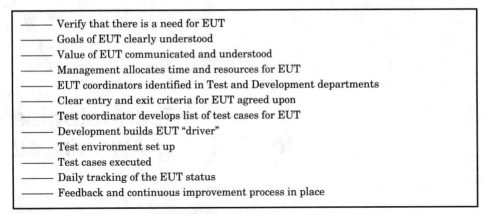

——— Verify that there is a need for EUT
——— Goals of EUT clearly understood
——— Value of EUT communicated and understood
——— Management allocates time and resources for EUT
——— EUT coordinators identified in Test and Development departments
——— Clear entry and exit criteria for EUT agreed upon
——— Test coordinator develops list of test cases for EUT
——— Development builds EUT "driver"
——— Test environment set up
——— Test cases executed
——— Daily tracking of the EUT status
——— Feedback and continuous improvement process in place

**Figure 6.6** EUT implementation checklist.

was first implemented. One had the feeling, Why do we need more bureaucracy when we do this stuff already?

The key point is that a good process—one that is worth using—will save you more time than it costs in the long run. If you are not spending any time bouncing code back and forth between Test and Development and engaging in rework, then you probably don't need EUT. But if you are, it means there is a problem. EUT is one way to get some leverage on that problem.

Figure 6.6 describes some of the steps we went through in our implementation of EUT.

## Suggested Readings

ANSI/IEEE Standard 1008-1987, *IEEE Standard for Software Unit Testing*, July 28, 1986.

Ayer, S., and Patrinostro, F. (1992) *Documenting the Software Development Process.* New York: McGraw-Hill. *If you are looking for technical detail on how to document processes, together with a comprehensive list of CASE vendors with process documentation tools, this book is for you.*

Distaso, J. (1980) "Software Management—A Survey of Practice in 1980." *Proceedings of IEEE,* 68(9): 1103–1119. *Though dated, the survey is useful for a historical perspective on variations of the waterfall development process in the 1970s.*

Metzger, P. W. (1981) Managing a Programming Project. Englewood Cliffs, NJ: Prentice-Hall. *This book describes the traditional phases of the waterfall life-cycle model and outlines the documents produced at each step.*

Pressman, R. S. (1988) *Making Software Engineering Happen.* Englewood Cliffs, NJ: Prentice-Hall. *An excellent book about how to apply software engineering techniques in the real world.*

Royce, W. W. (1987) "Managing the Development of Large Software Systems." *Proceedings of the 9th International Conference on Software Engineering.* IEEE Computer Society, pp. 328–338. (Originally published in *Proceedings of WESCON,* 1970). *One of the first articles to explain the software life cycle by using the waterfall chart.*

Whitten, N. (1990) *Managing Software Development Projects.* New York: Wiley. *Chapter 11 has a clear explanation of software test phases; also there is lots of good project management advice.*

# 7

# Technologies
# for Gaining Awareness

Perhaps the hallmark of the awareness stage is determining where you stand. In the last chapter we discussed the importance of documenting the development process in handbooks. We showed how such an effort can lead to immediate process improvement by helping identify where to focus effort (e.g., the EUT process change).

This chapter provides tools to bring even more leverage to bear on process understanding efforts. Moreover, because it is critical to know where you stand with regard to customers as well as processes, we describe satisfaction survey approaches we have used with our internal and external customers.

Table 7.1 summarizes these innovations, their objectives, and implementation pitfalls.

The satisfaction surveys help sharpen your quality focus. The joint application development (JAD) meeting technology provides a powerful approach to uncovering problems and reaching solutions in a group environment. Because it was originally developed to help produce more efficient product designs, it can also be used in conjunction with the survey data to attack quality problems at their source—the design stage of the development process. Finally, process modeling allows you to debug your process, detecting problems in the process flow diagrams before they occur in the real world.

## Innovation 8 (Tools): Satisfaction Surveys

### The objective

IBM has been conducting surveys of its customers for many years, but until relatively recently there was no standard format for the surveys. The problem with this approach is that it is very difficult to know whether customer satisfaction is increasing if the questions keep changing from year to year. In short, we lacked standard and consistent metrics for tracking customer satisfaction.

**TABLE 7.1   Stage: Awareness / Food Group: Technology / Objectives: Calibrate Quality Baseline and Lay Foundation to Address Quality Problems**

| Objective | Innovative approach | Implementation pitfalls |
|---|---|---|
| Use metrics for software quality | *External satisfaction surveys:* CUPRIMDO methodology<br>  Capability<br>  Usability<br>  Performance<br>  Reliability<br>  Installability<br>  Maintainability<br>  Documentation<br>  Overall | Improperly targeted survey population<br>Excessive focus on numbers not trends<br>Failure to take action |
| Gain a complete and accurate view of internal capabilities. | *Internal satisfaction surveys:*<br>  Skills<br>  Inventory and assessment innovations<br>  Morale | Survey fatigue<br>Not acting on survey information |
| Ensure ownership of quality problems. | *JAD*<br>  Methodology<br>  Meeting technology | Wrong parties at the table<br>Unstructured process<br>Poor preparation |
| Eliminate process failures causing:<br>  Product delays<br>  Cost overruns<br>  Customer complaints | *Process modeling methods and tools:* Process modeling methods that simulate problems *before* they occur. | Ad hoc modeling<br>No clear objectives or idea of leverage points<br>Buying tool du jour |

Moreover, as we got more and more involved in Baldrige criteria, we realized that we lacked these same consistent measurements for various groups and programs internal to IBM. As a result, we had an incomplete and possibly inaccurate view of both our customers and our internal capabilities.

## An innovative approach

Surveys are probably the most widely used method to obtain input and feedback. And there are good reasons for the widespread use of surveys. For one thing, surveys allow you to focus on just the issues of interest, since you have complete control of the questions that are asked. At the same time, open-ended questions provide flexibility for the survey to raise issues that you might not have thought important.

However, the primary benefit of surveys is probably that they are quantifiable. They provide a convenient way to bring the power of statistics to bear. Thousands of inputs can be summarized in a single number such as the percentage of customers satisfied or the number of defects detected. These simple statistics can feed into more sophisticated analyses which lead to powerful recommendations for quality improvement actions. Thus surveys are not only indicators in themselves, but also enablers of more sophisticated analysis techniques appropriate to organizations with higher levels of quality maturity.

Organizations in the software or electronics businesses are ideally equipped to improve the basic survey methodology by use of electronic tools. These tools can increase not only the speed and ease of gathering data but also the ease with which the data are analyzed and disseminated throughout the organization.

At Santa Teresa, we now conduct both external customer surveys and internal surveys. The external surveys are aimed primarily at determining customer satisfaction with our products, while the internal surveys address satisfaction with internal support activities, morale, skills, and our quality and innovation efforts.

For external surveys, the trick was to determine those factors that most affect customer satisfaction and to measure them consistently from year to year for all products. After some trial and error, IBM decided upon seven areas of customer satisfaction which are becoming something of a standard in the industry: capability, usability, performance, reliability, installability, maintainability, and documentation. These measures are referred to collectively as CUPRIMD (the first letter of each measure is a letter in the acronym). Figure 7.1 describes the components of CUPRIMD briefly.

When our lab took on responsibility for service and maintenance of our products, an eighth indicator was added to CUPRIMD—S, for service. Finally, in addition to the CUPRIMDS measures, there is an overall (O) measure of satisfaction. Customers rate each of the CUPRIMDSO measures on a scale ranging from 1 (very satisfied) to 5 (very dissatisfied). An example of a survey using the CUPRIMDS metrics for one of our products is shown in Fig. 7.2.

To better understand our *internal* customers, our lab conducted a variety of internal surveys that helped the staff and support organizations improve

---

**Capability:**   Function. Has necessary function to do user's job.

**Usability:**   Ease of use. Easy to use in terms of accomplishing desired tasks. Useful with regard to the amount and way in which function is implemented. Easy to learn. Design is consistent with other products. User can interact effectively with product to enhance productivity.

**Performance:**   Efficiency. Speed with which the product executes its functions. Overall throughput and response time.

**Reliability:**   Frequency, number and seriousness of incidents, program errors, and problems. Recovery attributes.

**Installability:**   Ease of installation. Easy to install and initialize software in terms of time required, number of problems encountered and ease of resolution, amount of customizing required, and ease of installation verification.

**Maintainability:**   Vendor support. Error diagnosis, response time and quality of fixes, manageability of maintenance, and installability of service.

**Documentation:**   All product information (formal, on-line, help screens, etc.) evaluated for accuracy, format, understandability, thoroughness and completeness, and time to find information.

---

**Figure 7.1**   CUPRIMD measures.

**IBM**    **CUPRIMDS**
**VM** SOFTWARE PRODUCT SURVEY
For further information or assistance with this survey, please contact our representative at 1-800-626-7953

1a. If VM is no longer installed, please check this box and return the form.  ☐
1b. Please list the CPUs licensed for VM at this site.

| | | | PRIMARY OPERATING SYSTEM | | | | | GUEST OPERATING SYSTEMS USED | | |
| NUMBER OF CPUs | CPU TYPE | MODEL NUMBER | VM/ESA (ESA) | VM/ESA (370) | VM/XA | VM/SP | HPO | VSE | MVS | Other (Specify) |
|---|---|---|---|---|---|---|---|---|---|---|
| _____ | _____ | _____ | ☐ | ☐ | ☐ | ☐ | ☐ | ☐ | ☐ | _____ |
| _____ | _____ | _____ | ☐ | ☐ | ☐ | ☐ | ☐ | ☐ | ☐ | _____ |

2a. How many system programmers support your VM system(s) (including subsystems)? _____ Operators? _____
2b. How many system programmers support your guest operating system(s) under VM? _____ Operators? _____
3a. How many years has VM been used at this site? _____
3b. When did you install your most recent release of VM?  (Month _____/_____ Year)

For the following questions please use the attributes defined below for your product evaluations.
C)  CAPABILITY:          Has necessary functions and ability to do user's job.
U)  USABILITY:           The "ease of use" attributes that allow the user to effectively interact with the product to do productive work.
P)  PERFORMANCE:         Speed with which product executes its functions; overall throughput and response time.
R)  RELIABILITY:         Frequency, number, and seriousness of incidents and program errors. Recoverability attributes.
I)  INSTALLABILITY:      Ease of product installation with associated service and initializing the product.
M)  MAINTAINABILITY:     Error diagnosis; manageability of maintenance; installability of service.
D)  DOCUMENTATION:       All product information (formal, on-line, help screens, etc.) evaluated for accuracy, format, understandability; thoroughness and completeness; time to find information.
S)  SERVICE:             IBM software service support includes the quality and timeliness of the assistance and the solutions provided. It also includes the technical ability and sensitivity of IBM service personnel.
O)  OVERALL:             All aspects of the product as a total evaluation.

**A** Please check (✓) the most current level in production, circle your satisfaction for ALL attributes using the rating scale provided, and check (✓) the attribute that needs the most improvement to increase your Overall satisfaction.

Satisfaction Rating Scale
1  =  Very Satisfied
2  =  Satisfied
3  =  Neither Satisfied nor Dissatisfied
4  =  Dissatisfied
5  =  Very Dissatisfied
N  =  Don't Know or No Opinion
☐  =  Attribute needing most improvement

EXAMPLE:
☐ V2.1
☑ V2.0
☐ V1.3
☐ V1.2
☐ Other

C)  1 ② 3 4 5 N  ☐
U)  1 ② 3 4 5 N  ☑
P)  1 2 ③ 4 5 N  ☐
R)  ① 2 3 4 5 N  ☐
I)  1 2 ③ 4 5 N  ☐
M)  1 ② 3 4 5 N  ☐
D)  1 ② 3 4 5 N  ☐
S)  1 2 3 4 5 Ⓝ  ☐
O)  1 ② 3 4 5 N  ☐

NOTE: Where it is necessary to indicate "Don't Know" or "No Opinion," use "N," instead of "3."

**B** If you rate any product attribute(s) less than satisfied, please explain why in the "comment" lines provided under each question.

4.  What is your satisfaction with the 'entire' VM System (including subsystems from IBM)?

C)  Capability       1  2  3  4  5  N  ☐
U)  Usability        1  2  3  4  5  N  ☐
P)  Performance      1  2  3  4  5  N  ☐
R)  Reliability      1  2  3  4  5  N  ☐
I)  Installability   1  2  3  4  5  N  ☐
M)  Maintainability  1  2  3  4  5  N  ☐
D)  Documentation    1  2  3  4  5  N  ☐
S)  Service          1  2  3  4  5  N  ☐
O)  Overall          1  2  3  4  5  N  ☐

Comment:_____
Please note that IBM may use or distribute this survey information without obligation, except that data linked to a specific customer will only be used internally in IBM. Aggregate data may be used without limitation.
January 94

**Figure 7.2**  Cover page of an IBM CUPRIMD Survey. (*Courtesy of IBM*)

their effectiveness. For example, the Site Services Customer Satisfaction Survey is conducted once a quarter by the Support Managers Council.

There is a version for managers and a version for nonmanagers. The questions all concern the services offered by the indirect support services departments including the groups and organizations shown in Fig. 7.3.

| | |
|---|---|
| Administrative support | Information systems |
| Cafeteria | Medical |
| Center for Software Excellence | Personnel |
| Communications | Security |
| Education | Site services |
| Facilities | Tools support |
| Finance and business planning | |

**Figure 7.3**  Lab support organizations.

The results were used to put together action plans to address areas where the support organizations could improve the quality of their services.

A second internal survey effort, the Skills Assessment Survey, was an attempt to categorize the skills of various employees at the lab for planning and resource allocation purposes. This may sound funny to a small department or an organization with less than one hundred people. But when you are a lab of 1700, skills assessments are serious business.

Conceptually, conducting a skills survey is as simple as asking all the managers in the organization to list the skills of their people. At a department level, the manager could ask each member of the department to describe her or his skills.

A skill survey in a large organization also involves locating core competency centers for different skills. A core competency center is just a department or group of people who are all experts in a particular area and could educate and advise other areas of the organization.

A third type of internal survey was recently conducted by the Center for Software Excellence to get a better idea of the deployment and perceived value of 66 of the best-known software development innovations at the lab—including most of those described in this book.

The numerical results and comments from the innovation survey were made available to the inventors of the innovations so that they could find ways to improve their software development techniques. The results also provided management with a clearer understanding of which software innovations were having the greatest impact on quality at the lab. (These results were also one of the criteria used in deciding which innovations to include in this book.)

Finally, IBM Santa Teresa conducts a yearly Opinion Survey which every employee is invited to take. The Opinion Survey includes topics such as employee morale, satisfaction with IBM as a company, and—since 1989— questions relating to our quality efforts.

## Costs, benefits, and risks

The costs for conducting a survey can be relatively small compared to the benefit of the information.

For external surveys, IBM Santa Teresa has one person who is the resident expert on CUPRIMD survey methodology. However, generally each product group takes some time to analyze and interpret its own results. The least costly approach is simply to include survey forms with the product when it is shipped to customers. An alternative approach, and the one we typically use, is to conduct periodic random surveys of existing customers.

The benefit of this periodic approach is that it lets our customers know that we are concerned with their ongoing satisfaction. It also provides a way to get feedback from customers which can be used as input to our development process at critical times, such as during the design of a new release. Most important, conducting surveys periodically with consistent measures allows us to gauge the effects of our long-term quality improvement efforts.

Internal surveys are conducted on-line typically, since every employee has access to a host computer system. The time to prepare and analyze the questions varies with the complexity of the survey and analysis, but we found that one programmer working full-time for 2 months was able to produce a survey and a series of reports.

The larger cost for IBM Santa Teresa was the time required to actually take the survey. If 400 lab members participate in a survey and it takes them 1 h to complete (the support survey had 116 multiple-choice questions), it requires 10 person-weeks to take the survey. The on-line nature of the survey neutralizes this time hit somewhat since it allows people to take the survey at their convenience.

Overall, we found the costs to be small compared with the benefits. For example, Fig. 7.4 lists some of the areas for improvement identified on the support survey. However, a key to getting value out of the survey is the development and execution of action plans that address the problem spots. Sample action plans are also listed in Fig. 7.4.

The primary risk to avoid is oversurveying the population. Customers are generally willing to provide feedback, but they get impatient if they are asked the same questions by five different groups within a short time. Coordinating your survey efforts through a central point of contact with customers is a good way to avoid this pitfall.

## Synergy

The different survey methodologies are synergistic with each other since many of the process steps involved in executing customer surveys are the same as those involved in internal surveys. Similarly, statistical techniques that are used to analyze the data from one type of survey can apply to the other types.

## Prerequisites

There are no prerequisites for conducting surveys.

**Administration:**   Perceived drop in administrative support due to attrition rate, inadequate skill level.

ACTION PLAN:   Skill assessments will be performed for all IBM and vendor employees. Plans to improve training and counter attrition.

**Cafeteria:**   Prices too high, lack of variety.

ACTION PLAN: New vendor chosen that commits to better selection and "budget meals."

**Center for Software Excellence:**   The Excellence Councils are viewed as cumbersome and costly.

ACTION PLAN:   Excellence Council process will be changed to be more effective.

**Communications:**   Employees want to hear more about employees and local news, less about executives and corporate management issues.

ACTION PLAN:   The lab-wide TV program will be continued with more focus on lab events, products, and employees. Employees will be directly involved, including being guest "anchors" for the show.

**Education:**   Low awareness of the lab's educational services offerings.

ACTION PLAN:   Meet directly with lab managers to communicate services. Develop plan with Communications department to publicize services. Give demonstrations in new Decision Support Center. Letter to lab management on facilitation team services.

**Facilities:**   No effective process for reporting facilities problems.

ACTION PLAN:   A hotline and E-mail ID will be established for reporting problems. A monthly site tour will be conducted to locate problems. Offices affected by moves will be painted.

**Finance and Business Planning:**   Capital process too cumbersome.

ACTION PLAN:   Users will be invited to meet to review the capital process and recommend changes.

**Figure 7.4**   Sample improvement areas and action plans from support survey.


## Implementation advice

Any organization that wants to conduct external customer satisfaction surveys must follow these basic steps:

1.   Design the survey.

2.   Execute the survey.

3.   Analyze the data.

4.   Distribute the results.

5.   Modify business practices and the survey questions in a cycle of continuous improvement.

There are some caveats about the way that surveys are distributed. For example, several years ago our lab distributed surveys to the managers in other companies whom our marketing representatives knew best. These individuals tended to be friendly to IBM but sometimes had little direct experience in using the products. As a result, satisfaction tended to be high.

Although it is gratifying to hear that customers like your product, the information that tends to be more useful is the reason why customers don't like your products.

What are their frustrations, their concerns? What new features would make their jobs easier and would increase the customers' effectiveness? This type of information is best obtained from the people who use the products on a day-to-day basis.

Note that these are often not the people whom the marketing representatives know best. Recognizing this, we changed the way in which our surveys were distributed in order to get them to the right people. Customer satisfaction dropped several points, but the amount of useful information greatly increased.

The lesson here for management is not to get too caught up in the numbers. Yes, it's nice to see high customer satisfaction numbers, but unless the organization is more interested in improvement than in short-term gratification, the organization can easily become the victim of self-delusion. At IBM, some managers were distressed by what they saw as declining satisfaction, after the change in survey methodology.

It is important to emphasize that improvement is the goal, and any time satisfaction seems too high, it is time to look for new ways to improve the survey methodology. The goal, after all, is to ferret out the areas where improvement will yield the most gain in satisfaction. If you start reaching a ceiling effect in the survey, the survey is no longer a useful instrument to measure the effects of process changes.

Internal surveys provide information that can give you leverage on problems within the organization. For example, a skills survey enables management to do a better job of assigning the right people to various projects. Moreover, management can analyze what skills are lacking at the organizational level, and you can build a skills strategy. The skills strategy includes both plans to acquire needed skills and a method to spread the skills from one center of core competency to another. With a skills inventory, an organization can do more with fewer resources. Hiring and training can be based on projected needs and the organization is less vulnerable to personnel changes.

The net result is improved quality since there is less variability in a process when it is executed by skilled professionals. Efficient assignment of skills ultimately frees resources for investment in other quality innovations.

The information obtained from innovation and opinion surveys, on the other hand, is more useful in tracking your organization's quality progress. For example, data from the innovation survey showed that 88 percent of the lab felt that the quality of IBM's products and processes had improved since the start of the quality journey in 1989. This information was significant because it showed that the quality transformation had been largely successful, despite a lot of resistance to specific techniques, such as the Excellence Council.

The opinion survey provided a way to monitor both morale and the buy-in of employees and management to the lab's market-driven quality efforts. We saw a steady decline in these measures during the awareness and control stages, followed by an upturn as some of the results began to be seen in the second half of the management stage of quality maturity.

The main risk in conducting internal surveys, as with customer surveys, is that employees can feel "oversurveyed" if every group does its own survey. At

IBM Santa Teresa we try to be sensitive to this issue by combining questions of interest to several groups in the same survey and by selecting different random samples for each survey so that the same people are not surveyed over and over.

The typical internal survey procedure at IBM Santa Teresa is to design a set of questions that can be asked on-line using an in-house computerized survey tool. The questions are multiple-choice, and often they involve scoring something (e.g., satisfaction) on a 5-point rating scale. Usually, there is a space to type in comments as well.

Summary statistics are calculated, and the comments are used for a more detailed analysis of the reasons for particular scores on various questions.

To ensure an adequate sample size, we try to survey at least 25 percent of the lab on most surveys and 100 percent of the lab on critical surveys such as the annual Opinion Survey. The people surveyed are chosen at random, subject to the constraint that the same people should not be chosen for a survey twice in the same year if at all possible.

Figure 7.5 contains some sample questions which are typical of the format used in most internal surveys including the support survey, the innovation survey, and the opinion survey.

It's worth describing the skills survey in some detail because it shows how a very specific type of data can be used on a very large scale. There were three steps in the skills inventory process.

First, we gathered the data on employee skills and core competencies by category. For example, some core competencies in IBM Santa Teresa's Center for Software Excellence include the defect prevention process, project management, benchmarking, and ISO 9000.

For each skill category, there were four levels of proficiency:

None (or nearly none)

Trained—been to class

Skilled—can use or execute

Expert—can teach and train others

For example, relative to process assessments, if you've completed a relevant class, then you're trained; if you can perform assessments, then you're skilled; and if you can teach or train others, then you're an expert.

Second, we distributed the list of skills to appropriate parts of the organization. Since our skills assessment was part of a multiple-site effort, our information together with information from other IBM sites went to headquarters.

Finally, a core competency council was set up to enhance the level of competency across several sites and to create a strategy for determining which competencies should be developed further.

In a very large organization different labs may sign up to be the center of competencies. The person with the most expertise in a particular skill for

1. How satisfied are you that Finance and Business Planning *effectively communicates* changes in the business process, as well as when business issues occur?
   *a.* Very satisfied
   *b.* Satisfied
   *c.* Neither satisfied nor dissatisfied
   *d.* Dissatisfied
   *e.* Very dissatisfied
   *f.* Don't know or no opinion
   (You may enter a comment below if you wish.)

   _____

   _____

   _____

2. Compared to 1989, the quality of the processes/products in your department has:
   *a.* Greatly improved
   *b.* Significantly improved
   *c.* Somewhat improved
   *d.* Not improved
   *e.* Degraded
   *f.* Don't know/No opinion
   (You may enter a comment below if you wish.)

   _____

   _____

   _____

3. *Connections* is a monthly newsletter for employees. Indicate one area below where you would like to see more emphasis:
   *a.* Tips about using VM/CMS, Office Vision, PhoneMail, etc.
   *b.* Stories about employees and their activities
   *c.* News about education, professional seminars, career development
   *d.* Articles about IBM customers
   *e.* Other (please explain below)
   *f.* Don't know/No opinion
   (You may enter a comment below if you wish.)

   _____

   _____

   _____

**Figure 7.5**  Sample survey items.

that lab is identified and becomes the coordinator in that skill for the organization. The role of the coordinator is to help the center

- Be an advocate for that skill across the organization.
- Determine how the skills fit into the organization's overall strategy and help satisfy development and process imperatives.

- Foster the spread of the skills across the organization.
- Benchmark and evaluate best-of-breed processes and tools.
- Measure the effectiveness of, and use of, the skill.

Such centers of competency are one way to leverage the knowledge of the organization. But note that it required coordination and standardization of survey efforts across several sites to be able to compare expertise on such a large scale.

In a random survey, when asked about the value of surveys in general (a survey about surveys, oh no!), members of the lab had this to say:

"OK, but there are lots of surveys these days."

"I think it is worth the time spent to answer the surveys in the hopes that the data will be used productively. I don't have concrete information on this."

"If the surveys result in appropriate actions, they have value; if they don't, no value added."

"Pitfalls: `Just another survey,' `oh no! Another survey.' People can get tired of this type [electronic/on-line] of survey. Face-to-face surveys put...some feeling into the process."

"This gives you a good indicator of your customers' problems."

"We need to maintain a regular, periodic set of surveys so progress can be measured."

In our view, the common theme of all the survey efforts should be to gather the most useful information with the least disruption to those being surveyed. Surveys told IBM Santa Teresa where we stood with regard to quality buy-in, morale, skills and abilities, satisfaction with internal suppliers, and innovation. That information was critical both at the awareness stage, to help point us in the right direction, and all along our quality journey, to help us recognize when we were making progress and where we were stuck. The trick is to get that information as painlessly as possible and then to make sure you use it!

Figure 7.6 lists some of the steps we went through in conducting our internal and external surveys.

## Innovation 9 (Tools): Joint Application Design Sessions

### The objective

As we collected more and more data from surveys and other sources, the challenges facing our lab began to sort themselves into two categories. There were those items which were clearly the responsibility of a particular department or organization (e.g., the items listed in Fig. 7.4), and there were problems which no one seemed to own but which resulted in a lot of finger-pointing and

———— Goals of survey clear; survey is best way to get information
———— "Customers" for survey data clear
———— Survey coordinator identified
———— Survey audience defined clearly; adequate sample size
———— Audience willing to participate; not oversurveyed
———— Clear plan for data analysis in place
———— Content driven by goals, audience, and data analysis plan
———— Survey as simple and short as possible to meet content goals
———— Distribution method set (e.g., phone, fax, mail, on-line)
———— Funding and resources for survey obtained
———— Review survey content and method for potential biases
———— Execute survey
———— Analyze results
———— Results easily accessible to data "customers"
———— Follow-up actions taken and communicated to survey participants
———— Feedback and continuous improvement process in place

**Figure 7.6**  Satisfaction survey implementation checklist.

passing of the buck. Some of these second-category problems arose even within a department where there was confusion or lack of ownership of certain departmental items.

The typical response to such challenges was to call a meeting, try to understand the different points of view, and hash out a solution. The problem was that our meetings didn't always go as well as they should. So we began to look at how we held meetings as a basic area for quality improvement. We reasoned that if the quality of meetings went up, so would the quality of all the decisions that were reached in those meetings.

### An innovative approach

In the awareness stage, we had not yet experimented with some of the high-technology approaches to meetings described in later chapters, but we were aware of a technique which has been around for a number of years called *joint application design* (JAD). With immediate action as our goal, we adopted JAD into our fold of quality innovations and began exploring its quality improvement potential.

Joint application design is a technique for conducting highly structured meetings by using a facilitator, a recorder (note taker), a special room configuration, and a clear set of meeting rules. The technique was originally developed for conducting design meetings for new products, but it can be used in any situation where there are many diverse points of view—especially if cross-functional or cross-site considerations play a role in reaching a decision. It is a process ideally suited for dealing with large and unwieldy problems which can get stuck in a logjam in conventional meetings.

Our version of JAD was adapted from the procedures laid out in Judith August's book (see Suggested Readings). We follow much of the advice for meetings explained in that book, and we have tailored the process to meet our needs.

For example, we have rules to make the meeting more effective by making sure that a decision is reached within a reasonable amount of time and that all parties are allowed equal representation. The *binary decision rule* says that you don't leave the room with a *maybe* or an *if*; you leave with *yes* or *no*. The *5-minute rule* allows anybody to say that he or she wants a particular issue resolved in 5 minutes.

Other critical aspects of JAD include a horseshoe-shaped table that allows everyone to see everyone else, but also allows the facilitator to intervene between two warring parties. The facilitator is trained to keep meetings on track, while the recorder acts as an impartial note taker and gives everyone a copy of the meeting minutes.

While some of the JAD techniques can be picked up from reading a book, successful facilitators recommend a one-week training course followed by a 6-month apprenticeship with experienced facilitators. At IBM Santa Teresa, it was a stretch just to get the time for the class, so we did our own apprenticeship program. The people who took the facilitator training acted as recorders and apprentices for each other back at the lab. It was not the ideal situation, but it is probably a realistic option given our schedule constraints.

### Costs, benefits, and risks

The main cost of JAD is due not to the facilitation training, but to the time of the people participating in the meetings. That's why it's important to make sure the facilitators receive as much training as possible. Assuming that you use JAD to replace conventional meetings that would have been held anyway, JAD should improve the overall effectiveness of the meetings and reduce the time consumed by them.

One major benefit of a JAD approach is that it results in a "big picture" understanding of all sides of a problem. With a skillful facilitator, you can increase teamwork and arrive at solutions that stymie conventional meetings.

The risks are that the meetings go off poorly due to lack of training or experience. Also, a poorly conducted JAD session is probably worse than none at all. Some of the keys to successful JAD meetings that minimize this risk include getting the right (highly motivated) people in the meeting, obtaining the backing of senior management, and making sure that the problem lends itself to a JAD type of resolution.

### Synergy

We have found JAD to be especially synergistic with our process modeling efforts, since this type of problem is large and complex and often involves cross-functional participation. Any problem with these same characteristics would probably work well with JAD.

**Prerequisites**

Management commitment to fund the training and enthusiasm on the part of the JAD trainees are the only prerequisites.

**Implementation advice**

We have used JAD to solve complex problems such as how to improve the planning process and the service support process for some of our database products. In the process, we stumbled over a few obstacles that you may encounter as well.

On the facilities end, it was difficult to find rooms of the right size with the right shape (horseshoe) of table. This may sound like a trivial point, but the configuration of the meeting rooms is actually an important part of JAD. We did what anyone would do—we adapted, jury-rigged, and made do.

Probably the toughest challenge was to get the right people in the meeting. Typically, our minimum process improvement efforts required a 3-day JAD session to really get to the core issues, then document and resolve them. And if you don't have the best people for those 3 days, you probably will be missing information and key issues. But, of course, the best people are also the hardest to schedule in a meeting of that length. The key is to get senior management commitment and work from there.

For example, in the case of improving the service support process, the manager had suffered so much frustration because of the existing process that he was willing to commit 12 to 15 days of his best people's time to rework the whole process. As it turned out, JAD got the thing done in 10 days, and he left a very satisfied internal customer.

A conventional meeting would not have worked in this case because there were too many external influences and because each department member had his or her own job which nobody else understood very well. The group needed a structured way of understanding what each member did and how the interactions were impeding the current process.

In a random survey, here are some of the comments and implementation advice offered by JAD participants:

"It is very valuable for ID [publications department] to be in on this effort. Generates good ideas early."

"It is a great way to get customers to buy into a product or a strategic direction—sometimes it is the only way."

"I am a JAD facilitator and was using this technique with external customers of IBM from 1990 to 1992. I received much positive feedback from them about its value. I also led JADs here at Santa Teresa. The reception was much less enthusiastic because the people here are so stressed with getting their work done and attending numerous unproductive meetings. They felt it was an imposition on them because their management didn't buy into it and didn't allow time for them to attend (i.e., didn't reassign their workload)."

"JADs help codify processes that currently sit in folks' heads."

"Make sure that everyone in the session is 'on the same bus going to the same destination,' or the effectiveness of the session will be defeated. Also a good facilitator is key."

Overall our own view of JAD is that if you have the right scope, goals, and people, JAD can help you reach consensus and document the decisions more efficiently than regular meetings. However, as pointed out above by the JAD facilitator, buy-in and a willingness to participate are also key.

Figure 7.7 lists some of the key steps we went through in our implementation of JAD. (If you choose to use external JAD facilitators, the items concerning facilitator training and apprenticeship do not apply.)

## Innovation 10 (Tools): Process Modeling Methods and Tools

### The objective

You can't improve your process unless you know what it is. The Baldrige assessment (Chap. 2) and the programming development handbooks (Chap. 6) are examples of formats to describe your process, but they don't tell you how to discover your existing process or how to design new ones. At our lab, we just assumed that we could muddle through, and we did. But had we brought more rigor to our efforts at process understanding, we would probably be much better off.

For example, take the case of getting a name approved for a new product. At IBM, it can take up to 6 months to do all the legal checks on new names. Our Expert Systems group found this out the hard way.

They were ready to release a product named Knowledge Tool, and they wanted to use the two-letter acronym KT. But some French company had

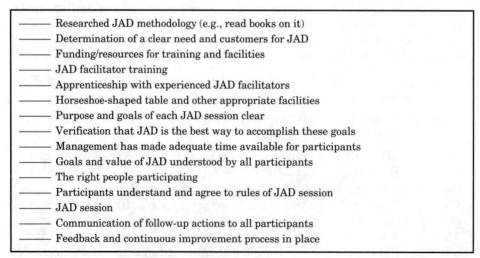

——— Researched JAD methodology (e.g., read books on it)
——— Determination of a clear need and customers for JAD
——— Funding/resources for training and facilities
——— JAD facilitator training
——— Apprenticeship with experienced JAD facilitators
——— Horseshoe-shaped table and other appropriate facilities
——— Purpose and goals of each JAD session clear
——— Verification that JAD is the best way to accomplish these goals
——— Management has made adequate time available for participants
——— Goals and value of JAD understood by all participants
——— The right people participating
——— Participants understand and agree to rules of JAD session
——— JAD session
——— Communication of follow-up actions to all participants
——— Feedback and continuous improvement process in place

**Figure 7.7**  Our JAD implementation checklist.

already registered all two-letter acronyms, and we would have had to pay them royalties. The whole thing was a big mess. Had the product team members understood the process for getting names approved better, they could have started earlier on solving the problem instead of risking a slipped schedule by dealing with it at release time.

When schedules slip, it costs thousands of dollars in lost revenue and market share. When a process glitch is the cause, it's particularly frustrating. For example, IMS's failure to conduct rigorous reviews and inspections (described in Chap. 11) resulted in the Test department taking 1.5 years instead of the 9 months allocated. That cost us, but it didn't need to.

Process modeling could have shown us the effects of each review—and of skipping steps in the process. Instead we had to learn the importance of doing code inspections the hard way. As a result of these experiences, we felt process modeling could provide a much needed service to the lab.

### An innovative approach

Any process understanding or modeling effort begins with identifying the process steps needed to produce a product or service. Then you step back and ask if the steps are really doing what they are supposed to be doing and if they are needed. This allows you to identify duplicate steps, and you can evaluate with data flow diagrams whether there is value added to a step. You can also determine, by simulating the process, where you are likely to get into trouble. Such simulation is far better than waiting for your customers to point out your process glitches.

For example, one of our products was presented to our customer support team as one big module. If there was any error in any part of the product, we had to ship a fix that was the equivalent of a re-release of the product. That meant that when another error occurred, our fix became a "programming fix in error."

But, according to our process, we could not ship a fix to the first problem until we also fixed the second problem. This procedure was supposed to prevent shipping a code fix that was known to have an error. Instead it resulted in all our customers, most of whom couldn't care less about minor error 2, waiting to get a fix for major error 1 until both errors could be fixed.

The solution was to present the product to our customer support team as several small modules instead of one gigantic one. Then errors in any one module could be fixed independent of the errors in the others. It sure would have been nice to figure this out with a process model instead of with our customers!

At our lab, the standard methodology for process modeling is to conduct a JAD session (see above) and use a process modeling tool.

For example, one of our organizations wanted to document their planning process. The methodology was to define the scope and goals of the effort, define who would participate, interview all participants to make sure they understood what JAD was all about, and then hold a 3-day JAD session stepping through the planning process.

The end result was a 15-step process with definitions and work products for each step. The process modeling tool produced a process flow document that had diagrams of the process and descriptions of each step. This process was then distributed to all managers as the new project planning process.

Other process modeling efforts produced development or test processes such as the one shown in Fig. 7.8.

Despite these successes however, process modeling never really caught on, primarily because of the perceived cost of engaging in the activity. The tools were difficult to use unless you were an expert, and most managers were hesitant to commit their 10 best developers to a 3- to 10-day JAD session.

### Costs, benefits, and risks

The greatest cost in process modeling is people time. We estimate that it takes one person working half-time to keep the process of a 100-person organization up to date. Add to that periodic meetings with developers, and you have a 1 percent of the resource maintenance cost.

But the start-up can be an even bigger obstacle. First, at least with KnowledgeWare's tool, there is a big learning curve before you become proficient. Plus you need to commit one person from every group included in your process for a 3- to 10-day JAD session. This time commitment scared off many of our managers unless they were being strangled by their current process. And for new products that keep changing their process, it sometimes seemed like the group lived in process modeling meetings.

We made another mistake by buying way too many process modeling tools. Much as we hate to admit it, we acquired over $100,000 worth of process modeling tools, which today are mostly gathering dust.

Learn from our mistakes! There is nothing wrong with starting small. And this applies to the modeling efforts themselves as well as to your tools. If you try to model all your processes at once, it is easy to become overwhelmed.

Our main caveat is to make sure that people understand the need for process modeling and agree with it. Process modeling has not been too successful at our lab, partly because we did not sell the problem well enough. The process modeling experts came from our Quality Assurance department, where the need for process modeling was already understood. What these experts failed to realize was that the rest of the lab needed education before they would be able to recognize process as the source of some of their problems. Unfortunately, process modeling is one of those things that you realize you should have done—*after* something goes wrong with your process. But it's tough to convince developers to sign up for something that looks suspiciously like more bureaucracy.

However, if you can get over the start-up hurdles, we've seen some benefits. First, people are able to communicate better once they share a common process vocabulary. We were surprised how many people throw around terms and don't really know what each other is saying.

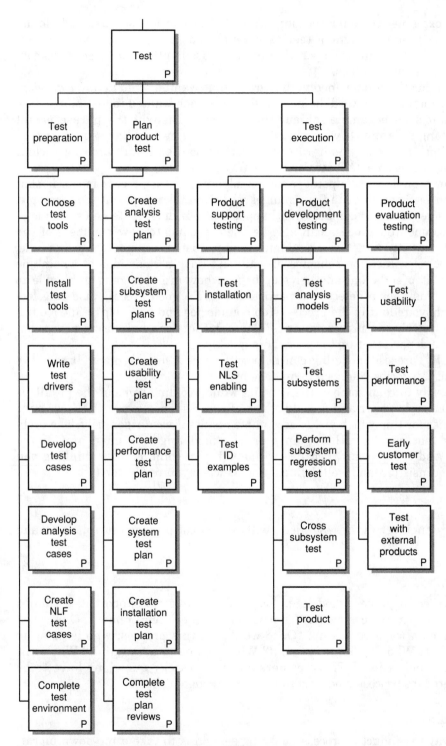

**Figure 7.8** Sample test process. (*Courtesy of IBM*)

For example, consider the phrases *test case* and *test scenario*. We found that one group thought a test case contained several scenarios whereas another department was operating from the assumption that a scenario contained several test cases.

A similar thing happened with a group that wanted to do *iterative development*—another buzzword du jour. At first everyone wanted to just plunge into it, but it soon became apparent that everyone thought the phrase meant something different. If we had just plunged in, we would have spent production time trying to understand each other, rather than reaching a clear understanding in a JAD session up front.

From a quality standpoint, another advantage of a process model is that you can see how the data flow changes when you take steps out. For example, with some tools, you can see what happens to your defect rate and schedule.

A documented process can also be used to educate new members of the department and to define meaningful in-process measurements. For example, in defect classification schemes, if you don't have a clear idea of where one process step ends and another step begins, how are you going to be able to assign blame for a defect to a particular step? A good process modeling tool will help you identify the process step boundaries and will help define a database for storing in-process metrics. These outputs can help bring new members of a department up to speed more quickly.

Finally, process modeling can help with project management. It can give you the categories you need to manage by.

One way to reap some of the benefits while avoiding some of the pitfalls is to do a simple paper-and-pencil version of process modeling. At IBM, we have a process for this which yields acceptable results if used rigorously. The problem is that people, rather than a process modeling tool, must provide the rigor. And rigor is key, because without it, you could end up thinking you have a consistent and well-defined process when you really don't.

## Synergy

Process engineering is synergistic with statistical process control, DPP, and JAD.

## Prerequisites

To succeed at process modeling, you need resources to support it, a trained expert, and a process owner. That is the toughest requirement. One set of questions always comes up: "Once we define this process, who is going to enforce it? Who is going to track it? Who is going to maintain it? Who owns the documentation?" These ownership and strategy questions have to be answered for process modeling to work on an ongoing basis.

## Implementation advice

One way to conduct a process modeling session is to take a top-down hierarchical approach. Here you are starting with the elements you think should be in the process and fleshing out the process tree with questions (e.g., Where's your planning? Where's your continuous improvement mechanism?"). When you get to the leaves of the tree, you start documenting data flow and describing processes in detail. Certain tools give you a static look at this detail. For example, Fig. 7.9 zooms in on the test subsystems stage from Fig. 7.8. Other tools allow you to change parameters and see how variables are affected—more of a spreadsheet approach.

Whichever tools you use, the goal is to identify the leverage points for improving the process.

You can also bypass computerized tools altogether and use the process analysis technique (PAT) methodology. This works for existing processes only and can be done with paper and pencil. For example, Table 7.2 illustrates the major steps in the PAT methodology by using a matrix technique that is itself part of the PAT methodology.

We used the PAT process with good results. PAT works with individual interviews and requires only 1 or 2 h per interview. The total cost might involve 10 interviews followed by one group meeting to validate it at the end. So it is much cheaper than a JAD session and KnowledgeWare tools in terms of resources.

In general, JAD is better when you have a cross-functional or cross-lab situation where you need to make big decisions. If you are dealing with a large and unwieldy situation, then JAD would be best. But if few decisions need to be made and it's just a matter of data collection, then a pencil-and-paper approach like PAT works well.

Whatever your process modeling approach, you'll want to make sure to consider three key elements of any process:

1.  Effectiveness (Are you doing the right thing?)

2.  Efficiency (Could you do things better?)

3.  Adaptability (If requirements change, what breaks?)

---

Test Subsystems

|  |  |
|---|---|
| *Inputs:* | *Outputs:* |
| Driver | Validated source code |
| Test environment | Test results |
| Test cases | |

*Purpose:* To validate that a subsystem produces the correct outputs for each input.

*Entry criteria:* The subsystem to be tested must have successfully exited Analysis Test. Each driver is provided by the agreed-to date. Test will slip on a day-to-day basis until the above criteria are met.

*Exit criteria:* Zero category 1 and 2 defects and no more than five category 3 and 4 defects; 100% attempted planned tests, 97% of tests have run successfully.

*Test subsystems:* Performance problems identified in normal subsystem testing will be brought forward.

*Note:* Development must provide any required complex scaffolding.

---

**Figure 7.9**  Test subsystems.

TABLE 7.2   PAT Implementation Steps

| Step | Owner | Consultant | Lead coordinator | Involved managers | Task experts |
|---|---|---|---|---|---|
| 1 | Decision to do PAT | — | | | |
| 2 | Bounding the process | A | | | |
| 3 | Document of understanding | A | I | | |
| 4 | I | Preliminary PAT | A | I | |
| 5 | I | Information meeting | A | I | I |
| 6 | | PAT interviews | A | | I |
| 7 | | Analysis and revision | A | | |
| 8 | I | A | Prototype revised process | I | |
| 9 | Decision to implement | A | A | | |

A = assist; I = involved.
(Partnership)

There are also a few warning signs that a process modeling effort is off track. You're in trouble if:

1. You find missing pieces in your process.

2. The participants in the process modeling effort lack enthusiasm or don't show up.

3. You can't get answers when you ask detailed process questions—an indication that you don't have the right people in the meetings.

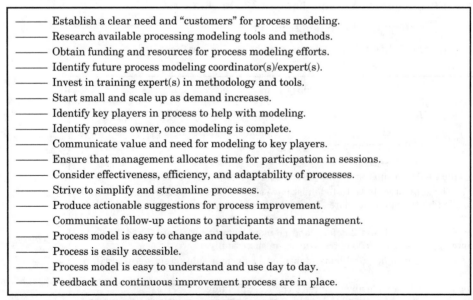

————  Establish a clear need and "customers" for process modeling.
————  Research available processing modeling tools and methods.
————  Obtain funding and resources for process modeling efforts.
————  Identify future process modeling coordinator(s)/expert(s).
————  Invest in training expert(s) in methodology and tools.
————  Start small and scale up as demand increases.
————  Identify key players in process to help with modeling.
————  Identify process owner, once modeling is complete.
————  Communicate value and need for modeling to key players.
————  Ensure that management allocates time for participation in sessions.
————  Consider effectiveness, efficiency, and adaptability of processes.
————  Strive to simplify and streamline processes.
————  Produce actionable suggestions for process improvement.
————  Communicate follow-up actions to participants and management.
————  Process model is easy to change and update.
————  Process is easily accessible.
————  Process model is easy to understand and use day to day.
————  Feedback and continuous improvement process are in place.

Figure 7.10   Process modeling implementation checklist.

If you can avoid the pitfalls, process modeling can be a powerful technique. But before you begin, make sure that a clear need exists and that you can communicate that need effectively to those who will be involved in the process modeling efforts.

Figure 7.10 provides an implementation checklist for process modeling.

## Suggested Readings

August, J. H. (1991) *Joint Application Design: The Group Session Approach to System Design.* Englewood Cliffs, NJ: Yourdon Press. *A good book that discusses the room setup and general procedures for conducting JAD sessions.*

Basili, V. R., and Rombach, H. D. (1987) "Tailoring the Software Process to Project Goals and Environments." *Proceedings of the 9th International Conference for Software Engineering.* IEEE Computer Society, pp. 345–357. *This paper describes a goal-based process improvement methodology that links defect profiles to process improvement.*

Curtis, B., Krasner, H., Shen, V., and Iscoe, N. (1987) "On Building Software Process Models under the Lamppost." *Proceedings of the 9th International Conference for Software Engineering."* IEEE Computer Society, pp. 96–103.

Humphrey, W. S. (1985) "The IBM Large-Systems Software Development Process: Objectives and Direction." *IBM Systems Journal,* 24(2): 76–78. *An introduction to some process-oriented modeling and measurement approaches used by IBM.*

Kellner, M. I. (1992) "Process Modelling." *Communications of the ACM,* 35(9): 75–90.

Kellner, M. I., and Hansen, G. A. (1989) "Software Process Modelling: A Case Study." *Proceedings of the 22d Annual Hawaii International Conference on Systems Science.* IEEE Press, pp. 175–188. *Relates experiences applying a specific process modeling technique to U.S. Air Force software support process.*

Krut, Jr., R. and Wood, D. P. (1991) *Evaluation of Process Modelling Improvements.* CMU/SEI Technical Report, CMU/SEI-91-TR-5, ADA24-4293. *A report on modifications to SEI's process modeling techniques.*

Pfleeger, S. L., and McGowan, C. (1990) "Software Metrics in the Process Maturity Framework." *The Journal of Systems and Software,* 12: 255–261, December.

Potts, C., ed. (1984) *Proceedings of the Software Process Workshop.* Los Alamitos, CA: IEEE Computer Society. *This first workshop on process modeling sponsored by the IEEE raised problems with traditional life-cycle models and suggested some alternatives.*

Radice, R. A., Roth, N. K., O'Hara, Jr., A., and Ciarfella, W. A. (1985) "A Programming Process Architecture." *IBM Systems Journal,* 24(2): 79–90. *This paper presents a software development framework including process management, analysis mechanisms, and quality reviews.*

Wood, J., and Silver, D. (1989) *Joint Application Design: How to Design Quality Systems in 40% Less Time.* New York: Wiley. *A detailed how-to description of JAD including what's needed to get started, who does what, and ingredients for success.*

# 8

# Stage 2: Coping

## Are You in the Coping Stage?

The second stage of quality maturity marks the transition from activities which are primarily aimed at raising quality awareness to activities that are aimed at bringing quality under some measure of control. In the coping stage, our Baldrige assessment scored from 500 to 625.

Table 8.1 shows specific indicators we saw in each of the seven areas covered by Baldrige. An organization exhibiting most or all of these signs is probably in the coping stage.

**TABLE 8.1  Baldrige Indicators of the Coping Stage**

| Baldrige area | Indicators |
|---|---|
| 1.0 Leadership | Senior leaders committed<br>First-line management unsure |
| 2.0 Information and analysis | Some data collected<br>Beginning to define quality measurements<br>External customer and/or supplier indicators defined but no data |
| 3.0 Strategic quality planning | Overall quality strategy/plan in place<br>Some departmental strategies/plans in place<br>Working to define repeatable strategic planning process |
| 4.0 Human resource development and management | Quality education courses available<br>Morale low, but participation in quality activities increasing |
| 5.0 Management of process quality | Initial efforts to understand and document processes<br>Focus on easy-to-fix process elements<br>Defect detection and test emphasis<br>Little or no focus on supplier processes |
| 6.0 Quality and operational results | Beginning to get data on quality levels<br>Lack of trend and competitor data<br>Little or no impact of quality efforts on operational results |
| 7.0 Customer focus and satisfaction | Developed systematic customer satisfaction measurements<br>Lack of comparison data with competitors |

## Objectives of the Coping Stage

The goal in the coping stage is to do something immediately to improve the quality of products and processes, while laying the groundwork for innovation that will lead to quality breakthroughs in subsequent stages.

The leadership challenge is to get more of the organization to buy into quality. Simple awareness of quality issues is no longer enough. Organizational systems must be created that ensure that people act to improve quality. These systems act as catalysts for change, facilitating the exchange of quality-related information.

The process challenge is to continue to understand and contain the quality "fires" via assessment and process improvements. The most immediate improvements can be achieved by using enhanced testing and defect detection techniques, so it makes sense to concentrate efforts here. These techniques are essentially reactive, in that they do nothing to prevent the occurrence of defects. However, they do prevent defects from reaching customers, so quality as perceived by the customer will increase. Also, improved testing is the least radical approach to quality improvement. It allows organizations at this stage of quality maturity to obtain quality results as quickly as possible.

In the technology arena, again the objective is to use tools that will produce immediate results with a minimum of restructuring of the organization. Better use of existing information is one of the highest-leverage quality activities possible. That is, it costs little to perform analyses of existing data, and the resulting information can greatly enhance the organization's effectiveness.

From a Baldrige perspective, Fig. 8.1 shows our lab's specific Baldrige focus items for the coping stage.

## Overview of Innovations for the Coping Stage

Table 8.2 summarizes nine innovations that can help organizations meet quality objectives in the coping stage.

As in the awareness stage, the leadership innovations for the coping stage emphasize obtaining deeper commitment to quality improvement activities.

---

1.2 Management for quality (especially communicating quality values throughout the company)

2.1 Scope and management of quality and performance data and information (especially selection of data for quality improvement)

4.2 Employee involvement (especially mechanisms to promote employee involvement and give feedback to employees)

5.1 Design and introduction of quality products and services (especially improvement of design and design review processes)

5.2 Process management: Product and service production and delivery processes (especially in-process measurements)

7.2 Customer relationship management (especially quality indicators and service standards)

7.3 Commitment to customers (especially how feedback from customers is used)

---

**Figure 8.1**  Baldrige items for improvement in the coping stage.

**TABLE 8.2   Coping Stage Innovations**

| Food group | Objective | Innovative approach | Implementation pitfalls |
|---|---|---|---|
| Leadership | Get line organization to take quality responsibility; promote organizational learning. | Create a group to act as a quality improvement catalyst and experience factory—the Center for Software Excellence (CSE). | Failure to evolve CSE. Lack of preparation for push-back. |
| | Get powerful informal "shadow" organization that has bought into quality. | Tap into informal organization via a management council system. | Wrong people staffing CSE. NATO—no action, talk only. |
| Process | Meet ISO 9000 requirements and use Baldridge. | Do both: Baldrige: Tell me. ISO 9000 Strategy: Show me. | Excluding one for the other; ignoring synergism. |
| | Promote design and code inspections. | Reinstate rigorous design reviews and code inspections. | Wavering on push-back, poor preparation, no follow-up or communications. |
| | Reduce cycle times; improve quality. | Use train method as part of early test involvement. | Giving up; focus on failures. |
| | Improve testing; increase effectiveness. | Integrate development and test in a combined line-item and functional test (CLIFT) program. | Failure to provide tools and education; no postmortems, no learning from mistakes. |
| Technology | Reduce errors in the field. | Error-prone module analysis statistically identifies problem code modules. | Failure to act on analysis; belief this is more bureaucracy. |
| | Predict and prevent error-prone code. | Determine "fingerprint" of error-prone code early via high-risk module analysis. | Failure of data collection mechanism; failure to act on information. |
| | Ensure we can answer: "Will our efforts improve customer satisfaction?" | Linking customer satisfaction to investment via data linkage analysis. | Using naive statistical analyses. |

However, the method for obtaining this endorsement is quite different. Whereas we focused on specific events to raise quality consciousness in the awareness stage, in the coping stage we add organizational systems that are meant to support and sustain a quality focus over a period of years. The Center for Software Excellence is a group whose mission is to serve as a catalyst for quality improvement for the rest of the lab. Similarly, the management council system is an organizational structure designed to get key managers to participate in ongoing communication and action related to quality improvement.

The process innovations for the coping stage emphasize assessment of processes by using ISO 9000 and enhancements to the testing, inspection, and review steps in the development process. These process enhancements reflect a dual strategy: (1) Continue to assess the existing process, and (2) do the process better via more rigor and better defect detection.

Coping technologies focus on statistical analysis techniques. *Error-prone module analysis* uses existing data on errors from the field to identify and focus effort on troublesome code modules. *High-risk module analysis* goes one step further and explores what the characteristics of error-free modules should be. Finally, *customer survey data linkage analysis* helps use customer feedback more effectively to drive product development efforts. A high-quality product should be both error-free and what the customers want.

Together, the leadership, process, and technology innovations provide immediate leverage on quality while laying the groundwork for more radical innovation in subsequent stages. Chapters 9 to 12 describe the nine coping stage innovations in greater detail.

## Obstacles and Pitfalls

In the coping stage, you are likely to see a lot of resistance to change. Few, if any, results are evident, and many people may view the focus on quality as a disruption of the "real work" that needs to be done.

The worst thing a leader can do in the coping stage is to let up the heat. People *must* push through the pain and the resistance if lasting change is to occur. Figure 8.2 shows some other common pitfalls that we fell into, or nearly fell into, during the coping stage.

## Signs of Progress

Despite a general lack of results, there will be some signs of progress that you can look for as your organization moves through the coping stage. One very positive sign is the appearance of in-process measurements and metrics. Another is the increased focus on testing and on design reviews and code inspections. Almost all software companies incorporate these activities somewhere in the development process. When developers begin to take these activ-

---

**Leadership pitfalls**

1. Letting up the heat
2. Failing to constantly communicate importance of quality and progress
3. Settling for small improvements, thereby signaling "We're there"
4. Worrying about unpopularity and resentment
5. Becoming alarmed that things will get worse before they get better

**Process pitfalls**

1. Settling for qualitative measures
2. Failing to encourage process redesign
3. Failing to encourage cross-functional communication
4. Failing to celebrate improvements, no matter how small

**Technology pitfalls**

1. Settling for "Whip 'em harder"
2. Lack of focus on test tools and automation
3. Failure to encourage innovation and breakthroughs

---

**Figure 8.2**   Pitfalls in the coping stage.

ities more seriously, it's a sign that they have woken up to the need for higher quality.

On the leadership front, look for increased resistance and push-back from the developers. You are in a quality race here, so if it isn't hurting, you probably aren't pushing hard enough. No pain, no gain.

Finally, look for successes—any kind of successes—and promote the hell out of them. The second half of the coping stage and the first half of the management stage are the toughest part of the journey, so it is doubly important to celebrate accomplishments along the way.

## Our Lab in the Coping Stage

Our lab received the bronze medal from IBM's Corporate Quality group in October 1990, signifying a Baldrige score above 500. We had completed two Excellence Council sessions in July and April, and the use of customer satisfaction surveys was being emphasized throughout the lab. Developers and support staff who had never heard of CUPRIMDS now could all recite: capability, usability, performance, reliability, installability, maintainability, documentation, and service—the categories of our customer survey.

At the same time, developers, many on their own initiative, had begun to implement a plethora of testing and inspection techniques in an attempt to reach the lab's 10-fold quality improvement goals. Despite these hopeful signs, however, the coping stage was plagued by the first signs of serious resistance to quality activities.

Many people still hoped secretly that quality would just go away. That hope was shattered when the GM put some teeth into the quality assurance process. At our lab, missing a ship date was the worst sin a product manager could commit. So when the general manager personally held up the shipment of a product because it failed to meet more stringent quality levels, that decision echoed like a rifle shot in the hallways throughout the lab.

Resentment began to set in and morale declined, reflecting a shift from denial ("This, too, shall pass") to resistance ("This is unreasonable!"). At the same time, the economy was just entering a worldwide recession. IBM's profits were down and sliding fast. Managers were being forced to slash their budgets on one hand and were being asked to invest in quality improvement activities on the other. The typical first response, under the circumstances, was: "You must be out of your minds!"

Yet little by little, management was realizing the seriousness of the quality challenge and increasingly recognized the need for process improvement. Awareness and recognition seem to trickle down, becoming more dilute as one got farther away from the GM's office. This situation was reflected clearly in the results of an opinion survey taken in the early coping stage (Table 8.3).

Two general trends were apparent in the data. First, both buy-in and participation tended to decrease as you got further from the top of the organization. This trend reflected the fact that the higher-level managers participated

TABLE 8.3    Results from Opinion Survey,
Coping Stage

| Management level | Buy-in index, % | Quality participation index, % |
|---|---|---|
| Third line | 90 | 100 |
| Second line | 95 | 85 |
| First line | 60 | 72 |
| Nonmanager | 41 | 63 |

in the Excellence Council and were more directly involved in the quality awareness activities than the rest of the lab.

Second, participation (with the exception of the second-line managers) was greater than buy-in. This reflected our general manager's approach: demand participation, buy-in will follow.

Although senior management had realized the significance of quality and the middle managers were under pressure to improve quality, the average software developer still had a deep mistrust of the quality initiatives that were popping up. There was a general feeling that quality was an intangible—something elusive that you either had or didn't have. The common refrain seemed to be: "Our quality is fine, if only management would leave us alone so that we could develop products."

Looking back, as the lab entered the coping stage, many of us still had a *Zen and the Art of Motorcycle Maintenance* view of quality. Sure it was important. Of course, customers wanted it. But somehow it seemed abstract, almost philosophical. Or else we thought we were already doing it. After all, we were IBM, weren't we? People were buying our products weren't they?

Today, especially in light of IBM's financial performance from 1991 to 1993, that attitude seems complacent. But in 1990 few believed that the company was in serious trouble.

Part of the problem was that we didn't know what we could do. Frankly, the goals of 10-fold improvement seemed impossible. It seemed as if senior management had lost touch with reality and was squandering resources on quality hype while IBM as a whole was reeling from the shock waves of the recession. It was a frustrating time for both managers and employees, and throughout the coping stage things just seemed to get worse and worse. If we had quit at this point and written a book about it, we would probably have recommended staying as far away as possible from TQM or anything to do with quality improvement. Fortunately we persisted, and results began to appear in the management stage.

## Suggested Readings

Conte, S. D., Dunsmore, H. E., and Shen, V. Y. (1986) *Software Engineering Metrics and Models.* Menlo Park, CA: Benjamin/Cummings. *A fairly comprehensive treatment of metrics and models that should be useful to anyone desiring to introduce measurements to the software development process.*

Curtis, B. (1980) "Measurement and Experimentation in Software Engineering." *Proceedings of IEEE*, 68(9): 1144–1157. *A survey of basic concerns that are relevant to organizations trying to understand their development practices in a systematic way.*

Davenport, T. H. (1993) *Process Innovation: Reengineering Work through Information Technology.* Boston: Harvard Business School Press. *A first-class book that provides a framework for achieving organizational change through process innovation.*

DeMarco, T. (1982) *Controlling Software Projects.* New York: Yourdon Press. *Explains how quality can affect software costs and describes how software metrics can help.*

Grady, R. B., and Caswell, D. L. (1987) *Software Metrics: Establishing a Company-Wide Program.* Englewood Cliffs, NJ: Prentice-Hall. *Two software experts at Hewlett-Packard describe how to set up a software metrics program.*

Harrington, H. J. (1991) *Business Process Improvement.* New York: McGraw-Hill. *An excellent introduction to process reengineering.*

Yacobellis, R. H. (1984) "Software and Development Process Quality Metrics." *Proceedings of COMPSAC '84.* IEEE Computer Society, pp. 262–269. *Early experiments at AT&T Bell Labs emphasize the importance of using software metrics.*

# 9

# Organizational Catalysts for Quality Improvement

While awareness-stage innovations like the Leadership Institute jolted people into a state of quality awareness, such jolts of enlightenment wear off quickly. To sustain consistent efforts at quality improvement, a large organization needs support in the form of encouragement, advice, and technical expertise. The Center for Software Excellence was conceived originally to provide this support. Later, as the lab's efforts became self-sustaining, the center evolved into an Experience Factory, capturing and communicating the innovations of various development groups throughout the lab.

The management council system represents a slightly different solution to the same basic problem of sustaining quality focus. Because a powerful informal network existed at our lab, the idea was to use this network to promote quality improvement activities. Key product and support managers were invited to participate in regular council sessions to address quality-related issues. Information could be shared and actions decided upon.

Table 9.1 summarizes these two innovations, the objectives they helped achieve, and some implementation pitfalls. Finally, we want to emphasize the importance of synthesizing all of the innovations we have discussed so far

**TABLE 9.1   Stage: Coping / Food Group: Leadership / Themes: Increase Buy-in at All Levels; Create Environment for Innovation; Create Institutional Foundations for Quality**

| Objective | Innovative approach | Pitfalls |
|---|---|---|
| Sustain quality focus<br>Transfer quality ownership to Development<br>Sustain and promote innovation | *Center for Software Excellence:*<br>Create a special group of quality experts to advise Development<br>Implement experience factory concept | Failure to evolve role of Center for Software Excellence<br>Failure to weather storms of resistance |
| Sustain quality focus in powerful informal organization | *Management Council System:*<br>Use council system to formalize the informal organization.<br>Councils to have quality focus. | NATO—No action, talk only |

(and some yet to be discussed) into a comprehensive approach to quality. Moreover, we believe that the quality innovations can be applied on a variety of scales. To illustrate how a single product developed a comprehensive approach to quality improvement, we have included a case study as a third topic in this chapter.

## Innovation 11 (Leadership): The Center for Software Excellence

### The objective

A major challenge facing our lab at the end of the awareness stage was that the development groups looked to the Quality Assurance department to take care of quality. Quality was just another step in the development process— another hurdle for a development manager to jump over in the race to get the product out the door, on schedule.

From the development manager's perspective, the Quality Assurance group was a small group of auditors who would rap you on the knuckles if your product didn't meet their standards. Then you'd fix the problems pointed out by the auditors and rush your product to market.

This approach was better than having no independent Quality Assurance group at all, but it could never help us make the kinds of drastic improvements in quality that we knew we must make. During the dozen or so years that the Quality Assurance group was in operation, quality levels had improved at a snail's pace. But what could a small group of auditors do in a lab of almost 2000 people?

The trick was to transfer ownership of quality from a small group of auditors to the development community at large.

### An innovative approach

The solution required transforming the Quality Assurance group to an entirely different kind of organization—a Center for Software Excellence.

At first, the center's mission was to act as a catalyst for change. It served as the arms and legs for senior management, spreading the gospel of quality improvement.

Once the word was out, the Center for Software Excellence (CSE) began honing its own core skills in areas such as Baldrige, ISO 9000, CleanRoom, statistical analysis, and process modeling. As it gained core expertise, members of the CSE began to teach and consult with development groups, providing them with the tools they needed to improve quality.

As the development groups learned, they began to innovate on their own, coming up with completely new approaches to quality improvement. At this stage, the Center for Software Excellence took on yet another role—that of a knowledge repository for the entire lab. It became an "experience factory"—a repository for the best innovations at the lab, with a mission of spreading these innovations to other groups who hadn't heard of them yet.

Finally, even as we write, the CSE is undergoing yet another transformation. The lab as a whole has assumed full ownership for quality, for innovation, and for the dissemination of such innovation internally. Consequently, the Center for Software Excellence is no longer needed as a catalyst. Instead it provides value now by focusing on two key areas. First, it leverages its quality expertise internally to carry out quality research and analysis. Second, externally it leverages these same skills, together with its in-depth knowledge of various quality innovations, to provide consulting services to customers outside IBM.

### Costs, benefits, and risks

The cost of creating the Center for Software Excellence ranged from 3 to 4 percent of the lab's resources. Because a quality assurance group already existed, that group was folded into the new organization, reducing the overall cost.

The immediate benefit of an organization like the CSE is a much more rapid and pervasive commitment to quality improvement activities. Later benefits include rapid spread of innovations due to the experience factory concept and the accumulation of knowledge that can be used for external as well as internal consulting.

The primary risk is that if senior management fails to back the new organization, it can succumb to resistance from Development. In the worst case, a half-hearted attempt to form an organization like the CSE might accomplish nothing except to anger developers and demoralize members of the center.

### Synergy

As catalyst, the Center for Software Excellence is synergistic with the Excellence Council, departmental quality strategies, and other leadership innovations emphasizing a quality transformation. As an experience factory, the CSE is synergistic with all the innovations in this book.

### Prerequisites

The key prerequisite for the CSE is unwavering commitment from senior management. There is also a size requirement. It would make no sense for a department of only 10 people to commission a separate organization to catalyze the adoption of quality values and techniques. The Center for Software Excellence works best at the site level. However, the principles of first catalyzing quality, building a base of expertise, and then leveraging that expertise to help both internal and external customers can be applied by organizations of any size.

### Implementation advice

It is ironic that while the Japanese Society of Engineers praised the CSE above all other innovations at the lab, and while the quality results described in Chap. 1 demonstrate the success of the CSE in its mission of spreading cultural change, the CSE received initially some of the harshest criticism from within the organization.

This paradox reflects the fact that the CSE often acted as a lightning rod. All the resistance and resentment that typically accompany rapid change strike first at the visible agent of that change—in this case, the CSE. It takes a tough and flexible leader to weather these torrents of criticism. Fortunately, the senior management team supported the CSE through the inevitable storms.

Ultimately, though, even harsh criticism melts in the face of concrete evidence of success. As improved quality results have begun to come in, Table 9.2 shows how the internal critics began to reevaluate their initial assessment of the Center for Software Excellence.

The complaints that we heard about the CSE followed a predictable pattern, mirroring the evolving role of the organization depicted in Table 9.3.

In the preawareness stage, there are no complaints because no one recognizes that quality is a problem and no one has been asked to do anything about it.

In the awareness stage, senior management recognizes that quality is a problem, but may still cling to the belief that the problem can be delegated to a quality assurance group. This group assumes the role of "cop" and lets the line organization know when quality falls below set standards. The most common complaint from Development here is: "Why do I have to go through this added bureaucracy of getting a quality certification? We know we have good quality." We were at this stage in 1989.

In the coping stage, senior management has realized that there is absolutely no way to improve quality significantly unless all of Development has bought into and made quality a top priority. The role of the quality assurance group—if it exists—must change at this point from cop to catalyst. The group must build expertise and share knowledge with Development. The most common complaint from Development during the building knowledge phase is: "If we are responsible for quality, what good is the Center?" The Center for Software Excellence must answer this question by providing value added in the form of internal consulting. Thus, the coping stage marks the emergence of the CSE in its role as an internal quality consulting agency. The foundations are also being laid for an operational experience factory—a mechanism for capturing and disseminating knowledge.

**TABLE 9.2  Satisfaction Ratings for the Center for Software Excellence**

| Survey date | Percent satisfied | Percent neutral | Percent dissatisfied |
|---|---|---|---|
| April 1992 | 16 | 39 | 45 |
| December 1992 | 46 | 41 | 13 |
| June 1993 | 54 | 35 | 12 |

**TABLE 9.3  Evolution of the Center for Software Excellence**

| | Preawareness stage | Awareness stage | Coping stage | Management stage | Integration stage |
|---|---|---|---|---|---|
| Senior management's view of quality | None | Quality is a problem that can be delegated | Quality is everyone's responsibility | Quality requires innovation and proactive approaches | Quality extends beyond the organization |
| Role of quality group | Does not exist | Quality assurance "Cop"/auditor role | Quality catalyst Internal consultant | Internal consultant Knowledge repository | Minimal internal role External consulting |
| Implementation issues/ownership | No implementation No ownership | Line organization sees Quality Assurance as a hoop to jump through Quality Assurance group owns the quality problem | Line organizations accepts ownership but asks Quality Assurance for help | Line organization makes progress and innovates Center's role shifts from internal consulting to documentation | Line organization has internalized quality CSE shifts toward external consulting |
| What our lab did | No action | Created a Quality Assurance group | Transformed Quality Assurance group into the Center for Software Excellence Emphasized education and process engineering | Emphasized strategic focus with quality strategy group Emphasized innovation with innovation council Emphasized documenting innovations | Reduced size of CSE Added external consulting function |

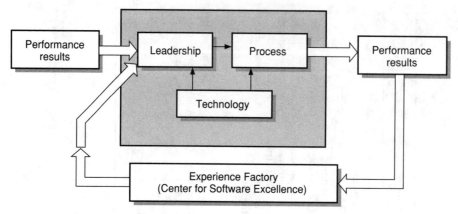

**Figure 9.1**   The experience factory concept.

In the management stage, senior management has begun to put the pressure on Development to deliver quality results. This pressure helps drive innovation. The CSE also tried to foster innovation through mechanisms such as the Innovation and Creativity Council (see below) and the addition of a Quality Strategy group. However, as the line organization becomes more and more competent, the common complaint becomes: "We can do this quality stuff ourselves. We don't need the Center's consulting." This signals yet another change in the Center's role from internal consultant and innovation sponsor to repository for the innovation of others. The Center's mission now is to spread good innovations to other parts of the lab. Its function as experience factory—capturing and passing on the innovations of others—now supersedes its role as innovator and internal consultant.

Finally, in the integration stage, there should be no need for a Center if it has done its job well. Quality values and the capacities for creating, documenting, and spreading quality-related innovations should all be internalized in the line organization. The overall organization has become a "learning laboratory" without the need for a separate CSE group. Theoretically, the Center could be dissolved or (as in our case) refocused on quality research, analysis, and external consulting.

Since the coping stage marks the emergence of the Center and the beginning of the experience factory concept, implementation at this stage is the most critical.

Assuming that you have a strong leader for the Center and the unequivocal support of senior management, the next most important ingredient is the right type of people. While an assurance organization requires cops, or "rules-driven" people, the Center needs to be staffed with quality zealots, or "principle-driven" people. The staff must have internalized the importance of responding to customer needs and of being service-oriented. Moreover, the staff should have quantitative skills, since Development can see the value of quantitative analyses immediately. Gaining credibility with Development by offering concrete analyses is an important step on the way to spreading the more nebulous gospel of a Baldrige or ISO 9000 style of quality transformation.

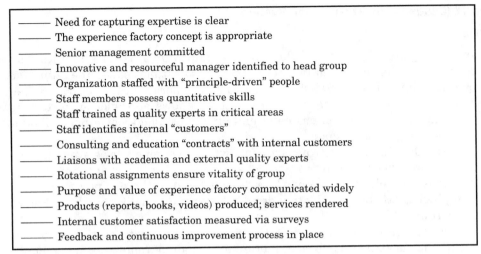

——— Need for capturing expertise is clear
——— The experience factory concept is appropriate
——— Senior management committed
——— Innovative and resourceful manager identified to head group
——— Organization staffed with "principle-driven" people
——— Staff members possess quantitative skills
——— Staff trained as quality experts in critical areas
——— Staff identifies internal "customers"
——— Consulting and education "contracts" with internal customers
——— Liaisons with academia and external quality experts
——— Rotational assignments ensure vitality of group
——— Purpose and value of experience factory communicated widely
——— Products (reports, books, videos) produced; services rendered
——— Internal customer satisfaction measured via surveys
——— Feedback and continuous improvement process in place

**Figure 9.2**   Center for Software Excellence implementation checklist.

Figure 9.1 illustrates the overall operation of the Center, viewed as an experience factory—a concept discussed by Guinan (1993), Basili (1993), and others. The business of software development should occur in a strategic context (described in Chap. 14). As the organization develops leadership, process, and technology innovations, these not only affect performance results but also feed into the Center. The Center, acting as an experience factory, then disseminates this knowledge throughout the organization.

As the organization reaches higher levels of quality maturity, the dissemination function, which originally was outside the development groups, becomes infused in the organization as a whole. When this happens, the organization has become what Professor Leonard-Barton of Harvard Business School has called a "learning laboratory." Continuous innovation and improvement have become values embedded in the fabric of the organization, and they go on constantly, at every level, from the general manager to the most junior employee.

People might well ask how it is possible that our lab went on to win IBM's most prestigious quality award—the gold medal—more than a year after the general manager who started our quality transformation left. Our answer is that Furey left, but his quality vision, which was embodied first in the Center for Software Excellence and ultimately in the entire lab, remained. In retrospect, although the Center changed its tactics constantly, it remained steadfast in its strategic purpose—to transfer a quality vision, and the expertise to execute that vision, from a few leaders and innovators to the lab as a whole. In 1993, shouts of congratulations echoed through the lab's halls as the entire lab celebrated (yes, with wine and beer—it's a new IBM) winning IBM's gold medal. The Center had done its job well.

Figure 9.2 describes an implementation checklist for the Center at the coping Stage.

## Innovation 12 (Leadership): The Council System

### The objective

In any organization there is the formal organizational chart structure, and there is an informal communication network, sometimes called the *grapevine* or *rumor mill.* The formal structure is usually hierarchical and looks something like a pyramid. The informal structure knows no rank, but instead is made up of many connections between individuals who know other individuals who can get things done.

In small organizations or departments where everyone knows everyone, the distinction between these two types of structures is unimportant. Small organizations are able to move quickly, precisely because there is no communication problem. If the organization decides to focus on quality, everyone knows in short order.

In large organizations, savvy CEOs know that the way to get things done in a hurry is *not* to use the formal, hierarchical chain of command. If you doubt this, consider which spreads faster: a juicy rumor leaked through the grapevine or some new bureaucratic procedure sent down through the chain of command.

The key to effective communication is to tap into the informal network and communicate via the "shadow organization"—the organization that never shows up in any organizational chart but which is responsible for most of the communication and work that gets done.

We needed to get quality improvement activities started in a hurry. So we tried to use the shadow organization, by inventing a new piece of organizational technology known as the *council system.*

### An innovative approach

The idea was to create a semiformal system of councils which could be laid on top of the informal network. Quality-related information could be transmitted to the councils which would then spread the information through the organization much more quickly than the formal reporting structure could.

The Excellence Council, described earlier, was the heart of this council system. It was designed to pump the quality message throughout the lab, beginning with the major arteries—the functional managers. It also served as a catalyst for all the quality transformation efforts. But not all the key players in the informal network would fit on the Excellence Council, and a single council did not seem the best way to address the diversity of concerns that could arise, so five other councils were formed.

The management vision underlying all of them was that of a cultural transformation that required a shift in the management system. Management had to shift from a bureaucratic and resistant hierarchical structure to a flexible, matrixlike structure. Figure 9.3 graphically illustrates this shift, while Fig. 9.4 identifies the six councils that helped make it happen and their linkages.

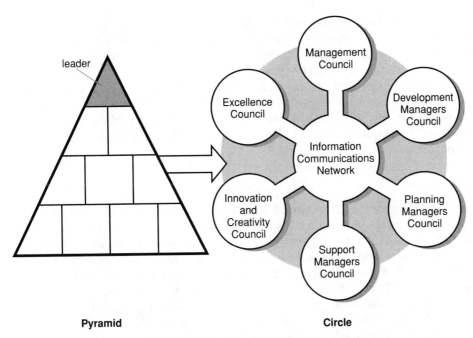

**Figure 9.3**  The organizational shift. (*Adapted from Heartwork, Inc. 1991*)

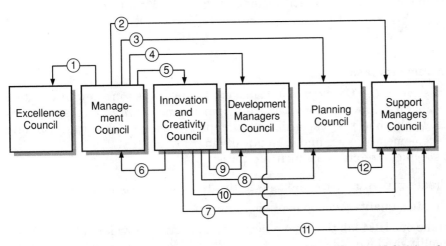

**Figure 9.4**  Council system and linkages. Linkages 1 to 5 provide guidance and decision; 6 to 9, recommendations for innovative projects; 10 to 12, recommendations and requests for support changes. (*Courtesy of IBM*)

These councils were conceived by the GM and implemented from the top down. However, in retrospect, there was no reason why the councils could not be self-organizing, as long as there was a critical mass of leaders who recognized the need for a quality improvement network.

Perhaps the best way to introduce the councils is simply to describe the vision and/or mission and goals of the councils at a moment in time when we were midway on our quality journey in 1991. The Excellence Council is described in detail in Chap. 4. Here is what each of the other councils said about itself:

## The Management Council

The vision of the Management Council was to make our lab a world-class leader in software technology. Its mission was to promote senior management focus and consensus on the overall laboratory mission, goals, and strategy. It was to promote the operation of the lab as an integrated management team and to foster senior management awareness of key business, technical, and people issues. It would recognize leverage points for achieving and maintaining world-class software product development leadership, and it would act as a court of appeals for issues brought forward from the other councils.

Specific "stretch" goals in 1991 included these:

1. The lab achieves 10-fold product quality objectives.

2. Gain recognition for our lab from IBM and the information processing industry as a world-class software lab.

3. The lab achieves gold-level IBM quality award.

The members of the council included the general manager and 14 of the senior and functional managers at the lab. The council met monthly for 2 hours.

## The Development Managers Council

The mission of the Development Managers Council was to review alternative proposals for achieving innovative development and service process improvements. It also had the responsibility to implement approaches to streamline the development process and dramatically improve quality.

Its specific "stretch" goals included these:

1. Create cross-functional linkages in the development community.

2. Create a quality development environment.

3. Make our IBM lab the most efficient and effective provider of the highest-quality products.

4. Reduce cycle time and attain significantly improved levels of customer satisfaction.

5. Focus on morale, empowerment, recognition/incentives, technical vitality, and appropriate use of critical skills.

6. Establish and use in-process metrics for productivity and quality.

7. Improve the tools and processes in use at the lab with an emphasis on CASE tools as a long-term strategy, eliminating rework, and building a management system for reuse.

8. Decide if we want a common process, by first understanding the current lab processes and then determining ownership for the development and service processes.

The members of the Development Managers Council consisted of the 10 senior product managers with development responsibilities. The council met semimonthly for 2 h at a time.

## The Planning Council

The vision of the Planning Council was to be the premier software planning organization with the right product, in the right market, at the right time.

The council's mission was to provide leadership to the planning community in transforming our lab to a market-driven culture.

Specific goals included the following:

1. Reach agreement on success criteria and measurement for planning.

2. Define and document the plan process and the linkages between the processes and the organizations.

3. Improve the planning process efficiency.

4. Create a consistent definition of planner jobs and/or responsibilities.

5. Make education available to the planning community to improve their skills.

6. Provide a set of tools for planners to communicate with each other throughout the lab.

The membership of the Planning Council included key product planners as well as representatives from Finance, Centralized Planning, and Quality. The council met every 2 weeks for 2 h.

## Support Managers Council

The vision of the Support Managers Council was to enable management efficiency.

Its mission was to create a smooth road for an effective management system, focused on resolution of tactical problems in support of the development of the lab's software products.

The goals were

1. To increase the efficiency of management systems, thereby reducing the frequency of the Support Managers Council meetings.

2. To encourage our customers to bring their problems forward.

The council had 12 members comprising various support functions within the lab (e.g., administrative support, legal, human resources). It met every 2 weeks from 7:30 to 9:00 a.m.

### The Innovation and Creativity Council

The vision of the Innovation and Creativity Council was for the lab to produce the highest-quality, innovative products in the industry by leveraging leading-edge technologies.

The mission of the council was to be a catalyst for innovation by nurturing, identifying, sponsoring, and rewarding innovative proposals for products, tools, or process improvements.

Specific goals included these:

1. The lab should be recognized by the marketplace as a creator and implementer of innovation.

2. Innovators should bring their ideas to the council, demonstrating that innovation is alive and well at the lab.

3. Proposals should be acknowledged, decided upon, and recognized in a timely fashion.

4. The existence of the council should be publicized monthly.

There were 15 permanent members of the council including the senior technical staff and members of a department chartered to promote innovation. Meetings were held monthly or as often as needed to accommodate new proposals.

In theory, all the councils were linked together and interacted as depicted in Fig. 9.4. In practice, the amount of interaction depended primarily on the degree to which the various councils actually succeeded in tapping into the informal shadow organization network.

Since our lab took responsibility for service of its own products in 1992, a Service Managers Council has also been added to the council system.

### Costs, benefits, and risks

The costs of the council system were significant when you consider that they required the time of precisely those managers whose time was in most demand. The time spent sitting in the meetings alone totaled well over a person-year. When the time for preparation, data gathering, administration, and everything else is added in, it is not unreasonable to expect the council system to consume 1 percent or more of a large organization's people resources.

However, the benefits are potentially great. Just one outstanding innovation discovered by the Innovation and Creativity Council, or one major process improvement uncovered by one of the other councils, could pay for the cost of the whole system many times over.

There is another type of benefit which is harder to quantify but perhaps more significant. On the surface, there is an exchange of information that leads to more efficient action on the part of the organization. But at the same time, bonding takes place as a result of the council system. For example, any group of presenters who has gone through the process of the Excellence Council comes out with a deeper sense of commitment to quality and to teamwork.

These feelings are simply a by-product of having been actively engaged in quality activities in a way where success depends critically on other people. The contacts and relationships that are nurtured in the course of preparing for an Excellence Council remain long after the last overhead transparency projector has been turned off.

The risk, of course, is that no great discoveries are made and that, instead of bonding, managers grow to resent the council system as yet another series of useless meetings.

### Synergy

The council system is synergistic with the other awareness stage innovations inasmuch as it represents a means of spreading the quality message to every function of the organization. The council system is also synergistic with many of the innovations described later in the book simply because it provides a forum for gaining wide exposure to, and promoting acceptance of, new ideas coming out of various operational units in the lab.

### Prerequisites

In retrospect, a thorough mapping of the informal shadow organization—inasmuch as such a mapping is possible—would be extremely helpful in identifying the right membership for the various councils. Unless the right players can be identified and persuaded to participate, the system has little chance of producing anything worthwhile.

### Implementation advice

Quite frankly, the results of the council system at our lab have been mixed. Here are some of the comments we culled from a survey conducted 3 years after the first council meetings:

"OK, but overdone. Some never had clear objectives."

"I'm not sure that I have seen anything come out of these councils that could not or does not come from good management."

"Make sure that someone 'owns' every action and that there are target dates. There also needs to be understanding that if a representative cannot attend a meeting, they need to send a backup. Management focus on the product of the councils helps greatly."

"These are great at coordinating matrix management and communicating stuff throughout the lab."

Overall, those councils that seemed to do well, and that have persisted without any external driving influence, tended to be those with concrete operational responsibilities and with a no-nonsense results bias.

The Support Managers Council is a case in point. You could almost predict the success of this council by looking at their vision statement back in 1991. It was only three words long: "Enable management efficiency." And if you look at the goals, instead of management rhetoric, you find that the council wants to make itself obsolete. There was probably a final clue in the fact that the council met for only $1\frac{1}{2}$ h—before 9 a.m.—whereas the other councils met for 2 h during the workday. If council members are willing to start their days an hour and a half earlier, you can bet that they aren't going to put up with any nonsense. It probably also means you've got the right set of people on board.

The Support Managers Council did not invent a new relational database technology, but they did knock down all kinds of obstacles that got in the way of the developers who were working on the next generation of products. For example, at one point a lack of speaker phones was causing all sorts of havoc in the lab. Twelve developers would be crowded into a manager's office because, for some bureaucratic and inane reason, managers were the only ones authorized to have speaker phones. This situation kept both managers and software developers busy in an unending game of musical offices. No one could get work done efficiently this way.

The issue was raised at the Support Managers Council. Next thing you knew, anyone who needed a speaker phone had one.

On the other hand, the Innovation and Creativity Council was an example of a group that died and resurrected itself several times with various different organizational structures, but never really seemed to get off the ground. In one incarnation, the mistake seems to have been to invite too many of the wrong people to sit around without a clear idea of what the council's function was. By the time it was finally established that the purpose was to award money to good proposals, the good technical folks had stopped coming to what they perceived as a worthless meeting. This made it hard to get the word out that funding was available, and few new proposals came in.

The council format was changed, and a steering committee was established with operational responsibility. This worked better for a time, and the steering committee actually produced some beneficial results such as a lab-wide Quality Week (see Chap. 14).

Although there has been some debate as to whether a centralized council like the Innovation and Creativity Council could ever be effective, this question was never put to a fair test because of three implementation issues that affect all the councils to varying degrees.

First, the right people have to be identified and persuaded of the value of the particular council's activities. Specifically the council members should be well connected in the informal shadow organization, and they should be temperamentally suited to the council's purpose.

Second, the council must have a concrete and operational focus. Trying to use the council simply as a forum for ideas and concerns without giving it concrete operational responsibilities will result in a series of time-wasting meetings and no action.

Third, the councils should be adapted to the organization's needs—not the other way round. Trying to force-fit teamwork or a matrix organization where there is no true need for such an organization is like trying to push water uphill.

If these three issues are considered carefully when the council system is first implemented, the system can be a very powerful leadership catalyst for cultural transformation. Figure 9.5 summarizes our implementation advice for the council system.

## Overcoming Learned Helplessness: A Case Study

Learned helplessness occurs when people stop trying because they no longer believe their actions will have any positive effect. People who habitually say things like "Nothing will help" or "It won't do any good" have learned to be helpless. Change may become possible, but these people have stopped trying.

We faced this challenge at IBM with one of our major products. Senior management had challenged the product team to improve quality and was willing to back the team with whatever resources were necessary. But the team refused to take ownership. Instead, it continued to look to senior management for solutions.

Over the years, because it had been working on a complicated product that was difficult to change, the product team had become used to letting senior management make all the decisions. They had given up on innovation, and they had accepted the idea of maintaining the product as it existed. They had learned to be helpless in an environment where changes seemed extremely difficult to make and carried high risk with little or no reward.

---

———— Clear vision of organization's quality strategy
———— Commitment of senior leaders to quality strategy secured
———— Appropriate councils formed
———— Key players in organization's informal network identified
———— Participation of key players on councils obtained
———— Action-oriented council chairperson
———— Vision, mission, and goals for each council clear
———— Every council with an operational focus and responsibility
———— Ongoing evaluation of usefulness of each council
———— Elimination or modification of ineffective councils

**Figure 9.5**  Council system implementation checklist.

## Objective

Of course, senior management recognized that quality improvement wasn't a matter of a single technical fix. Dozens of small innovations would be required. More importantly, no technical solution would last for long if the more basic problem of learned helplessness wasn't solved.

The goals were to increase customer satisfaction with the product, improve the quality and vitality of the product, and improve team morale. With the lowest morale in the lab and customers who were beginning to question whether the product was dead, achieving these goals was a matter of survival.

## Innovative approach

The approach was to leverage the latent ability of the product team to innovate and create solutions. Management knew that the team had some of the best programmers around; those programmers needed a clear direction, education, tools, and most importantly a sense that change was both possible and absolutely critical to survival.

The first step was to establish a clear vision. Without a clear set of goals and priorities, it's difficult to get team members moving in the same direction, and coordinated teamwork is essential to large software development efforts. But teamwork doesn't mean that the entire product team develops the vision.

Senior management for the product conducted a series of round-table interviews with the product developers. After listening to the key technical staff, the senior management team sat down and put a vision together. Then, the entire product team was involved in figuring out how to achieve the vision.

The next step was to build the leadership team. In this case, that meant creating a core group of development managers who understood the vision and who were willing to learn about the business and about what customers really wanted from the product.

The third step was to divide and conquer. By focusing on the most important changes first, and worrying about how to integrate everything later, developers were able to make progress without being overwhelmed.

Teams were a key element in the divide and conquer strategy. For each critical objective or product function, a team was formed. But people were not brought onto a team just to perform a specific task. Instead, each team member was selected not only for specific technical skills but also for quality-related "team skills."

For example, one team member might have a very strong business background, another might have a strong technical background, a third might be an expert on workstations, and a fourth might have a good knowledge of the industry and competitive products. Together, the team members would have all the skills not only to do a good technical job but also to address the larger quality issues that involve customer satisfaction, comparison with competitors, and financial results.

In all, there were seven different teams, with two managers sponsoring each team. Within a team, the members decided together how they would improve the quality of a component that the team owned from start to finish.

The fourth step was to provide support for the teams in the form of tools and technology. For example, one problem is that it is very difficult to know how a design is going to work until the code is actually written and tested. But CASE tools allowed some of the teams to simulate the performance of designs beforehand. By using these tools, developers were able to change designs instead of having to patch code. The result was higher quality code in less time.

While tools were very important, success depended upon tapping the creative abilities of the product developers. That meant getting understanding and buy-in to the quality vision. Education in the form of systematic Baldrige training and participation in the Excellence Council (see Chap. 4) was part of the answer. So was customer contact through programs like the Quality Partnership Program (see Chap. 21).

Since Baldrige emphasized customer satisfaction, developers began to talk to customers more frequently. When they did, they saw, often for the first time, the real world environments in which customers used the product. They understood the implication of an outage for customers, and the importance of quality.

In short, developers stopped programming in a black box and began to program with the customer's environment in mind.

Once developers understood the necessity for quality improvement, and began to take hesitant steps in this direction, publicity and the reward system played an essential role.

First, management applauded every step in the right direction, no matter how small, thus sending the message that management supported and encouraged innovation for quality improvement. Management also "put its money where its mouth was" by precommitting to monetary awards for teams who could meet very aggressive quality goals and schedules.

As innovations began to appear, communication vehicles were needed to assure the rapid spread of good ideas. Informal, bimonthly chalk talks on innovations and technical subjects, bulletin boards, newsletters, and frequent round-table discussions all helped to spread new ideas.

Finally, management practiced what it preached. Managers ranked each other in terms of teamwork, cooperation, innovation, and communication twice a year.

To sum up, the strategy for overcoming learned helplessness involved vision, building a leadership team, building development teams to "divide and conquer," tools support, education support, customer contact, publicity, rewards, communication, and integrity.

### Costs, benefits, and risks

The costs for implementing this strategy are difficult to estimate because the approach was not rolled out as one specific technique. It was pervasive, affecting everything the developers did. In that sense, the cost was 100 percent of the development budget because the approach to product development was completely changed. Quality became the job—not something that could be tacked on after the code was developed.

The primary benefits include a rejuvenation of the product development organization, increased customer satisfaction, higher product quality, and improved team morale. A secondary benefit is the development or customization of innovations for quality improvement such as those sketched below and discussed elsewhere.

A secondary benefit is that an organization which overcomes learned helplessness serves as a role model for other "helpless" organizations. Peer achievement is frequently more effective than management exhortation or coercion.

The main risk is that without a clear direction and clear communication of priorities no change will occur. At our lab, many developers experienced a sense of uncertainty as they underwent the transition to a team-based organization focused on quality. People began to question their jobs, and were unsure of what they should do. We discovered that this uncertainty is a natural companion of real change and represents an opportunity to lead the organization out of the cage of learned helplessness.

## Synergy

The particular case discussed above demonstrated how innovations such as the Excellence Council, the Quality Partnership Program, CASE tools, quality publications, and team-based approaches can work synergistically to achieve quality improvement results. A critical success factor is the ability to keep a broad perspective at all times. Success requires focusing on defect reduction, but also on customer satisfaction, teams, and communication. More fundamentally, the leadership activities of management should be synergistic with the process improvement innovations and the technology innovations that the teams develop.

## Implementation

Product developers have always had an insatiable appetite for tools. However focus is often lacking. Once our developers realized that quality improvement and product re-architecture were the technical goals, they began to focus their search on tools to help achieve these ends.

An organization that has learned to be helpless will give up if no existing tool seems to meet the product development needs. This state of affairs had persisted for years, since our product and process were too complicated to be addressed by any single CASE tool. However, once the organization began to overcome its learned helplessness, developers looked for CASE tools that could help with specific parts of the development process.

Similarly, once the members of the organization began to talk to customers and learn about competitive products, they recognized the needs to reduce cycle time, improve performance, move into new markets, and keep customers satisfied. Solutions to these problems took the form of several process innovations that are detailed elsewhere in this book.

For example, years of success in the marketplace had served to distance the developer from the customer. The organization had forgotten how critically dependent customers were on the product. Yet the product's quality objectives emphasized that customers should be the final arbiter of product quality. The solution was a quality partnership program with customers.

Each customer in the program was assigned a customer advocate at our lab, whose principal role was to "worry" about that customer's wants, problems, and difficulties. The program served to rekindle the awareness of what we were in business to do and to highlight many of the common oversights in our internal development cycle. In its partnership efforts with customers, the organization not only learned how to improve its approach to development but also demonstrated its commitment to quality and to its customers.

A second example concerns measurement innovations. Developers recognized that the approach of testing quality into the product was not working well. In fact, fixes injected late in the development cycle tended to destabilize the product.

Think of the code as a small piece of metal. Every time the code is patched, it's like bending the metal. Eventually, the metal fatigues and it breaks. This is just what was happening to modules of code that needed too many fixes late in the development cycle.

The solution was to develop measurements that could indicate problem areas early in development, without having to discover all the problems in test. The Center for Software Excellence developed a "rework index" that measured how many times a piece of code was reworked. This index helped us monitor when too many fixes might cause quality problems. Another measurement innovation, orthogonal defect classification (see Chap. 22), helped identify problems with code early in the development cycle when they were easier to fix.

A final process example that reflected the rejuvenation of the organization was the wholesale adoption of the "train" development process. In the past, product planners would identify functions that should be added to a new release of the product. Inevitably, the entire release would be held up, waiting for the most complicated new piece of function (called a "line item") to be finished. This procedure led to a host of problems.

Many of the smaller line items were completed and shelved for long periods of time—thus subject to technology or staff atrophy. These items would have to be pulled off the shelf and reworked, sometimes multiple times, before they were shipped. Meanwhile, customers often needed the ability to exploit new hardware technology long before its release. This meant we had to ship small programming enhancements in an expedited release to run concurrently with the major release. These expedited releases proved to be error-prone, because they were not put through the rigors of a full development process.

The train concept (see Chap. 11) was a dramatic solution to these problems. Instead of waiting for completion of line items, each release would ship on a predetermined schedule like a train leaving the station. Those line items that were complete would be added to the release like cars on a train. Those that missed the train would have to make the next train.

Although simple in concept, the train process represented a radical re-thinking of our development process. Its adoption signaled that the organization had overcome learned helplessness, and had begun to take a proactive approach to product quality.

Finally, an important part of any quality program is the feedback and tuning process, often referred to as continuous improvement. The members of the product development team realized that constructive self-criticism is a key to improvement. This idea was implemented through frequent informal identification of new process approaches, through monitoring of weekly goals and process control limits, through ongoing meetings between the management and technical leaders of all releases, and through an annual post-mortem analysis of all major activities of the year.

Together, the leadership, technology, and process approaches sketched above encouraged an organization that had learned to be helpless, to seize control of its future and become one of the leading sources of quality innovations at the lab.

## Suggested Readings

Bardwick, J. M. (1991) *Danger in the Comfort Zone.* New York: Amacom. *One of the books we found helpful dealing with the learned helplessness syndrome.*

Basili, V. (1993) Personal communication.

Charan, R. (1991) "How Networks Make Organizations Boundaryless—and Deliver Superior Results." *Harvard Business Review,* September–October.

Cooper, J. D. (1978) "Corporate Level Software Management." *IEEE Transactions Software Engineering,* 4(4): 319. *Raises some of the issues that might be discussed at high-level council meetings.*

Garvin, D. (1988) *Managing Quality.* New York: Free Press. *Interesting outline of the evolution of quality management; some parallels to the evolution of the Center for Software Excellence.*

Guinan, P. (1993) Personal communication at Boston University.

Kotter, J. P., and Heskett, J. L. (1992) *Corporate Culture and Performance.* New York: The Free Press. *Another book that can be helpful in overcoming learned helplessness in an organization.*

Leonard-Barton, D. (1992) "The Factory as a Learning Laboratory." *Sloan Management Review,* 34(1): 23–38. *Although the case study presented concerns a steel mill, the same underlying principles discussed here can be applied to software organizations.*

Levitt, B., and March, J. G. (1988) "Organizational Learning." *Annual Review of Sociology,* 14: 319–340. *Theoretical literature review of the field of organizational learning; many references to key scientific papers.*

March, J. G. (1988) "Variable Risk Preferences and Adaptive Aspirations." *Journal of Economic Behavior and Organization,* 9:5–24. *A theoretical model describes factors that might influence the amount of risk people are willing to take.*

March, J. G. (1991) "Exploration and Exploitation in Organizational Learning." *Organization Science,* 2(1): 71–87. *A theoretical look at the organizational tradeoffs between exploring new possibilities and exploiting old ones.*

Peters, T. (1992) *Liberation Management.* New York: Alfred A. Knopf. *A leading guru looks at how current trends require a new management style.*

# Process Assessment with ISO 9000

The process focus in the control stage is on assessment and on doing the existing steps in the process better. Although Baldrige remained our primary assessment tool, the necessity of ISO 9000 registration caused us to integrate the ISO requirements into our quality assessment activities.

Fortunately our work with Baldrige (Chap. 2), the Excellence Council (Chap. 4), and process documentation (Chaps. 6 and 7) provided much of what we needed for ISO 9000 registration. Our strategy, using prior efforts as much as possible while also using ISO 9000 evaluations to tell us where to focus future improvement activities, ultimately proved successful, resulting in ISO 9000 certification in 1994.

## Innovation 13 (Process): Our Lab's ISO 9000 Strategy

### The objective

The problem, as perceived by many developers in the lab, was that the whole world was rushing to adopt ISO 9000 as a quality standard, and here we were, messing around with Baldrige! What could we do to integrate ISO 9000 with our existing Baldrige efforts, and should we drop Baldrige in favor of ISO?

### An innovative solution

After some heated debate, a number of facts emerged. First, ISO 9000 (short for International Standards Organization 9000 series) addresses only process quality, not the quality of products, or customer satisfaction, or business results, or public responsibility, or benchmarking, or any of a number of areas covered by the Baldrige template. Moreover, if you are doing Baldrige, you are already doing a lot of the things you will need to do for ISO 9000; but the reverse is not true.

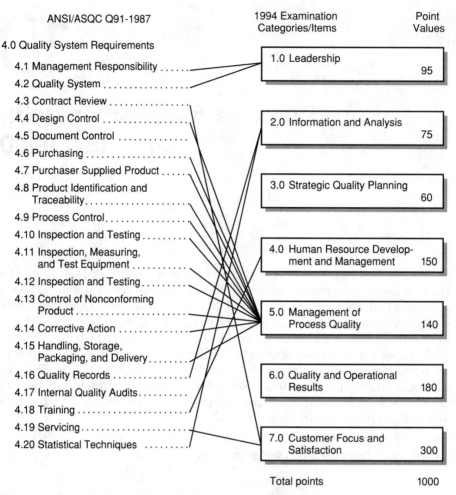

**Figure 10.1** Comparison of ISO 9000 and Baldrige. (*Courtesy of IBM*)

Figure 10.1 expresses how we see Baldrige and ISO 9000 fitting together. Note that ISO 9000 is largely contained in Baldrige. Specifically, it is heavily process-oriented, with more than 50 percent of its content mapping to category 5 of Baldrige. However, other areas of Baldrige (e.g., category 6) are completely ignored by ISO 9000.

An important difference is that ISO 9000 has a "show me" focus since registration depends upon showing external auditors evidence of conformance. While Baldrige examiners visit the top sites applying for the national award, most Baldrige assessments are evaluations done on paper or in a presentation. As a result, Baldrige tends to have more of a "tell me" focus. Once we understood these differences, we began to look for ways in which ISO 9000 and Baldrige could complement each other. Each has strengths and weaknesses, so an organization is better off understanding both.

## An ISO 9000 Overview

ISO 9000 is a series of quality standards that were published in 1987 by the International Standards Organization (ISO), based in Geneva, Switzerland. Since more than 90 countries are members of the ISO, the standards carry some weight, especially in Europe where ISO 9000 certification is fast becoming a requirement for doing business.

Despite the recent fuss about ISO 9000, the standards actually date from U.S. military standards during World War II. The British changed these around a bit and produced something called British Standards 5750 in 1979. Then, in 1987, when the ISO formed a task force to look for an international standard of quality, the task force took BS5750 and turned it into ISO 9000.

The ISO 9000 series includes 9001, 9002, 9003, and 9004. The first three standards are meant to support contractual agreements between companies, whereas 9004 is only for self-assessment purposes. Since 9001 is the most stringent and covers development life-cycle types of operations (e.g., software development), it is the standard that our lab has been primarily concerned with. There is also a document ISO 9000-3 (not to be confused with 9003) which provides guidelines for the application of ISO 9001 to the development, supply, and maintenance of software. (This document would be of interest to software companies and is referenced at the end of this section.)

### Costs, benefits, and risks

The costs of initial ISO registration at the lab were estimated to be $45,000 to $50,000, and about 50 person-years (45 nonmanagement, 5 management). Since ISO requires ongoing internal audits, these figures would decrease to about 15 person-years when the lab goes into maintenance mode. These numbers translate to about 3 percent of the lab's people resources to get certification and 1 percent to maintain it.

Despite the fact that these costs represent a significant chunk of resources, we have encountered nowhere near the resistance to ISO 9000 that we encountered with Baldrige. For example, here were some sample comments from a random survey:

"I believe ISO 9000 will provide a view that has been missing with our other quality assessment methodologies—it asks for 'proof' that you are doing what you say you are doing. It uses objective auditors, who come back to ensure that you are still doing it 6 months or a year after the first time, and most important it provides a *basic* quality management system that will yield improved results if followed."

"We are still building our process information, but as we go, we find useful information on what needs improvement in our department and over our location."

"Just beginning to apply this. It is going to be a great value in getting the department organized and unified for documentation. Much more buy-in from the masses than market-driven quality."

We think there are three critical factors in the relatively warm reception developers gave to ISO 9000. First, the benefits of ISO are clear and immediate. British Telecom requires ISO registration *now,* so we need it if we want to do business with them or with most of the European Community. NATO and the U.S. Department of Defense will require ISO 9000, as will Britain's Department of Trade and (probably) the governments of Australia, Canada, Japan, and others.

It is true that, so far, ISO requirements have applied mainly to hardware. But it's clear that the requirements on software will not be long in coming.

Second, ISO 9000 is simpler and requires less effort than Baldrige. Given that anything detracting from actual code production tends to be viewed by programmers as "evil," ISO 9000 is perceived as the lesser of two evils when compared with Baldrige.

Third, the survey revealed some excitement about ISO 9000's function as a useful quality management system. Of course, one could speculate as to how much of this feeling ought to be attributed to ISO itself and how much to 3 years of Baldrige indoctrination.

Despite these arguments, it is clear that ISO 9000 offers some real benefits and that it is likely to become a necessity for conducting business in any case.

### Synergy

ISO 9000 is synergistic with the Malcolm Baldrige template as well as with other process assessment activities.

### Prerequisites

The prerequisites are management commitment and buy-in.

### Implementation advice

The strategy for implementing ISO 9000 at our lab, from the ISO coordinator's view, looks something like what is shown in Fig. 10.2. The strategy starts by leveraging our existing quality system—the Baldrige—and by making use of the data we have gathered for our Excellence Councils (Chap. 4). The ISO 9000 requirements for quality policy, management review, quality plans, data collection and record keeping, continuous monitoring, quality records, and training were all part of our existing quality system.

Many of the other requirements including process documentation and record keeping, design control, document control, inspection and testing, etc. were documented in our programming development handbooks (Chap. 6). As a result, we focused our efforts on tailoring existing information to the ISO 9000 format and on setting up an internal ISO 9000 auditing program.

The auditability box in Fig. 10.2 shows that we concentrated on documentation, internal audits, and preparation for external audits. Our document control system consisted of a quality manual, a set of procedures, and work instructions—all of which were based to some degree on the information in our programming development handbooks.

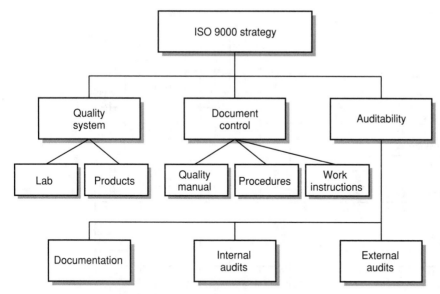

**Figure 10.2**   Our ISO 9000 strategy. (*Courtesy of IBM*)

In short, we discovered that ISO 9000 could be viewed as another way to package the processes that we were already using (and improving) to achieve our quality objectives. Figure 10.3 shows a matrix we used to map our lab's existing development process to the major ISO 9000 elements. Such a mapping can be done by any organization and is an essential step in preparing for an ISO 9000 audit. Simply list all your existing process documentation, quality plans, standards, etc., along one dimension and the criteria of ISO 9000 along the other dimension. Put an X in the cells where the two converge. A completed matrix allows you to see at a glance where your ISO 9000 exposures are.

One of the key features of ISO 9000 is the requirement of auditing by external, objective auditors, who have the power both to grant and to revoke ISO 9000 certification. This is different from Baldrige, where there is a team of national examiners who can perform a site visit, but who do not revisit the site and revoke the award after you've won.

With regard to internal audits, the ISO criteria insist that the internal auditor not be a part of the department or organization being audited. There should also be a management representative on the internal audit team.

We had about 9 lead auditors and 20 internal auditors to handle a lab of 1700. But scaling the number of auditors up or down should not be a problem. IBM's Mid-Hudson Valley facility did ISO with a site of 1000 people while IBM Rochester did it with a site of 8000.

The critical success factors for ISO 9000 include having a rollout strategy, ISO 9000 education, and training; interfacing ISO 9000 with Baldrige; and obtaining management and employee buy-in. Table 10.1 shows the ISO 9000 areas that IBM has identified as the most common source of audit failures.

| ISO elements | Chapter 4 Quality System: Framework | 4.1.1.2.1 Responsibility and authority | 4.1.1.2.2 Verification | 4.1.1.2.3 Management responsibility | 4.1.1.2 Management review | 4.1.2 Purchaser's responsibility | 4.1.3 Joint reviews | 4.2.1 Quality systems, general | 4.2.2 Quality system documentation | 4.2.3 Quality plan | 4.3 Internal audits | 4.4 Corrective action | Chapter 5 Quality System: Life Cycle Activities | 5.1 General | 5.2.1 Contract—general | 5.2.2 Contract items |
|---|---|---|---|---|---|---|---|---|---|---|---|---|---|---|---|---|
| 2 Exposed | | | | | | | | | | | | | | | | |
| 3 Does Not Apply | | | | | | | | | | | | | | | | |
| 4 Quality Manual | | | | | | | | | | | | | | | | |
| 5 Program development handbook | | | | | | | | | | | | | | | | |
| 6 Redbook guidelines | | | | | | | | | | | | | | | | |
| 7 System plan/project management | | | | | | | | | | | | | | | | |
| 8 Quality/production plan | | | | | | | | | | | | | | | | |
| 9 Build plan | | | | | | | | | | | | | | | | |
| 10 IBP/FPS/design workbook | | | | | | | | | | | | | | | | |
| 11 Product publications | | | | | | | | | | | | | | | | |
| 12 Contract DOU | | | | | | | | | | | | | | | | |
| 13 Phase/checkpoint reviews | | | | | | | | | | | | | | | | |
| 14 Reviews and inspections | | | | | | | | | | | | | | | | |
| 15 4* module analysis | | | | | | | | | | | | | | | | |
| 16 FVT/PVT/SVT/IVT | | | | | | | | | | | | | | | | |
| 17 QPP/ESP/CACs | | | | | | | | | | | | | | | | |
| 18 DPP/Postmortems | | | | | | | | | | | | | | | | |
| 19 Self-assurance procedure | | | | | | | | | | | | | | | | |
| 20 Program director review | | | | | | | | | | | | | | | | |
| 21 Quality certification | | | | | | | | | | | | | | | | |
| 22 RFA/Ts&Cs | | | | | | | | | | | | | | | | |
| 23 Service supplementary plan | | | | | | | | | | | | | | | | |
| 24 Ser/L1/L2/L3 | | | | | | | | | | | | | | | | |
| 25 RETAIN/SPA | | | | | | | | | | | | | | | | |
| 26 APARs/PMRs/PTFs/Process | | | | | | | | | | | | | | | | |
| 27 MDQ/5-ups/10X Plan | | | | | | | | | | | | | | | | |
| 28 LCS/CLEAR | | | | | | | | | | | | | | | | |
| 29 Program objectives | | | | | | | | | | | | | | | | |
| 30 Requirements/quality function deployment | | | | | | | | | | | | | | | | |
| 31 Program standards | | | | | | | | | | | | | | | | |
| 32 Design change request | | | | | | | | | | | | | | | | |
| 33 Quality management systems | | | | | | | | | | | | | | | | |

**Figure 10.3**  Mapping ISO 9000 to an existing development process. (*Courtesy of IBM*)

**TABLE 10.1  Most Common Series
of ISO 9000 Audit Failures**

| Item | Percent failures |
|---|---|
| Document control | 20 |
| Process control | 18 |
| Quality records | 15 |
| Corrective action | 12 |
| Internal assessment | 10 |

---

——— Clear on purpose and goals of ISO registration

——— Management buy-in and commitment

——— ISO registration coordinator identified

——— Training/infrastructure for internal ISO auditors in place

——— Copies of ISO 9000 and 9000-3 obtained

——— Research on others' ISO experiences (e.g., books and/or seminars)

——— Need and value of ISO registration communicated widely

——— Overall ISO registration strategy and timetable developed

——— Funding and resources obtained

——— ISO 9000 education organization-wide

——— Leverage information gathered for Baldrige

——— Execute rollout strategy

——— Feedback and continuous improvement process in place

**Figure 10.4**  ISO 9000 implementation checklist.

When you are preparing for ISO 9000 registration, we recommend paying particular attention to these areas.

Finally, Fig. 10.4 shows some of the steps we went through during our ISO 9000 implementation.

## Suggested Readings

ANSI/ASQC Standard Q91-1987, *Quality Systems—Model for Quality Assurance in Design/Development, Production, Installation, and Servicing.* Available from the American Society for Quality Control. *This is our primary ISO 9000 training document.*

Burrows, P. (1992) "Behind the Facade of ISO 9000." *Electronic Business,* pp. 40–44, January 27. *An interesting look at what ISO 9000 is all about.*

Durand, I. G., Marquardt, D. W., Peach, R. W., and Pyle, J. C. (1993) "Updating the ISO 9000 Quality Standards: Responding to Marketplace Needs." *Quality Progress,* 26(7): 23–28. *Of interest to practitioners trying to anticipate the latest changes to ISO 9000.*

Dzus, G. (1991) "Planning a Successful ISO 9000 Assessment." *Quality Progress,* pp. 43–45, November. *Advice for those interested in ISO 9000 registration.*

Lamprecht, J. L. (1991) "ISO 9000 Implementation Strategies," *Quality,* pp. 14–17, November. *Overview of some ISO 9000 implementation issues.*

Lamprecht, J. L. (1992) *ISO 9000: Preparing for Registration.* Milwaukee, WI: ASQC Quality Press; New York: Marcel Dekker. *More detailed advice for those preparing for ISO 9000 registration.*

Lofgren, G. Q. (1991) "Quality System Registration." *Quality Progress,* pp. 35–37, May. *Discusses issues relevant to ISO 9000.*

*Quality Management and Quality Assurance Standards—Part 3: Guidelines for the Application of ISO 9001 to the Development, Supply, and Maintenance of Software.* Available from the American National Standards Institute (ANSI). Order ISO 9000-3:1991(E) or latest revision.

Rabbitt, J. T., and Berg, P. A. (1993) *The ISO 9000 Book: A Global Competitor's Guide to Compliance and Certification.* White Plains, NY: Quality Resources; New York: AMACOM. *A recent and fairly popular book on ISO 9000.*

# 11

# Improving the Software Development Process

Rigorous code inspections and design reviews are an example of doing the steps in our existing process steps better. Combined line-item and function test (CLIFT) and early test involvement represent attempts to modify and improve the development process itself. Although the focus of these process innovations is still on defect detection, they represent a drive to detect bugs earlier and earlier in the development process.

Table 11.1 summarizes each of these innovations, the objectives they helped achieve, and implementation pitfalls.

**TABLE 11.1   Stage: Control / Food Group: Process / Themes: Modify and Improve Existing Processes; Introduce New Processes**

| Objective | Innovative approach | Implementation pitfalls |
|---|---|---|
| Revamp code/design inspections<br>Reduce error rate | Rigorous reviews and inspections<br>Reinstate: more rigorous and disciplined<br>  Code inspections<br>  Design reviews | Wavering on resistance and push-back.<br>Inspections as job performance input<br>Sloppy preparation and process<br>No follow-up or communications |
| Reduce cycle times for waterfall<br>  process<br>Improve quality | *Early test involvement:*<br>Implement train/locomotive<br>  methodology<br>Introduce:<br>  Parallelism<br>  Early engagement of test and<br>    documentation teams<br>  Cross functional teams | Easily discouraged<br>Focus on what didn't work, *not* on<br>  learning |
| Improve testing effectiveness<br>Shorten test cycle | *CLIFT:*<br>Combined line-item and functional<br>  test (CLIFT)<br>Integrate development and test | Failure to address cross-functional<br>  education and tool development<br>Failure to learn from mistakes,<br>  e.g., not having postmortems |

## Innovation 14 (Process): Rigorous Code Inspections and Design Reviews

### The objective

Code inspections are probably one of the earliest process steps known to humans—computer scientists anyway. In cave-dwelling days, you had to submit programs as batch jobs at night because that was when the computer rates were at their lowest. The next morning you'd get a printout, and all day you'd code-inspect, code-inspect, code-inspect until midnight, when the rates dropped again. Machine time was so expensive, and people time was so cheap, that rigorous code inspections were a matter of simple economics.

Then came interactive computing, good compilers with fancy editors and debuggers, and cheap computing time. And out went the idea of code inspections. After all, why should you sweat the bugs out when a high-powered edit/compile/debug tool can find them for you?

You shouldn't. As long as there is a cheap automated way of catching bugs, that's certainly preferable to slogging through the code, line by line. The problem is that there are still some situations in which code inspections make good economic sense. Unfortunately, many developers have gotten out of the code inspection habit, and they don't understand why rigorous inspections are really necessary.

This was the case with the developers of our database product, IMS, back in 1983. The IMS developers had decided to discontinue code inspections because an executive decision had just dumped an incredible workload on the Development group. The management and technical people thought they could not afford to go through formal code reviews on all the code and still meet the deadlines. So they skipped some of the code inspections.

By 1985, they were paying the price. New development was at a standstill because the release with the skipped inspections was running into all kinds of problems during system test in Poughkeepsie, New York. Key developers in San Jose, California, were jetting back and forth to Poughkeepsie, trying to work out all the problems. Meanwhile new work ceased.

Getting the release through test successfully became everyone's number 1 priority, but a side effect was that quality suddenly was on everyone's mind. A number 2 priority became to investigate whether code inspections really could solve some of the IMS quality problems.

### An innovative approach

The first step was to perform a causal analysis to see why previous code inspections had failed. The analysis revealed that the right people didn't show up, the people who did show up used the sessions to learn about the code instead of to inspect it, and there was no follow-up on the recommendations of the code inspectors. So we created a new code inspection process that fixed those things.

Next, because code inspections had been around (and ignored) for years, we needed a new name so that people would know this was not business as usual. We called the new process *rigorous code inspections* to give it a different ring. Finally, we had to conduct a study to determine whether the new process was actually of any benefit.

We began with the simple graph shown in Fig. 11.1*a,* a defect depletion curve. The graph shows defects removed per 1000 lines of code (KLOC) on the $y$ axis and our development process stages on the $x$ axis. The curve portrays how many defects are removed at each stage of the process. The area under the curve represents the total defects found in a given release.

Notice that roughly 60 percent of the total defects in the product are discovered and corrected before the formal test stage. The remaining 40 percent are found during testing and in the field (by service). Thus the product in Fig. 11.1*a* relies heavily on formal testing to ensure quality.

We had two goals:

1.  Over the long term, we wanted to reduce the area under the curve by injecting fewer defects. This reduction would depend upon process changes and innovations described later in this book.

2.  We wanted to shift the shape of the curve to show that we were detecting and correcting the defects as close to the point of injection as possible.

This second goal was what we hoped to accomplish with rigorous code inspections and design reviews. Figure 11.1*b* illustrates this shift. Note that it shows a situation where 90 percent of the defects are removed prior to formal testing by more rigorous design reviews and code inspections. Because most of the defects are found earlier in the development process, they are easier and cheaper to fix, as we discussed in Chap. 1. At least this was the theory. But would it work in a busy development lab with schedule pressures and all the day-to-day obstacles that software developers face?

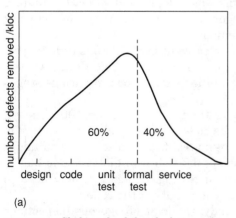

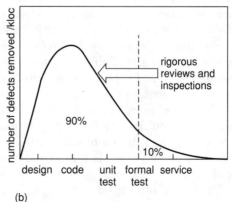

(a)                                             (b)

**Figure 11.1**  Shifting the defect depletion curve.

TABLE 11.2    Results from Rigorous Inspection Study*

|  | Functions | Tested | New or changed code | Total |
|---|---|---|---|---|
| Inspection sessions | 11 | 10 | 40 | 61 |
| Major errors | 22 | 59 | 376 | 457 |
| Minor errors | 51 | 123 | 1267 | 1441 |
| Total KLOC | 4 | 7 | 36 | 47 |
| Total hours | 197 | 386 | 1017 | 1600 |
| Major errors per KLOC | 5.5 | 8.4 | 10.4 | 9.7 |
| Hours per major defect | 9.0 | 6.5 | 2.7 | 3.5 |

*60 inspectors, 14 teams; inspection results by code type.

To find out, we ran a study. Sixty programmers on 14 teams conducted 61 rigorous inspections on a release of code. The time spent in the inspections and the number of major and minor errors detected were recorded. Table 11.2 shows the results.

The "functions" column in Table 11.2 shows the results of inspecting code that had already gone through the entire development and test process. The "tested" column shows the results for code that was currently in testing and the "new or changed code" column shows the results for new code that had not yet reached the test phase of the development process.

The first finding, apparent if you read across the hours per major defect row, was that it took longer to find major defects in tested code than in newly developed code. That was what we expected, since testing should remove most of the more obvious defects and inspectors must look harder to find the remaining defects.

More important, on average, it required only 3.5 h to find each major defect in the code by using the rigorous inspection methodology. Since we already knew we were spending between 15 and 25 h to find a major defect in the Test department, that meant rigorous inspections could boost the efficiency of defect detection by over 400 percent. This was a big enough effect to convince management that we ought to adopt rigorous inspections as one of the ways to help meet our 10-fold quality improvement goals.

For those who already believed in the effectiveness of rigorous code inspections, the data in Table 11.2 answer another question. The data give you some baselines for how much time to spend inspecting code in various stages of development.

For example, if you are spending more than 3 h inspecting 1000 lines of new code and haven't found any bugs, the code may be ready for testing. On the other hand, if you haven't found a bug in *tested* code after 3 h, you might want to persist since it takes an average of 6.5 to 9 h to discover one bug in code that has already gone through formal testing. (*Note:* You may need to adjust these findings depending upon the complexity of the code.)

Although we have not run a formal study, the logic of rigorous inspections applies also to conducting more rigorous design reviews. If we put more effort into conducting rigorous design reviews, we should catch more defects in design, rather than waiting for them to show up in the coding or test stages.

Similarly, the idea of early rigorous inspections can apply to other areas such as planning, test case development, and information development (publications). While we do not have concrete results from these efforts yet, logic dictates that rigorous early inspections will improve the efficiency and quality of processes and products.

## Costs, benefits, and risks

Rigorous code inspections require about $\frac{1}{2}$ day of process training for everyone involved, plus moderator training. Ideally, moderators and reviewers should go to the same class, so that everyone knows what everyone else's role is. There is some cost involved with this initial training, and you also need a continuous training program to keep everyone up to date on the process.

There is little dollar cost to conducting the rigorous code inspections themselves. The cost is almost solely the time of the developers who participate in the meetings. But as our data show, you can invest a little extra time early in rigorous reviews and inspections, or you can invest a lot of extra time later in the test stage.

The potential benefits of rigorous inspections as compared with those of test range from a conservative 1.5-fold efficiency improvement estimate (assuming code that is already in the field and a super-efficient test group) to a 10-fold efficiency improvement (assuming brand new code and a not-so-efficient test group). In either case, rigorous inspections seem a better approach than trying to test quality in to the product.

Here are what some the participants in the rigorous inspection study had to say in 1985:

> "This type of program should be continued. Management must allow ample time to do this in the future for new code."

> "More emphasis on module/function education is needed in the areas to be inspected."

> "Need similar rigor at the design level."

> "Definitely a beneficial exercise, found a lot of defects."

Eight years later, in 1993, we did a random survey of the lab and got these comments:

> "Commitment and prep time are critical to this being successful. There also needs to be a process in place to make sure that appropriate follow-up is done."

> "For code quality all code must be inspected. New modules should have formal review with a few people getting together after each has reviewed the module at their desks. Modules which have minor changes can just be

given a desk check. Time has shown that the line items with the best quality have made sure all the code was inspected either formally or informally."

"Reviewers must be knowledgeable in the area, or the review won't be effective."

"[Design reviews] are where the time and money spent pay off."

The risks of the program have mainly to do with presenting the program in the right way, keeping people enthusiastic, and making sure that the right people are in the meeting. (We discuss some approaches to these problems below.)

Another risk is that detecting a lot of defects in inspection does not guarantee fewer errors in the test stage or in the field. Other factors, such as requirements changes during the test phase, can inject new defects into the product, after it has left the development phase. If you do a great job of inspecting a release only to have the requirements for the release changed all around at the eleventh hour, you can pretty much count on new defects appearing. So rigorous inspections need to be used in conjunction with other quality management techniques.

It's a classic case that argues for a comprehensive quality management system. You may have a high-quality development process, but unless you have a high-quality customer requirements process, and high-quality planning, and high-quality communication between the organization's functions, one of the inputs to the development process can screw up the quality that you worked so hard to achieve during development. Minimizing this risk is one of the reasons the lab chose Baldrige. No group can think of itself as an island if the organization expects to achieve world-class quality levels.

## Synergy

Rigorous reviews and inspections are synergistic with computer-supported team work spaces, on-line document reviews, error-prone module analysis, and statistical process control (SPC) techniques.

## Prerequisites

Before you can conduct rigorous inspections and reviews, you must have a clear understanding of your development process so that you can know when these reviews and inspections would be most appropriate. Ideally the process should be documented in something like the programming development handbooks (see Chap. 6).

## Implementation advice

Figure 11.2 lists the 11 steps in the rigorous review process we implemented for our IMS product starting in 1985.

- *Training:*  How to inspect, Insp/Mod
- *Document:*  How module works, interfaces, and purpose
- *Educate:*  Module education—prepare inspectors
- *Analyze:*  APAR/PTM errors—create error-type checklists
- *Overview:*  Inspection purpose for each session
- *Preparation:*  For each inspection session
- *Inspect:*  Inspection session
- *Rework:*  Defects found, duration will depend on number of defects
- *Closure:*  Review resolutions, major defects, unresolved assignments
- *Integrate:*  Rework fixes, minimum number of integrations
- *Test:*  Rework fixes, after integration

**Figure 11.2**  Steps in our rigorous reviews and inspections.

A successful inspection or review begins by having the right people in the meeting. They must be knowledgeable both about how to conduct an inspection and about the code being inspected.

Next comes preparation for the inspection. The inspection is not a training session. Unless people prepare, it becomes an exercise of opening up the code and reading through it line by line. This is a waste of people's time. But if everyone has prepared by reviewing the code a couple of days before the inspection and by making notes, the inspection is spent talking about the problem areas everyone has uncovered.

We use on-line reviewing tools (see Chap. 17) to help with the preparation. People can review the code on-line, make comments, and read other people's comments. Everybody knows who is saying what. This is where a lot of experience sharing and education take place.

Because on-line review comments are out there for everyone to see, the procedure causes people to think more deeply to avoid looking foolish on the system. The result is that a lot of education takes place before the actual inspection, not when everyone's time is involved.

Ideally the review itself should last no longer than about 3 h. Data from our studies show that the effectiveness tends to decrease with longer reviews. But this doesn't mean you should rush through the code. In the IMS study, we also found that the number of defects found is roughly proportional to the time spent inspecting. That is, those groups who inspected code at the (optimum) rate of 300 lines of code per hour found more defects than those who inspected at a rate of 600 lines of code per hour. Take the time needed to do a thorough job of inspection.

A trained moderator should keep the inspection on track. She or he makes sure that the appropriate areas are covered in the review, records the defects and concerns uncovered in the meeting, and ensures that there is follow-up.

Follow-up includes getting the inspection team together after the fixes have been put in place and reviewing the fixes with the team. This serves as a final check, but more importantly it reinforces that the inspection accomplished something. It sends the message: "Hey, we achieved something! Here are the defects we found, and here's what became of them."

There are several pitfalls that we can warn you about. First, you may encounter some resistance in trying to get the program off the ground. At our lab, many experienced developers had seen code inspections fall by the wayside and believed management would not support them. Ironically, management was more ready to support them than the "old guard" believed. (Having the cost-per-defect numbers from the IMS study above—which included preparation time—helped convince management.)

The problem is that if time is not allowed to prepare for an inspection during normal work hours, people will not come to the inspection prepared. The result is an unproductive inspection. The complaint we heard over and over in 1985 was: "Yeah, that's an effective way to get defects out, but management will never give us the time to do it!" So you have to sell management, and you have to tell the programmers that you've sold management.

Assuming you've got the rigorous inspections and reviews program launched, a key to success is maintaining a positive attitude on the part of the participants. If they feel as if they've been herded into a room just to check off some step in someone's process, then they really won't want to participate. You may get their bodies, but not their hearts and minds. It is a communication challenge to express why the inspection is important and to explain that it is not about counting beans.

On the other hand, you must collect data. So the challenge is to explain why *we* are collecting the data. *We* are collecting the data to help *us* determine when *we* are doing a good job—not *they* are collecting the data to *evaluate* us or to put up on a chart.

After all, if the data show that we are getting a defect out only with 20 h of people effort, there is no reason for doing this work. Code inspections are boring, boring, boring. But if we are getting defects out with only 3 to 4 h of effort, it's worth doing this work, because it's saving us time and effort in the long run.

Finally, one of the nice things about rigorous reviews and inspections is that the procedures can be implemented pretty much independent of the size of the organization. Unlike some of the other innovations, small is actually easier in this case, since it is easier to get all the right players in a meeting. With large development organizations spread out in two or more physical locations, teleconferencing and/or video conferencing can help make sure that all the right players are involved. Although it can seem like a lot of effort to set up a video conference and to coordinate schedules, our experience has been that you save time in the long run because those same experts will just have to be tracked down later when bugs are found in the test phase. It is better to catch them early.

Figure 11.3 presents an implementation checklist for rigorous reviews and inspections.

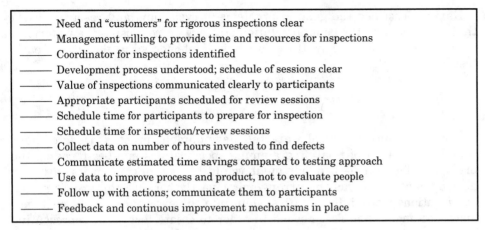

———— Need and "customers" for rigorous inspections clear
———— Management willing to provide time and resources for inspections
———— Coordinator for inspections identified
———— Development process understood; schedule of sessions clear
———— Value of inspections communicated clearly to participants
———— Appropriate participants scheduled for review sessions
———— Schedule time for participants to prepare for inspection
———— Schedule time for inspection/review sessions
———— Collect data on number of hours invested to find defects
———— Communicate estimated time savings compared to testing approach
———— Use data to improve process and product, not to evaluate people
———— Follow up with actions; communicate them to participants
———— Feedback and continuous improvement mechanisms in place

**Figure 11.3** Rigorous reviews and inspections implementation checklist.

## Innovation 15 (Process): Early Test Involvement

The advantage of a strictly serial development process is that it is very modular. The interfaces between development stages are clear and well defined. Everyone knows exactly what his or her job is. But two disadvantages became increasingly problematic as we pushed to improve quality.

First, in a serial process, lengthening any of the stages lengthens the total development cycle. That meant that quality improvement activities that added a step (e.g., extended unit test) or lengthened a step (e.g., rigorous inspections) could be done only by increasing the length of the development cycle. We were caught in a classic tradeoff that all software developers are familiar with: We can ship now and have poor quality; or we can wait for good quality, but our schedule may have to slip.

Initially, our GM took a firm stand on the side of quality, but no organization can continually let schedules slip and get away with it. We had to find a way to achieve higher levels of quality *and* shorter development cycles.

And we did it by collapsing our highly serial waterfall process into a more parallel process.

Reduced cycle time is one advantage of introducing parallelism, but we soon discovered another advantage as well. Parallel development could actually be more efficient because sources of error could be caught sooner in the development process and fixed when they were cheaper to fix. In addition, some of the same steps were repeated at each stage of the development process by different professionals. For example, designers, coders, and testers each had to have meetings to understand what the code was supposed to do. But if designers, testers, and coders could discuss it in one meeting instead of in three separate meetings, then redundant effort and potential sources of miscommunication could be eliminated.

Having described the general problems of cycle time and resource waste that we faced, and the general solution strategy of "collapsing the waterfall," we now take a look at how the strategy is implemented in the case of early test involvement.

## The objective

According to our standard waterfall development process, Development would create a set of final programming specifications and begin coding the product before the Test department would begin working on its test case development. This was the arrangement partly because the programming specifications were difficult to translate into the external view, or customer view, document that Test needed in order to create test cases representing how the customer would use the product. Also, if Development made changes to the product that weren't in the final programming specifications, Test would not always be aware of the changes, so it was safer to wait until Development had nearly finished with coding before starting work on the test case development. Figure 11.4a represents this standard, highly serial, waterfall process approach.

However, there was a problem. With increased pressure to get the product out more quickly, Test was beginning to feel rushed. And the rush corresponded with a demand for increased quality, which put even more pressure on Test. Together these pressures simply could not be handled by our existing process. So Test "collapsed the waterfall," as shown in Fig. 11.4b.

The result was reduced cycle time to develop the product and better communication between Test, Development, and Information Development.

## An innovative approach

Test couldn't collapse the waterfall by itself, because the Test department was dependent on the technical writers in the Information Development department for the external view document that served as the basis for creating test cases. Test also needed the cooperation of Development, because Development would have to work more closely with both Test and Information Development right from the very early stages of product development.

Fortunately, the Leadership Institute focus on cross-functional teamwork and on quality and innovation had laid the cultural groundwork for this kind of cooperation. The technical writers can produce better documentation because they are involved with the product earlier and have more time to understand the product. The testers get an external view document that they can work with earlier and so can develop better test cases. And the developers are forced to learn how the users are going to apply the function, which often results in better coding decisions. The result is that each group does a better job, the product is of higher quality, and the cycle time is shorter.

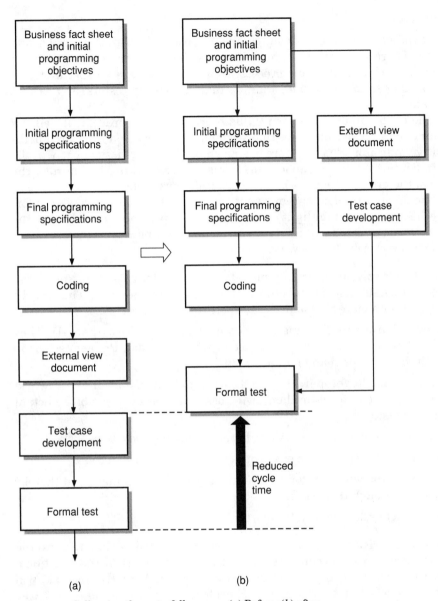

**Figure 11.4**   Collapsing the waterfall process. (*a*) Before; (*b*) after.

## Costs, benefits, and risks

The costs of making a process change like collapsing the waterfall are hard to estimate. There is certainly some initial cost in trying to start up and get everyone to understand a new process. However, there are no specific training costs other than the product training that developers, testers, and writers might take anyway.

For one of the products following this process, reports are that it delivers more function in a shorter time. Improvements in regression tests are another positive indicator. Finally, more design change requests issued early in the cycle indicate that the feedback mechanisms are working to improve the quality of the product before it is made generally available to customers.

Comments on a random survey about the value of early testing were informative because they highlight both a generally positive attitude and the problems that accompany any change where groups have to work more together more closely. Here's what people said:

"Early test involvement usually means that the tester gets more knowledge of the internals, and potentially of weak spots in the code. This can be translated into more thorough, less superficial test cases."

"It's even harder to get time and commitment from Test than ID. They hardly showed up at all, but were useful when they did. Problem seems to be both test personnel and management."

"Tough to get developers to see Test as an extension of their work. Developers tend to focus on their own work, and workers are a bit reluctant to involve testers."

"This is very important if you want to reduce testing cycle time."

"The earlier the testing, the easier it is to change the design/code."

"The earlier the exposure for testers, the better they can plan, and thereby the more thorough their testing."

"The product cycle time will be shorter."

The primary risk in the early test approach, assuming that testers and developers can learn to cooperate, is that drastic changes in the functional specifications can lead to a lot more rework because both ID and Test will have to change what they've done. Therefore, it is critical that all three groups work closely together and, with planning, keep on top of changing requirements.

## Synergy

Early testing is synergistic with the cross-functional teamwork leadership innovations. It is clear that as you move to a more parallel development process, teamwork stops being just a buzzword and starts becoming a necessity. As long as departments treated each other as black boxes, there could still exist lip service to cross-functional teamwork and isolationist departments. But the shift in process requires a shift in culture as well. That's why this book emphasizes the interrelatedness of leadership, process, and technology.

## Prerequisites

The main prerequisite is a change in management style. Managers must be willing to go with a cross-functional team approach and must be willing to trust their cross-functional teams.

## Implementation advice

We found the most efficient way to implement the early test involvement concept was to create mini cross-functional teams, each consisting of developers, testers, and technical writers. Each team is responsible for a line item in a release, and team members must work together to get the line item ready in a timely manner.

One way to view this process change is to think of the product release as a train. The train is going to pull away from the station at a certain time (ship date), and it's going to take as many cars as are attached. Figure 11.5 illustrates this idea.

Each line item is a car, and the mini cross-functional teams are each responsible for getting their cars on the train before it pulls out of the station. One of the advantages of this iterative development concept is that it is possible for shorter trains to leave the station, before the final departure for testing efforts, in the middle of the development cycle.

In order for the train concept to work smoothly, there must be a set of operating procedures that specify who is responsible for getting cars on the train

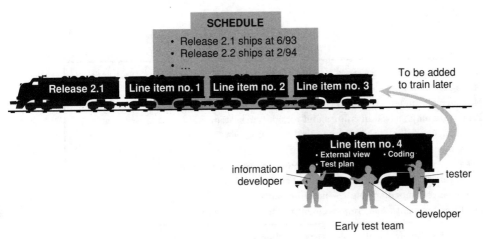

**Figure 11.5**   The train concept for early test involvement.

- Everything in build plan currently on train.
- Confirm dates in build plan for Development, ID, and Test.
- If any checkpoint date is missed, the line item is "off the train."
- These items go into one of two buckets.
- One bucket is for mandatory items; the other is for "should have" items.
- Person who missed checkpoint date is responsible for creating, driving, and getting agreement on a recovery plan.
- All other team members must agree to recovery plan and it must be approved by first-line management and team leads.
- For all items that fall into the mandatory bucket, it is the responsibility of the first-line manager to ensure that the recovery plan is created and agreed to within 1 week.
- Recovery plans will probably require those who missed commitments to help the other line-item team members to contain dates or help other line items teams to free up other personnel.
- Train procedures administered by product manager.

**Figure 11.6**   Train procedures for early test involvement.

and what to do if a deadline is missed. Figure 11.6 lists some sample process requirements for running an effective train.

As a parting word of advice, be prepared for some resistance if you try to implement these concepts. In our experience, every time something goes wrong, a certain subset of people will want to return to the old way of doing things, and it can be frustrating to have to justify the new changes—especially when they aren't perfect. The key is to get people to focus not on the problems with the new approach, but on the overall picture. If you are serious about decreasing cycle time and improving quality, the old serial process just isn't an option. Early testing isn't perfect either, but it has the potential to move you forward on your quality journey.

Figure 11.7 presents our implementation checklist for early test involvement.

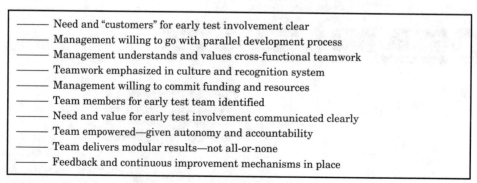

——— Need and "customers" for early test involvement clear
——— Management willing to go with parallel development process
——— Management understands and values cross-functional teamwork
——— Teamwork emphasized in culture and recognition system
——— Management willing to commit funding and resources
——— Team members for early test team identified
——— Need and value for early test involvement communicated clearly
——— Team empowered—given autonomy and accountability
——— Team delivers modular results—not all-or-none
——— Feedback and continuous improvement mechanisms in place

**Figure 11.7**   Early test involvement implementation checklist.

## Innovation 16 (Process): Combined Line Item and Function Test

### The objective

Ironically, one reason for increased cycle time and poorer quality may be a technique which was originally conceived as a way to improve quality. For years, various parts of IBM have employed an adversarial approach to testing. The Test group and Development group were separate with very different missions. Tom DeMarco (1982) described the situation vividly in his book *Controlling Software Projects:*

> The now-legendary "Black Team" was a separate test group that worked in a particularly quality-conscious environment at IBM. The team was unique at the time in that it made active use of its adversary position. According to the (possibly apocryphal) stories, team members took positive delight in destroying code that had been written by perfectly nice people. They were fiendish. They stressed the code in ways that would never occur to anyone whose mind wasn't horribly devious and more than a little bit nasty. They reduced poor programmers to tears. They prided themselves on being able to make almost any program crash a few dozen different ways before breakfast.

The theory went that with groups like the Black Team testing the code, developers would pay extra attention to quality so as not to give the testers the satisfaction of finding any defects. Like most theories, it had some merit and some problems. On the positive side, there is clearly an advantage to having someone other than the developers test the code so as to get an external perspective. The testers are to the developers what reviewers and a good editor are to an author—external sanity checks and sources of advice.

One problem is that *adversarial* testing can lead to adversarial relations as easily as it can lead to increased motivation. The "throw the code over the wall and let Test worry about the bugs" approach of some development groups at our lab illustrates how easily relations can degenerate—especially in an environment where everyone is rushing to meet schedules. Moreover, contrary to the elite status of the Black Team, the reality at our lab was that many testers were perceived as second-class citizens.

A second problem is that to use adversarial testing is to assume that quality can be improved by motivating developers to pay more attention to their work. This assumption is not always true. Often the developers are missing critical information about the way customers will use the product. Ironically, the testers are usually better informed in this area and could share that information if there was a cooperative relationship between Test and Development.

But the biggest problem with adversarial testing was that it proved to be just plain inefficient. Every error found by Test was written up formally as a program trouble memorandum (PTM) and was sent back to Development with a detailed description of just how the error occurred. The turnaround time for PTMs could be considerable, especially if Test and Development were on adversarial terms.

Test would want to make sure that it produced ironclad PTMs that Development could not argue with. By the time the PTMs arrived, developers were already on to something else and would have to backtrack to try to recreate the context of the error and then fix it. But when the developers sat down to fix the error, many of the complex interactions between modules would have become a bit hazy, since the developers were now working on other parts of the code. As a result, new errors were often introduced in the process of fixing the original error. Test would eventually find (some of) these new errors, write them up, and send them back. Code might bounce back and forth between Development and Test seven or eight times in this manner before the code was approved.

The net result was increased development cycle time and bad feelings between the Test and Development departments. Despite the legends about the Black Team, adversarial testing just wasn't working at our lab. Specifically, for certain releases of major products at the lab, every time new code (line items) was added to the base of already developed code, the entire product would crash. Clearly something was wrong with the way that the code was being tested in Development.

## An innovative approach

At our lab, the major testing phases for many products included the line-item test (conducted by developers) and function verification test, product verification test, system verification test, and installation verification test—all conducted by testers.

In Chap. 6, we described the extended unit test (EUT) which was a formal method that ensured that Development conducted more rigorous testing on its code before passing that code on to Test. EUT was anchored in the principle that the earlier you can catch a problem, the less expensive it will be to fix. And it seemed to be working.

Our description of early test involvement (above) offered an entirely new paradigm for Test, where test work done in small teams is iteratively added to a release. Combined line-item and function test (CLIFT) is somewhere in between these other two innovations.

CLIFT emphasizes teamwork between developers and testers, but it does not require an iterative development model. As the name suggests, CLIFT made testing a team effort between testers and developers by combining two previously separate steps in the development process—the line-item test and the function test. It, too, collapses the waterfall.

Since both developers and testers had previously been conducting many of the same tests, the team approach reduced duplication of effort. But more importantly it increased sharing of tools and knowledge between testers and developers.

For example, the testers had tools, automation, and standards that were completely alien to Development. Prior to CLIFT, each development department would test in its idiosyncratic way, typically throwing away test cases after they had been used.

The testers, who had rigorous standards for the development of test cases and who saved most test cases in an automated "test bucket," were shocked by this behavior. They helped the developers understand the importance of following test case standards and of test case reuse.

For their part, the developers educated the testers about the function of the code. They were equally surprised to learn that the testers would test code without having a clear idea of what it was doing or why. Once testers began to have a better idea of certain code internals, the testers were able to design much more relevant test cases and find more errors.

A CLIFT team not only tested the code more thoroughly, but also ended up with a "bucket" of test cases that could be used to test any future changes to the code automatically.

Although the CLIFT concept sounds ridiculously simple, it is important to remember that it represents something of a heresy. Traditional wisdom states that there are developers—who understand the workings of the code—and black box testers—testers who don't need to understand anything about how the code works, but who are good at breaking things. Testers on the CLIFT teams are quick to point out that they don't want to become just like developers in terms of their knowledge of the internal workings of the code, but they also recognize the tremendous advantage of knowing a little more about the internal workings.

For example, in one product, a new keyword shared a byte with an existing keyword. The developers on the CLIFT team told the testers that this was a tricky situation that was easy to screw up. As a result, the testers knew to pull extra test cases that used the existing keyword. Without the CLIFT team and the resulting close communication between developers and testers, there is a good chance that several errors would have slipped past the line-item and function test stages.

Similarly, the testers bring an awareness to developers of how the customers are likely to use the code. This awareness sometimes changes how developers choose to implement certain functions, and it influences how Development designs its own test cases. What would have been considered heresy 10 years ago is proving to be a more effective way of developing higher-quality code in less time.

## Costs, benefits, and risks

CLIFT can be a frustrating process. At our lab, developers had to learn a whole new set of tools, and they were forced to write the test cases in an automated way. From Test's perspective, the coordination of a CLIFT team (10 or 15 people) is a much bigger headache than simply working with one or two developers as in the past.

Education can be a significant cost. It takes about 2 days to introduce developers to the automated testing tools and to the basics of constructing reusable test cases. But this is just the beginning. There is a 2-week learning curve on most of the test tools, and testers have to be available to coach developers who get stuck.

On the other hand, the benefits seem to far outweigh the costs. On one product, one CLIFT team produced 173 test cases for a function of which 98 percent were automated and running in the overnight regression test bucket. Not only does that save developers a lot of time, but also developers can pull these test cases whenever they change something in the code. Because these test cases run continually, as soon as a new error is introduced accidentally into the code, developers know it.

The CLIFT concept can also provide added motivation for Test to accelerate its automation efforts. At our lab, what used to take Test 2 weeks—writing and debugging a test case—now takes 2 days because of automated tools.

Even more important, although more difficult to quantify, are the improved communication and sense of teamwork that CLIFT has fostered. Instead of shooting program trouble memorandums (PTMs) at one another, the members of a CLIFT team get together and talk it out. Developers and testers understand and respect each other more.

In the two postmortems that have been done on pilot CLIFT groups, 18 of the 20 CLIFT participants said they would do it again. Two abstained. In a lab-wide survey, here are some of the comments about CLIFT:

"Speeds up the development/test cycle but needs test resources."

"CLIFT has to be very well defined up front. Define up front who is responsible for writing how many test cases. CLIFT is one of the single biggest factors in the escalation of tensions between developers and testers....There was a *lot* of resentment, developers felt that by going with CLIFT the test workload shifted from Test to Development, and no one had included the extra time in their schedules."

"I think the key is close teamwork between your developers and testers to maximize test coverage with a given resource."

"There is some overhead in trying to coordinate the effort, but I think it pays off in the long run by reducing redundancy in test effort, creating automated test cases, and getting good test case coverage."

"CLIFT provides better information, earlier, about upcoming design changes. That saves Test time."

Despite the general positive comments about CLIFT, there are a few risks which can be minimized by recognizing them at the outset. First, the tools for producing automated test cases can be slow and complicated. Acknowledging this problem and allocating time to deal with it are important. One of the pitfalls we fell into was suddenly asking developers to add more testing to their immediate workload without letting schedules slip. Understandably, this caused some resentment.

Second, the primary mission of most developers is code development. Testing tends to be viewed as a low priority. Even if developers learn about test tools, unless they apply what they've learned right away, they come back at the eleventh hour having forgotten how to use the tools. So the testers on the CLIFT team need to be prepared to reeducate and hold hands.

Third, there needs to be flexibility. In general, testers seem more receptive to the CLIFT idea than developers—perhaps because they recognize the value of testing more easily. If you try to force developers to be part of a CLIFT team, inevitably you will run up against developers who feel that they can't participate for one reason or another. Perhaps the developer owns a piece of code that is always getting hit with errors and is fighting just to keep his or her head above water. Or there may be timing considerations, where developers become more or less available to participate on CLIFT teams depending upon what else is happening with their release of code.

In an ideal world, developers and testers would make CLIFT their highest priority. In reality, the teams that worked best were those that had some flexibility—those that allowed, e.g., for developers to cover for each other. The willingness of testers to cover for developers when things get hectic has also been a critical success factor in CLIFT teams. In short, CLIFT really requires a team effort.

## Synergy

CLIFT is synergistic with extended unit test, automated testing, and early test involvement.

## Prerequisites

The team has to understand the goals of CLIFT:

1.  Increase the quality of the test plan.

2.  Reduce duplication of effort.

3.  Work more closely as a team.

4.  Automate test cases.

Development and Test must each understand what is expected and the time commitment involved.

## Implementation advice

A critical step in implementing CLIFT is the establishment of its value. CLIFT can eliminate redundant testing effort, increase teamwork between developers and testers, leverage the synergistic expertise of developers and testers working together, and result in better-quality automated test plans. Paradoxically, CLIFT will also probably lengthen the development cycle the first time it is implemented because of the learning curve involved in mastering the test tools, learning about test case standards, and understanding the philosophy of the function test (e.g., emphasis on externals and more of a customer's perspective).

Once you have established value, you might follow a process like the one we used:

1. Identify who is going to be on the CLIFT team from Development and Test. Traditionally only one or two developers were the "Test type of people"

in Development who would do most of the testing. One approach is to pick these same two or three people in Development and have them be in the CLIFT. Another approach is to use the developers who have already learned to use the automated test tools. A third approach is to spread the test cases among the entire development team, but this will increase the coordination and education needed from the testers.

2. Identify a tester to be team coordinator. The Test owner and the Development owner (of the line item) must work very closely together. Some testers don't want the overhead of the administrative work just as some developers don't want the overhead of learning new tools. A key is picking people who see the value: a higher-quality test plan, an increase in productivity once you learn the tools, a reduction in duplication of effort, automated test cases, and a closer working relationship between Test and Development.

3. Assign who works on what. Since development crises often disrupt the initial assignments, it is important to document CLIFT work so that new developers or testers can pick up where their predecessors left off. In our first efforts, we tried to not switch ownership at all, but this was completely unrealistic. In practice, we had one CLIFT where Development did most of the work because all Test's resources were tied up. At other times, Development lost resources so Test covered.

4. The Test owner should coordinate development of test scenarios. He or she requests scenarios, ideas, thoughts, etc., from the CLIFT team. Here is where testers can learn a lot from the developers by asking questions about how the product works and where the weak spots of the code are.

5. The Test owner comes up with a strategy that includes schedules, scope, objectives, regression areas that need to be tested, error projections, and the algorithms used for coming up with error projections. The test cases are also described at a high level.

6. The CLIFT team documents test cases.

7. The CLIFT team writes the code for the test cases.

8. The CLIFT team runs the test cases.

9. Conduct postmortem activities with the CLIFT team after all test cases have been run.

One device that has been helpful to our CLIFT teams has been the construction of a matrix that maps internals (e.g., module names, key words—nitty-gritty aspects of the code itself) to externals (the functions and commands that users see). Such a mapping allows developers and testers to see at a glance which internal components of the code would be affected by executing any external component. While such a matrix makes perfect logical sense, it was not created until the testers (who were steeped in an external or customer's view of the product) teamed up with developers (who typically thought of the product in terms of its internal components).

Another useful technique has been to incorporate the test cases into a "test bucket" that runs automatically—even before the code goes into the base code libraries. This allows the team to find problems early, rather than waiting until code is integrated into the overall base code. Then, once the code is integrated into the base libraries, the test bucket is executed until the code achieves a preset level of stability. Finally the test cases are moved into the overall test bucket for release.

A final note concerns the size of the software development organization. In large organizations, a pilot program might be worth considering. Also expect more resistance to and misunderstanding of CLIFT procedures in large organizations than in small organizations. Incorporation of CLIFT procedures into documentation of the development processes (e.g., see programming development handbooks in Chap. 6) is one way to minimize some of the communication problems.

In small organizations, the idea of CLIFT can be implemented quite easily, simply by encouraging the individuals responsible for function and line-item tests (or their equivalents in your organization) to work jointly on their test plans. The advantage of formalizing the process instead of just "leaving it to teamwork" is that you end up with a process that has institutionalized cooperation. When personnel changes occur, you have engineered a development environment that will naturally foster teamwork and cooperation. This is a more stable situation than depending on the characteristics of the individual programmers alone.

Of course, ultimately success depends on the individuals involved. Our point is simply that the process ought to encourage the right behaviors and help set the right tone.

Figure 11.8 shows our implementation checklist for CLIFT.

———— Clear need for CLIFT
———— Purpose and goals of CLIFT clear
———— Test and Development "owners" identified
———— Management commitment obtained
———— Funding and resources (time) obtained
———— Trust exists between Test and Development groups
———— Need for and value of CLIFT understood by both departments
———— Agreement on overall CLIFT plan with entrance and exit criteria
———— Participants in CLIFT identified
———— Roles and responsibilities assigned
———— Education on test tools for developers
———— Education on development issues for testers
———— Test owner develops overall test strategy
———— Test owner coordinates test scenario development
———— Matrix maps code internals to Test externals
———— Test cases documented
———— Test cases written
———— Test cases run
———— Postmortem on CLIFT. Continuous improvement process in place

**Figure 11.8**   CLIFT implementation checklist.

## Suggested Readings

Ackerman, A. F., Buchwald, L. S., and Lewski, F. H. (1989) "Software Inspections: An Effective Verification Process." *IEEE Software,* 6(3): 31–36. *An excellent brief introduction to inspections and how to perform them.*

ANSI/IEEE Standard 829-1983, *IEEE Standard for Software Test Documentation,* August 19, 1983.

ANSI/IEEE Standard 1012-1986, *IEEE Standard for Software Verification and Validation Plans,* February 10, 1987.

Christel, M. G., and Stevens, S. M. (1992) "Rule Base and Digital Video Technologies Applied to Training Simulations," *SEI Technical Review,* available from the Software Engineering Institute, Pittsburgh, PA. *Description of an interactive video course for conducting code inspections that uses artificial intelligence and multimedia—very impressive.*

DeMarco, T. (1982) *Controlling Software Projects.* Englewood Cliffs, NJ: Yourdon Press/Prentice-Hall.

Fagan, M. E. (1976) "Design and Code Inspections to Reduce Errors in Program Development." *IBM Systems Journal,* 15(3): 182–211. *One of the original papers on software code inspections; useful for historical context.*

Fagan, M. E. (1986) "Advances in Software Inspections." *IEEE Transactions on Software Engineering,* 12(7): 744–751. *More useful information related to code inspections.*

IEEE Standard 1028-1988, *IEEE Standard for Software Reviews and Audits,* March 10, 1988.

Jones, C. (1986) *Programming Productivity.* New York: McGraw-Hill. *A shorter book than Jones'* Applied Software Measurement *which has some thought-provoking things to say about how defects should be counted and measured.*

Musa, J. D., and Ackerman, A. F. (1989) "Quantifying Software Validation: When to Stop Testing?" *IEEE Software,* 6(3): 19–27. *Relevant for anyone involved in testing.*

Russell, G. (1991) "Inspection in Ultralarge-Scale Development," *IEEE Software,* 8(1): 25–31. *Practical introduction to code inspections from an author with lots of hands-on experience at Bell-Northern research.*

Smith, P. G., and Reinertsen, D. G. (1991) *Developing Products in Half the Time.* New York: Van Nostrand Reinhold. *Chapter 9 describes techniques to create highly parallel development processes; many other good ideas as well.*

Weinberg, G. M., and Freedman, D. P. (1984) "Reviews, Walkthroughs, and Inspections." *IEEE Transactions on Software Engineering,* 10(1). *A description of several formal technical review procedures.*

# Statistical Approaches to Software Quality Improvement

The technological theme in the coping stage is analysis. In the previous chapter we showed how doing the same steps in a process more rigorously or collapsing the waterfall process could lead to higher quality. In this chapter, we show how inexpensive analyses can help identify and correct soft spots both in processes and in code.

Error-prone module analysis is a highly successful technique for identifying trouble spots in code. When it is used in conjunction with the defect prevention process (see Chap. 15), it has great potential for improving the quality of products and processes. It also serves as the basis for the more advanced high-risk module analysis, described in this chapter. Finally, data linkage analysis provides a rigorous approach to link customer feedback data to investment and design decisions. We show that the simplistic approach of improving what customers report being most dissatisfied with is sometimes not the best way to increase customer satisfaction.

Table 12.1 summarizes each of these innovations, the objectives they helped achieve, and implementation pitfalls.

## Innovation 17 (Tools): Error-Prone Module Analysis

### The objective

The primary challenge that any development laboratory faces lies in trying to attack quality on many potential fronts with only limited resources. Statistical techniques can be a cheap way to gain leverage by telling you where these limited resources should be invested for maximum effect.

Since the later they are detected the more errors cost to fix, it is particularly important to identify potential sources of error as early as possible.

Intuitively, product developers know that some code modules give you more trouble than others. Often, error reports from the field are traced over and over to the same module. We call such error-prone modules *four-star modules* because to qualify as error-prone at least four problems or errors from the

**TABLE 12.1    Stage: Coping / Food Group: Technology / Themes: Low-Cost, High-Yield Statistical Analyses for Quality Improvement of Products and Processes**

| Objective | Innovative approach | Implementation pitfalls |
|---|---|---|
| Reduce field discovery of errors | *Error-prone module analysis:* Four-star methodology Early, a priori, identification of error-prone software | Failure to act Belief this is more bureaucracy |
| Predict error-prone code "Blue print" good code Allocate effort to high leverage points in development process | *High-risk module analysis:* Categorize high- and low-risk module Determine characteristics of error-prone and error-free code Target early stages of development process | Failure to act Belief this is more bureaucracy |
| "Will our efforts improve customer satisfaction?" | *Data linkage analysis:* statistical regression Linkage to customer satisfaction | Using statistical analysis naively Failure to invest in areas with maximum leverage on customer satisfaction |

field have to be traced back to the module. An efficient quality strategy involves identifying four-star modules early—even before they have four problems, if possible—and spending extra resources to make the modules as error-free as possible.

Four-star module analysis began with the assumption that errors in the field are predicted by errors found at the lab. There are many theories in the literature that say this should be so, but we wanted empirical confirmation with our own products. More importantly, we wanted to develop a statistical methodology that we could use for any product to help us identify potentially troublesome modules *before* they became really troublesome.

We suspected that defective modules remain defective from one release to the next, from one test phase to another test phase, and from the lab to the customer's shop. If so, this meant that we were wasting development time and money—not to mention increasing customer and developer frustration—by not focusing on troublesome modules early in the development cycle.

The challenge was to develop a method that would confirm or disconfirm our suspicions and that could provide useful input to other innovations to correct these quality problems.

## An innovative approach

Our efforts to identify and "fingerprint" troublesome modules of code evolved in three stages. The initial four-star analysis approach was reactive. We would wait and see which modules got the most errors in the field, and these would be classified as troublesome. Then we would try to take corrective action for the next release. The approach was far better than accepted practice at the time (which essentially relied on a programmer's intuition), but it was far from being proactive enough.

Just as the key to proactive process improvement lies in developing in-process measurements instead of waiting for error reports from the field, so, too, early identification of error-prone modules meant finding other factors that correlated with errors from the field. These factors needed to be recognizable early in the development process and had to be good predictors of how many errors the module would ultimately have in the field.

The second stage of refinement was to add program complexity metrics (e.g., Halstead metrics). In our version of complexity metrics, the total number of *unique* operators and/or operands and total number of operators and/or operands in the module determined the level of complexity. Modules with higher complexity tended to be more difficult to program, change, understand, and service. Such modules also proved to be statistically more error-prone. This approach helped, but still wasn't quite what we were looking for.

Then a bright young programmer said, "Hey, why don't we see if the number of problems reported in line-item test, function test, and system test are correlated, and whether they predict errors in the field?" If this proved to be true, it would mean that we could look at modules still under development and have a pretty good idea of which were most likely to give us trouble both in Test and subsequently in the field. Then we could reallocate resources appropriately.

This hypothesis led to the third stage of four-star module analysis—our current procedure. (The complexity approach evolved into a separate innovation, HARM analysis, which we describe below.)

A recent use of our improved four-star procedure was to evaluate our popular relational database product DB2. The analysis revealed that common defect modules were found from one test phase to the next and from release to release. Moreover, errors in the field were positively correlated with the error-prone modules. Specifically, modules with three problem reports in Test (three-star modules) averaged one error apiece in the field. Modules with four problem reports in Test (four-star modules) averaged 1.5 field errors apiece. And five-star modules averaged 2.29 field errors apiece.

Even more significant were the following results:

1. Of a release's four-star modules, 82 percent had already received two problem reports when they were still in development and before formal testing began.

2. Overall, 55 percent of the modules that were found defective during testing later had errors in the field.

Our four-star analysis showed how to generate a list of error-prone modules and demonstrated that the more problem reports a module had, the more likely the module was to have an error in the field. More important, the analysis suggested that by looking at the problem reports while the module is still in development, we can predict, and therefore compensate for, errors that are likely to show up later in testing or in the field.

### Costs, benefits, and risks

The primary cost for each of these stages of error-prone module identification comes down to the resource of having a person with very basic statistical skills spend time performing the analyses. (A statistical tool such as SAS, VM/AS, or Personal/AS is helpful.) Provided you already have the data for analysis, the cost can be as little as 1 or 2 person-weeks per product release. If you don't have these data, the analysis will require more effort—but you should be tracking these data anyway.

Theoretically the benefits of the methodologies include the following:

1. They predict errors in the field which allows intelligent planning of service resource allocation.

2. They predict errors in testing which allows more efficient allocation of test resources.

3. They predict errors in Development which allows more efficient allocation of development resources.

4. Improvements can be quantified by measuring the number of four-star modules with reduced and/or improved product quality.

However, mixed comments from a lab-wide survey indicated that these benefits should be tempered by real-world considerations. Here are what some developers had to say:

"Helps prioritize effort."

"Error analysis concentrates on where the fixes went, not necessarily where they originated. Quite often fixes are not put where the error is created but where it is easiest to correct the symptoms of the error. [Thus,] the error is not really corrected."

"Marking modules as four-star helped in that we were more careful when doing work on that module. But it was not enough to ever get that module to the point where it was considered for redesign and recoding."

"The results of four-star analysis for components that I owned yielded no breakthrough discoveries. Since I had spent the past few years fixing errors in the same set of modules, I didn't need statistical analysis to tell me which modules were error-prone."

There is little risk involved in this technique since the cost is so low. However, the pitfalls mentioned in the survey comments should be avoided. Moreover, the product developers should be aware that the information being analyzed is going to be used to help improve the product, not to beat up module owners. This is one of the reasons for having a member of the development team conduct the analysis, rather than an outside group such as the Quality Assurance department.

## Synergy

These methodologies are synergistic with multiple regression analysis, customer satisfaction data linkage analysis, and other statistical techniques. The same statistical knowledge can be leveraged multiple times by using each of these methodologies.

It is important to remember that a defect analysis by itself cannot improve the quality. To benefit from the results of the analysis, the results must be used to improve the process. Therefore, the innovation would work very well with the defect prevention process (DPP). DPP is a method for performing causal analysis which can lead to preventive measures against four-star modules.

## Prerequisites

The main prerequisite is the possession of the defect data which are input to the analyses. There must be a defect tracking mechanism which tracks defective modules consistently through the product life cycle.

## Implementation

Any group thinking of implementing this innovation should decide what it is going to do with the results of the analysis. If group members just want to understand their status, then something like the following process should be sufficient. If they want to improve the development process by using the result of the four-star module analysis, then they should educate themselves in the defect prevention process (see Chap. 15) and form causal analysis and action teams. Management must also give employees the time needed to implement the corrective actions.

The four-star module analysis process begins with data collection. For each release of the product which we want to study, we collect the number of times each executable module has a problem report during Development and Test. We put everything in tabular form and do the following:

1. Identify the four-star modules for each test phase, and identify those modules that are hit by four or more problem reports in multiple test phases.

2. Identify the common defective modules between releases.

3. Identify the modules that are hit by a total of four or more problem reports, and compare these modules with the modules that are found defective in the field.

4. Group the defective modules by components to understand the distribution of the defective modules.

5. Identify how many four-star modules were actually hit by two or more problem reports during extended unit test (see Chap. 6). This allows us to ider.tify the potential four-star modules before formal testing starts.

For example, Table 12.2 shows the results of performing steps 1 through 4 for two releases of one of our products. Note that, with a few exceptions, the

**TABLE 12.2    Results of an Error-Prone Module Analysis**

| Component | Release 1 | | Release 2 | |
|---|---|---|---|---|
| | In-process problems | Field errors | In-process problems | Field errors |
| 1 | 299 | 118 | 51 | 5 |
| 2 | 267 | 81 | 224 | 36 |
| 3 | 128 | 47 | 88 | 11 |
| 4 | 73 | 24 | 28 | 8 |
| 5 | 51 | 19 | 42 | 7 |
| 6 | 29 | 19 | 5 | 2 |
| 7 | 19 | 14 | 6 | 2 |
| 8 | 17 | 2 | 11 | 0 |
| 9 | 7 | 3 | 17 | 1 |
| 10 | 3 | 24 | 0 | 1 |
| 11 | — | — | 466 | 32 |
| Other | 46 | — | 53 | — |
| Total | 939 | — | 1043 | — |

pattern of field errors mirrors the pattern of in-process problems. That is, if a module has a lot of in-process problems, it also tends to have a lot of field errors.

We are working toward automating these steps which would substantially reduce the time needed to perform the four-star module analysis.

There is not much training needed for implementing the four-star module analysis. The person responsible for the implementation needs access to a defect database with the necessary data. If you don't have that, now is the time to start collecting those data. (It'll improve your Baldrige score as well.)

The four-star module analysis is best implemented at the release level. A separate four-star module analysis should be conducted for each release of the product.

One potential pitfall lies in trying to gather new data when you already have some data that you can use. Once you embark on a data-gathering program, you have just taken on a job that is 10 to 100 times as large as analyzing existing data. Of course, if you have no data on your errors and problems, then you're stuck. But if possible, squeeze as much action as you can out of analysis of whatever data exist before you begin to collect new data.

A second caveat is that the person performing the analysis should be part of the development team or should work very closely with them. Our experience is that the recommendations of "outsiders" are not easily accepted by developers working under tight deadlines. Besides, "outsiders" are less likely to have all the relevant data for their analysis.

The implementation can easily be scaled up or down. However, the implementation should be at least at the product release level; otherwise there might not be enough defect data to perform a meaningful analysis and to draw firm conclusions.

Centralization has both advantages and disadvantages. The main advantage is that analyses resulting from different products can easily be shared.

The disadvantage is that centralization often means setting up a separate organization which is removed from the immediate concerns and expertise of the developers.

One of the great features of four-star module analysis, if it is implemented at the product release level, is that it takes very little resources. In roughly 2 person-weeks, you can have a useful analysis, provided you start with the data.

Figure 12.1 portrays our process graphically, while Fig. 12.2 presents our implementation checklist for error-prone module analysis.

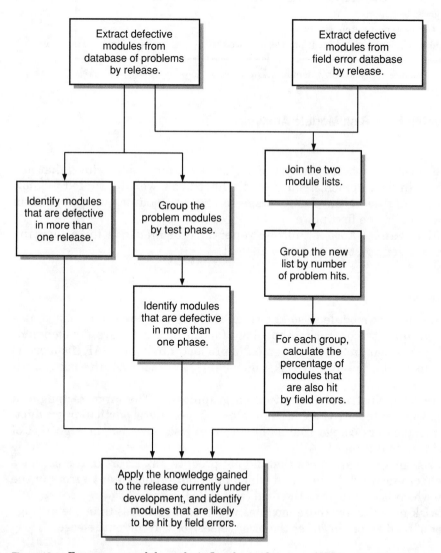

**Figure 12.1** Error-prone module analysis flowchart. (*Courtesy of IBM*)

—— Clear need for four-star analysis established
—— Defect data collection system exists
—— Management support and funding for analysis obtained
—— Coordinator with statistical skills identified/trained
—— Value and benefits of analysis communicated to development team
—— "Catcher" in development identified for analysis results
—— Analysis adapted to maximize use of existing data
—— Four-star code (code with more than four defects in a development stage) identified
—— Four-star code linked statistically with defects found in field
—— Extra design/coding/test effort recommended for certain modules
—— Analysis followed by action
—— Results of actions communicated widely
—— Feedback and continuous improvement process in place

**Figure 12.2**   Error-prone module analysis implementation checklist.

## Innovation 18 (Tools): High-Risk Module Analysis

### The objective

While error-prone module analysis demonstrated that code modules that had bugs early in development tended to still have bugs, we still wanted to know what we could do at the design stage to prevent modules with bugs from being written in the first place.

We also wanted to expand our repertoire of methods for allocating resources to service, test, and development.

### An innovative approach

High APAR* risk module (also known as HARM) analysis is envisioned as a statistical quality control methodology for the full software development cycle. The basic approach is to segment a product into high APAR (field error) risk components, low APAR risk components, and zero APAR risk components.

Figure 12.3 illustrates this situation graphically. The large rectangle in Fig. 12.3 indicates all the code modules comprising a particular product. These modules are categorized as having zero risk, low risk, or high risk of producing a field error (APAR).

Zero-risk modules are those that did not produce any errors in the previous release (zero forward fit hits) and which have not produced any errors in the release which is currently in the field (zero APAR hits).

Low-risk modules are those modules which produced less than the average number of field errors in *either* the prior release *or* the current release.

---

*Authorized programming alteration request—IBM's terminology for field errors.

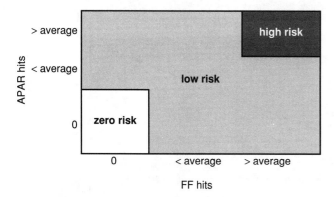

**Figure 12.3** Assigning modules to risk categories. Zero risk: modules with no APAR (authorized programming alteration request—a defect found in the field) and forward fit (FF) hits. Low risk: modules with below average APAR or FF hits. High risk: modules with above average APAR and FF hits. (*Courtesy of IBM.*)

High APAR risk modules—HARMs—are those which produced more than the average number of field errors in *both* the prior release and the current release.

Next the HARM analysis categorization scheme is applied to the new release under development. At each phase of development for this new release, the different types of modules are treated differently in order to ensure the highest levels of quality.

For example, in Test, high APAR risk modules (HARM) receive more testing than zero APAR risk modules. In addition, the HARMs are broken into smaller submodules whenever possible since research indicates that oversized modules are correlated with high field error (APAR) risk.

In coding, HARMs may be analyzed by using syntactic complexity measurements. For example, data such as those in Fig. 12.4 show a correlation between complexity (using Halstead's difficulty metric—see Suggested Readings) and the number of in-process problems. Despite the variation in the data, the correlation coefficient for this set of data is 0.53 and is statistically significant.

Based on analyses such as these, those modules which seem overly complex are coded with extra care or are redesigned to reduce the complexity.

Finally, every effort is made to determine the design characteristics of HARMs, as compared with zero-defect modules, so that designers can avoid creating future HARMs in the design stage.

Ultimately we hope to develop new design rules which lead to easy-to-code designs and which result in higher-quality code. We are still experimenting in this area.

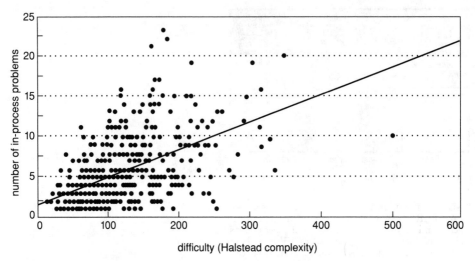

**Figure 12.4** Code difficulty/complexity versus in-process problems. (*Courtesy of IBM*)

## Costs, benefits, and risks

The cost of implementing HARM analysis is relatively low. It requires one person, with some statistical training, to work for perhaps a month—assuming that the defect data have already been collected.

The potential benefits are great. They fall into three areas. First, testing can be tailored based on HARM analysis so that modules with a high risk of field errors receive extra testing effort.

Second, developers may be able to spend extra effort inspecting modules with a high-risk profile. Finally, HARM analysis can lead to better module designs and to rules for reducing the complexity—and thus the error risk—of modules.

Although HARM is still relatively new, two people commented on it in a lab-wide survey:

> "Combines several techniques for identifying error-prone modules. Good way to prioritize in-process correction efforts."

> "Same problem as four-star [error-prone module] analysis, it tells you what you already know and it may not indicate the real problem."

There is little risk to HARM analysis, since the cost is relatively low and since the decision about how to act upon the results ultimately rests with the design, development, and test groups. Our feeling is that even if HARM is not completely accurate or as useful as one would like, it points you in the right direction. Even confirming what you already "knew in your gut" is useful information.

## Synergy

HARM analysis is synergistic with error-prone module analysis, CleanRoom techniques, orthogonal defect classification, ISO 9000, rapid prototyping, and rigorous design reviews and code inspections (Chap. 11).

## Prerequisites

Defect data need to be collected for HARM to be effective.

## Implementation advice

HARM is implemented slightly differently at each phase of the development process. In the test phase, a defective product's impact on the customer is minimized by optimizing test to catch as many defects as possible before the product is shipped and by reducing the total number of defects by controlling the module size. The test process itself can be subjected to statistical control by periodically checking the rate of problems that are uncovered.

In the development phase, the objectives of HARM analysis are to detect as many HARMs as possible before they reach testing. The number of defects can be reduced further by keeping the design document current and by simplifying modules as much as possible.

In the development phase, there are three general implementation steps:

1. Segment program modules according to problem intensity into homogeneous clusters. As a first pass, look for those modules that have had above-average numbers of field errors for two consecutive releases. These are your high-risk modules. Those with below-average levels of field errors are your low-risk modules. Finally those with no field errors are your zero risk modules.

Figure 12.5 shows the results of this type of analysis for one of our products composed of 289 code modules. Approximately 5 percent of these modules were classified as high-risk.

2. Profile each risk category in terms of the characteristics of the modules it contains. We have found the module's size (in terms of lines of code) and the number of "hits" at various stages of testing to be discriminating factors. Table 12.3 shows the characteristics of modules in each of three risk categories for one of our major products.

3. Periodically verify that the design documentation is up to date and that the modules are not becoming oversized. That is, check the module size against the criteria in Table 12.3.

These same steps are carried out in the design phase, with a few modifications. For example, high-risk modules in design might be identified by the number of design change requests in addition to the number of hits received in testing. The amount of time required for design reviews is another variable that can be correlated with hits in testing and eventual field errors. By using

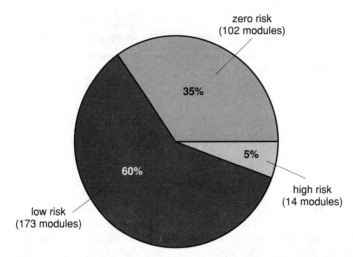

zero risk
(102 modules)

35%

5%

high risk
(14 modules)

60%

low risk
(173 modules)

**Figure 12.5**   Results of HARM analysis for 289 code modules.
(*Courtesy of IBM*)

**TABLE 12.3    Three Risk Profiles for Code Modules**

| | Module profile | | | | |
|---|---|---|---|---|---|
| Module type | Avg. module size (LOC) | Line-item test (#PTM*) | Function verification test (#PTM) | System verification test (#PTM) | Total test (#PTM) |
| Zero risk | 116 | .33 | .13 | .06 | .5 |
| Low risk | 274 | .88 | .62 | .24 | 1.7 |
| High risk | 618 | 1.74 | 2.50 | .50 | 4.7 |

*PTMs are problems found during testing.

criteria such as these, it may be possible to identify high-risk modules in the design stage, before any testing has occurred at all.

Ultimately our goal is to derive guidelines for constructing zero-risk modules from the start. Of course, if you have inherited tangled "spaghetti code," some reengineering and redesign of modules may be involved. Even so, HARM analysis can help point out which modules need to be redesigned.

Finally, it is worth mentioning that HARM analysis works best when the analysis is implemented in close cooperation with the development team. Ideally, developers would perform the analysis or work closely with the statistical expert.

Figure 12.6 summarizes some of these points in an implementation checklist.

—— Purpose of analysis clear
—— Development wants analysis
—— Analyzer with statistical knowledge identified
—— Modules segmented by problem frequency and intensity
—— Correlation between field errors and test problems
—— Correlation between coding problems and test problems
—— Correlation between design problems and coding problems
—— Profile high-risk versus low-risk designs for modules
—— Communicate results clearly
—— Actions recommended
—— Follow-up
—— Feedback and continuous improvement process in place

**Figure 12.6**   High-risk module analysis implementation checklist.

## Innovation 19 (Tools): Customer Survey Data Linkage Analysis

### The objective

How do you know where to invest resources to maximize customer satisfaction? It sounds like a simple question, and we try to answer it by conducting surveys in which we ask customers to rate their satisfaction with specific aspects of our products. We also ask customers to give us an overall rating of their satisfaction with our product.

Initially, our approach was to invest in those areas where customers rated us lowest. But soon we realized that there were problems with this approach. Improving the areas with the lowest scores did not necessarily boost overall satisfaction. As we wrestled with this puzzle, we adopted a more sophisticated approach to analyzing survey data which we call *customer survey data linkage analysis*.

### An innovative approach

The goal of data linkage analysis is to link survey results to product planning and investment decisions in the most accurate way possible. A key insight was the realization that customer satisfaction is not affected equally by all the things you may ask about on a survey.

For example, customers may give a low rating to performance; but if what they really care about is reliability, then improving performance is not going to boost customer satisfaction as much as improving reliability—even if reliability is already pretty good. Unfortunately, customers cannot always tell you what factors weigh most heavily in their assessment of satisfaction. Moreover, the weighting of factors is likely to vary from customer to customer.

Statistical techniques are needed to examine the linkage between each survey question and overall satisfaction across many customers. Data linkage analysis simply uses statistics to determine which areas affect overall customer satisfaction the most. Because these areas are often *not* the areas with the lowest score on surveys, this analysis can lead to much better investment decisions than simply working on the lowest-scoring survey items.

### Costs, benefits, and risks

Assuming that you already gather data on the elements that affect overall customer satisfaction, the cost of customer satisfaction data linkage analysis is the cost of devoting part of a person's effort to conducting the analysis. Provided the person has a background in statistics, the analysis shouldn't take more than a couple of weeks per product. The much more significant cost will come from the changes required to improve the product itself.

The benefits are well worth the cost, provided survey data exist to analyze. The main benefit lies in having a principled way of deciding where to invest future development resources. The savings—from accomplishing more in terms of improving customer satisfaction with less development expense—should more than cover the cost of the analysis.

Here are some of the comments from a lab-wide survey on the usefulness of CUPRIMDS (our customer satisfaction survey) data linkage analysis:

"Points out interesting links; not in a position to use data to set priorities. This must come from top project managers."

"The current survey is too generic....You need specifics to take any action."

"In order for this to be useful, a large customer base is needed."

"The data assist us in focusing on the most critical customer needs."

"This is an easy way to prioritize product improvement efforts based on impact on overall satisfaction."

The main risk is that you may encounter resistance to the methodology if it is not well understood. For this reason, it is important that the development group be involved in the analysis. Otherwise, you may find yourself in the awkward position of having an outsider spend 2 weeks analyzing data and then telling development that they need to completely reprioritize their efforts. It takes a very open-minded development organization to accept that.

### Synergy

Data linkage analysis is synergistic with survey work, with other statistical methods (e.g., orthogonal defect classification), with competitive analysis, and with the quality partnership program for customers.

### Prerequisites

Data are a prerequisite for analysis. One source of these data is the customer surveys described in Chap. 7. Some knowledge of statistics and a close working relationship with development are other critical success factors.

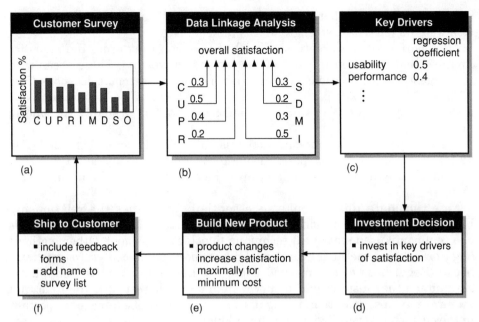

**Figure 12.7** Data linkage analysis process. (*a*) to (*f*) are consecutive steps in the process. (*Courtesy of IBM*)

## Implementation advice

Figure 12.7 sketches the process for data linkage analysis. It begins with gathering survey data that cover questions about overall satisfaction as well as individual components of satisfaction (Fig. 12.7*a*).

Next data from many respondents are put into a statistical analysis package that performs a multiple regression analysis (Fig. 12.7*b*). Multiple regression is a general statistical technique that asks: How do we weight a set of variables so that they best predict the value of another variable that we are interested in?

Specifically, in our case we wanted to know how much weight to give each of the CUPRIMDS areas covered on our survey so that if we knew how each area were scored, we could predict what the overall satisfaction would be. [Readers interested in the mathematical process for carrying out such an analysis are referred to standard texts on statistical analysis, such as Hayes (1981).]

For example, we might find that usability had a larger regression weight than performance for a particular product. If so, the analysis would be saying that we would get more "bang for the buck" (in terms of improving overall customer satisfaction) by investing in usability improvements than we would get by investing in performance improvements. Note that it is not the absolute score on performance or usability that matters. What drives our investment decision is the strength of the linkage between performance and overall satisfaction or between usability and overall satisfaction. The regression weights tell us the strength of this linkage.

After performing the regression analysis, we can rank-order the areas for improvement based on the size of the regression weights. Those areas with the largest weights become the key drivers of our investment decisions (Fig. 12.7c and d). For example, if two line items cost the same to build and one affects a key driver of customer satisfaction, that is probably the one to build.

Once the new product and/or function is built (Fig. 12.7e) and shipped (Fig. 12.7f), a new survey can be performed and the analysis repeated. In this way, you continually improve and adjust investment decisions to the needs of customers.

Note that data linkage analysis essentially quantifies the relationship between survey information and overall satisfaction. Multiple regression is one commonly used statistical technique to achieve this goal. Other methods (e.g., orthogonal methods) can be found in more advanced statistical textbooks. Regardless of the method used, the key is to avoid the simplistic assumption that just because a survey item scores lowest, it is the item that requires the most attention. It might score low and still be fairly unimportant in the customer's overall view of your product.

We have conducted data linkage analysis for a number of products, including our database programs IMS and DB2 and our FORTRAN language product. The approach has also been validated by mathematical experts across IBM.

In general, the response to the analysis has been quite positive, but whether actual changes have occurred in the product plans is another story.

The problem here is cultural rather than technological. For many established products, it is easy to run into the situation where the old-timers already feel that they know where the improvements should be made and simply are not receptive to new analyses.

Alternatively, the analysis may confirm what they already know—that the product has certain areas in desperate need of improvement. But for a variety of reasons, including fear of slipping schedules or the risk involved in redesigning existing code, the problems are quietly ignored.

Finally, there may legitimately be a number of other concerns that figure into product plans besides customer survey data. Competitors' plans, overall strategy considerations, and competing quality concerns all feed into the product planning process.

Our advice is to pursue data linkage analysis because it provides information needed to develop better products. But let the analysis also be sensitive to organizational issues. In linkage analysis, the technical challenges may be overshadowed by the challenges of integrating new knowledge into an existing culture.

Figure 12.8 presents our implementation checklist for survey data linkage analysis.

——— Survey data exists
——— Purpose of analysis clear
——— Development wants the analysis
——— Analyzer (knows statistics) identified
——— Analysis methods (e.g., regression, correlation) selected
——— Several analyses converge on product areas to improve
——— Results of analysis communicated clearly
——— Follow-up actions for product improvement in place
——— Feedback and continuous improvement process in place

**Figure 12.8**    Data linkage analysis implementation checklist.

## Suggested Readings

Chan, S. (1993) *4\* Module Analysis Process.* Working Paper, IBM Santa Teresa, February 1993. *Our most recent documentation of the four-star process at IBM Santa Teresa.*

Crane, G. F., and Garth, J. M. (1991) *Four-Star Modules: A Methodology for Quality Management Using AD/Cycle.* Technical Report TR 03.395, IBM Santa Teresa, March 1991. *A description of IBM Santa Teresa's four-star efforts in the CASE tools arena.*

Halstead, M. H. (1975) *Software Physics: Basic Principles.* Technical Report RJ1582, IBM Research, San Jose, CA, May. *Early investigation into issues (e.g., complexity) affecting software development.*

Hayes, W. L. (1981) *Statistics,* 3d ed. New York: CBS College Publishing. *A popular text on statistics with explanations of regression and multiple regression.*

Lo, B. (1991) *High APAR Risk Module (HARM) Analysis.* Technical Report TR 03.400, IBM Santa Teresa, May 1991. *A more detailed (technical) look at the HARM process described above.*

Martin, J. (1990) *Information Engineering.* Englewood Cliffs, NJ: Prentice-Hall. *A three-volume, comprehensive treatment of information engineering that contains some concepts relevant to the design of low-error-risk modules.*

Selby, R. W., and Porter, A. A. (1988) "Learning from Examples: Generation and Evaluation of Decision Trees for Software Measurement Analysis." *IEEE,* 14(12): 1743–1757. *Provides an alternative approach that gets at the same issues as four-star analysis.*

Tang, K., and Lo, B. (1993) "Determination of the Optimal Process Mean When Inspection Is Based on a Correlated Variable." *IEEE Transactions,* 25(3): 66–72. *Theoretical foundation for the data linkage analysis work with a manufacturing example and literature review.*

# 13

# Stage 3: Management

## Are You in the Management Stage?

You know you're in the management stage when your organization begins to take a proactive approach to quality. To reach this stage, an organization must already have controlled its quality problems to some extent. The organization should understand its processes and have made some effort to improve quality through process improvements such as enhanced testing or more rigorous code inspections.

To accomplish the shift from a reactive mode of defect *detection* to a proactive mode of defect *prevention* requires teamwork. Serial development models like the waterfall process tend to create rigid departmental boundaries, and the leadership challenge in the management stage is to break down those boundaries and create a new culture of cross-functional teamwork. So the leadership theme in the management stage is proactive teams, while the technology and process themes are innovation and defect prevention.

At this stage, our lab scored in the 625 to 750 range on the Baldrige template. Table 13.1 shows specific indicators we saw in each of the seven areas covered by Baldrige. An organization exhibiting most of or all these signs is probably in the management stage.

## Objectives of the Management Stage

The overall goal in the management stage of quality maturity is to make quantum improvements in quality—not just the incremental gains that can be obtained by doing the same thing with greater focus on quality. In our experience, these quantum improvements demand radical process change as well as unprecedented levels of teamwork and innovation. Unless the organization has realized the limitations of incremental approaches to quality in the coping stage, it is unlikely that people will be willing to support the experimentation and longer-term focus required by the management stage.

TABLE 13.1    Baldrige Indicators of the Management Stage

| Baldrige area | Indicators |
| --- | --- |
| 1.0 Leadership | Commitment consistent at all levels of management |
| 2.0 Information and analysis | In-process quality measurements defined<br>Internal/external data collected<br>Some data analyzed; attempts to improve data analysis techniques |
| 3.0 Strategic quality planning | Strategic planning process defined<br>All departmental strategies/plans in place<br>Working to improve strategic planning process<br>In-process measurements are strong and widely used |
| 4.0 Human resource development and management | All employees had quality education<br>All employees have some participation in quality activities<br>Team-oriented measurement and rewards |
| 5.0 Management of process quality | Processes well understood<br>Critical processes documented<br>Focus on defect prevention<br>Some focus on supplier quality<br>Strong cross-functional teams widely deployed<br>Broad-scale process reengineering<br>New technology to support all processes |
| 6.0 Quality and operational results | Good data on product quality levels<br>Some trend and competitor data<br>First tentative signs of positive quality impact on operational results |
| 7.0 Customer focus and satisfaction | Good data on customer satisfaction<br>Beginning to gather data on customer satisfaction with competitors' products |

In the earlier awareness and coping stages, a few visionaries pushed a quality agenda and the organization reacted. In the management stage, most of the organization should be driving the quality efforts. The leadership challenge is no longer to focus attention on the organization's quality problems, but to support innovative and proactive approaches to these problems. Supporting teamwork and initiative in the context of an overall strategic focus are the key goals for leaders in the management stage.

From a process perspective, the management stage represents a shift in focus from defect detection (by doing the existing process better) to defect prevention (by analyzing and changing the existing process). Process goals for the management stage include developing the ability to critically analyze internal processes and to benchmark processes against other companies.

With regard to technology, the goal is develop tools that make the team development of code more efficient and error-free. The code should also match the customer's needs which means technology should support rapid prototyping efforts. Finally, the code should be reusable so as to improve the quality and efficiency of subsequent development efforts.

The specific Baldrige items corresponding to these objectives in the management stage are shown in Fig. 13.1.

2.3 Analysis and use of data:   Focus on analyzing and using data to improve quality.

3.1 Strategic planning:   Link quality measurements to business plans.

4.4 Employee performance:   Make sure the employee recognition system is in accord with quality goals and plans.

5.3 Process management support:   Focus on quality management for support functions.

6.1 Product and service quality:   Focus on measuring and improving product quality results.

6.3 Business and support results:   Focus on measuring and improving quality results in the indirect (support) organizations.

7.1 Customer expectations:   Improve your process for determining customer requirements.

7.5 Customer satisfaction results:   Measure and improve your customer satisfaction levels.

**Figure 13.1**   Baldrige items for improvement in the management stage.

## Overview of Innovations for the Management Stage

The leadership innovations in the management stage include strategic focus, empowerment, and Quality Week. These programs represent a pincer movement on quality. From the top down comes a strategic approach to ensure that we are building the products that customers really want. From the bottom up come innovation, teamwork, and grass roots leadership.

The process innovations include the defect prevention process, process benchmarking, and competitive analysis. The central thrust is to improve processes: first, by analyzing the cause of quality problems and, second, by comparing internal processes (and products) to the best of class in the industry. The ultimate aim is to prevent defects via these process improvements instead of relying on defect detection schemes.

The technological innovations include several IBM inventions such as computer-supported team work spaces and electronic meeting technology. On-line review tools and local-area network (LAN) library control systems help computerize the software development process, while object-oriented methods, rapid prototyping, and clean-room techniques represent new paradigms for software development.

Table 13.2 summarizes the objectives, innovative approaches, and pitfalls for the management stage. All these leadership, process, and technological innovations are described in detail in Chaps. 14 to 18.

## Obstacles and Pitfalls

The management stage is probably the most difficult passage to navigate successfully. Whereas initial enthusiasm and commitment can carry you through the first two stages, by the time you hit the beginning of the management stage, morale may be at an all-time low while quality results still have not surfaced. The positive note is that things should improve steadily as you work your way up through this stage, as long as you avoid certain critical pitfalls. Figure 13.2 lists some of the pitfalls that we fell into or narrowly avoided during the management stage.

TABLE 13.2    **Management Stage Innovations**

| Food group | Objective | Innovative approach | Implementation pitfalls |
|---|---|---|---|
| Leadership | Provide strategic focus and integration with quality. | Large-scale strategic planning, education, and tools; Baldrige assessment of planning groups and strategic focus initiatives. | Failure to take a business perspective. Not shifting from production quality to strategic quality. |
| | Generate innovations and breakthroughs. | Emphasize and reward empowerment. | Yo-Yo management style; settling for incremental progress. |
| | Improve morale, achieve deep quality deployment, encourage bottoms-up activity. | Showcase innovations, tools, teams, and progress in a grass roots Quality Week. | Not making it fun; low relevancy, anemic content, less than total participation. |
| Process | Shift from defect detection to defect prevention. | Root cause analysis as part of the defect prevention process. | Expecting immediate results, failure to implement recommended actions. |
| | Ensure we can answer: "Are our processes world-class?" | Process benchmarking. | No benchmarking plan and preparation. Limiting benchmarking to one industry. |
| | Ensure we can answer: "Are our products competitive?" | Competitive analysis. | Failure to identify right market segments. Unactionable analyses. |
| Technology | Improve meeting productivity. | Computerized team work spaces. | Skepticism, funding issues. |
| | Eliminate problems in participation, productivity, prioritization. | Electronic meetings (TeamFocus®). | Unskilled moderator, poor session preparation. |
| | Eliminate unproductive code reviews. | Revufile technology enabling online reviews. | No cross-functional participation. |
| | Reduce coordination problems with team code development. | LAN library control systems. | Impatience, lack of training and education. |
| | Reuse code. | Object-oriented programming and design | Learning curve. |
| | Fast "proof of concept." | Rapid prototyping. | Appropriate tool selection. |
| | Improve on the waterfall process. | CleanRoom techniques. | Lack of education, insistence on "whole hog" deployment. |

## Signs of Progress

As with the other stages, your Baldrige score is a key indicator of progress. Our score on the Baldrige template continued to climb during both Excellence Councils held in the management stage. On the other hand, morale steadily declined through the first half of this stage and only began to increase again as we neared the threshold of the integration stage.

Part of this decrease in morale reflected our inability to communicate the vision of the quality transformation to the entire organization. There are few

**Leadership pitfalls**

1. Failure to reward teamwork
2. Failure to support innovation and encourage risk taking
3. Giving in to increasing resistance
4. Expecting bottom-line results immediately
5. Viewing low morale as an immediate indicator of failure

**Process pitfalls**

1. Settling for incremental process improvement
2. Failure to experiment with processes
3. Focusing on defect detection at the expense of prevention
4. Failure to benchmark best-of-class processes
5. Failure to have closed-loop processes
6. Lack of in-process measurements

**Technology pitfalls**

1. Developing technology that increases individual productivity at the expense of teamwork
2. Failing to develop rigorous analysis techniques for customer satisfaction data
3. Spending money on vendor tools without pilot-testing them first

**Figure 13.2**   Pitfalls in the management stage.

things as demoralizing as feeling that you are being forced to change for reasons that you don't agree with or don't understand. On the other hand, any organization undergoing rapid change is likely to experience a drop in morale. Change is not always pleasant, and one often doesn't feel good about it until the results are in. For this reason, morale is likely to lag behind quality improvement efforts, not lead them.

Innovation, however, is a leading indicator of progress. If the technical people in the organization are not pursuing innovative approaches to software development, it is almost impossible to make the quantum improvements necessary to progress through the management stage. Doing the same things more rigorously just isn't enough at this stage of maturity. Management needs to look for and encourage new approaches.

Evidence of cross-functional cooperation and teamwork is also a positive sign. We knew we were making progress when developers and testers began to speak of quality from an overall product perspective instead of from the perspective of people who owned individual line items or test cases.

## Our Lab in the Management Stage

In 1993, our lab neared the end of the management stage of quality maturity. In early 1992, we were awarded the silver-level market-driven quality award by IBM's corporate headquarters. This reflected a Baldrige score greater than 625. In 1993 we prepared a Baldrige submission, using the 1993 guidelines, which attained the gold level, reflecting a Baldrige score greater than 750.

Both morale and customer satisfaction with our products increased overall. But the path to the gold level was fraught with obstacles, and we have come to believe the saying, "The night is never blacker than just before the dawn."

During the early phases of the management stage in 1991, our Baldrige score was up, but everything else was down. Morale at the lab dropped to an all-time low, and the grumbling about quality presentations, the Excellence Council, and Baldrige assessments was ubiquitous.

The grumbling was understandable. Everyone was overloaded with the added demands of quality programs while still trying to meet aggressive product ship dates. The results of the earlier quality efforts would not be evident for several months since it took time for reports to filter back from customers. And it would be a year or more before we knew the true quality of our latest releases. A year seemed a long time to wait.

During that year, probably everyone in the lab, with the possible exception of our general manager (who at least didn't show any outward signs of weakening), probably considered throwing in the towel on quality. There was a lab-wide case of quality burnout.

At such times, milestones and in-process measurements of quality play a critical role as motivators. Despite lab-wide discontent, we watched our Baldrige assessment score climb. Logic told us it was only a matter of time before these results began to be manifested in bottom-line measurements. So we persisted.

We also knew that, while uncomfortable, the burnout meant the focus on quality had finally percolated through every department in the organization. No one was untouched. If we grumbled, at least we were grumbling while using the Baldrige vocabulary.

This was the sort of thinking that allowed us to hang on and round the corner. Fortunately not all of us rounded the corner at the same time, and by the time the bulk of the lab began to look optimistically toward the future, the innovators had already developed leadership techniques like strategic focus, deployed processes like the defect prevention process (DPP), and invented technologies like computer-supported team work spaces.

Then finally, at the end of 1992, three years after the beginning of our quality journey and after two stage transitions, the fruits of our labors finally began to appear.

Throughout the journey we had been able to gauge our progress, using the Baldrige assessment tool. However, the bottom-line results that counted most showed up last. It was not until mid-1992, when we were solidly in the management stage, that these measures began to improve.

Despite an industry-wide recession, increasing competition in the software business, and generally horrendous results for IBM as a whole, we saw our costs decrease and revenues rise. Defects both in the field and in the lab decreased. Most importantly, customer satisfaction increased.

Employee morale finally improved, too—last of all. This was not surprising, considering the stress that all the changes had created. Ironically, our customers recognized the benefits of our quality efforts before many of our own employees did.

However, once the improvement numbers were in, a core contingent of "I'll believe it when I see it" employees finally had to face the evidence. Yes, the 100-fold improvement plans still sounded outlandish, but there was no denying that something was working. In retrospect, it may have been those 100-fold goals, unrealistic as they seemed, that forced us to let go of our old tools and methodologies and invent new ones. Today this approach is sometimes called reengineering. In 1989, we didn't know what to call it, but it worked.

## Suggested Readings

Bayer, J., and Melone, N. (1989) *Adoption of Software Engineering Innovations in Organizations,* Software Engineering Institute Technical Report, CMU/SEI-89-TR-17, DTIC no. ADA211573. *Results and analysis of a survey of 75 defense contractors who adopted new software engineering technologies.*

Firth, R., Mosley, V., Pethia, R., Roberts-Gold, L., and Wood, W. (1987) *A Guide to the Classification and Assessment of Software Engineering Tools,* CMU/SEI Technical Report, CMU/SEI-87-TR-10, ADA213968. *Describes a tool classification technique that helps determine where a tool fits in the development process.*

Gilman, J. J. (1992) *Inventivity: The Art and Science of Research Management.* New York: Van Nostrand Reinhold. *A look at what it takes to manage researchers, together with analysis, advice, and insight that would be useful to anyone interested in fostering invention.*

Raghavan, S. A., and Chand, D. R. (1989) "Diffusing Software-Engineering Methods," *IEEE Software,* 6(4):81–90, July.

Rogers, E. M. (1983) *Diffusion of Innovations,* 3d ed. New York: Free Press. *This book should be of interest to anyone trying to help foster innovation and the spread of innovations throughout an organization.*

# 14

# Transforming Quality into Business as Usual

While the leadership challenges in the awareness and coping stages were to jump-start and catalyze quality improvement, in the management stage the goal is to create an environment where quality is seen as business as usual. That means finding ways to embed a quality focus in the day-to-day operations of the organization.

Table 14.1 summarizes three leadership innovations that come at this goal from different directions. Strategic focus comes from the top down. It recognizes that customer satisfaction is the ultimate goal of the quality improvement activities, and that customers will be satisfied only if the organization has a strategy to build the right products.

**TABLE 14.1  Stage: Management / Food Group: Leadership / Themes: Create Environment for Innovations in Process and Technology: / Encourage Cultural Transformation to Proactive, Cross-Functional Teams and Closed-Loop Processes; Sustain Momentum Coping Stage**

| Objective | Innovative approach | Pitfalls |
|---|---|---|
| Provide strategic focus in the business and integration with quality initiatives | Major initiatives on strategic management and integration with quality initiatives<br>Baldrige assessment of planning groups<br>Large-scale strategy planning, education, and tools | Failure to take a business perspective<br>Not shifting from production quality to strategic quality |
| Foster innovations and breakthroughs | Create empowered environment<br>Deploy new processes and technology<br>Emphasize new reward system | Allow mistakes, but learn from them<br>Settle for incremental progress<br>Yo-Yo management style |
| Foster buy-in at all levels to drive innovations | *Quality Week:*<br>Showcase:<br>  Innovations<br>  Tools<br>  Teams<br>Bottom-up activity | Not making it fun<br>Low relevancy<br>Anemic content<br>Not having all disciplines participate |

*Empowerment* is a term that is probably overused these days, but it represents the idea that management has to loosen the reins and encourage risk taking if innovation is to flourish.

Finally, Quality Week provides an example of empowerment in action. The grass roots innovation fair and other quality-related events illustrate what is possible when management just steps out of the way.

## Innovation 20 (Leadership): Strategic Focus

### The objective

One of the biggest challenges facing software companies today is the rapid pace of technological change. Even the futurists can't stay far ahead of it. For example, consider these words from world-renowned futurist Alvin Toffler (1981):

> To my pleasure I found I could master the machine in a single short session. Within a few hours I was using it fluently. After more than a year at the keyboard, I am still amazed at its speed and its power. Today, instead of typing a draft of a chapter on paper, I type on a keyboard that stores it in electronic form on what is known as a "floppy disk." I see my words displayed before me on a TV-like screen....I press a button, and a printer beside me makes a letter-perfect final copy at vision-blurring speeds.

Today, when you can read about computerized "hypernovels" in the New York Times *Book Review,* it's hard to imagine a futurist getting so excited about a word processor—especially one that used floppy disks, lacked an LCD screen, and couldn't be taken with you on an airplane. But much has changed since 1981.

Today it is the software industry that moves at vision-blurring speed. As computing shifts from the mainframe to workstations, proprietary standards are yielding to open systems. Telecommunications and networking software has become fundamentally important to customers in almost all installations. Alphanumeric screens are disappearing, and graphical screens are the rule. Customers are demanding nonproprietary systems with industry standards for interoperability. Whereas in the past software was either procured from the systems vendor or made in-house, today the shrink-wrapped market is of vast size and reach.

Companies like IBM scramble to hook up with business partners, while increasingly educated customers have become very choosy about where to spend their decreasing information system budgets.

These changes compel software companies to be responsive to their customers to an unprecedented degree. It is no longer enough to build a high-quality product. It has to be the *right* high-quality product. There is no point in building a bug-free product that nobody wants.

Recognizing that building the right product was as much a part of quality as reducing defects led the lab to ask questions like these: What do customers value? Who are our competitors? What is the configuration of the industry at large? Where do we want to compete in the marketplace? Where should we concentrate our investment?

To answer these questions, we had to completely overhaul our planning process and develop our skills to create what we call *strategic focus*.

## An innovative approach

Strategic focus consisted of a four-step process.

First, we anticipated future demands for products, using an analytical and systematic approach. We segmented the market and built quantitative models based on our analysis of the market structure. We implemented on a broad scale a process that we found to be the most effective in reflecting customer needs. We codeveloped software with customers, and we held customer advisory councils on a worldwide basis.

Second, we tried to develop and prioritize the right mix of functions to meet customer needs. The technique of conjoint analysis proved extremely helpful at this phase. Conjoint analysis is a statistical process that permits a planner to determine the mix of the most important attributes from the customer's perspective. We used this process in major releases of our most important products.

Third, we tried to invest in the right products, based on our analyses. We had market forecasts of how many licenses we expected to sell for existing products, and we created investment models which calculated the expected return on investment for over 100 product investment decisions. Then the top planners who were skilled in technology and finance at the lab, together with professors we knew at Stanford University, developed a portfolio model that helped guide our overall investment strategy. The planners implemented a *capital asset pricing model* (CAPM) based on market research data and the key projects at the lab.

Fourth, we applied the Baldrige criteria, both in principle and in actual assessments, to the entire planning organization. The assessment helped us zero in on our strengths and weaknesses. It led to investments in graduate MBA-level skills development for the planning community, to the adoption of a policy of "management by facts," and to intensive analytical modeling efforts based on market research. The result has been a major improvement in the early stabilization of product specifications and better allocation of resources. Significantly, employee morale went up along the way.

## Costs, benefits, and risks

The number one cost is management time. Other significant costs include investment in education and tools and in obtaining a quality staff. Our costs to deploy the strategic focus program ranged from 3 to 5 percent of the organization's resources.

The benefits can be summed up by saying that strategic focus increases the probability that the development organization will build the right products for the market. This translates to higher customer satisfaction and better financial performance in the marketplace. The literature and research show clearly that strategy is necessary to achieve these goals. And IBM's corporate Baldrige examiners apparently agree, since they awarded the gold medal award for excellence to our lab—in part for these strategic planning efforts.

The number one risk is lack of management resolve and myopia, resulting in a short-term perspective. To expect that bug-free code and short-term actions alone will result in sustainable competitiveness would be a serious mistake.

A secondary risk is that with poor implementation, the program can waste money and lead to flawed analysis and conclusions. To minimize this risk, each of the pitfalls discussed in the implementation section should be addressed.

### Synergy

Strategic focus is synergistic with the Baldrige template, with customer involvement activities, with analysis and modeling techniques, and with the experience factory concept described in Chap. 9.

### Prerequisites

The main prerequisite is a recognition of the need for, and a commitment to, a strategic approach to planning. The organization must be ready to abandon simplistic thinking of the "buy low, sell high" variety and embrace analytical approaches that produce real insight and improved knowledge of customer needs and market competitiveness.

### Implementation advice

Figure 14.1 lists the top 10 pitfalls that must be avoided in implementing a strategic focus approach.

Not surprisingly, our implementation advice focuses on avoiding these pitfalls. First, get a good leader. A proactive person who knows strategy and software is required.

Next, staff the organization with the best people you can find, and equip them with the education and tools they need to collect and analyze data. The goal is to produce information based on rigorous market research that can be used to make decisions. Avoid data collection for data collection's sake. The analysis must be actionable. Always ask yourself, What is the decision that I will make with this analysis?

Emphasize that mediocrity will not be tolerated in the organization. To transform an inwardly focused bureaucratic or technocratic organization into a market-focused strategic organization, driven by the wants and needs of customers, requires 100 percent effort from everyone. No matter how defect-free the code is, if the strategy of the organization is off, the organization can-

1. Lack of a real leader who understands strategy, planning, and software
2. Settling for an internal view of quality, e.g., focusing only on defect reduction instead of on customer wants and needs
3. Settling for a piecemeal approach to strategy; failure to adopt an integrated, Baldrige-like approach
4. Settling for a rear-view mirror approach; focusing on historical trends instead of the current and future market
5. Excessive focus on cost and expense control instead of focusing on increasing revenue and customer satisfaction
6. Ignoring stakeholders; failure to get customers, business partners, and developers actively involved
7. Letting technology rule; building leading-edge technology regardless of customers' wants and needs
8. Letting bureaucrats rule; failure to take calculated risks; mindless adherence to process
9. Being "penny-wise and pound-foolish"; failure to invest in the tools and education needed to do the job
10. Failure to fire the incompetent; wasting resources and time avoiding decisive personnel actions

**Figure 14.1**   Top 10 implementation pitfalls for strategic focus.

not succeed. For this reason, a view of quality that includes operational results and strategic planning—such as Baldrige—works hand in hand with strategic focus.

Figure 14.2 presents an implementation checklist for strategic focus.

## Innovation 21 (Leadership): Empowerment

### The objective

Let's face it. The types of employees who are attracted to large corporations such as IBM tend to be those who like hierarchical organizations. And these organizations, with their strict chains of command, seem the very opposite of creative entrepreneurial organizations that foster innovation.

It's no accident that Steve Jobs and Steve Wozniak started Apple Computer in their garage, rather than at IBM. At IBM, they would have needed to get

_____ Executive management committed to strategy
_____ Strong, skilled leader identified
_____ Adequate resources allocated
_____ Hand-picked professional staff of top caliber
_____ Career paths for professional staff clearly visible
_____ Strategic focus goals clearly communicated
_____ Analysis—not just data collection—group in place
_____ Tools in place
_____ Strategic education plans in place
_____ Stakeholders engaged via advisory councils, reviews, etc.

**Figure 14.2**   Implementation checklist for strategic focus.

approval from four levels of management and endorsement from scores of other parties. On their own, they simply sold their car for start-up capital and did some fast talking at a computer hobby shop to get started.

The challenge facing us was to foster innovation within a hierarchical organization.

## An innovative approach

In a way the challenge was nothing new. It simply meant rediscovering part of the heritage that made IBM great. Despite IBM's stuffy blue-suit image, there has always been some toleration for eccentric and adventurous spirits. Tom Watson, Jr., IBM's chairman for many years, put it this way in *A Business and Its Beliefs: The Ideas That Helped Build IBM:*

> In IBM we frequently refer to our need for "wild ducks." The moral is drawn from a story by the Danish philosopher, Soren Kierkegaard. He told of a man...who liked to watch the wild ducks fly south in great flocks each fall. Out of charity, he took to putting feed for them in a nearby pond. After a while some of the ducks no longer bothered to fly south; they wintered in Denmark on what he fed them. In time they flew less and less. When the wild ducks returned, the others would circle up to greet them but then head back to their feeding grounds on the pond. After three or four years, they grew so lazy and fat that they found difficulty in flying at all.
>
> Kierkegaard drew his point—you can make wild ducks tame, but you can never make tame ducks wild again. One might also add that the duck who is tamed will never go anywhere any more.
>
> We are convinced that any business needs its wild ducks. And in IBM we try not to tame them.

There are two interesting things about this quotation. First, it shows that IBM has long recognized and appreciated the need for innovative and entrepreneurial spirits. Second, it implies that the way to get innovation is to hire wild ducks, or avoid taming the ones you already have. The notion of encouraging tame ducks to fly again just doesn't seem realistic.

Perhaps that's why the authors of this book are somewhat divided on the issue of empowerment. One of us believes that the empowerment folks are on the wrong track altogether. You can't turn a tame duck wild, and this is what most empowerment programs try to do. The truly wild ducks are going to be wild no matter what you do, and the others are a lost cause.

Another of us argues that empowerment is a way of supporting wild ducks. And for ducks on the fence—not quite wild and not quite tame—empowerment may provide the impetus to fly wild instead of becoming tame.

Finally, the third author believes that starving a tame duck will force it to fly again.

Despite our disagreements over empowerment, our lab has gone ahead—like most of U.S. industry—and implemented a bunch of programs under the general heading of employee empowerment. So we'll tell you what we did, and you can decide for yourself whether you think it makes any sense.

First, we have to get clear about what we mean by empowerment. In our research for this section, we discovered that feminist organizations, George Bush, Chicano political activist groups, nurses, and quality gurus all talk about empowerment. But each group defines it slightly differently.

To us, *empowerment* means sharing power and increasing autonomy throughout the organization. It means giving all employees the authority to make more judgments and reach more decisions without checking with superiors. But it also means delegating accountability and responsibility along with that authority.

Employee empowerment takes many forms. At its simplest it can be a verbal agreement between manager and employee that the employee should actively try to make more autonomous decisions and can count on the manager's support for such actions. The manager agrees that mistakes will be viewed as part of the learning process, and the employee agrees to try to avoid mistakes that are fatal.

If this sounds like good management practice, it is. But empowerment goes beyond standard management practice in that it stretches the trust between superior and subordinate. Empowerment says, "Let's make an active effort to trust each other more, because both of us will learn from the experience, and if we are successful, the overall efficiency of organization will increase."

When applied to teams instead of to individuals, empowerment means allowing team members greater authority and responsibility for managing themselves. The recent surge in books on self-directed teams (see Suggested Readings) reflects this notion of team empowerment. In fact, one of our product areas completely reorganized itself into self-directed teams.

## Costs, benefits, and risks

The short-term cost to empowerment is that the organization is likely to make more mistakes. If your empowerment program is working, the rate of failures is going to be the first thing to increase. After all, you're asking people to make decisions that they've never made before, and you are asking them to accept responsibility at an accelerated rate. If they're not failing, they probably are not really exercising the power that has been granted them in the name of empowerment.

The cost of these mistakes is highly variable and depends upon the skill with which managers delegate decisions. The trick is to delegate to the point where employees are slightly uncomfortable making decisions but are still competent. By stretching people a little beyond where they are comfortable, you maximize learning without overwhelming anyone. The location of this point varies from employee to employee and from situation to situation. We don't have any magic formula to offer except to stress that good communication between manager and empowered employee or team is critical.

Empowerment has to be seen as an investment. For the price of more initial mistakes, ultimately you end up with more competent employees who are willing and able to take more initiative. The organization runs more smoothly and efficiently because there are fewer levels of bureaucracy to gum up the works.

The other thing that empowerment (arguably) brings, is increased levels of innovation. For example, one of our most successful innovations started with a couple of programmers sneaking around at night and working weekends on a pet project. These were employees who empowered themselves! Yet management support and empowerment were ultimately necessary to turn a pet project into something that could be shown to the general manager, installed at locations throughout lab, and marketed to customers. If nothing else, our emphasis on empowerment allowed these developers to bring their idea out into the open earlier and gave the sponsoring manager a leg to stand on when he went to the financial officer to beg for prototyping funds.

The risk—the one managers are all afraid of—is that some empowered employee will go crazy and really screw things up. In our experience, this risk is more imaginary than real—but this does not make it any less scary. As long as responsibility and accountability are delegated along with power and authority, you get failures—but usually not catastrophes.

A more real risk is the yo-yo empowerment syndrome. What happens here is that well-meaning managers empower employees initially, but return control and authority to upper levels of management in response to tight economic conditions. It's an understandable reaction. When times get tough, there is less tolerance for mistakes that might affect the bottom line. Mistakes that might have been merely annoying in a good economic climate can be disastrous in recessionary times. Yet, yanking control back up to the top is the one sure way to kill an empowerment program. It sends the message that management was not really serious about delegating authority, and it breeds distrust. It would be better to delegate less authority and to proceed more cautiously with empowerment than to jerk employees around.

## Synergy

We would like to say everything goes better with empowerment, but that would sound like a Coca Cola commercial. We've found there are certain areas where empowerment seems to have worked really well and other areas where it hasn't. Usually it comes down to a question of scope. For example, Excellence Council participants were empowered with regard to the way they could construct their presentations, but they did not have control over the fact that the presentations were required or that each had a maximum length.

With regard to specific innovations, the Leadership Institute is probably most synergistic with employee empowerment. The Leadership Institute emphasizes independent action and leadership—areas that are at the heart of empowerment.

## Prerequisites

The prerequisites for empowerment are mutual trust and the ability to keep empowerment commitments to employees and teams even under adverse economic conditions.

## Implementation advice

Our implementation advice for empowerment can be summed up in the empowerment strategy shown in Fig. 14.3. This was the strategy that enabled IBM's Rochester site to develop the AS/400 computer in record time.

Conceptually, it's simple. First, you have to excite people; motivate them to take risks and reward people when they are successful. Second, you have to enable them; provide them with the latest technology and process improvements so that they have the very best working environment. Third, you have to empower; just let go of micromanaging while delegating authority *and* responsibility. Finally, you step out of the way and make sure to publicize the successes widely.

Specific activities can help in each of these various stages. For example, it can help to clearly communicate what outstanding performance looks like. We are continually amazed at how many managers fail to achieve results simply because their employees don't understand the desired goal state. Both at IBM Rochester and our lab, an effort was made to define criteria for outstanding performance at every level for every position in the lab. These criteria were then circulated in the form of guidelines so that employees could have some objective way of evaluating where they stood.

Providing education and tools is another important step in empowerment. For example, we could not expect people to participate in Baldrige without first investing heavily in Baldrige education. Similarly, developers working on process innovations like CLIFT or extended unit test required training on automated test tools.

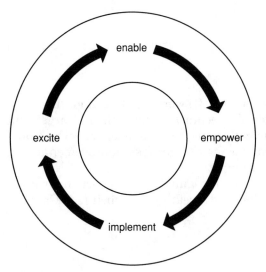

**Figure 14.3** Empowerment strategy. (*Courtesy of Oxford University Press*)

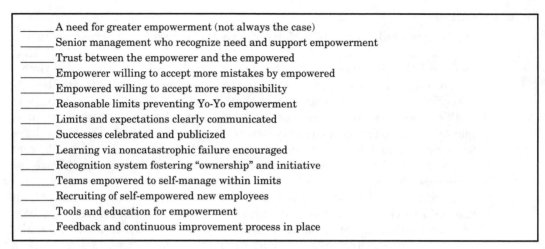

_____ A need for greater empowerment (not always the case)
_____ Senior management who recognize need and support empowerment
_____ Trust between the empowerer and the empowered
_____ Empowerer willing to accept more mistakes by empowered
_____ Empowered willing to accept more responsibility
_____ Reasonable limits preventing Yo-Yo empowerment
_____ Limits and expectations clearly communicated
_____ Successes celebrated and publicized
_____ Learning via noncatastrophic failure encouraged
_____ Recognition system fostering "ownership" and initiative
_____ Teams empowered to self-manage within limits
_____ Recruiting of self-empowered new employees
_____ Tools and education for empowerment
_____ Feedback and continuous improvement process in place

**Figure 14.4**   Empowerment implementation checklist.

Finally, the simplest step—letting go of micromanagement—is often the hardest for managers to do. Yet time and time again, we've found that the technical professionals in the lab were more knowledgeable and better equipped to innovate than managers. Managers need to ask themselves, What's the use of hiring good people if they are kept shackled by bureaucracy? If managers expect employees to take risks, then managers must be willing to take a risk themselves in delegating responsibility and authority.

Figure 14.4 provides a checklist for some of the empowerment issues we considered.

## Innovation 22 (Leadership): Quality Week

### The objective

While the Excellence Councils (phases I and II) were effective at getting management to buy into quality, they left the technical folks at the lab largely out of the picture. Yet it was the technical people, not management, who would ultimately have to invent the technologies and process improvements that would get us to 10-fold quality improvement.

The lab needed a mechanism to both recognize and support innovation. Recognizing this need, the Innovation and Creativity Council (see Chap. 9) invented Quality Week.

### An innovative approach

Quality Week was our local version of National Quality Month. The idea was to have a week of activities all emphasizing quality. Quality Week demonstrated the lab's recognition of, commitment to, and expertise in innovation and quality activities.

At the lab, Quality Week kicked off with a recognition buffet lunch for all the inventors in the lab who had submitted patent applications. As authors of several patent applications ourselves, we can attest to the amount of work and rework that goes into a patent. Yet unless the patent is crucial to a product that has a ship date, patents are typically seen as something one does on one's own time. The overworked IBM attorneys often can provide only symbolic assistance. And so the programmer who feels she or he has invented something worthwhile—more often than not on personal time—is left to slog through the bureaucracy of getting the patent together.

Ideally, the patent process should be revamped—there would be more lawyers to help and more time for patents. But while you are waiting for the complete revamping of your organization's legal system, there is something simple and effective you can do. Start by recognizing the efforts and perseverance of the intrepid inventors who had a vision and stuck with it long enough to file a patent on behalf of the company. We held an inventors' reception and lunch with the general manager as one way to accomplish this.

The Innovation Fair was the highlight of the second day of Quality Week. The fair was an innovation itself—inspiration for this idea came from the science fairs that many high schools hold. The idea was to have booths concentrated in the cafeteria but also spread throughout the lab. At each booth, a programmer or team of programmers demonstrated an innovative project. Sometimes the project was related to an actual IBM project under development, but often programmers dug out tools and projects that they had been working on in their spare time.

Since all the top managers of the lab made the rounds of the booths, the fair was an opportunity to get exposure, and perhaps even funding, for a pet project. But much of the motivation was that the whole thing was just plain fun.

The Tools Expo was the more formal counterpart to the Innovation Fair. Most of the electronic tools that different groups had developed to automate the software development process were on display. In addition, IBM products and non-IBM tools that might be of interest to software developers were demonstrated.

The climax of Quality Week was Team Day—an opportunity to bring the entire lab together in the central plaza, to celebrate our successes, and to encourage teamwork. The highlight of Team Day was an all-hands meeting with the lab GM followed by a talk by three-time winner of the Iditarod Alaskan dog sled race, Susan Butcher.

### Costs, benefits, and risks

The costs of Quality Week were fairly substantial. Once again, time costs were the critical factor. For a lab of our size, just taking 1 day off to celebrate quality and teamwork costs over 6 person-years. That's enough resources for some small-niche companies to develop an entire product! Compared with this time cost, the speaker fees and other preparation expenses for Quality Week were insignificant.

Nevertheless, there are ways to keep out-of-pocket costs down. For example, booths for the Innovation Fair were assembled on a shoestring budget. A member of the steering committee went to K-Mart and bought 50 poster boards and some clamps. These materials, together with a page of suggestions on how to assemble a booth, were distributed to each booth presenter. The presenters handled getting their own booths ready, often after hours.

The benefits of Quality Week included celebrating our quality progress, recognizing innovation, and exposing people to many new ideas in a very efficient way. Comments from employees surveyed randomly 2 years after the first Quality Week were uniformly positive, although some pointed out the need for follow-up. Here are some samples:

"A quick way to show people what's available."

"Events like the Innovation Fair show that innovation can be fun. People really seem to enjoy this event."

"It was nice to see nontechnical areas able to participate in both [the Innovation and Tools Expo] fairs to show off some of the innovative things happening in their organizations."

"Management really needs to get behind some of the ideas presented during Quality Week, to promote new product ideas as well as new process ideas."

"While I do think these [fairs] are a good idea, we haven't translated much of what we saw into our day-to-day work."

As mentioned in some of the comments, one risk is that an event such as Quality Week can be seen as fun but of not much real value to the lab. In the awareness stage, an event that simply popularized quality would have been fine, but in the management stage, the organization should also derive some operational benefit. The key is follow-up. If there are good ideas that come out of the closet to be displayed in the innovation or tools fairs, then management has a responsibility to follow up and push these ideas forward.

A greater risk is that the event may not even be fun, particularly if it is overcontrolled by management. For example, the whole idea of the Innovation Fair was to have a grass roots, carnival-type atmosphere. We almost made the mistake early on of insisting that there be rigid, high standards for the appearance of the booths. However, when we realized that this attitude would keep some of our more creative, scruffy innovators away from the event, we canned the notion of pretty standards.

## Synergy

Quality Week is synergistic with most of the innovations in this book since all of them could have booths at events like the Tools Fair or Innovation Fair.

## Prerequisites

The main prerequisite for a successful Quality Week is a willingness on the part of the organization to participate. We gauged the enthusiasm at the lab by talking informally with people and lining up potential presenters for the Innovation Fair and Tools Fair in advance.

## Implementation advice

Quality Week at the lab was launched officially during the first week in October 1991 to correspond with National Quality Month. However, in retrospect, we probably should have launched it even sooner—at the beginning of the coping stage rather than at the end.

The week was coordinated by a team of five volunteers—one for each of the four events plus an overall coordinator reporting to management. The volunteers believed in the concept enough to take time from their other work activities. This was significant, because the whole spirit of the week hinged on a sense of enthusiasm and voluntary participation.

The inventors' reception was held outside on a sunny day and provided a chance for the general manager to personally recognize the patent producers at the lab.

The Innovation Fair, held the next day, had a carnival atmosphere complete with popcorn, balloons, and a road-rally event with a prize drawing for those who visited a certain number of booths. The presenters at the booths got a certain amount of logistical support, but it was essentially a grass roots operation. At a company that usually conjures up images of blue suits and starched white shirts, the Innovation Fair was a refreshing change. Best of the all, the turnout was incredible, with more than half of the lab catching some part of the fair.

In the preparation stages, it was difficult to judge how many people would want to participate and whether the spirit of the event would really catch on. But after a few presenters signed up for booths, word spread, and a sort of friendly competition emerged between departments. We ended up with over 30 booths.

The most frequent comment we got on surveys, which doubled as entries for a prize drawing, was that the Innovation Fair was fantastic but too short. We had scheduled it for only half a day, including a guest speaker on creativity. But people were not able to spend as much time as they would have liked at the booths.

The fair was a success in another sense as well. It allowed software developers to share ideas and tools with their peers. On more than one occasion it turned out that one department had invented a tool that another department needed but didn't know about. Exposure to high levels of management in an informal setting was also a win-win situation for programmers and their managers. Both groups saw new sides of their organizations.

Having said all these positive things, we must add a few caveats. First, everything depends on the attitude of the presenters and how they perceive

Ad/Cycle Change Control—tracks changes to product, process, etc.

AD/REQ—IBM's requirements tracking system for products and services

Boblingen Building Blocks—a code reuse scheme

BACHMAN tool (business partner)

CADREA tool (vendor)

CASE/390—CASE for large systems

CLEAR—library management system for product and system development

LLMS—*LAN library management system*

CODEPRTX—turns code into a reviewable text document

CRE—provides for software reuse across organizations

CVF/WITT/TASC2—testing system for system and application software

EAGLE SCAN—automatically analyzes assembler and PL/x applications

EASEL (vendor)

ECD—*edit/compile/debug* tool for PL/x

COSLD—*cooperative source level debugger* for PL/x on workstations

EXCELERATOR (vendor)

EXMAP—*execution time mapping*, a test-case coverage tool

ICOC—a corporate focal point group for tool integration at IBM

KNOWLEDGEWARE (vendor)

LOTUS FREELANCE/NOTES (vendor)

OOTC—group focused on internal use of object-oriented technology

OFFICE VISION TOOLS—IBM's office productivity tool set

PAS/2—project management that runs on OS/2

RDM—redistribution management tool set

REVUFILE—application to review documents (see Chap. 16)

SLD—*source level debug* for PL/x, PL/AS, and assembler applications

SMALLTALK (vendor)

TESTCOUNSELLOR—tells you if product is ready or needs more testing

The Integrated Reasoning Shell (TIRS)—expert system/AI development system

Tool Requirements Expo Collection Device—feedback collection tool

VICOM Source Debugger (VSD) for MVS

WITT—fast, flexible application testing on the workstation

**Figure 14.5** Sample tools at our Tools Fair.

the event. We purposely tried to make the event as grass roots as possible. In fact, senior management didn't even know about it until the plan was put together and 20 presenters had been lined up. Even then, we were careful not to let it turn into a propaganda event. The fair was really a way for the programmers to show off to each other and to management, and it was an excuse to have a good time. Because this was the spirit of the event, it was a tremendous success. Sometimes the best thing management can do to support innovation is to do nothing.

Whereas any innovation, no matter how scruffy or bizarre, was fair game for the Innovation Fair, the Tools Fair focused on demonstrations of existing internal tools and vendor tools that could aid productivity and quality. Figure 14.5 lists the tools demonstrated at one of our Tools Fairs.

Participants at the Tools Fair were able both to try out the tools and to submit requirements to the developers of the tools. So people became more aware of quality improvement tools, and the quality of the tools themselves was improved.

Quality Week ended on a strong upbeat with addresses by our general manager and guest speaker Susan Butcher. Butcher reinforced the theme of teamwork by pointing out that finishing the Iditarod, the annual dog sled race from Anchorage to Nome, Alaska, is really a matter of teamwork.

Winning the race, and sometimes just surviving, requires a tremendous amount of communication between a musher and her dogs. This communication has to be two-way.

Of her many stories, the one we like best reveals how listening to the lead dog saved her life. She was traveling over a frozen lake when the lead dog kept veering off the track. She kept jerking him back, somewhat puzzled because this dog was one of her best leaders.

When the lead dog veered off for the third time, Susan decided to just let him go his own way. It was a gut decision, born of thousands of grueling hours of training with her team of dogs. It was a decision based on trust, not reason. She said that she had no idea why the lead dog was behaving so strangely. On top of that, she was behind in the race and needed desperately to make up time. Yet she let the sled veer off track anyway.

Moments later a large section of the freshly frozen ice collapsed. She had come within inches of plunging herself, the dogs, and the entire sled into the freezing water. At $-20°$, that would have been fatal.

Something caused her to slack off the reins at the critical instant. And that something—call it leadership, trust, respect, love for her dogs, or whatever you like—is why, instead of freezing to death in the Alaskan wilderness, she was telling us this story on a sunny day in California and getting paid thousands of dollars for it. From our perspective, our money couldn't have been better spent.

Figure 14.6 lists some of the steps we went through in our implementation of Quality Week.

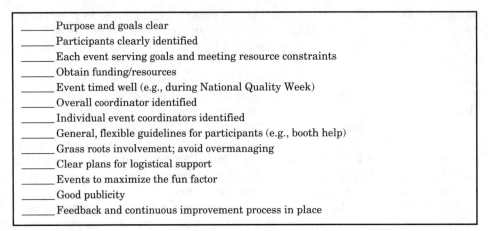

_____ Purpose and goals clear

_____ Participants clearly identified

_____ Each event serving goals and meeting resource constraints

_____ Obtain funding/resources

_____ Event timed well (e.g., during National Quality Week)

_____ Overall coordinator identified

_____ Individual event coordinators identified

_____ General, flexible guidelines for participants (e.g., booth help)

_____ Grass roots involvement; avoid overmanaging

_____ Clear plans for logistical support

_____ Events to maximize the fun factor

_____ Good publicity

_____ Feedback and continuous improvement process in place

**Figure 14.6**   Quality Week implementation checklist.

## Suggested Readings

Alster, J. and Gallo, H., eds. (1992) *Leadership and Empowerment for Total Quality*. Symposium sponsored by KPMG Peat Marwick. New York: Conference Board. *A popular report.*

Bauer, R. A., Collar, E., and Tang, V. (1992) *The SilverLake Project*. New York: Oxford University Press. *The inside story of the AS/400 including the strategic principles and techniques that made that product so successful.*

Byham, W. C., with Cox, J. (1990) *Zapp!: The Lightning of Empowerment: How to Improve Productivity, Quality, and Employee Satisfaction*. New York: Harmony Books. *A popular book on empowerment.*

DeMarco, T., and Lister, T. (1987) *Peopleware: Productive Projects and Teams*. New York: Dorset House. *A book on teams and people from authors with an extensive background in software.*

Fisher, K. (1993) *Leading Self-Directed Work Teams: A Guide to Developing New Team Leadership Skills*. New York: McGraw-Hill.

Frohman, A. L., and Johnson, L. W. (1993) *The Middle Management Challenge: Moving from Crisis to Empowerment*. New York: McGraw-Hill.

Gilbert, G. R., and Nelson, A. E. (1991) *Beyond Participative Management: Toward Total Employee Empowerment for Quality*. New York: Quorum Books.

Ketchum, L. D., and Trist, E. (1992) *All Teams Are Not Created Equal: How Employee Empowerment Really Works*. Newbury Park, CA: Sage Publications.

Metzger, P. W. (1987) *Managing Programming People*. Englewood Cliffs, NJ: Prentice-Hall. *Try this one for a less trendy view of what's involved in managing programmers.*

Mills, H. (1983) *Improving Software Productivity*. Englewood Cliffs, NJ: Prentice-Hall. *A collection of Mills' papers from the 1960s and 1970s that put programmer team organization into perspective.*

Mullender, A., and Ward, D. (1991) *Self-Directed Groupwork: Users Take Action for Empowerment*. London: Whiting & Birch.

Ohmae, K. (1982) *The Mind of a Strategist*. New York: McGraw-Hill. *Provides an excellent methodical approach to identify critical issues in the formulation of strategies.*

Porter, M. E. (1980) *Competitive Strategy: Techniques for Analyzing Industries and Competitors*. New York: Free Press. *A useful analytical approach that addresses the structure of an industry, competition, and competitive strategies.*

Porter, M. E. (1985) *Competitive Advantage: Creating and Sustaining Superior Performance*. New York: Free Press. *Develops the value chain as a pivotal element in the formulation of competitive strategies.*

Plunkett, L. C., and Fournier, R. (1991) *Participative Management: Implementing Empowerment*. New York: Wiley.

Stevenson, H. H., and Gumpert, D. E. (1985) "The Heart of Entrepreneurship," *Harvard Business Review*, 63(2): 85–94. *Describes the characteristics of entrepreneurial organizations; relevant to empowerment and grass roots efforts.*

Thomsett, R. (1990) "Effective Project Teams," *American Programmer,* pp. 25–35, July/August.

Toffler, A. (1981) *The Third Wave.* New York: Bantam Books. *A popular futurist outlines future trends as seen in 1981.*

Vogt, J. F., and Murrell, K. L. (1990) *Empowerment in Organizations: How to Spark Exceptional Performance.* San Diego: University Associates.

VonHippel, E. (1988) *Sources of Innovation.* New York: Oxford University Press. *Seminal study that convincingly demonstrates that innovation occurs most frequently outside the firm among users and suppliers.*

Wellins, R. S., Byham, W. C., and Wilson, J. M. (1991) *Empowered Teams: Creating Self-Directed Work Groups that Improve Quality, Productivity, and Participation.* San Francisco: Jossey-Bass. *A popular book on empowerment and self-directed work teams.*

# 15

# Creating a Self-Improving Software Development Process

The management stage requires a shift from reactive to proactive processes. For example, enhanced maintenance is a completely reactive approach because it waits for customers to find problems and then tries to solve them. Enhanced testing is better because the errors are found before they leave the lab, but such approaches are still reactive in that they focus on defect detection. Proactive approaches to quality improvement try to improve the development process itself to avoid injecting bugs into the software altogether. Such processes support the ultimate aim of building the best products in the marketplace.

Once a proactive process has been developed, it must be continuously improved if it is to retain its competitive advantage. The software industry changes so quickly that unless self-improvement mechanisms are built in from the start, processes can become obsolete almost before they are fully understood and implemented.

Table 15.1 summarizes three management-stage process innovations that helped us meet the challenge of creating proactive, continuously improving processes that lead to highly competitive products.

The defect prevention process (DPP) is a general and highly effective methodology for process improvement aimed at preventing defects in any type of process.

Process benchmarking is a method for accelerating process improvement by determining what the best-of-class processes in the industry are.

Finally, competitive analysis is a methodology for better understanding the products of the competition. Because the task of process improvement can be so overwhelming, it is important to prioritize efforts to address those areas in need of most improvement (compared with the competition) first.

**TABLE 15.1   Stage: Management / Food Group: Process / Themes: Shift from Correction to Prevention; Deployment of Benchmarking; Initiate Process Reengineering**

| Objective | Innovative approach | Pitfalls |
|---|---|---|
| Make the shift from correction to prevention model. | *Defect prevention process (DPP):* Root-cause analysis and process redesign<br>Deployment in cross-functional teams | Expect immediate, dramatic results<br>Failure to redesign processes<br>Using process to assign blame instead of learning |
| Are we world-class? | *Process benchmarking:* Benchmarking initiatives<br>Benchmark both competition *and* world-class processes | Limit benchmarking to competitors in your industry<br>Mindless deployment for improvements without preparation |
| Do our processes make us more competitive? | *Competitive analysis:* Help focus on building the right features/functions in products | Failure to identify target markets to provide context<br>Engage in "unactionable" analysis |

## Innovation 23 (Process): Defect Prevention Process

### The objective

The challenge at our lab was to prevent errors by improving the software development process. Because each development team had customized its development process, and because the Baldrige view of quality includes support processes as well as development processes, the requirement was for a general method that could be applied to any process. But the method had to be powerful, and it had to be easy to teach to developers and support staff with a wide variety of backgrounds.

### An innovative approach

We found a solution to all these constraints in a method called the *defect prevention process* (DPP). DPP starts from the premise that if an error has occurred, it will happen again *unless* we do something to stop it! DPP is a closed-loop method that detects errors, analyzes them, and then changes the process to prevent their recurrence. With DPP, you may make an error once. But if you are implementing the method correctly, the first time you make the mistake will be the last time.

This quick organizational learning can literally be a matter of life and death. For example, one of the DPP instructors at the lab (who happens to be married to a nurse) likes to point out that defects in the medical profession, such as giving the wrong medication to a patient, can be fatal. Software errors are usually not quite as catastrophic, but DPP can prevent them just as effectively. In fact, DPP is general enough to be tailored to almost any business.

While IBM Raleigh developed DPP primarily to prevent bugs in computer software, DPP is now used by IBM sites worldwide for a variety of purposes. For example, managers at our lab use DPP to prevent "bugs" in employee-manager communications. Companies outside of IBM including U.S. West,

GTE, and Motorola have expressed interest in DPP while Boeing has begun its own DPP training program.

One of the reasons for this growing interest may be the simplicity of DPP. In the early 1980s, DPP was known as the 1-2-3 process because practitioners followed three simple steps:

1.  Determine the cause of the defect.

2.  Determine what will prevent the defect from recurring in the future.

3.  Implement preventive actions.

Although the implementation is more sophisticated today, DPP is still simple enough to cross organizational boundaries and bridge the communication gap between management and technical professionals. IBM managers support DPP because they understand and use it themselves. Similarly, DPP provides a common framework and vocabulary that allow synergistic quality efforts between organizations.

DPP at the lab currently uses a two-team approach, supported by kickoff meetings and database tools. Figure 15.1 illustrates how these four major components of DPP interact:

1. A *causal analysis team* identifies defects and suggests actions that might prevent their recurrence. Members of this team should be the actual

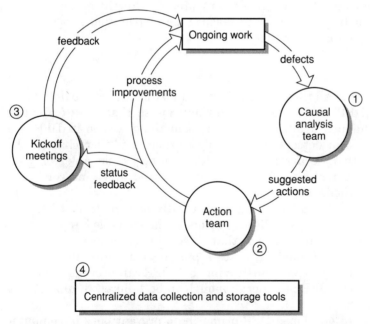

**Figure 15.1** How DPP works: (1) Causal analysis team identifies defects and suggests preventative action. (2) Action team prioritizes and implements process improvements. It provides feedback on the status of pending improvements. (3) Kickoff meetings provide feedback about process changes to the developers. (4) Database and data collection tools track the defects and suggested actions.

developers of the product or providers of the service. The members meet periodically to analyze problems that arise and to discuss prevention of their recurrence. Because these discussions work best in a completely open environment, some teams work with no managers present. Other teams say they prefer a management presence. However, all teams produce a list of preventive actions and suggested process improvements which are forwarded to an action team.

2. The *action team* prioritizes the suggested improvements and ensures their implementation. The action team needs authority and good communication skills, so management participation on this team is usually critical. Management support is especially helpful when suggested actions cross departmental or functional boundaries. Typically, several causal analysis teams feed a single action team, which handles actions for an entire organization.

3. *Stage kickoff meetings* support the teams. For staged development processes, kickoff meetings are held at the beginning of each stage to review any improvements in the development process. These meetings provide an opportunity for developers who have been doing causal analysis to get feedback from the action team on the status of recommended process changes. This review also ensures that any process changes or potential pitfalls in the upcoming development stage are fresh in everyone's mind.

4. Centralized data collection and storage tools make it easy to tell which defects occur repeatedly—even if they occur in different development groups. A database also ensures that suggested corrective actions are not lost, clarifying which items are outstanding for the action team.

## Costs, benefits, and risks

One of the nice things about DPP is that its cost is scalable. The minimal investment is the cost of 1 or 2 days of training for each member of a department or development group. Those people could begin using DPP immediately in their existing meetings to make those meetings more effective.

At the other extreme, you could conduct DPP training for the entire organization, hire a full-time DPP consultant, and create new meetings to perform DPP analysis on a wide variety of processes. A reasonable middle course would be to invest in DPP training, and perhaps a part-time consultant, for a pilot project. As the results begin to accrue from the initial pilot program (typically within 6 months to 1 year), the methodology can be extended to other parts of the organization.

The benefits of DPP include improving the efficiency of processes, making processes more customer-oriented, and fostering a shared vocabulary and approach for improving quality.

Groups that have implemented DPP cite fewer, more productive meetings. One external measure of DPP's success is that the Quality Assurance Institute has selected our DPP program for its Best of the Best Award three times in a row.

Empirical studies reported in an *IBM Systems Journal* article (May et al., 1990) concluded: "Reductions in defects by more than 50% [were] achieved at a cost of about one-half percent of the product area's resources." Additional benefits included savings in tester effort, increased esprit de corps, improved communications, and heightened quality awareness.

The most significant evidence of DPP's success is that from the humble beginnings of a few scattered pilot projects, it has spread to the point where over 45 percent of the work force has been trained in DPP, including 30 percent of the managers. The product development group for DB2 alone logged over 700 suggested process improvements. In a recent survey, here is what some users of DPP had to say:

"Integrate it into your process...it really works."

"It's easy to be overwhelmed by creating more actions than can be done. Make sure some action is taken, and don't expect to solve all problems. Focus."

"DPP has been outstanding in helping us understand and avoid future recurrences of problems."

"Excellent tool. Get cross-function participation. Follow through on action items."

"Make sure that DPP is incorporated into your process and it is not considered an add-on. For example, my old department did causal analysis on [errors] immediately following the code review for these items. You have the right people in the room, when the problem is fresh in their minds. This is a lot more efficient than asking people to go back after the fact and figure out why a problem occurred."

"Pick a few significant things that are worth spending time on, to get started."

Despite the mostly positive comments, there are some dangers in implementing DPP. First, it's important to remember that DPP is aimed at process improvement, and it typically takes at least one development cycle for the results of process improvements to show up. For this reason, DPP should be considered a long-term investment in quality, not a quick fix.

Second, the most common problem with DPP is that corrective actions are generated by the causal analysis team, but the action team is unable to implement the process changes quickly enough or effectively enough. The key to minimizing this risk is to make sure that management is fully committed to DPP and that the action teams are composed of capable, action-oriented individuals.

Third, DPP seems to work best when integrated into your process. If the process involves several departments, all should use DPP.

Finally, make sure that DPP is not used as a witch hunt—to blame people. The whole point is to improve the process.

## Synergy

DPP works well with any process or method that has a postmortem step, because DPP provides a mechanism for transforming postmortem results into process improvements.

Any kind of process documentation activity works well with DPP because the process documents can be kept current by regular DPP activity. Similarly, DPP complements process modeling activities.

DPP also works well with orthogonal defect classification (see Chap. 22), because it shows how to improve the areas that have been identified as trouble spots.

## Prerequisites

DPP works more easily when the processes to be improved are first understood and documented. Management support, especially with regard to the action team, is required.

## Implementation advice

Ironically, enthusiastic participation in DPP can create new challenges. Faced with a growing backlog of suggested process improvements, DB2's action team searched for ways to increase DPP's efficiency.

One effective strategy was to focus on eliminating several related defects with a single improvement. For example, many defects could be traced to communications problems between the development and service organizations which were physically separate from each other. The solution: Move the groups together and add rigor to the communications process with a checklist.

Other organizations at the lab tell similar stories. One manager describes how causal analysis led to innovations in overnight testing procedures, a new team structure where developers and testers work together to resolve customer complaints, and rotational assignments that allow developers more contact with customers. Another cites three new automated tools that were developed to improve the coding process.

One key to implementing a successful DPP is to have an experienced DPP practitioner and/or educator serve as a consultant to groups that are just beginning. Our internal DPP consultants perform a variety of services, listed in Fig. 15.2.

An effective consultant also helps keep the enthusiasm of the teams high and helps ensure that action teams are not overwhelmed with off-target action requests which waste time and dilute DPP's effectiveness.

You know you're on the right track with DPP if you see a majority of the positive signs listed in Fig. 15.3. On the other hand, Fig. 15.4 lists some common signs that something is wrong with DPP.

While DPP is implemented slightly differently from group to group within the lab, certain implementation issues cropped up consistently. Figure 15.5 addresses these issues by providing some sound general advice for the implementation of DPP.

Assistance with initial integration of DPP into existing meetings
Guidance on effective use of DPP techniques
Facilitation services for DPP meetings
Analysis of actions; product versus process focus
Feedback to DPP teams and management
Analysis of DPP progress and impediments
Measurement of DPP effectiveness versus costs

**Figure 15.2**   DPP consultant services.

Teams like it and don't want it to go
Significant problems coming in
Groups able to prioritize problems with consensus
Documentation base is growing or being revised
Actions getting done
Actions integrated into the process
All elements of DPP cycle executing
Management feels it's worth funding and rewarding with awards

**Figure 15.3**   DPP: Signs of progress.

People stop showing up at meetings
People come to meetings not sure what kinds of problems they should be discussing
Backlog of actions; not enough people to implement; problems prioritizing actions
Problems getting right resources for action team

**Figure 15.4**   DPP: Signs of trouble.

_____ Need for DPP clear
_____ Management commitment to DPP
_____ Obtain funding and resources for education and action items
_____ Management education in DPP
_____ Employee education in DPP
_____ Development process well understood and documented
_____ Doers with appropriate knowledge on the action team
_____ Focus on specific processes to improve
_____ Prioritize; avoid overwhelming the action team
_____ Implement DPP during stable organizational period
_____ Rotate assignments to action teams (3 to 6 months)
_____ Administrative support to log items, schedule meetings, etc.
_____ DPP done on DPP; continuous improvement process in place

**Figure 15.5**   DPP: General implementation checklist.

## Innovation 24 (Process): Process Benchmarking

### The objective

One of the most costly lessons a company can learn is that it is absolutely necessary to subject plans and processes to a reality check on a continual basis. The cost of failure in this area is threefold. You can end up reinventing processes that others have already discovered—an unnecessary expense. You can fail to push your competitive advantage when you are ahead, thus losing *potential* market share. Or worst of all, you can fail to realize that you are behind and settle into a bureaucratic complacency, thus guaranteeing you will lose *actual* market share.

Even if you realize that you need to change, without detailed knowledge of best-of-class competitors, it is easy to pour resources into problems which are easy to recognize but which may not be the most critical.

IBM made just about all the mistakes it is possible to make in this area, as evidenced by the company's dismal performance in the early 1990s, but three stand out as especially devastating. First, IBM had an ego problem. *We* had the best practices. *We* had the best products. If it wasn't invented at *IBM,* then it couldn't possibly be any good.

Second, when we did look outside the company, we tended to look at only competitors in the same businesses we were in. In truth, we were doing well in those businesses. The problem was that the whole market structure was shifting. Our studies showed that we had the nicest berth on the *Titanic.* What the studies failed to show was that the entire ship was going down.

Finally, like most of the industry, when we compared ourselves with others, we tended to compare our products, not the processes that led to the development of these products. The problem, of course, is that in a rapidly changing industry, it is one's *capacity* to develop new products of high quality in a timely fashion, not one's current product set, that is the best predictor of success.

The challenge was to come up with a method that allowed us to leverage the knowledge of other companies to help us improve our processes as quickly and with as little cost as possible. When we looked outside IBM at companies like Xerox and AT&T, we discovered that others already had a name for what we were looking for—*process benchmarking.* So we began by borrowing what was already out there and evolved our own formula, described below.

### An innovative approach

The word *benchmark* brings to mind *Consumer Reports*–style evaluations that show which processor can crunch the most numbers or whose spreadsheet is the easiest to use. But the term *benchmark* can refer to processes as well as products. In fact, process benchmarking is probably the more important type of comparison for an organization trying to improve its quality levels. Figure 15.6 lists three definitions of benchmarking that appeared in our quality publication, *Innovations,* and that capture the spirit of what we mean.

"Benchmarking is the continuous process of measuring products, services and processes against the toughest competitors or those companies recognized as industry leaders."—*Xerox CEO David Kearns*

"Benchmarking is the search for industry best practices that lead to superior performance."—*Robert C. Camp, Benchmarking*

"[Benchmarking is] the continuous process of analyzing the best practices in the world for the purpose of establishing and validating process goals and objectives leading to world-class levels of achievement."—*IBM definition*

**Figure 15.6**   Three definitions of benchmarking.

With process benchmarks, what you are looking for is knowledge about how the best organizations develop their products, relate to their customers and suppliers, and ensure quality. One advantage of this process focus is that it frees you to look beyond your immediate industry to find the very best practices.

For example, when we wanted to benchmark our service practices, we contacted L. L. Bean because that company has a reputation of being the best in customer service. When we were interested in benchmarking processes more specific to software development, we chose Hewlett-Packard because of both its outstanding reputation and its proximity to Silicon Valley.

Benchmarking is not a one-shot deal. It is an ongoing process, a corporate habit of comparing your organization continually to the best organizations that you can find.

Partly to demonstrate its long-term commitment to benchmarking, our lab hosted IBM's Fourth Worldwide Benchmarking Conference in April 1992. The conference included 174 attendees representing 55 IBM locations, 9 countries, and 4 visiting companies. Two of the visiting companies were winners of the Malcolm Baldrige Quality Award. Since then, the lab has participated in a wide range of benchmarking efforts.

The partnership idea is critical to successful benchmarking. In contrast to competitive understanding where your competitors may not even be aware that you are evaluating their products or services, benchmarking is a cooperative process in which both partners share information about their processes. Often the sharing extends to the sharing of metrics and more general experiences as well.

Legal concerns can be solved usually with simple nondisclosure agreements and/or agreements that no material disclosed during the benchmarking sessions will be of a confidential nature. However, another option, in cases where you may be uncomfortable with benchmarking competitors, is to conduct internal benchmarks against other divisions, or organizations, within your own company.

For example, one IBM group came to our benchmarking coordinator because it knew its processes were inefficient and conflict-ridden. The group members were somewhat skeptical of the whole process at first but ended up becoming strong advocates of benchmarking—so much so that they eventually involved six other IBM sites in an internal benchmark and are now conducting external benchmarks.

## Costs, benefits, and risks

The cost of benchmarking is highly variable depending upon whether the benchmarks are internal or external, whether travel is involved, and whether the benchmarking process is well established or not. We have one full-time benchmarking coordinator who works on a team with employees from the group desiring the benchmark for a period of 2 to 6 months per project. Typically small teams of two to four people work best, and the time required of each team member might average 5 to 10 hours per week.

These estimates yield an average cost of 1 to 2 person-months for an internal benchmark and 2 to 4 person-months for an external benchmark. The travel costs and overhead tend to be higher for external benchmarks, although there are some strategies for reducing these costs.

For example, when we sought approval to benchmark Hewlett-Packard in Colorado, we also checked to see if we could do the same thing locally with Hewlett-Packard in Palo Alto, California. Video conferences and teleconferences are other ways to keep travel expenses down, especially for internal benchmarks. Finally, it is often unnecessary for the entire benchmark team to travel to the external location. Our benchmarking coordinator often prepares one member of the team who does the actual travel. Afterward, the entire team discusses what was learned and how to implement changes to existing processes.

As a final note on cost, we were particularly impressed with the remarks of our benchmarking coordinator, Cleo Lepori-Costello, when we first approached her on this subject:

> Cost? What did it cost for IBM not to look outward when Apple started producing the products they began producing? It cost us market, it cost us customers, it cost ideas that had to be reinvented because we were so busy looking inward that we missed all kinds of developments and breakthroughs. What is the hidden cost of ignoring the ideas that are breaking all around us? These hidden costs are what IBM should be concerned about. And my guess is that they are quite high.

The main benefit of process benchmarking is that it provides a way to escape the hidden costs described above. It is much cheaper to benchmark the process leader in a given area than to try to invent the best-of-breed process yourself. Benchmarking also allows much more rapid improvement than the invent-your-own-process approach. In a rapidly changing industry, this time factor can provide a critical competitive advantage.

Benchmarking can focus process innovation efforts where they are most needed. When a company becomes too internally focused, it is easy to forget that it is not absolute merit, but merit relative to competitors, that determines success in the marketplace. Benchmarking can help set investment priorities according to which process areas lag behind the competition.

It is worth noting that approximately 25 percent of the points in the Malcolm Baldrige criteria are directly related to benchmarking. It is probably not overstating the case to say that an organization cannot reach world-class quality levels without some sort of benchmarking process.

Here are some of the comments from a lab-wide survey that asked about the value of benchmarking:

"Each department should go through this process once just to get an idea of where they are with [regard to] the rest of the world....We found out that we were better than most sites within IBM. This prompted us to look into benchmarking with our IBM partners and companies external to IBM."

"I think benchmarking is the right way to evaluate yourself against the best, and to get critical success factors for improving your own process."

"The cost for any benchmarking effort is very high. I am sure there are so many things we can benchmark; however, we have to prioritize benchmarking studies to fit our critical needs first."

"Emphasize that the goal of benchmarking is not just to compare yourself to other people, but to take actions to improve your process if the other group is doing something better. Too often I hear people refer to benchmarking as if it only meant going out to study other people's processes. There is not enough emphasis on (1) What did you learn after doing the benchmark? (2) What (if anything) will you do differently as a result of the benchmark? (3) What (if anything) did you learn that we are doing right and should continue to do?"

One of the risks in conducting benchmarking activities is overbenchmarking. Just as customers tire of never-ending customer satisfaction surveys, best-of-breed companies may not welcome the twelfth invitation to participate in a benchmarking study as readily as they did the first. We encountered this situation with L. L. Bean—the poor company was being bombarded with requests for benchmarking at the time that we initiated our request.

There are two measures that can minimize the risk of overbenchmarking. First, make sure that there is coordinated effort on the part of the company as a whole. If one organization is benchmarking company X, your organization can get that report and probably spend your effort better by benchmarking company Y.

Second, look for companies that have established programs for sharing information. For example, all winners of the Baldrige Award agree, by accepting the award, to share their knowledge with other companies. So past Baldrige Award winners are often good benchmarking candidates.

## Synergy

Competitive analysis, on-line reviews, process modeling and process documentation efforts, and ISO 9000 are all areas that are synergistic with process benchmarking.

## Prerequisites

There are no formal prerequisites for benchmarking. But we should point out that the "Best Practices Report" of the American Society for Quality Control (ASQC) recommends that benchmarking not be attempted until the company has reached a significant degree of quality maturity. Benchmarking too early, the report argues, could discourage the organization by setting the bar too high at a time when fundamentals need attention.

Our own view is that benchmarking is most useful once processes have been understood and documented. Some education about benchmarking methods can also be helpful.

## Implementation advice

Our lab's benchmarking process requires a partnership between two principals in the organization: the benchmarking expert or coordinator and the process owner.

The benchmarking coordinator needs a basic understanding of the process that is to be improved and expertise in the area of process documentation. The process owner is the person in the organization with primary responsibility for updating and documenting the particular process to be improved. Figure 15.7 illustrates the roles of these two principals in the benchmarking process.

The benchmarking process itself consists of four major stages: organization and planning, data collection, analysis, and implementation. Figure 15.8 presents more detail on each of these stages in a process flow diagram.

The benchmarking process begins with an initial period of research and planning. During this time the benchmarking coordinator works with the

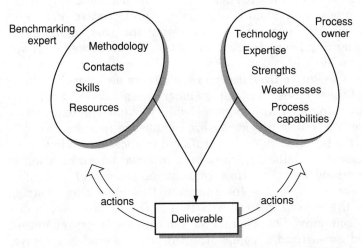

**Figure 15.7**  Anatomy of benchmarking deployment. (*Courtesy of IBM*)

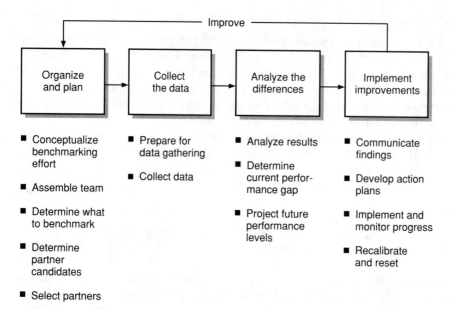

Figure 15.8  Our benchmarking process. (*Courtesy of IBM*)

process owner to define the goals and scope of the effort and to select potential internal and external benchmarking partners. The coordinator generally assists in writing a brief proposal that identifies which aspects of a process are to be benchmarked.

In terms of assembling the benchmarking team, our experience has been that less is usually more. Some of our best benchmarking experiences involved only the coordinator, the process owner, and a single contact at another company. Small teams foster personal relationships between individuals at the two companies or sites participating in the benchmark activity. Small teams also promote individual responsibility and initiative. For these same reasons, benchmarking has worked very well at the group and department levels. Benchmarking is one innovation that works quite well, perhaps even best, on a small scale.

Conversely, some of the more troublesome benchmarks have involved larger teams. In some of these cases, the team members were not really committed but saw benchmarking as a way to gain visibility. When the team members retired or moved on to new projects before completing their benchmarking responsibilities, the benchmark projects suffered unnecessary delays.

IBM maintains computer bulletin boards and internal documentation of prospective benchmarking partners. However, outside sources of this information also exist. For example, the International Benchmarking Clearing House, a service of the American Productivity and Quality Center, is one source open to any company. The Council for Continuous Improvement—a Silicon Valley–based consortium of companies dedicated to quality improvement—is another source of benchmarking leads. Other sources include data-

TABLE 15.2    World-Class Benchmarking Candidates

| Function | Company |
| --- | --- |
| Benchmarking | Xerox |
| | Motorola |
| | Ford |
| | Florida Power & Light |
| | IBM/Rochester |
| | DEC |
| Billing and collection | American Express |
| | MCI |
| Customer focus | Xerox |
| | GE (plastics) |
| | Westinghouse (furniture systems) |
| Design for manufacturing assembly | Motorola |
| | DEC |
| | NCR |
| Employee suggestions | Millikin |
| | Dow Chemical |
| | Toyota |
| Empowerment | Millikin |
| | Honda of America |
| Flexible manufacturing | Allen-Bradley/Milwaukee |
| | Motorola/Boynton Beach |
| | Baldor Electric |
| Industrial design | Black & Decker (household products) |
| | Braun |
| | Herman Miller |
| Leadership | GE: Jack Welch |
| | Hanover Insurance: Bill O'Brien |
| | Manco Inc.: Jack Kahl |
| Marketing | Procter & Gamble |
| Quality process | Florida Power & Light |
| | Toyota |
| | IBM/Rochester |
| Quick changeovers | United Electric Controls |
| | Dana Corp./Minneapolis |
| | Johnson Controls/Milwaukee |
| R&D | AT&T |
| | Hewlett-Packard |
| | Shell Oil |
| Self-directed work team | Corning/SCC plant |
| | Physio Control |
| | Toledo Scale |
| Supplier management | Levi Strauss |
| | Motorola |
| | Xerox |
| | Ford |
| | 3M |
| | Bose Corp. |
| Total productive maintenance | Tennessee Eastman |
| Training | Square D |
| Waste minimization | 3M |
| | Dow Chemical |

SOURCE: Adapted from *Industry Week,* July 15, 1991, p. 16.

_____ Need and "customers" for process benchmarking clear
_____ Obtaining funding and resources
_____ Benchmarking education for team
_____ Determining benchmarking goals and process
_____ Identifying scope and developing benchmarking questionnaire
_____ Identifying key contact in group desiring benchmark
_____ Identifying best-of-class benchmarking partners
_____ Researching local and low-cost benchmarking options
_____ Objectives of benchmark being communicated to partners
_____ Gathering data from benchmark
_____ Analyzing data
_____ Recommendations being distributed to group requesting benchmark
_____ Follow up on recommendations
_____ Follow up with benchmark partners
_____ Feedback and continuous improvement process in place

**Figure 15.9**   Process benchmarking implementation checklist.

bases with company information (e.g., Dun & Bradstreet, Nexis, Lexis, FIND-EX, Compustat), industry analysts, corporate customers and suppliers, business books and newsletters, business school reports and professors, consultants, and lists of quality award winners (e.g., Baldrige Award winners).

Even popular magazines can be sources of benchmarking partners. For example, Table 15.2 shows an updated version of a list of some world-class benchmarking candidates that appeared in *Industry Week* in 1991.

Keys to successful benchmarks include putting in work up front to make sure that the process runs smoothly and staying on top of participants. For example, clearly specifying in the proposal exactly what each participant might expect to gain out of the benchmarking activity can save a lot of headaches in the long run. And taking action immediately once a partner has agreed to participate sets an action-oriented tone that usually speeds up the benchmarking process.

However, sometimes, running a top-notch benchmarking program requires a pinch of ingenuity. When our coordinator thought she was getting more lip service than action, she instituted the BBC—Benchmarking Breakfast Club. Now key managers are invited to breakfast to lay out concrete plans for benchmarking activities. So far, it seems to be working.

Finally, for those interested in benchmarking the benchmarkers, IBM, Xerox, AT&T, and DEC are all reputed to have best-of-breed processes for benchmarking. Figure 15.9 presents our implementation checklist for process benchmarking.

## Innovation 25 (Process): Analysis of the Competition

"If you know your enemy and know yourself, you need not fear the outcome of a hundred battles."—*Sun Tzu, Chinese General, 500 B.C.*

## The objective

One of the most difficult challenges facing any software company today lies in determining which products to develop and where to invest resources. In the early 1980s, IBM was still primarily a technology-driven company. That is, we poured millions of dollars into research and development and into hiring the best people we could find. When these people came up with a good product idea, that's what we produced.

Partly because the products were good and partly because our customers didn't have much choice, we sold a lot of hardware and software. However, increased competition now requires software companies to produce not only high-quality products, but also products that meet specific market needs better than the competition. IBM's recognition of this shift in the marketplace was captured in the phrase heard so often in the late 1980s: *market-driven quality.*

While meeting market needs must be considered part of quality, unfortunately how to do this was less clear.

One place to start is to understand what your competition is doing, and then plan to beat them. This approach is reflected in the Malcolm Baldrige Quality Award criteria, which continually ask about comparisons with competitors and which have a 70-point item devoted entirely to customer satisfaction comparison with competitors (see Chap. 2). The approach is also reflected in our leadership initiative of strategic focus.

We had always done some comparisons on an informal basis. In fact, a certain amount of competitive comparison and market understanding is a prerequisite for making the business case for a new product. However, the new challenge was to develop a much broader, more systematic, and more effective approach to understanding the competition which could help drive our product planning strategy and process.

## An innovative approach

Competitive analysis at our lab is based on three key principles: market assessment, competitive product evaluation, and early involvement.

Market assessment addresses these questions: Where do we want to compete? What do our customers need? What do they want? What competitive products should we be looking at?

Market segmentation—division of the marketplace into categories of customers—is probably the single most important part of assessing the market.

There are many ways to segment a market. A standard approach has been to use industry "SIC" codes. But we have also invented our own market segment categories, with names like *technological wizards* or *medium-size followers*, reflecting the propensity of different groups to incorporate new technology into their businesses.

The particular way you segment the market is less important than the fact that these segments create a context for understanding what your customers and your competitors are doing at a strategic level. Without a clear under-standing of the overall marketplace, understanding the competition quickly degenerates to a set of arbitrary comparisons between products. Some of these comparisons might be relevant and informative, but others could be unimportant and misleading.

Another important benefit of market segmentation is that it provides a way to measure progress, in terms of market share from year to year. If last year 17 percent of the technological wizard market segment bought your product and this year 25 percent bought it, you are making progress (assuming you have chosen to pursue that segment). But this kind of year-to-year tracking is possible only if you have a market segmentation that you use consistently.

The difference between companies that have done market assessment work and companies that haven't is the difference between navigating with a map and navigating solely by gut feeling. It's a simple matter of competitive advantage. If everyone else has a map and you don't, you're probably going to be left behind. But if you develop the map first, you have a good chance of leading the competition in your chosen market segments.

Market assessment sets the stage for effective application of the principle of *competitive evaluation*. The principle is simple: Look at what your competi-tion is doing. But to be maximally effective, there should be a process for doing this.

The competitive evaluation process answers the questions How should we evaluate our competitors' products? and Who should do the evaluating? Knowing that we want to go for Y percent market share in segment X allows us to choose which of our competitors' products we need to evaluate.

The actual evaluations are conducted both by using the products and by reading reports of evaluations by independent parties (e.g., magazine com-parison articles).

A competitive evaluation group performs broad-scope evaluations of com-petitive products. For example, the group might look at the range of function offered by a product. But if it becomes necessary to understand the function of a competitor's product at a deeper, more technical level, developers with expertise in the relevant area are asked to help with the evaluation.

Finally, there remains the question of when the competitive evaluations should be performed. The principle of *early involvement* says that the earlier such competitive evaluations are performed, the better. The rationale is much the same as that used to argue for early test involvement (Chap. 11). It is much more efficient to understand the marketplace and the competition before the product is built than to try to patch the product and make it more competitive later in the development cycle. However, competitive evaluation must also be an ongoing process, especially since the software market changes so rapidly.

For example, in the application development and CASE arenas, new prod-ucts appear from competitors almost weekly. The manager of Workstation Interactive Test Tool (one of our CASE products) insists that each of his developers play with competitive products on a regular basis. It's the only way to get a good feeling for what the competition is doing in an exploding market.

## Costs, benefits, and risks

The market segmentation and strategy work that is so necessary to focus the competitive evaluations themselves is done by various planning groups at the lab. Because our organization is large and the strategy work is seen as vital, we devote a significant amount of resources to these planning efforts. Smaller organizations might be able to get much of the same benefit by using existing market research materials from consulting or market research firms. The cost here will depend primarily on the scope and depth of the effort (e.g., how many markets are involved and the level of detail required for each).

Factors affecting the cost of the actual competitive evaluations themselves include how you choose to perform your evaluations, how many competitors you have, and who is expected to perform the evaluations. A low-cost approach is to use "paper evaluations."

For example, we have gotten much of our information about competitors from talking to consultants, from going to conferences, from brochures we obtain, and from articles that are published. However, our best competitive information came from our customers. They were not shy about telling us where we were short of the mark and who was better.

If you feel that you need more detail, the best way to get it is to actually use the competition's products. The problem here is that the cost goes up in proportion to the number of competitors—especially if special hardware is involved.

In general, it will be cheaper to perform competitive evaluations in-house rather than subcontracting them. But if you feel you need an outside opinion or if you simply cannot spare developers' time, vending is an option. Note the advantage of having a developer actually use a competitor's product: It provides a very concrete point of comparison. It's a lot easier to know whether your product measures up if you've actually used the competition's product.

The benefits are basic but critically important. If you don't know the competition, you don't know how to effectively allocate your development effort to produce a successful product. You could have high-quality development processes, great customer-requirements information, highly efficient programming tools, and a terrific marketing force—all this—and still fail, simply because the competition came out with a better product sooner.

In a lab-wide survey, the value of competitive analysis was unquestioned. Comment after comment emphasized the need for understanding the competition. However, there were also some concerns with how it should be carried out. Here are some sample comments:

"You can't be competitive without knowing what's out there."

"You can't tell if you have a valuable product or service unless you look at what somebody else has."

"You can't expect to be best of breed if you do not know what else is out there. [The] Team has to have the initiative to do this, i.e., read the trade press, go to conferences, make the extra effort to look at other tools. I question whether a [separate] competitive analysis [group] can do this work effectively across a variety of products because you really need to have an in-depth technical understanding to really assess the strengths and weaknesses."

"Process still needs more rigor and better follow-up to know that we're taking advantage of what we learn."

"Need to be sensitive to intellectual property issues with regard to obtaining and doing hands-on evaluation of competitive products, such as licensing terms and conditions."

This last comment raises an interesting risk in conducting hands-on competitive analyses. For a long time IBM took the ultraconservative position that we would not even bring competitive products into the workplace for fear of "contamination." Essentially what this meant was that IBM didn't want to be sued if some developer happened to be influenced by the design of a competitive product that she was using.

In today's environment—when you can put Microsoft Windows and a MacIntosh side by side and hardly tell the difference—such an attitude seems positively ludicrous. But it dates back to an era when IBM was viewed as a potential monopoly player in the computer industry and was plagued with antitrust suits.

Because most products are now released OCO (object code only), the concern over contamination is not as great as it once was. Still, certain safeguards can be built into a competitive evaluation center which your legal counsel can probably help with.

A different kind of risk is the risk that the people conducting the evaluation may not possess the necessary technical expertise, as suggested in one of the comments. The lab's strategy for minimizing this risk has been to try to conduct both less technical "breadth" evaluations and more technical "depth" evaluations. The breadth evaluations are conducted by the competitive evaluation department. The more technical depth evaluations depend upon experts in the different product areas.

## Synergy

Conjoint analysis and other techniques for gathering customer requirements are synergistic with understanding the competition. Similarly, any process related to planning, strategy, and customer satisfaction management will probably have a competitive understanding aspect.

## Prerequisites

A product planning process is a prerequisite for effective use of competitive understanding information.

## Implementation advice

One of the recurring questions at the lab was, "Who is going to own the competitive understanding mission?" The right answer is: "Everyone." The problem with that answer is that it encourages diffusion of responsibility—the notion that if everyone is accountable, no one is accountable.

At the lab, a small group of people is held accountable for knowing what specific competitors are doing and what their strengths and weaknesses are. Still, these competitive understanding team members cannot possibly become experts on the hundreds of competitive products that exist. At best, they can provide general information about those competitive products, with detailed evaluations of a few that fall within their range of technical expertise.

This situation is not a function of the organizational infrastructure at the lab. It simply reflects the complexity of the marketplace. For that reason, unless your products are aimed at an extremely narrow-niche market, everyone will probably have to take some responsibility for competitive understanding in your organization, too.

That doesn't mean everyone has to run around conducting head-to-head, hands-on evaluations. It does mean that everyone needs to maintain a sensitivity to what competitors are doing. And if expertise is needed to understand a particular competitive product, that expertise should be made available.

In choosing members for a small, organization-wide team, it is important to choose people with good analytical skills. For example, we have a market research library at the lab, but all the literature in the world is useless if you lack the research and analytical skills to assemble it into a meaningful picture of the competition. The goal of team members should be to become good enough at competitive understanding that other areas (or outside companies) are willing to pay for that expertise.

Courage and honesty are two other requirements for team members. Those conducting the competitive understanding cannot be afraid to tell the truth. If the competition is really better, the product planners and developers need to hear that. What you want are messengers who will report what they see, whether they are shot at or not.

Finally, two caveats. The first caveat is that it takes time for the benefits of competitive understanding to become apparent. We began new market segmentation efforts in earnest in 1991, but the full effect of these efforts, on our investment decisions and on our products, may not be apparent until 1996.

The second caveat is that understanding the competition is not a substitute for innovation. Once you know what your competitors are doing, you still face the challenge of invention. Understanding the competition can bring you to the boundaries of the known and point you in the right direction, but to go beyond still takes a creative leap.

Figure 15.10 presents some of our implementation steps for competitive analysis.

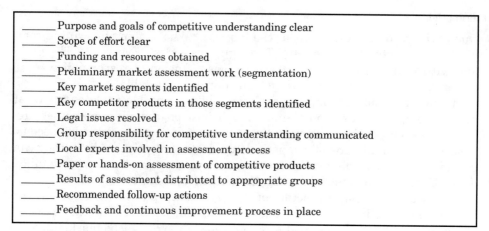

_____ Purpose and goals of competitive understanding clear
_____ Scope of effort clear
_____ Funding and resources obtained
_____ Preliminary market assessment work (segmentation)
_____ Key market segments identified
_____ Key competitor products in those segments identified
_____ Legal issues resolved
_____ Group responsibility for competitive understanding communicated
_____ Local experts involved in assessment process
_____ Paper or hands-on assessment of competitive products
_____ Results of assessment distributed to appropriate groups
_____ Recommended follow-up actions
_____ Feedback and continuous improvement process in place

**Figure 15.10**   Competitive analysis implementation checklist.

## Suggested Readings

"The Benchmarking Bandwagon," *Quality Progress,* January 1991, pp. 19–24.

Camp, R. C. (1989) *Benchmarking: The Search for Industry Best Practices that Lead to Superior Performance,* White Plains, NY: Quality Resources. *Our lab's benchmarking coordinator highly recommends this book.*

Dunn, R., and Ullman, R. (1982) *Quality Assurance for Computer Software.* New York: McGraw-Hill. *A good book that has withstood the test of time; includes a chapter on defect prevention.*

Gale, J. L., Tirso, J. R., and Burchfield, C. A. (1990) "Implementing the Defect Prevention Process in the MVS Interactive Programming Organization," *IBM Systems Journal,* 29(1): 33–43. *Documents experiences at IBM putting defect prevention process theories into action.*

Jones, C. L. (1985) "A Process-Integrated Approach to Defect Prevention," *IBM Systems Journal,* 24(2): 150–167. *One of the early papers on causal analysis—the method that later evolved into DPP.*

Kitson, D. H., and Masters, S. (1992) *Analysis of SEI Software Process Assessment Results 1987–1991,* CMU/SEI Technical Report, CMU/SEI-92-TR-24. *Reports the process maturity of 59 government and industry sites that were assessed using SEI's process maturity model—useful for process comparisons.*

Mays, R. G., Jones, C. L., Holloway, G. J., and Studinski, D. P. (1990) "Experiences with Defect Prevention," *IBM Systems Journal,* 29(1): 4–32. *Explains DPP and presents data on DPP's effectiveness from 6 years' worth of implementation experience.*

Phillips, R. T. (1986) "An Approach to Software Causal Analysis and Defect Extinction," *IEEE Globecom '86,* 1(12): 412–416.

Sirkin, H., and Stalk, Jr., G. (1990) "Fix the Process Not the Problem," *Harvard Business Review,* pp. 26–33, July/August. *Good case study of quality improvement at a paper mill that focuses on process improvement.*

Stevick, G. E. (1990) "Preventing Process Problems," *Quality Progress,* pp. 67–73, September.

Zimmer, B. (1989) "Software Quality and Productivity Analysis at Hewlett-Packard," *Proceedings of COMPSAC '89,* pp. 628–632, September 20–22. *This paper may be useful in terms of understanding the kind of quality-related information that benchmarking partners might share.*

For more information about benchmarking, contact the Council for Continuous Improvement: 1-408 441-7716.

# 16

# Computerizing Teamwork

As we stoked the fires of innovation in the management stage, new ideas began boiling up from the creative imaginations of the lab's developers. These ideas tended to condense around a few core challenges that faced the lab, distilling into several inventions that promised to revolutionize the way we developed software.

Table 16.1 summarizes two of these innovations—one invented at our lab, the other an IBM product. Some background helps put these two innovations in perspective. First, consider that many of our products already had a base of millions of lines of code and that this base had to be made upwardly compatible with each new release. Add to that constantly changing customer requirements and demands for unprecedented levels of function, and you had a quality assurer's nightmare.

Whatever the answers to this challenge might be, it was clear that the old model of one programmer, working in isolation on his or her piece of code, wasn't going to work. The complexity of possible interactions between modules in these large programs was far too great for a single mind to model reliably. Development had to become much more of a team activity.

Ironically, this lone programmer model was embedded in the very architecture of the buildings at our lab's site. The lab was composed of eight distinct towers which held, in turn, a rabbit warren of individual offices, each with a

**TABLE 16.1  Stage: Management / Food Group: Technology / Themes: Technology Deployment for Improvements in Development Productivity, Cross-Functional Integration, Teamwork**

| Objectives | Innovative approach | Pitfalls |
|---|---|---|
| Capture (comprehensively) key decisions and action plans of complex cross-functional meetings | Computer support team work spaces <br> Knowledge mining centers (KMC) <br> Real-time, multimedia, computer, and communications assisted meeting rooms | Allowing initial start-up expenses to inhibit trying <br> Lack of courage; skepticism <br> Continue to rely on bureaucratic processes |
| Improve three Ps: productivity, participation, prioritization | Electronic meetings <br> TeamFocus™ <br> Nonverbal, computer and message-based anonymous meeting format | Lack of preparation prior to meetings <br> Using unskilled moderator |

door that could be closed against the world. The tower layout fostered sharp divisions between products (e.g., IMS was in one tower, DB2 in another), while individual offices meant that developers had to seek out interaction with their peers.

The architectural solution might have been to redesign the lab with cubicles rather than offices (something we may still do someday). However, as might be expected of a software development lab, our solution was to fix it with software. Specifically, we adopted two new technologies for computerizing teamwork. One was a homegrown solution that has exploded from an idea in a couple of programmers' brains to become the most pervasive innovation at the lab, used by everyone from programmers to planners to secretaries to the general manager. The other was a technology for holding electronic meetings that was so effective that IBM now markets it as a product.

## Innovation 26 (Tools): Computer-Supported Team Work Spaces

### The objective

The idea for building computer-supported team work spaces evolved from a very specific development problem at the lab. The DB2 relational database product had a requirement to add a feature called *referential integrity*. This feature was complex enough that it required the coordination of a team of programmers who would write and test approximately 60,000 lines of new code. This new code had potential interactions with much of the existing code base—a total of 1.5 million lines of code.

Given the complexity of the task, teamwork became a critical priority. The developers soon found that most of their time was being spent in meetings, discussing computer printouts, making notes, and shuffling a lot of paper. Finally, they would leave a meeting to work on their separate pieces of code. In the next meeting, they would discover that they had failed to communicate or understand some critical piece of information. Frustrated, they would try to hack out the code dependency issues one more time.

Progress was being made during the meetings, but the pace was maddeningly slow. Two of the developers decided that there had to be a way to use computer technology to make the meetings more effective. From this conviction, the first computer-supported team work space, known locally as a *knowledge mining center,* was born.

Today knowledge mining centers (KMCs) are ubiquitous at the lab and are used for a wide range of meetings. The consensus at the lab is that if you have a problem that requires people to get together and exchange information, the problem can probably be solved better by using a knowledge mining center.

### An innovative approach

In its simplest form, a KMC consists of a comfortable meeting room, a computer connected to relevant information, and a way to project the computer screen on the wall. When the right people meet in this environment, they can reach consensus and capture solutions to problems on-line in real time. If more information is needed, the group uses the computer (connected to databases), phone, fax, or video technology to access the information and reach a decision.

Figure 16.1 illustrates these basic concepts, but neither the figure nor the description does justice to what happens when the right group of people assemble in the room and start working as a team.

In the case of the DB2 development team, the code was brought up on the computer and projected on a large wall screen for the entire group to see. Rather than flipping through printouts and having each team member make his or her own notes, notes and changes were made on-line in real time. If someone made a comment or suggestion, it was captured immediately for all to see. This not only encouraged participation but also reduced misunderstandings, because everyone could see immediately the exact comments or code changes that were being made.

Productivity increased because KMCs eliminated the old method of talk, separate note taking, off-line data entry, duplication of hard copy, and more talk. In KMCs, the code wasn't just discussed. It was changed, documented, annotated, reviewed, and sometimes actually run. When people left the meeting, everyone knew that real work had been done, because everyone had seen the changes to the code being made on the huge projection screen.

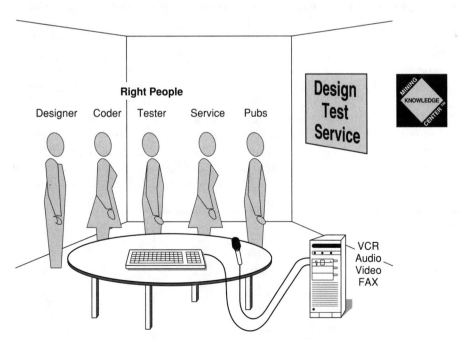

**Figure 16.1**  Basic concepts of the knowledge mining center. The essential concepts are (1) a computer-supported collaborative work space, (2) the right people in the right place at the right time, (3) capture of group consensus, (4) effective use of workforce and time, and (5) documentation of results.

Quality increased because the work done in the KMC was validated by all the minds in the room, not just by a single programmer who might not know all the ramifications of a code change.

Finally, there was an unexpected additional benefit. People seemed more enthusiastic and more ready to participate in meetings that took place in a KMC. At first we attributed it to the fact that KMCs were a new idea. But the enthusiasm has not seemed to diminish with time. One frequent participant in KMCs offered this interpretation:

"There is something about seeing your ideas go up on the big screen for everyone to see. It makes you more willing to participate because you know that your idea is going to be captured. But it also makes you think a little bit harder, because you don't want your idea to appear foolish. I guess with KMCs you just get a sense that your ideas are important and that something is actually being accomplished, whereas in most meetings, you don't."

General Manager Tom Furey seemed to share this sentiment, calling KMCs a "breakthrough process leading to tremendous gains in quality and productivity." In fact, the name *knowledge mining center* came from Furey. According to one local legend, the general manager saw a demonstration of the invention and then spent a mostly sleepless night trying to think of a name. When he finally did fall asleep, it was only to wake in the wee hours of the morning with the name *knowledge mining center*. The name stuck.

Since then, KMCs have been demonstrated to IBM's board of directors as well as to scores of IBM customers ranging from Fuji Bank to Mrs. Field's Cookies. In 1991, the lab had a hard time building KMCs fast enough to meet demand—partly because new uses kept being discovered for them. Since their invention, KMCs have been used to facilitate product design, code reviews and inspections, joint application development, team planning, problem correction, document revision, code documentation, and product performance improvement. Some additional uses are shown in Fig. 16.2.

The KMC project team feels that KMCs could be useful in a wide variety of business environments besides software development. Any task requiring team synergy and fast access to information is a good candidate for a KMC. In fact, one of the inventors envisions a group of doctors meeting to discuss a patient's unusual case history. With a computer connected to an on-line data-

- Product design
- Code reviews
- Education
- Test-case construction
- Technical planning
- Financial reviews
- Design reviews
- Problem determination
- Process development

**Figure 16.2**  Some uses of KMCs.

base of medical cases, they are able to quickly bring up relevant information on screen that everyone can see and discuss.

We have used KMCs ourselves on numerous occasions while preparing the lab's quality submission document for IBM's internal version of the Malcolm Baldrige Award. Normally, preparing such a document requires an exhausting number of revisions because over 20 different managers are involved. With the KMC, we got the key players in a room and captured their revisions on-line in real time. By the time the meeting was finished, we not only had a document, but had a document that everyone agreed on, right down to the phrasing.

Another occasion when knowledge mining centers saved our bacon has become almost legendary among certain groups of developers at the lab. A major Japanese bank wanted a 12-hour turnaround on any severe problems with its 18 million transactions-per-day IMS software system.

To prevent problems from occurring and to ensure rapid resolution if they did occur, we had to link programmers in Raleigh, North Carolina, Poughkeepsie, New York, San Jose, California, and Tokyo, Japan—all of whom had a hand in developing the code. These programmers had to be able to view code together, make changes in real time, and discuss the effects of these changes. KMCs and CVIEW (see below) allowed instant group development meetings without flying the participants to a central location.

How effective were these meetings? Well, the last time this large Japanese bank had an outage was over 4 years ago. That's 18 million $\times$ 365 days $\times$ 4 years, or over 26,280 million transactions ago.

### Costs, benefits, and risks

The costs of building a KMC are highly variable. The initial prototype was cobbled together from spare computer parts and hooked up to a BARCO overhead screen projection system. The inventors worked nights and weekends for several months and put the thing together for under $10,000.

Since then, over a dozen KMCs have been built by using outside contractors. These KMCs are the ergonomically designed progeny of that original scruffy ancestor. Some feature soundproofing, comfortable chairs, fancy audiovisual equipment, speaker systems, fax machines, teleconferencing capabilities, scanners that allow any chart to be instantly scanned and projected electronically, whiteboards that copy themselves onto paper at the touch of a button, and price tags running into six figures. However, even at a cost of several hundred thousand dollars, most managers feel the KMCs pay for themselves in short order.

For example, one senior manager described his conversion experience. An error report had come in from the field on DB2. The responsible programmer fixed the error, but since the product contained 1.5 million lines of code, no one was absolutely certain that the fix wouldn't adversely affect other parts of the product. The manager decided to get the top developers together in a KMC and examine the fix. Because everyone was able to see the code at once—not only the fix, but any part of the 1.5 million lines of code, instantly—the group discovered not only that the fix was in error, but that it would have created at least 10 additional errors.

The manager did the math. Errors in this product could cost up to $50,000 each to fix if they are discovered in the field. And that's not even counting the inconvenience to our customers. So he figured 2 hours in the KMC had just saved IBM $500,000 and a lot of goodwill. That just doesn't happen very often in conventional meetings.

A senior programmer at the lab offers a corroborating view of KMC effectiveness. He conducted an informal study which concluded our software lab could save up to 15 percent of its direct labor costs simply by conducting design sessions, code reviews, document reviews, and other team-oriented meetings in KMCs.

Even greater savings, up to $25,000 per meeting, result when KMCs are coupled with teleconferencing techniques that allow developers worldwide to examine and dynamically change the same code without having to travel to a central meeting location.

For example, Fig. 16.3 illustrates the potential for virtual meetings held in more than one location simultaneously. A software program called CVIEW allows KMCs in multiple locations to share information. Thus, developers in Westlake, Texas, can see the same code or document projected in their KMC as developers at our lab in San Jose, California. When one group makes a change on-line, all the groups see the change in real time in their KMCs. With speaker-phone and fax capability, KMC-to-KMC virtual meetings have become cost-effective ways to coordinate teams of developers in multiple locations.

With all these benefits, together with the savings in service costs and increased customer goodwill resulting from higher-quality products, it is easy to see why the GM authorized construction of thirteen KMCs in 1991. By conservative estimates, the KMCs paid for themselves within the first 6 months of operation.

Word has spread, and other sites at IBM are beginning to catch KMC fever. Figure 16.4 shows that KMCs are now popping up worldwide.

Overall, KMCs are one of the most successful innovations at the lab with users from all major product groups. In fact, sometimes the only thing more difficult than finding someone at the lab who has not spent some time in a KMC is finding someone who disliked the experience. On a lab-wide survey, we received pages of write-in comments. Here are some samples:

"An interpretation of the office (and home entertainment) of the future. No better way to do all kinds of business when folks come together in a meeting."

"An effective place to hold reviews. More, smaller KMCs would be useful. Quite often only need room for 3 to 5 people but unable to get KMC because they are all booked."

"Contributes greatly to long technical reviews. A better atmosphere and focuses on hi-tech—the way our business should be operating. Excellent

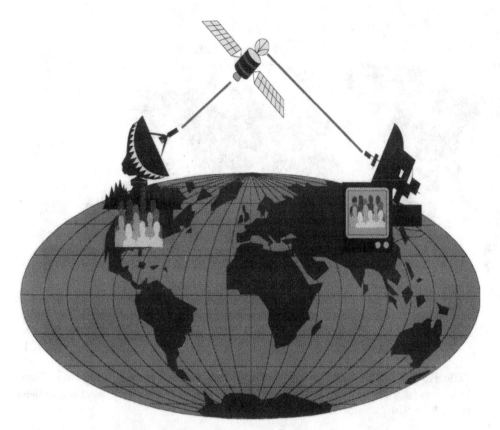

**Figure 16.3**  Virtual meetings via knowledge mining centers. (*Courtesy of IBM*)

addition to Santa Teresa. Hard to schedule and people don't cancel space when time/dates change. Some of the rooms are poorly ventilated. You run out of air long before you run out of material to review."

"Every conference room should have many of the KMC facilities."

"Good for group review."

"Great!"

"Don't have silly rules like no foil projectors in the room. You should use whatever communications means are necessary to get the job done."

"It is useful when you want someone to take meeting notes on-line as you are in the meeting."

"Nice rooms. [I] think a lot of the equipment has gotten less use after the initial honeymoon. Need to see sustained usage, not just a fad."

"Some of the technology (primarily the PC and BARCO) is highly useful, and recording a meeting is great. Technology does *not* solve group dynamics problems though, and without a skilled meeting leader, I think many of the rooms are not used appropriately."

**Figure 16.4**    Worldwide knowledge mining centers at IBM. (*Courtesy of IBM*)

"The KMCs are a must now. I can't see how we did it any other way. They have saved a lot of time and effort. The need for many tools also decreased when the KMCs came into being."

From hard-nosed developers, these reviews are about as glowing as they get. With such a groundswell of support for KMCs at our lab, it is difficult to anticipate the risks that other organizations might face with the concept. A conservative approach would be to start small with a single, fairly spartan KMC. By the time demand for the room outstrips the available number of hours, you should have a good idea of which features are most needed in your future KMCs.

## Synergy

KMCs are synergistic with many of the other innovations described in this book, primarily because so many of them have a team and/or meeting component. For example, DPP causal analysis and action team meetings are routinely held in KMCs. Similarly, there are very few rigorous code reviews or inspections that are not held in KMCs. Budget meetings, documentation reviews, CLIFT meetings, and even meetings with customers routinely take place in KMCs.

## Prerequisites

There are no formal prerequisites for a KMC, but as with any meeting, participants should know why they are meeting and what they hope to accom-

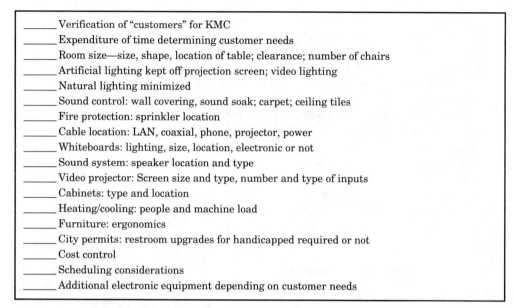

_____ Verification of "customers" for KMC
_____ Expenditure of time determining customer needs
_____ Room size—size, shape, location of table; clearance; number of chairs
_____ Artificial lighting kept off projection screen; video lighting
_____ Natural lighting minimized
_____ Sound control: wall covering, sound soak; carpet; ceiling tiles
_____ Fire protection: sprinkler location
_____ Cable location: LAN, coaxial, phone, projector, power
_____ Whiteboards: lighting, size, location, electronic or not
_____ Sound system: speaker location and type
_____ Video projector: Screen size and type, number and type of inputs
_____ Cabinets: type and location
_____ Heating/cooling: people and machine load
_____ Furniture: ergonomics
_____ City permits: restroom upgrades for handicapped required or not
_____ Cost control
_____ Scheduling considerations
_____ Additional electronic equipment depending on customer needs

**Figure 16.5**  KMC implementation checklist.

plish so that the technology can be put to the best possible use. It goes almost without saying that no meeting technology can produce good results if the meeting participants don't like each other or are unwilling to cooperate.

### Implementation advice

All KMCs include a meeting table, comfortable chairs, an overhead screen projection system, and a workstation. Most also include video cameras, VCRs, speaker phones, a variety of software programs, and whiteboards. Fancy sound systems, electronic whiteboards, fax machines, more computers, scanners, and other electronic goodies can be added upon demand.

All this high-technology equipment is designed to help with two primary jobs: information access and information capture.

*Information access* means having the right people in the meeting and providing them with the ability to instantly call up whatever information they need to support their work process. On-line databases, documents, program listings, diagrams, pictures, faxes—even teleconferencing facilities—are all ways of getting information to the people who need it, quickly.

*Information capture* means capturing revisions, ideas, code changes, or questions immediately. KMCs use the computer, video and audio taping, and whiteboards equipped with photocopiers to create a permanent record of IBM's most valuable resource—the knowledge and ideas of its employees. Information capture also means that much of the work that used to be done individually after meetings is done right in the KMC.

The ergonomics of designing a good KMC are much trickier than one might expect. We learned (the hard way) that good programmers don't necessarily make good architects. There are an amazing number of factors—heat caused by the computers, lighting, acoustics, and aesthetic factors. What you're striving for is a way to have access to all kinds of information. But you still want a spartan-looking conference room that is comfortable enough for long meetings. Achieving that balance is a real art. For this reason, it might be worthwhile to get an architect's or professional designer's opinion before you build.

Finally, a creative attitude helps. People have brought their spreadsheets into KMCs to project them on the wall for discussion. This idea never occurred to the inventors of the first KMC, but they recognize that it is perfect for some kinds of meetings. We like to think that one of the reasons KMCs have been so successful is that the core idea is very simple but there are almost endless variations.

Figure 16.5 describes some of the key design points to consider when you are implementing a knowledge mining center.

## Innovation 27 (Tools): Electronic Meetings

### The objective

By some estimates, 17 to 25 million corporate meetings are held every day. But go to any corporation, and you are likely to hear complaints about meetings. At our lab, many complaints about meetings stem from what we call the "3P problem areas"—productivity, participation, and priority. Table 16.2 illustrates some typical complaints about these problem areas.

Productivity complaints are probably the most common. No one likes sitting in a meeting wasting time when he or she could be getting some "real work" done. Yet despite a large number of books written about how to hold more productive meetings, certain productivity problems seem to be inherent in any gathering of large groups of people.

Perhaps the most basic problem is the fact that the information transfer rate (bandwidth) of spoken speech is quite small compared to people's ability to process information. The result is that one person speaks while nine people

**TABLE 16.2   Types of Common Complaints about Meetings**

| Problem area | Examples |
| --- | --- |
| Productivity | "Meetings take too much time." <br> "Group-think is too slow." <br> "Lots of talk, but no action." <br> "People forget what was decided." |
| Participation | "The same people always dominate." <br> "Not everyone is engaged." <br> "People are afraid to speak openly." <br> "Too many ego battles." |
| Priority | "The few good ideas get lost in a flood of distractors." <br> "Lack of focus. We wander off topics." <br> "Poor decisions are made because the most important issues aren't always the ones that get addressed." |

fade in and out. If what is being said is interesting, you might devote full attention. If not, you may daydream, doodle, or prepare what you are going say. If little was said that was of interest, you quite rightly come away with the feeling that the meeting was a waste of time.

There is a related problem. Because only one person can speak at a time, who speaks becomes critical. Unfortunately, who speaks is not necessarily correlated with who has the best or most interesting ideas. Instead who speaks seems to be correlated with who likes to talk and who is in the position of authority. Moreover, some people with very good ideas are simply afraid of speaking up for fear of looking foolish. These facts lead to a second area of complaints related to participation problems.

Finally, even meetings with enthusiastic and democratic participation can falter if there is no way to focus on the most important ideas that are generated. There are two problems here. First, just keeping track of all the ideas can be difficult. Second, one rarely knows what the other participants think of all the ideas. Without this knowledge, the group tends to focus on those ideas endorsed by the person in authority or by the loudest champions. When such ideas are given the highest priority—even though they may not be the most important to the group—there is a priority problem.

As this brief analysis shows, many of the complaints about meetings stem from basic facts of human information processing and interpersonal dynamics. Facilitators and rules for meetings can try to minimize the negative consequences of these facts, but can't eliminate them. For example, the "5-minute rule" of JAD sessions (see Chap. 7) can limit discussion of any topic to 5 minutes. But you still waste 5 minutes. Similarly, a good facilitator tries to include everyone in the group and to keep the meeting on track. But the best facilitator is not a mind reader, and will still skip over potentially good ideas. Moreover, even facilitators think twice before telling the boss to shut up.

Faced with limitations stemming from human information processing and from interpersonal dynamics, IBM began investigating new ways to conduct meetings by using computer technology. Today the fruits of that research are available in a product offering called TeamFocus. Figure 16.6 shows what a TeamFocus session looks like in action.

### An innovative approach

While knowledge mining centers started as a homegrown solution to a specific programming problem, TeamFocus technology represents a high-powered, IBM-wide effort to solve some of the age-old problems of interpersonal communication. IBM began funding research in this area at the University of Arizona in 1986. By 1990, the company had built 18 electronic meeting rooms incorporating the TeamFocus technology. Our lab began experimenting with the approach in 1991.

The TeamFocus approach uses computer hardware, software, a facilitator, and a structured process to overcome the three problem areas. Meeting participants gather in a room equipped with PS/2 workstations that are net-

**Figure 16.6**   TeamFocus in action. (*Courtesy of IBM*)

worked together by using a local-area network (LAN). The workstations run special software that allows everyone to type at once. As people type, the text is displayed on a big projection screen that everyone can see.

The special software allows anonymous brainstorming. Each person can generate ideas as fast as she or he can type, and the ideas are displayed anonymously on the big screen. A group of 20 people might generate 300 to 400 ideas in 15 minutes. That's an order-of-magnitude (10-fold) productivity advantage compared to the best-run conventional meetings where generating and recording 30 ideas in that amount of time are rare.

Once the ideas are generated, the TeamFocus software allows each participant to rank the importance of the ideas. In seconds, the ideas can be displayed for all to see, ordered by importance. The software also allows participants to vote on proposals. These features go a long way toward solving the prioritization problems common to many conventional meetings.

Because the activities are done anonymously via the computer, the software solves major participation problems. Shy people, aggressive people, senior managers, and junior employees all have equal opportunity to participate. Ideas are not elevated or ignored based on who advanced them. Instead, ideas are evaluated based on their perceived merit.

The abilities to generate many more ideas, to prioritize these ideas quickly and objectively, and to gain everyone's participation lead to better-quality decisions and ultimately to competitive advantage.

## Costs, benefits, and risks

The cost of a TeamFocus solution includes the cost of the computer workstations, the cost of the LAN, the cost of the software, the cost of the facilitator(s), and the cost of the participants' time. Our experience has been that TeamFocus centers are more expensive to set up than knowledge mining centers and can easily run to more than $100,000. A key factor in cost is whether you can use existing workstations and a LAN. If existing computers are used, the cost will be significantly lower.

Since TeamFocus software is an actual IBM product, you can get an accurate cost by calling IBM (see Suggested Readings). As for facilitators, we use lab employees who received special training and practice over a period of weeks. They generally spend only part of their time facilitating, depending upon the demand for the TeamFocus meetings. Finally, there should be zero cost for the time of the meeting participants—assuming that the participants would have gone to a traditional meeting anyway. In fact, here is where you can expect to derive some savings.

Because TeamFocus was developed as a product, it has been evaluated extensively and used by many companies outside of IBM. An early study by IBM and the University of Arizona found TeamFocus meetings to be 55 percent faster than traditional ones. A more recent, independent study by Boeing, reported in *The Wall Street Journal,* "found that the total time involved in meetings was cut 71 percent. The calendar time required for team projects involving meetings was cut a whopping 91 percent."

Other companies have found similar benefits. According to a *Business Week* article (June 11, 1990), the Phelps Dodge Mining Co. collapsed a planning meeting that usually takes days into 12 hours by using the TeamFocus technology.

We have used TeamFocus with generally positive results. For example, one functional area at the lab was having problems with morale. A TeamFocus session allowed members of the area to share their ideas and opinions about how to improve management anonymously. Some of these ideas were implemented, and morale improved by 18 percent on the next survey.

TeamFocus has also been useful with customers, helping to capture and clarify customer requirements. One of the most useful features in this context is the automatic documentation of every idea generated during the session. Designers can capture a much more complete set of customer concerns in shorter customer visits.

Overall, benefits include the following:

1. Efficient use of time
2. Anonymous exchange of ideas
3. Equal participation
4. Focus on content, not personalities
5. Parallel and simultaneous communication
6. Complete record of meeting
7. Increased productivity due to prioritized focus

Figure 16.7, courtesy of the product developers, summarizes the key aspects of the product leading to these benefits.

For a less biased assessment, we asked users what they thought of the product. Here's what some of them said in a lab-wide survey:

"Good for sensitive emotional topics....Generates a huge pile of data, though that is hard to assimilate. I wonder how much follow-up happens."

"A super way to capture the team's view of the world, as opposed to the dominating person's view."

"Excellent group process tool!"

"Good stuff. Very useful to promote the team and flat organization. Removes the clout of those with loud voices or high positions."

"I am a TeamFocus facilitator for Santa Teresa. I have seen many organizations utilize this software tool along with a facilitator to enhance their teams, come to a decision quicker, have more productive meetings. I must caution everyone though—TeamFocus is not a magic wand. You cannot expect to force 3 days' worth of meeting agenda into a 4-hour or 8-hour session and get quality results and have people feel good about it. But TeamFocus can make your meeting much more effective and result in quicker decisions with more buy-in from the group making the decision."

"Our organization was the first to use TeamFocus to address employee morale issues. It was extremely helpful and has had a positive effect on improving our overall morale."

"This is a 'fun' tool and has some value for those who can't or won't tell the truth to their peers and/or management."

"This is OK, but tends to be oversold, as do many technology solutions."

"What did IBM and its customers ever do without TeamFocus? I used it *many* times when I was in the field with customers and internally and have participated in several sessions at Santa Teresa. It takes time to set up the session properly, so know your specific objectives in advance."

The main risk with TeamFocus is that users of the technology may have inappropriate expectations. Because it is a new technology, we have had groups try to address issues that they would have never tried to address in a regular meeting. It's important to realize that while TeamFocus can lead to more efficient meetings with fuller participation, it is not a cure-all. Some

---

- Better ideas: brainstorming with anonymous participation
- Clear results: brainstorming, voting, topic commenter
- Instant documentation: meeting notes as you leave the session
- Worthwhile meetings: facilitator, agenda, meeting printouts

**Figure 16.7** How does TeamFocus work?

problems just do not lend themselves to resolution in a couple of meetings—even if the meetings are high-technology. The key to minimizing these risks is to set expectations realistically by exploring the capabilities of TeamFocus clearly and then communicating what the technology can be expected to do.

### Synergy

TeamFocus is synergistic with other group meeting technologies such as the knowledge mining center (above) and JAD sessions (see Chap. 7). TeamFocus has also helped with departmental quality strategies (Chap. 4), ISO 9000 (Chap. 10), process modeling (Chap. 7), DPP (Chap. 15), and the quality partnerships (Chap. 21). Action plan development, requirements definition and analysis, team building, customer partnership planning, morale issues, and strategic and tactical planning are other general areas where TeamFocus has been used successfully at the lab.

### Prerequisites

There are no formal prerequisites for TeamFocus.

### Implementation advice

The components of TeamFocus are as follows:

1. *The TeamRoom.*  The TeamRoom is a conference room equipped with (IBM PS/2) workstations for all meeting participants and a large-screen projection system for displaying information. Up to 20 (IBM PS/2) workstations are connected on a local-area network (LAN).

2. *A TeamGuide.*  The TeamGuide is the person instrumental in planning the meeting and conducting the session. The TeamGuide helps bring structure to the meeting, keeps participants on track, and is knowledgeable about the TeamFocus software, how to apply it, and how to conduct productive meetings.

3. *TeamKit/2.*  The software tools called TeamKit/2 serve as a catalyst in the meeting, promoting an energetic exchange of ideas between participants and the capability to sort and condense those ideas into an organized format. The tools also provide the ability to elaborate on ideas and to vote on them. TeamKit/2 is a collection of tools which can be applied to a variety of scenarios depending upon the characteristics of the team, the format, and objectives of the meeting. For example, Fig. 16.8 shows a screen from the electronic brainstorming tool. Many users can read each other's comments and add ideas simultaneously.

After brainstorming for a while, the ideas can be brought to an electronic vote to help determine which ones have the highest priority. A screen from the electronic voting tool is shown in Fig. 16.9.

4. A TeamFocus process that can be customized depending on the objectives of the meeting. For example, a typical meeting might have the following

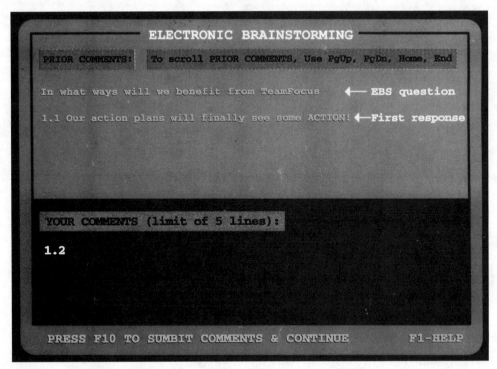

**Figure 16.8**  Electronic brainstorming using TeamFocus. (*Courtesy of IBM*)

stages: brainstorming, organizing ideas, voting and prioritization, evaluating alternatives, and action planning. However, a meeting whose purpose was to choose a name for a new product might focus on just two of these stages—brainstorming and voting.

Part of our process includes a presession meeting between the TeamFocus facilitator and the requestor of the TeamFocus session. Expectations about the session, the purpose of the session, and issues of who will be participating in the session are addressed in this meeting. Other issues, such as what to do if some participants can't type well, can also be addressed.

Customizing the TeamFocus session to match the needs of the participants is critical for a successful meeting. We end every TeamFocus session with a quick informal survey so that the facilitators can decide how to improve their process.

Finally, in evaluating whether to invest in TeamFocus, it's worth calculating roughly how much time your organization spends in meetings. Compared to knowledge mining centers or other groupware programs on the market, TeamFocus is a relatively high-powered offering. It has nice features, but also requires the overhead of a facilitator. Organizations holding lots of meetings that are suffering from problems of productivity, participation, and prioritization would probably find the investment worthwhile. However, for those

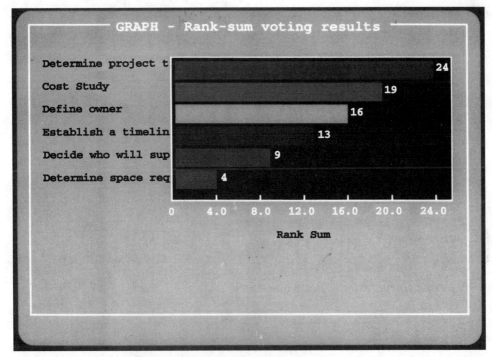

**Figure 16.9**   Electronic voting using TeamFocus. (*Courtesy of IBM*)

wishing to just dabble with the concept of groupware, or to hold less structured meetings, a stripped-down KMC and/or purchase of some of the many
groupware software packages that are now appearing might be the right initial step.

Figure 16.10 describes some of the TeamFocus implementation steps we
went through.

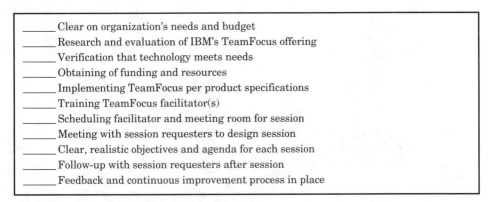

**Figure 16.10**   TeamFocus implementation checklist.

## Suggested Readings

"At These Shouting Matches, No One Says a Word," *Business Week,* June 11, 1990. *A high-level look at electronic meetings.*

Bulkeley, W. M. (1992) "Computerizing Dull Meetings Is Touted as an Antidote to the Mouth that Bored," *The Wall Street Journal,* January 28, p. B-1. *Another high-level look at electronic meetings.*

Doyle, M., and Straus, D. (1976) *How to Make Meetings Work,* New York, NY: Jove Publications. *A popular book on improving meetings; good background.*

Johansen, R. (1988) *Groupware: Computer Support for Business Teams,* New York, NY: Free Press. *A popular book on groupware.*

"Using the KMC to Build a Better Programming Environment," *Reflections,* April 1991, IBM Santa Teresa Communications Department. *An overview of computer-supported team work spaces (also known as knowledge mining centers, or KMCs) during their early development.*

Zahniser, R. A. (1990) "Building Software in Groups," *American Programmer,* pp. 50–56, July/August.

For more information on TeamFocus software or its successor provided, Group Systems V, call:

IBM's hotline—1-800 955-7474

Ventana Corporation—1-800 368-6338

# 17

# Computerizing the Software Development Process

With the increased emphasis on teamwork and team development efforts in the management stage, we began to think about ways to use technology to directly support steps in the software development process. Computer-supported team work spaces and electronic meetings were great, but they still required everyone to be engaged in the same activity at the same time. In our search for ways to boost productivity, the lab discovered two innovations that supported asynchronous team development efforts. These are summarized in Table 17.1.

## Innovation 28 (Tools): On-line Reviews

### The objective

We don't know any product developers who actually like review meetings. Perhaps it's because the meetings often go like this:

Any person who might possibly have anything to do with the product receives a fat binder on design specifications to review. No one is left out, and our nation's forests are several trees poorer.

TABLE 17.1   Stage: Management / Food Group: Technology / Theme: Support Specific Activities in the Software Development Process

| Objective | Innovative approach | Pitfalls |
|---|---|---|
| Reduce cycle time for software reviews<br>Circumvent difficulties scheduling meetings<br>Improve code review efficiency | *On-line reviews:*<br>REVUFILE technology<br>Cross-functional, on-line, asynchronous review of code | Lack of cross-functional participation<br>Tool availability issues |
| Capitalize on shifting development environment<br>Facilitate coordination of large teams of programmers | *LAN library control system:*<br>Adopt LAN technology<br>Run library control software with versioning and disaster recovery on LAN | Faulty estimates of system use<br>Hardware and software availability issues<br>Lack of adequate training |

A few conscientious reviewers actually go through the document, page by page, making comments in the book or on self-stick notes. Most reviewers take a look at the size of the binder, groan, and quickly flip to a few sections that seem most relevant.

Next comes the review meeting, or rather numerous attempts to *schedule* the review meeting. At last a time is found when most of the reviewers can be present. Some of the reviewers who have been invited actually show up. Each lugs a fat review binder, like Sisyphus with his rock.

Then comes the waiting, the doodling, the wondering whether there is time to make a quick run for a cup of coffee, before the review meeting reaches the one section where you have scrawled a comment. You decide to wait, but the review meeting ends before the group reaches your section. Another meeting will have to be scheduled, and if for some reason you can't make that meeting, there's always the code review, and the documentation review, and....

## An innovative approach

Our solution was not to have review meetings at all—at least not when we can accomplish the same thing far more efficiently by using a local invention called REVUFILE.

REVUFILE is an on-line review tool that allows multiple reviewers to read and add comments to a document. The document could be a design specification, a module of code, a user's manual with graphics, a business proposal, or just about anything that can be created by using IBM's text editors and graphics programs for its VM operating system.

Instead of going to a meeting, reviewers read the sections of the document that they feel are most relevant and add their comments directly to the text. What's more, they can read the comments of everyone else who has already added comments, so they can make comments on other people's comments. Best of all, reviewers can review the document at their convenience.

The net result is a dramatic increase in the efficiency of the reviewing process. Since its invention, REVUFILE has spread like wildfire through IBM sites from San Jose, California, to Cary, North Carolina, to Rome, Italy, and Perth, Australia. As of March 1993, REVUFILE was being used at more than 40 IBM locations worldwide and had more than 2750 users, with more signing up every day. That's not bad for a homegrown tool with no marketing except word of mouth. In fact, the tools group that invented REVUFILE is so pleased that it has a workstation version under development and is planning to make REVUFILE available to external customers.

## Costs, benefits, and risks

The cost of REVUFILE, or similar on-line review tool, is the cost of the software plus the cost of the time required to install it. In the case of REVUFILE, these costs are slight since the software is maintained by our tools group and gaining access to the tool is as simple as issuing a single command from any terminal in the lab. On-line manuals and tutorials for REVUFILE are available just as easily.

While other generally available programs were not specifically designed with software developers in mind, much of their functionality overlaps with REVUFILE. In our opinion, the cost of such off-the-shelf software will probably be slight compared with the savings in meeting time. Of greater concern would be the costs in time to install and maintain the software. These costs are likely to vary by vendor, so it is worth some careful research.

The benefits of REVUFILE (and, by extension, of other good on-line review tools) include

1.  The ability to add comments to a document at one's own leisure and to read and comment on the comments of others.

2.  The ability to sort, organize, or filter comments in various ways so that the reviewer can easily focus and comment on information most relevant to his or her expertise.

3.  The ability to handle graphics and a wide variety of text documents.

4.  The elimination of the requirement for multiple review meetings. In many cases, no meeting is needed at all.

5.  Savings in travel costs when reviewers are at different sites.

Two surveys in our DB2 product area reported a 90 percent satisfaction level with REVUFILE. Respondents on a lab-wide survey were almost unanimous in their endorsement of the concept:

"Great!!!"

"Has revolutionized review process. Biggest hurdle is reluctance of some reviewers to use it."

"An invaluable tool that saves lots of rework and eliminates data loss."

"Can be overused—missing the synergism which can happen in a face-to-face meeting. Danger of assuming 'if it's out on REVUFILE, everyone has read it' which may not be true. Very easy to use—well worth the small effort required to learn to use it."

"Captures decisions immediately. Excellent way to track progress and correction. Saves time—lets you read other comments at your leisure. Assures closure on all items."

"Excellent method of review which saves time by removing duplication, yet it generates more ideas because of the extended period people have to look at each other's ideas."

"I don't know that the tool makes for better reviews (thus improving quality), but it certainly improves productivity and reduces costs (travel costs, e.g., for people who can now review remotely)."

"REVUFILE is the single most valuable tool I use to improve quality while reducing the time it takes to get resolution to a design or change. It is simple to use and a very effective tool to get improved communication."

REVUFILE or similar on-line review programs involve relatively little risk. They can be tried out in a pilot program, perhaps in one department. If successful, they are generally easy to scale up.

## Synergy

On-line review tools are synergistic with anything that requires review of a document. For example, we use REVUFILE to help with review of our ISO 9000 documentation efforts (see Chap. 10).

Moreover, by customizing the general tool, it is also possible to create new synergies. For example, REVUFILE plus another tool (inspection repository system) allows us to classify errors according to the orthogonal defect classification (see Chap. 22) categories in an efficient way. Or, by adding some statistical capabilities to REVUFILE, we can gather and analyze statistics on the reviews. These statistics can help us track how effective the reviews are.

## Prerequisites

There are no prerequisites other than hardware and system requirements which vary depending upon the on-line review software chosen. REVUFILE currently requires a host system running the VM operating system.

## Implementation advice

As with many groupware technologies, the benefit tends to increase with the size of the group. This reflects the fact that coordination of meetings becomes more and more of a problem as the number of participants increases. On-line review tools skirt this problem by allowing any number of users to participate in a review asynchronously.

This logic suggests that for very small product development teams, on-line review tools are probably not necessary. If you can get the entire team in a meeting relatively easily and have a productive meeting, why complicate things?

On the other hand, for large development teams or for teams with developers physically separated by great distances, on-line review tools make good sense. If you decide to implement an on-line review tool, we recommend first conducting an informal analysis of where your biggest review problems are. Then check out a variety of tools to see which meets these requirements best. As of this writing, REVUFILE is under beta test on the Software Mall system in Tampa, Florida. Other products, typically LAN-based, are available off the shelf from a variety of sources (see Suggested Readings).

Figure 17.1 presents some of the implementation steps we recommend for a tool like REVUFILE.

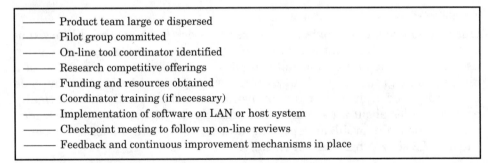

——— Product team large or dispersed
——— Pilot group committed
——— On-line tool coordinator identified
——— Research competitive offerings
——— Funding and resources obtained
——— Coordinator training (if necessary)
——— Implementation of software on LAN or host system
——— Checkpoint meeting to follow up on-line reviews
——— Feedback and continuous improvement mechanisms in place

**Figure 17.1**   On-line review implementation checklist.

## Innovation 29 (Tools): LAN Library Control Systems

*Note:* This innovation will probably be of greatest interest to organizations that are currently developing software on a mainframe host and are considering switching to a LAN development environment. If you already use a LAN environment with a good library system (e.g., version control, that is, the ability to keep different updates of a software program separate from each other in an organized fashion, and disaster recovery), you may want to skip this section.

### The objective

To meet customer demand for increased function, software products are becoming larger, which means they are increasingly developed by teams of programmers. Our very large projects may have dozens of programmers, each responsible for different parts of the code.

Whenever you have multiple programmers on a project, you run into problems of version control, changing data sets, and other difficulties in communication and coordination of effort. These problems were compounded in our case by a move from a mainframe, host-based development environment to a workstation environment.

The challenge was to develop technology that would enable team development of code on workstations while improving both efficiency and quality. Obtaining the workstations themselves was not a problem, since every employee already had a technical workstation or PS/2 in her or his office. But making sure that every developer had the most recent version of the code (or document) to work on was more difficult. The replication and updating of test tools and test cases for each developer on every workstation were also problems.

Moreover, even if an efficient process could be found for distributing the updates, storing the same information in multiple workstations was redundant and consumed valuable storage space.

## An innovative approach

Our solution was to combine a local-area network (LAN) with a library control system. The LAN put executable programs, tools, and other information used by the same group in a common place, accessible to every member of a development group. The library control system provided a common code repository and a development environment with formal (automatically enforced) rules about accessing and changing code. The system also provided a mechanism for problem reporting and tracking and disaster recovery. Figure 17.2 shows this solution visually.

## Costs, benefits, and risks

The primary cost associated with the LAN library control system is the initial training cost for users and for the LAN administrator. If the organization does not already have the hardware required for a LAN, there will be secondary hardware costs as well.

In our experience, it generally took users about a day to install the LAN software and to become familiar with it. However, the LAN administrator required 3 to 4 weeks of training and spent several months getting things up and run-

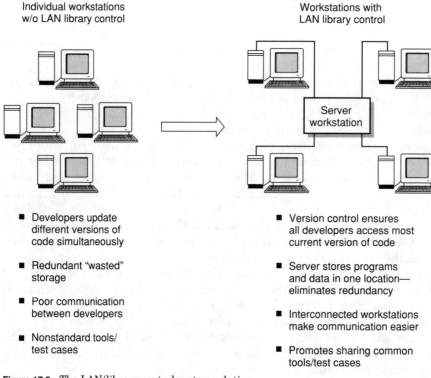

Individual workstations
w/o LAN library control

Workstations with
LAN library control

Server
workstation

- Developers update different versions of code simultaneously

- Redundant "wasted" storage

- Poor communication between developers

- Nonstandard tools/ test cases

- Version control ensures all developers access most current version of code

- Server stores programs and data in one location— eliminates redundancy

- Interconnected workstations make communication easier

- Promotes sharing common tools/test cases

**Figure 17.2**   The LAN/library control system solution.

ning initially. Once the bugs are worked out, we've found that it requires about one person at 25 percent effort to support a LAN with 50 people.

Benefits of the LAN library control system include improved communication between developers; easier sharing of code, documents, and tools; and reduced storage requirements. Some of these benefits derive from the interconnectivity of the LAN, others from the fact that workstations offer advantages over host-based environments.

For example, the LAN allows users to access code, data, or documents from one central place. When code or documents are changed, they are changed once—in the central location—eliminating the need to replicate the changes for every member of the development group. Having one central LAN server for all the critical information also simplifies the administration required to protect and support the information needed by the group.

Compared with a host-based environment, networked workstations offer graphical user interfaces and a wide variety of software development tools that are easier to use. Here are sample comments from a lab-wide survey:

"A big productivity boost."

"Depends on the LAN performance."

"Getting off the host control system provides us with much more flexibility. You must be prepared to resource this, but it does provide significant cycle time improvements."

"Good."

"LAN library control was the key to our source control and workstation builds."

The main risks with LAN library control relate to possible frustration at changing modes of development and trying to get the bugs worked out of the system. These risks can be minimized by implementing the system on a pilot basis first and avoiding switching to the system during critical points in the development cycle.

### Synergy

The LAN library control system is synergistic with code reuse efforts and on-line code reviews because it provides an electronic pathway and software that facilitate sharing of code and information. Similarly, a LAN provides a good communication vehicle for quality-related information such as departmental quality strategies (Chap. 4) or ISO 9000 (Chap. 10) activities.

### Prerequisites

There are no prerequisites for LAN library control, but having a well-documented set of development procedures and protocols for team development will help things go smoothly. In particular, it is unrealistic to expect that just because you get a LAN and some software you can suddenly do team software development. The technology is a facilitator of communication—not a substitute for good communication and team skills.

Whoever designs the LAN system should be very familiar with the application software that implements the library control system as well as with the needs of the development group.

## Implementation advice

The first step in setting up a LAN library control system is to assess system requirements in terms of the number of users in the group, data volume, and types and levels of activity. The system designer should also decide which tasks the administrator will carry out (e.g., security checks and system backup). This initial design stage is probably the most critical in terms of the overall effectiveness of the LAN system. We found it very useful to communicate with experienced LAN administrators and system designers at this stage.

In general, the smaller the group using the LAN, the easier LAN will be to set up. Part of the setup involves hardware—workstations, servers, LAN cards, and the wiring within and between the offices and/or buildings to be served by the LAN. Our entire site is served by one master LAN that spans buildings and development groups. Within the master network are smaller networks with local servers.

Once the hardware is in place, a variety of software is available to make the LAN run. For example, most of our workstations are IBM PS/2s that have Token-Ring Cards (Token-Ring is the name of IBM's LAN solution). If the PS/2s are running the AIX (Unix) operating system, we use TCP/IP as LAN software. If the PS/2s are running the OS/2 operating system, we use OS/2 LAN requester and server software. There are also a variety of non-Token-Ring LAN options such as Digital's ETHERNET system.

In our implementation—PS/2 workstations and an IBM library control product called configuration management version control (CMVC)—we found the limitation for one server to be about 30 to 50 users, depending upon the volume of data. For groups with more than 50 users, we use two servers. We also found that the complexity of the system administration and management increases significantly for groups with more than 200 users.

Once the system requirements have been determined, hardware and software availability issues and funding issues should be resolved. In several cases, our move to a LAN library control system was delayed because we failed to resolve these issues ahead of time.

Finally, the LAN administrator and users should be trained. Part of the training should include a clear understanding of what the administrator's responsibilities will be and what will be left up to the users.

At our lab, users were usually responsible for getting their own hardware (Token-Ring cards, cables, and servers—a dedicated workstation). The LAN administrator defined the LAN software and what information could be accessed on the LAN. The administrator also oversaw the establishment and

_____ Clear need and target users identified
_____ LAN system designer identified
_____ Scope and usage of system estimated
_____ LAN software and hardware options researched
_____ Library control software researched
_____ LAN strategy developed and verified to meet needs
_____ Funding and resources obtained
_____ Critical development efforts not endangered by timing
_____ Roles and responsibilities of administrator/users defined
_____ Hardware infrastructure in place
_____ Rollout of pilot system
_____ Education of administrators and users
_____ Rollout of full system
_____ Feedback and continuous improvement process in place

**Figure 17.3**   LAN library control system implementation advice.

maintenance of user accounts and handled tasks such as the periodic backups of the LAN software and information.

Figure 17.3 describes some of the steps we went through in establishing LAN library control systems at the lab.

## Suggested Readings

Berson, A. (1992) *Client/Server Architecture.* New York: McGraw-Hill. *A comprehensive treatment of the client/server model that includes discussion of local-area networks.*

Chorafas, D. N. (1989) *Local Area Network Reference.* New York: McGraw-Hill. *A thick book that discusses many technical topics of interest to LAN implementers and others involved in the design and use of LANs.*

Kauffels, F. J. (1991) *Network Management: Problems, Standards, Strategies.* Reading, MA: Addison Wesley. *A technical book on LANs that has gone through three German editions and one international edition.*

Naugle, M. C. (1991) *Local Area Networking.* New York: McGraw-Hill. *A compact and technical treatment of LAN implementation issues.*

# 18

# New Paradigms for Software Development

Once the obvious improvements to the existing software development process have been made (e.g., improved testing, collapsing stages in the waterfall process, and adding technology to do each step faster), there comes a point when you have to throw away your existing process and risk trying something completely new. In the management stage, our leading-edge development groups reached this point and began experimenting with new paradigms of software development, using the technologies summarized in Table 18.1.

Experiments with object-oriented design and coding reflected a growing concern with trying to produce more highly structured, reusable code. Rapid prototyping efforts complemented the focus on object-oriented technology because many of the prototypes were built by using object-oriented languages. Both technologies also supported increased customer involvement early in the development cycle—an important step toward increasing customer satisfaction with the final products.

**TABLE 18.1  Stage: Management / Food Group: Technology / Themes: Investigate New Paradigms of Software Development and Focus on Defect-Free Code, Reuse, and Customer Involvement**

| Objective | Innovative approach | Pitfalls |
|---|---|---|
| Foster code reuse<br>Foster clearer methods of expressing customer requirements | *OO design and coding:*<br>Object-oriented design to capture requirements and coding for reuse | Lack of expertise/training in OO methods<br>High learning curve |
| Speed "proofs of concept"<br>Include customer feedback *early* in the development cycle | *Rapid prototyping:*<br>Use rapid prototyping tools and get feedback from customers on prototypes | Learning curve for prototyping tools<br>Poor match of tools to needs |
| Speed progress toward zero defects<br>Foster customer involvement and teamwork | *CleanRoom techniques:*<br>Adopt specific CleanRoom techniques: iterative development, statistical testing, rigorous design, customer involvement | Failure to invest in education and training<br>Trying to do too much too quickly |

CleanRoom technology is often considered a process, but we implemented it as if it were a technology. While the "right way" to do CleanRoom technology is to use a set of techniques together in a coherent system, in practice different development groups ended up picking and choosing techniques that worked for them. This approach may be offensive to CleanRoom purists, but it seemed to work. At any rate, since there are a number of books already describing textbook implementations of CleanRoom technology, our contribution in this chapter will be to examine some of the pragmatic issues that complicate real-world implementation.

## Innovation 30 (Tools): Object-Oriented Design and Coding

### The objective

Every programmer has probably tried to reuse someone else's code at one time or another, only to decide that she or he would be better off just writing something new. In fact, there have been research studies that suggest it is often easier to write code from scratch than to decipher what someone else has already done.

However, besides the fact that often you don't have the option of redesigning a piece of software from scratch, there is the persistent logical thought that it *should* be easier to reuse someone else's code, if only....

At this point there comes a long list of requirements, most of which boil down to "if only the person who wrote the code I want to reuse thought the same way I did."

Designers of new programs face similar problems. A program design starts as a simple idea, capable of being implemented by one or two programmers. But as the design gains acceptance, more and more features are added, requiring more and more programmers. What starts out as a relatively clean design can turn out looking like the Winchester Mystery House.

Because each programmer tends to implement functions in an idiosyncratic way, the overall program becomes very complicated and beyond the ability of a single programmer to figure out.

### An innovative approach

Since the trend is for programs to become increasingly complex to provide added function, the problems described above can be solved only by coming up with a better way to develop the code and designs. Object-oriented (OO) programming and design techniques represent one approach to complexity.

Our lab obviously didn't invent object-oriented programming. But for us, it was innovative to begin designing and coding some of our products by using OO techniques. We'd like to share some of our experiences along these lines.

First, we should probably review what seem to us to be the central features of an object-oriented programming language.

1. Data and code are packaged together in a capsule called an *object*.

2. Information and instructions are passed between objects in the form of *messages*.

3. Objects of a similar type are grouped together in *classes*.

4. Objects can inherit *characteristics* (data and procedures) from other objects in their class.

One way to think of objects is to anthropomorphize them. Think of them as little people. Send the object the right message, and it will do all sorts of things for you. Send the wrong message, and it just sits there. Like people, objects inherit characteristics from their ancestors. And like people, each object can add to these inherited characteristics its own repertoire of behavior. Objects can send each other messages and can send different messages depending on the behavior of other objects.

Now, at some level, all these things *could* be done with a procedural language or even an assembler. The point is that these things are easily and more elegantly done with object-oriented languages.

From a code-reuse perspective, inheritance is probably the most significant feature of OO programming. What it means is that you have a programming language that, to an unprecedented degree, has modularity and reusability built into its fundamental structure.

For example, while procedures are dependent on the larger context of the program in which they are embedded, objects have more of an independent identity. Objects, like people, have a repertoire of behavior. Different behaviors ensue depending upon which messages are sent.

OO principles at our lab are being used in two ways. First, we use OO principles to design products and the user interfaces for products. For example, we use the Booch methodology (see Suggested Readings) to design parts of our expert systems products. We also use another methodology, developed by Coad and Yourdon (see Selected Readings), to design the user interfaces for some of our other products.

In both cases, the advantage is that OO principles provide a cleaner way to conceptualize and organize the design of a complicated product.

When OO programming is used for coding, the result is a library of reusable objects that can be accessed by all the programmers working on the project and that can be borrowed by programmers working on other projects.

Although OO programming is still very experimental at the lab, the productivity advantages are conceptually clear. Many at the lab are convinced that OO programming is the wave of the future. As one programmer put it, "It's not a matter of justifying investment in OO. It's more a matter of justifying why you aren't investing in it."

### Costs, benefits, and risks

The costs of object-oriented programming stem from (1) the time needed to bring programmers up to speed, since this is a new approach to programming, and (2) the time needed to build a useful library of object classes that can be shared.

Because OO programming is substantially different from standard programming languages like COBOL, C, or Ada, there is a significant learning curve. Moreover, the efficiency of OO programming languages depends upon having a well-developed library of objects (and classes). Until this library is developed, much of the development time is spent building the infrastructure to make the programming language more effective.

With regard to design, OO principles provide a disciplined way to conceive of program design. The learning curve here is less steep, but still represents a cost. For one product at the lab using an object-oriented analysis for design, the cost in design was higher than that of other methods, but the investment was felt to be worthwhile because it simplified the coding stage and allowed more potential flaws to be identified in design.

All in all, users of object-oriented programming tools and design methods warn that several months may be needed by programmers unfamiliar with OO programming to get up to speed. On top of that, the first project should be considered part of the learning experience. Despite these costs, those who have used OO design seem generally positive, although they emphasize the learning curve. Here are some representative comments from a lab-wide survey:

> "Get proper training. Expect to mature over at least a couple of design cycles. Each individual will require time to shift to this paradigm, and that can take months."

> "Object-oriented design provides better, reusable code. It is easy to maintain but hard to learn."

> "Takes more design time up front, but is very valuable for code reuse."

> "Make sure someone in your organization knows object-oriented design and object-oriented analysis. Knowing C++ is not good enough."

> "The main benefit I see is in the recognition up front of the reusability of data and code [methods]. The technique encourages it, although it is still possible to do a nonreusable design if you try hard enough."

> "Takes practice. High learning curve."

In general, the advantages of object-oriented programming languages and design methods include reusability, increased productivity, ease of maintenance, abstraction, encapsulation, modularity, hierarchy, and readability. Object-oriented languages can

1. Improve quality, ease maintenance, enable reuse
2. Reduce development cycle time and cost through reuse
3. Lower maintenance costs through implementation of objects
4. Develop objects by using modularity and information hiding

Looking toward the future, we note that many of the programmers coming out of school now have object-oriented programming experience. By programming in these languages, a group can attract the best and most technically vital new hires.

However, OO programming still has risks:

1. Some of the programming languages still contain bugs—more so than time-tested languages such as COBOL, PL/I, FORTRAN, etc.

2. With large numbers of object classes, it is difficult to keep track of what has been developed. A better sort of library control needs to be developed.

3. Not all the interactions between OO code and customers' systems have been tested

4. If the wrong OO language is selected, e.g., one for which most of the required objects must be created from scratch, you invest huge amounts of time in creating the object classes you need, before you enjoy much benefit.

### Synergy

As one might expect, OO technology is synergistic with code reuse. It is also synergistic with rapid prototyping (see below) and rigorous design reviews (see Chap. 11).

### Prerequisites

There are no formal prerequisites for OO technology. However, choosing the right OO tool is important.

### Implementation advice

OO technology has been used by programmers working on huge database programs like IMS, and smaller, relatively new projects like TIRS (the integrated reasoning shell). Everyone has encountered a learning curve, yet most agree that OO programming is one of the key programming technologies of the future.

Small teams have had the best success since, like many new technologies, OO programming requires lots of communication and sharing of experiences during the learning phase. In general, developers seemed to feel that OO technology was better suited to developing a new application from scratch than to adding a small component to an existing program.

Because certain OO techniques are easy to overuse, some groups hired an OO programming consultant to help get them started. The lab has also hired several OO contract programmers to work on specific projects, including rapid prototyping of user interfaces.

With regard to OO languages, C++ has emerged as the favorite of developers, while Digitalk's SMALLTALK has gained popularity with the user-interface designers and those requiring lots of graphical capabilities. More specific OO programming tools, such as graphical user interface (GUI) builders, are available for specific programming jobs.

In general, such tools are excellent as long as they are used to build the fairly narrow range of applications for which they were designed. However, trying to adapt a specific OO programming tool to a new purpose can lead to months of writing new object classes. The golden rule of OO programming is to select tools that have already defined most of the object classes you will want. It's like buying a language that has all the right stuff in the libraries. It saves months of writing code.

The advantage of an object-oriented analysis is that it allows designers to translate requirements into a form that clearly shows what code is reusable and what code will be application-specific. Interactions between objects, potential efficiencies, and potential stumbling blocks can be seen much more clearly than in a traditional list of requirements. Moreover, once an object-oriented analysis is complete, it can be fleshed out in one or more steps to become actual code for the objects.

Figure 18.1 presents some of the implementation steps we went through for object-oriented design and coding.

While object-oriented programming technology has not yet become a mainstream development tool, we feel it holds great promise. One good way to get into the object-oriented game, without the risk of having to ship code in OO languages right away, is to begin using OO programming for rapid prototyping. The next section describes some of our experiences and some of the advantages of this approach.

## Innovation 31 (Tools): Rapid Prototyping

### The objective

Some of the same problems that motivated object-oriented design also motivated our rapid prototyping efforts. For example, it was difficult to anticipate many of the interactions of a complex design simply from a paper specification. Waiting for the product to be built took too long, so we needed a way to mock up the design quickly.

```
_____ Pilot project identified: new project, flexible schedule ideal
_____ OO programming team members identified
_____ Available OO tools and methodologies researched
_____ OO training complete
_____ Class hierarchies of selected tool appropriate to project needs
_____ Commitment for more design time up front obtained
_____ Project planned to maximize code reuse
_____ Rapid prototyping used to gain immediate feedback
_____ Feedback and continuous improvement process in place
```

**Figure 18.1**  Implementation checklist for object-oriented techniques.

There were other factors driving prototyping as well. Changing customer requirements have been, and continue to be, a major injector of errors into code. It goes like this:

Developers hack out a design, code it, test it, recode it, retest it, and finally make it error-free. Just then, the customer requirements change. But it's too late to redesign the product from scratch, so new code gets tacked onto the original design to cover the new requirements. This tacked-on code is inelegant and error-prone. The result is poor quality.

Some changes in customer requirements are inevitable, but other changes stem from communications problems between IBM and its customers. Often neither the customer nor IBM is really to blame. All that has happened is that we've asked customers and developers to look at specifications on paper and try to decide if what they've got looks good. But there is no way that a complex design on paper can be understood in the same way as the final product. You can't take a specification out for a test drive. So what looked good on paper doesn't always look so good once it's built. Sometimes what's built does not even seem recognizable from what is on paper.

This problem crops up especially in the design of user interfaces, where current practice is more art than science. The accepted practice in the world of software human factors is to run usability studies to determine whether a new design is any good. Unfortunately, usability studies can be run only *after* you have a product. And by then, even if the product is found to have horrible "ease of use," it is too late in the development cycle to do much about it.

## An innovative approach

One solution to these problems of usability and poor quality due to changing requirements is rapid prototyping. In essence, the idea is to build a mock-up of the product, which simulates the look and feel of the interface and brings many of the complex interaction problems out into the open.

Once such a mock-up exists, you can show it to customers to determine if it was what they really had in mind. If not, it is still early enough in the development cycle to redesign and still make the ship date. Even if customers like it, it may not be that easy to use.

But with a prototype, you can find out. Just run a usability study on the prototype's user interface, and you can have your answer in time to change the design if necessary before the product is shipped.

## Costs, benefits, and risks

The cost of rapid prototyping varies depending on the tools used, the degree of functionality required in the prototype, and the experience of the prototypers. However, as the term *rapid prototyping* implies, the development of the prototype should take only a fraction of the development cost and should be completed in a fraction of the time required for the development of the industrial-strength product.

Benefits of rapid prototyping include

1. Better understanding of the complexities involved in actually programming the product
2. Better communication between the development organization and customers, using the prototype to elicit feedback
3. Better ease of use for products, since the prototype can be tested with real users before the final interface design is set
4. Faster development time for the actual product—especially if some of the prototype code can be incorporated into the final product (varies with the tools used)

Here are what some developers had to say about prototyping:

"A prototype should be put together by a small group of people (1?), so that it may be fast and effective. The others should be educating themselves, learning about customers, etc., and have information of their own to contribute to the information learned via the prototype. Don't try to build on top of the prototype. Consider it valuable for the lessons you've learned and the mistakes you will avoid because of it. Then go off and design your product."

"Iterative prototyping has allowed us to improve cycle time. The key has been in using prototypes to explore feasibility and going through the extra effort so that the prototype can be enhanced over time and ultimately becomes the product—i.e., don't throw prototypes away."

"Do more of it!"

"The benefit is that you can get feedback on an interface, a function, and performance before expending effort to do a complete product."

"Management seems to think that once code is prototyped, it only needs a little work to make it shippable. This is a bad assumption. Prototypes contain only main path code...."

"Prototypes are essential for groups tackling projects that are relatively unknown to the group. It provides much-needed feedback in order to do proper design."

"Prototyping is a great way of getting early feedback on the feasibility of an architecture. I think there should be customer involvement in the prototyping effort. In my case, demonstrations of the prototype were given to various customers."

As is apparent from these comments, philosophies of prototyping vary. Some developers believe in throw-away prototypes, while others hope to turn the prototypes into the product. However, none of the people surveyed expressed regret at undertaking prototyping efforts.

Risks of rapid prototyping include being sucked into an effort that proves anything but rapid and creating expectations that the real product can't fulfill. The key to avoiding the first problem is to pick the right prototyping tool and to recognize that there is a learning curve with most tools. The second risk can be minimized by making sure that the entire development team has had a chance to use and evaluate the prototype before it is shown to customers.

## Synergy

Rapid prototyping is synergistic with object-oriented design because many rapid prototyping tools are object-oriented in nature. It is also synergistic with efforts to gather customer requirements and feedback and with any efforts to improve usability.

## Prerequisites

The main prerequisite for a rapid prototyping activity is a good understanding of the strengths and weakness of the various tools.

## Implementation advice

Rapid prototyping at the lab is done by product developers, by user-interface designers, by research groups, and by many others. What all these groups share is the need for tools that allow a lot of function and visual information to be developed in a short time. Specifically, Smith (1991) lists the items in Fig. 18.2 as being tool requirements for rapid prototyping. Our observation is that object-oriented *languages* tend to satisfy most of the constraints in Fig. 18.2 quite well.

For example, if the goal is to rapidly prototype a user interface for a product, there are several graphical user interface (GUI) builder tools available. Most of these tools have the ability to create windows, buttons, icons, or other GUI objects with a single command or click of the mouse. When you use a GUI builder, as long as you stick with the problem of assembling a prototype of a user interface, you have a very powerful tool that can do in a day what might take a C programmer months of effort.

---

1. Readability: code easy to read and understand
2. Writeability: terse, compact code syntax
3. Interpretation or fast compilation: eliminates waiting for code to compile and link
4. Good error-checking and/or debugging: speeds development
5. Good run-time performance: helps user evaluate prototype
6. Modularity: speeds development; helps with interfaces
7. Power: higher-level languages are better
8. Extendibility: similar to modularity
9. Reusability: improves quality and saves development time

---

**Figure 18.2**  Rapid prototyping tool requirements. (*Adapted from Smith, 1991*)

The secret lies in the object class hierarchies that come with the tool. These class hierarchies can be thought of as libraries of specialized information—information about how to build windows, icons, and so forth. As long as you have the right information (e.g., classes) in the library, you can build complex designs very rapidly.

But what if you want to build something other than a graphical user interface with the standard features? In this case the effectiveness of the rapid prototyping tool would depend critically on whether it contained the right classes of objects for what you wanted to do. If it had the right classes, great. If not, you'd have to develop them yourself, and this is where rapid prototyping becomes just plain old prototyping. Without the right classes, the development time for a prototype can sometimes approach the development of an actual product.

What is true for GUI builder tools is true for rapid prototyping tools in general: They are terrific as long as the tool—specifically the object classes that come with an object-oriented tool—matches what you want to do.

One of the lab's products has a nice GUI interface primarily because of rapid prototyping efforts. The interface was developed in about 12 months, but is of far greater sophistication than what we could have developed by using a conventional design approach.

One advantage of rapid prototyping efforts is that they are cumulative. Once a member in a group begins to do rapid prototyping, the reusable objects in the object-oriented system begin to grow. This means that theoretically each subsequent prototyping effort should get faster, in proportion to the number of objects that are reusable.

The lab has an interface design group for our CASE tools that has been using object-oriented techniques to do rapid prototyping for over 3 years now. The speed with which new prototypes can be built has increased steadily, and the objects and classes of the tools are now being shared with other IBM locations.

According to the developers in this group, the beauty of object-oriented rapid prototyping tools is that the more you use them, the faster they get.

Figure 18.3 presents our implementation checklist for rapid prototyping.

| | |
|---|---|
| _____ | Prototype project selected |
| _____ | Type prototype clear (e.g., throw-away versus reusable) |
| _____ | Purpose clear (e.g., usability testing, show customers) |
| _____ | Key team members identified |
| _____ | Comparison and evaluation prototyping tools |
| _____ | Capabilities of selected tool appropriate to project needs |
| _____ | Commitment to invest in training on tool |
| _____ | Prototype-created expectations fulfillable by product |
| _____ | Prototype code/experience transferred to other projects |
| _____ | Use of data gathered from prototype to improve product |
| _____ | Feedback and continuous improvement process in place |

**Figure 18.3** Rapid prototyping implementation checklist.

## Innovation 32 (Tools): CleanRoom Techniques

### The objective

Progress had been made in improving the quality of software in earlier stages of quality maturity via techniques like early test involvement, rigorous code inspections and design reviews (Chap. 11), and error-prone module analysis (Chap. 12). While these techniques helped products stretch toward 10-fold quality improvement goals, the products still were embedded in the old software development process. However, as the lab looked toward more ambitious quality goals—100-fold improvement and zero-defect software—it became apparent that entirely new software development methods would be needed. Traditional wisdom that errors were inevitable and needed to be "tested out" was questioned. Instead a view began to emerge that formal specification and rigorous inspection might be the keys to developing error-free code.

Certain components of this view had already gained popularity under the name of rigorous code inspections (Chap. 11), but the challenge was to try to forge these components into a completely new way of developing software. Specifically the new method should eliminate all major design errors and provide a way to know, statistically speaking, when a software product had zero defects with a high probability.

### An innovative approach

Often you do not invent solutions yourself, but borrow them from outside the organization. This was certainly the case with CleanRoom software engineering whose roots date back to work on structured programming done by Harlan Mills, Richard Linger, and others in the 1970s. More recently a book by Michael Dyer has done much to popularize the methodology.

The methodology was used successfully at IBM as early as 1987. Our lab became seriously involved with CleanRoom software engineering in 1990, but with mixed results. Of the eleven teams that completed formal CleanRoom training, four teams went on to develop and test at least one increment of actual product code using the methodology. Two teams began with CleanRoom techniques and then dropped them. One team voted not to begin with CleanRoom technology. The remaining teams either worked on products that were canceled or are just getting started with CleanRoom technology.

As one might expect from this mixed track record, opinions about CleanRoom technology vary greatly at the lab. Some champions feel that it is absolutely the right way to develop software, and they have worked harder to promote these techniques than just about any other innovation champions at the lab. Others complain that CleanRoom technology is too slow and too costly and involves too many meetings. To understand the position of both the champions and the doubters, one needs to recognize first that CleanRoom software engineering represents a fairly radical departure from the traditional waterfall process of software development.

In the waterfall process, code is designed, coded, and then tested in a series of testing stages. These stages begin with unit test, where code is debugged by developers. Next comes function test, where several code units are integrated and tested. Finally comes system test, where the code is tested in an environment that is supposed to be more like the customer's environment.

In the CleanRoom approach, the code is specified formally and reviewed by teams as they develop it. There is no unit test. Instead the code is run for the first time in a system test environment. No private debugging is permitted. Figure 18.4 contrasts our traditional sequential development process with the CleanRoom approach.

With CleanRoom software development, the idea is that the code will be of zero-defect quality by the time it is first run, because of the rigorous design and inspection work done during development. The goal of system test is not to test in quality, which is completely counter to the CleanRoom philosophy. Instead, system test becomes a series of incremental certifications that the software is, in fact, error-free as specified.

Another difference between CleanRoom software development and the traditional process concerns who is involved in the various development activi-

**Traditional**

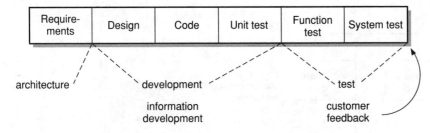

**CleanRoom**

Requirements / Specifications (S) / Design (D) / Verify (V) / Certify

Successive increments

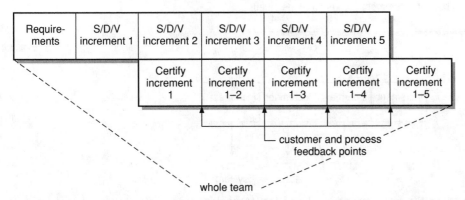

**Figure 18.4** Traditional versus CleanRoom software development. (*Courtesy of IBM*)

ties. In the traditional approach, different people worked at different phases of the development process. However, in the CleanRoom approach, the whole team—developers, testers, documenters, and customers—is involved at points throughout the development cycle.

One of the key ideas in the CleanRoom approach is that the code is developed and certified incrementally. Figure 18.5 illustrates this process.

The first increment of code may include only the most minimal function such as installation procedures, sign-on, and sign-off. However, it will be completely coded and tested in a system test environment before the next increment is coded. Each subsequent increment of code fleshes out the function which was "stubbed" in previous code increments.

By the time the final increment is finished, you have a fully functional product that has already been certified as having high quality. Moreover, the earlier (and most critical) increments have been tested many times since they keep getting tested each time new increments are added. Quality statistics

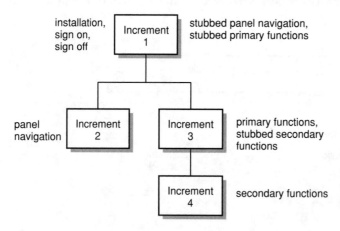

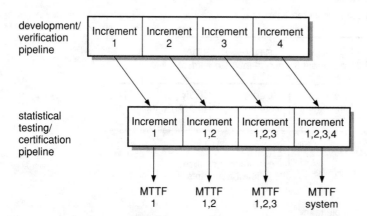

**Figure 18.5**  Incremental development in CleanRoom technology. (*Courtesy of IBM; adapted from Linger, 1993*)

such as the mean time to failure (MTTF) are gathered as way of determining whether the development process is working or needs to be adjusted.

Because the whole process starts with a rigorously specified design and because the interfaces between increments are tested at every stage of development, errors due to major design flaws or interface problems between code units are rare. CleanRoom software specifications typically use an object-based technology of box structures, similar to the object-oriented design methods mentioned earlier. The box structures have a number of features that result in a much more rigorous design than traditional designs, which often are just natural-language descriptions that can be quite vague. For example, the box structures allow the mathematical checking and validation of designs. One contention of CleanRoom advocates is that this rigorous verification of design produces quality results superior to unit testing and debugging.

## Costs, benefits, and risks

CleanRoom technology is expensive. The first cost is training. At our lab about 150 people attended 10 to 11 days of CleanRoom training. Twice that number attended a briefer, overview class on CleanRoom software development. We estimated that the lab invested a minimum of 7 to 8 person-years just in training.

In addition, implementation required input from CleanRoom experts for several months. Finally, there was a perceived additional time cost of developing specifications using the CleanRoom methodology. One team leader reported that writing the box specification took much longer than a traditional specification would. The team had allowed 6 weeks for the specification. It took 12 weeks using CleanRoom technology.

But many developers seem to feel the up-front time spent developing rigorous specifications paid for itself in fewer errors and more trouble-free development. As one team member said regarding the mathematical completeness reviews of the design, "This type of review takes time, but it is not wasted time."

The overall experience of our lab and of other sites using the CleanRoom methodology seems to corroborate this observation. For example, Table 18.2 shows some quality results that have been achieved with CleanRoom technology at IBM.

Despite additional time spent in the design phase, it is worth noting that at least one of the CleanRoom projects finished ahead of schedule, many reported productivity gains, and all reported quality improvements over previous baselines. To put these results in perspective, traditional software projects typically exhibit 30 to 50 errors per 1000 lines of code (KLOC) when they are first tested in unit test. CleanRoom technology does not have a unit test phase, but the error rates in Table 18.2 reflect the errors found in the first test of CleanRoom software. None of the errors rates are above 6 errors per 1000 lines of code. Overall, it seems that the CleanRoom projects average about 10 times fewer errors when they are first tested than traditional projects do.

**TABLE 18.2   CleanRoom Quality Results**

| Year | Technology | Project | Quality/Productivity |
|------|-----------|---------|---------------------|
| 1987 | CleanRoom software engineering | IBM Flight Control: Helicopter Avionics System Component 33 KLOC (JOVIAL) | Certification testing failure rate: 2.3 errors/KLOC<br>Error-fix reduced 5X<br>Completed ahead of schedule |
| 1988 | CleanRoom software engineering | IBM COBOL Structuring Facility: Product for automatically restructuring COBOL programs 85 KLOC (PL/I) | IBM's first CleanRoom product<br>Certification testing failure rate: 3.4 errors/KLOC<br>Productivity 740 LOC/PM<br>Deployment failures 0.2 error/KLOC, all simple fixes |
| 1989 | Partial CleanRoom software engineering | NASA Satellite Control Project I 40 KLOC (FORTRAN) | Certification testing failure rate: 4.5 errors/KLOC<br>50 percent improvement in quality<br>Productivity 780 LOC/PM<br>80 percent improvement in productivity |
| 1990 | CleanRoom software engineering | University of Tennessee: CleanRoom tool 12 KLOC (Ada) | Certification testing failure rate: 3.0 errors/KLOC |
| 1990 | CleanRoom software engineering | Martin Marietta: Automated documentation system 1.8 KLOC (FOXBASE) | First compilation: no errors found<br>Certification testing failure rate: 0.0 errors/KLOC (no errors found) |
| 1991 | CleanRoom software engineering | IBM system software First increment 0.6 KLOC (C) | First compilation: no errors found<br>Certification testing failure rate: 0.0 errors/KLOC (no errors found) |
| 1991 | Partial CleanRoom software engineering | IBM system product Three increments, total $10^7$ KLOC (mixed languages) | Testing failure rate: 2.6 errors/KLOC<br>Productivity 486 LOC/PM |
| 1991 | CleanRoom software engineering | IBM language product First increment 21.9 KLOC (PL/X) | Testing failure rate: 2.1 errors/KLOC |
| 1991 | Partial CleanRoom software engineering | IBM image product component 3.5 KLOC (C) | First compilation: 5 syntax errors<br>Certification testing failure rate: 0.9 error/KLOC |
| 1992 | CleanRoom software engineering | IBM printer application First increment 6.7 KLOC (C) | Certification testing failure rate: 5.1 errors/KLOC |
| 1992 | Partial CleanRoom software engineering | IBM knowledge-based system application 17.8 KLOC (TIRS) | Testing failure rate: 3.5 errors/KLOC |
| 1992 | CleanRoom software engineering | NASA Satellite Control Projects 2 and 3 170 KLOC (FORTRAN) | Testing failure rate: 4.2 errors/KLOC |
| 1993 | CleanRoom software engineering | IBM device controller First increment 39.9 KLOC (C) | Certification testing failure rate: 1.8 errors/KLOC |
| 1993 | Partial CleanRoom software engineering | IBM database transaction processor First increment 8.5 KLOC (JOVIAL) | Testing failure rate: 1.8 errors/KLOC<br>No design errors, all simple fixes |
| 1993 | Partial CleanRoom software engineering | IBM LAN software First increment 4.8 KLOC (C) | Testing failure rate: 0.8 errors/KLOC |

*Note:* All testing failure rates are measured from first-ever execution where correctness verification has taken the place of unit testing and debugging.
KLOC = thousand lines of code. PM = person-month.

Other benefits stem from the rigorous approach to testing that complements the rigorous design. Statistical *usage testing* is designed to test the software the same way users will use it. That is, those functions used most by users receive the greatest testing focus. Functions that are used less frequently receive proportionately less effort. The result is that the MTTF, or the average time a piece of code can be used without anyone encountering an error, for CleanRoom code tends to be much higher for CleanRoom projects than for code that doesn't use statistical usage testing. In fact, some experts claim that statistical usage testing is more than 20 times more effective at extending MTTF than more traditional coverage testing.

In a lab-wide survey, here is what the developers at our lab had to say about CleanRoom technology:

> "CleanRoom techniques are hard to get used to in the beginning; it took us a lot of time up front to start using the techniques. However, once we got used to it and [to] what steps needed to be taken, we found that it greatly increased our quality in the design phase and we found a lot less bugs in the coding phase. We reduced our PTMs [errors] per KLOC tremendously."

> "Almost impossible to apply to legacy code. Techniques from the process can be used but not the process as whole."

> "You should use the whole process. Don't try to use only parts of the tool."

> "Requires education, and commitment to follow principles and practices *as a team*. Definitely improves quality of output. Expect a learning curve at the beginning—it isn't easy. Consultant help during initial application of the methods is extremely helpful."

> "Too much 'administrative work.' Spending a lot of time writing specification/documentation. Little time for coding. Not suitable to shorten development cycle. Time-consuming."

Some of the risks inherent in CleanRoom technology should be apparent in these comments. First, although there is general agreement that quality improves, there is also consensus that a substantial investment in training, in rigorous design work, and in consultants is needed up front. There is also little evidence that CleanRoom technology will shorten the development cycle—at least during its initial use. Because of these considerations, an organization should be prepared for an investment and for a learning curve. If expectations are not too high initially, team members will persist and the quality benefits will come.

There is also the issue of whether CleanRoom technology is best implemented as a total package or whether pieces of CleanRoom techniques can be used successfully on their own. Our view is that the success of CleanRoom software as a package probably depends on an organization's level of quality maturity.

The lab first began experimenting with CleanRoom software development when we were still in the coping stage. In retrospect, we were probably asking too much of developers, who were just becoming convinced of the need for process improvement, to adopt a new approach to software development whole hog. What happened was that specific aspects of CleanRoom technology were adopted, according to what developers felt would be useful. This allowed them to take steps toward quality improvement without abandoning sacred steps in the old development process such as unit test. Of course, the CleanRoom purists feel that such piecemeal adoption of CleanRoom techniques is heresy.

One way around this dilemma is to introduce CleanRoom technology as a total methodology only after the organization has become accustomed to process change by moving through the earlier stages of quality maturity. Individual techniques that build toward CleanRoom technology (e.g., rigorous reviews and inspections) can be introduced at earlier stages where they have a better chance of acceptance.

### Synergy

CleanRoom technology is synergistic with early test involvement, rigorous design reviews, and rigorous code inspections (Chap. 11); knowledge mining centers, on-line reviews, and rapid prototyping; and object-oriented design.

### Prerequisites

You need to be willing to invest effort, time, and money up front for training and for "toughing out" the learning curve.

### Implementation advice

Figure 18.6 summarizes the overall CleanRoom process. You can do each of the steps or pick certain parts that fit your development process. The process begins with customer requirements which are translated into a function specification and a usage specification. The function specification ultimately gets translated into code, whereas the usage specification forms the basis for user-oriented testing. Formal design techniques and statistical testing result in code that can be statistically certified to be of a certain level of quality. The level of quality can be expressed in terms of MTTF estimates and 6 $\sigma$ (a low rate of defects per million lines of code).

Our implementation advice is derived from the guidelines supplied by the CleanRoom coordinator at the lab, Joan Keller, who has encountered (and overcome) just about every obstacle imaginable. In her technical paper *CleanRoom Software Engineering: Santa Teresa Laboratory Teams' Implementation Results,* she offers important considerations for implementing CleanRoom technology, which we reprint here:

1. *Decide to do it.* A Manager must commit resources to start up. Individual employees are NOT empowered to do it alone. A team must be allowed time to be trained together, and managed to work effectively as a team, applying the CleanRoom principles and practices. Be prepared for cultural changes.
2. *Form a CleanRoom team.* Steps must be taken to: educate all team members, get team buy-in, organize for team ownership of components and prod-

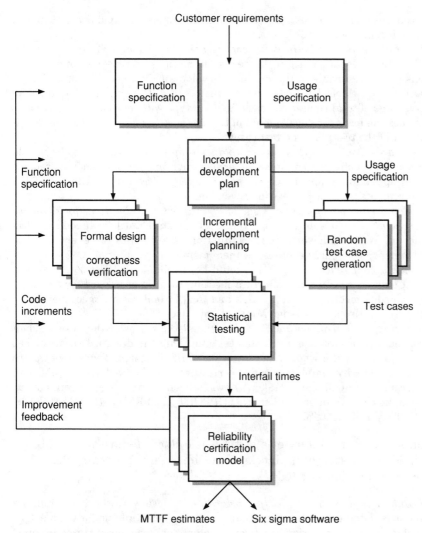

**Figure 18.6**  Our overall CleanRoom process. (*Courtesy of IBM*)

ucts (sub-teams of 3–4 people, in larger teams of up to 15 worked best), identify and train key people with whom your team will interact.

3. *Understand the requirements and objectives for the product to be developed.*
   Categorize and prioritize them. Mark the "fuzzy" ones for early work.

4. *Understand the System Environment.*   "Draw a box" around the product or
   product parts to be owned by the team. Completely define the boundaries of
   the box; all users, all tasks, all stages of use, all inputs (called "stimuli" in
   CleanRoom terms) and all outputs ("responses" in CleanRoom terms). Use
   prototyping to investigate interfaces which are not known.

5. *Write a CleanRoom specification.*   Document the externals using the Box
   Structure method. Define all stimuli and responses (the black box). Define
   data needed to create responses from stimuli (the state box). Then define the

procedures (the clear box). Use step-wise refinement to expand the clear box into sub-component black boxes.

6. *Plan for statistical reliability certification.* Involve Test...[and the Publications Department] in the design discussions and reviews of specifications for all externals of the product. Develop an Expected Customer Usage specification which describes how the customer will use the product and the percentage of total time [that] each function type will be used. This document becomes the basis for development of the customer publications and for development of the test plan and test cases.

7. *Create an incremental development plan.* Plan each increment to be usable for some level of testing in a customer-like environment. Use each increment as an opportunity for customer feedback regarding the fulfillment of his requirements, and for process improvement.

8. *Develop verifiable software designs of procedures and objects using step-wise refinement.* Each step expands the level of detail until final code level is reached. Write concise "intended function" statements for every level of refinement, which are verifiable by team members.

9. *Provide a conference room.* [It should be] available at least ½ day, every day. CleanRoom is a team effort...a meeting room is necessary for frequent, spontaneous meetings of sub-teams and [for] formal review meetings of the whole team. Use a Knowledge Mining Center [see Chap. 16].

10. *Develop effective teamwork.* Have individuals do pieces of the design. Then hold team reviews to correct, enhance, and verify the design. Establish that after the review the whole team owns the verified design. Team reviews are intended to verify completeness and correctness, not just to "find bugs." Team reviews replace Unit Test. Make reviews happen at every step of refinement, and make them frequent and short. SUPPORT AND REWARD TEAMWORK AND TEAM SUCCESS!!

Based on surveys and interviews of the CleanRoom teams at the lab, we also identified seven stumbling blocks to avoid. Again, these are described well by the paper previously cited:

1. *Schedule pressures and conflicting priorities.* These were the two inhibitors listed most often on our surveys. Team members not available for team activities, due to conflicting priorities, [were] the problem most often stated in interviews.

2. *Requirements changes.* Of the eleven pilot projects, two projects were cancelled, and two projects delayed the planned start of their CleanRoom releases to add function or to do quality upgrades on prior releases. All had ongoing changes of requirements for function and schedule.

3. *Re-organizations.* Of the eleven teams participating in the pilot projects, five had a change of management, four had a change of team leader, and all but one had members leave or new members join the team after the completion of training.

4. *Lack of conference rooms.* On the first survey, 11 people listed lack of conference rooms as one of the top two inhibitors to CleanRoom success. Implementation of several Knowledge Mining Centers has greatly reduced this problem.

5. *Personalities and egos.* By attending team meetings and interviewing individual team members, we observed the following:

*a.* Some programmers resisted change, some openly, some passively.

*b.* Some programmers preferred to work alone most of the time. CleanRoom teams spend 40–50% of their time in team or sub-team meetings. This was very uncomfortable for some people, but positive for others.

*c.* Some team members were reluctant to speak up in meetings, or to ask questions or give opinions. Some were very reluctant to expose their work to review by others, and [were] embarrassed when errors were pointed out.

*d.* Some team leaders were better than others at ensuring that all team members were encouraged to speak up, and at reaching true consensus in design discussions and verifications. We concluded that additional training in teamwork and in team leadership is needed for nearly all teams.

6. *Old habits and expectations.* We frequently observed minor problems in communication with others, not trained in CleanRoom. In most cases, we found that the source of the problem was that the Waterfall Process checkpoints or terminology [see Chaps. 3 and 7] were expected. Team status reports had to find ways to bridge from the old process to the new.

   Many programmers fell into the habit of describing internal structure, instead of external behavior, in the specification. Many jumped too quickly into coding, before externals were completely defined...which often resulted in re-work.

7. *Input from experts.* The second survey indicated that on-site input from experts is essential, at least for the first time through each major step. Box Structure specification, incremental planning, design through step-wise refinement, and team verification are skills which must be learned and practiced. Guidance and feedback at each new step [are] very beneficial. All teams reported that they made much more rapid progress when CleanRoom experts participated in the implementation.

Figure 18.7 summarizes the key points in an implementation checklist.

_____ Purpose of pilot project clear

_____ CleanRoom literature researched

_____ Pilot project selected

_____ Management commitment (first to evaluate the new technology, then to actually produce a product) and funding obtained

_____ Experts available for consultation

_____ CleanRoom team members identified and educated

_____ Conference rooms scheduled for daily use

_____ Product requirements understood and prioritized

_____ System environment understood

_____ CleanRoom specification written

_____ Expected customer usage defined

_____ Incremental development plan specified

_____ Test plan specified

_____ Verifiable designs for procedures and objects

_____ Team reviews

_____ Results measured and communicated

_____ Team recognition

_____ Feedback and continuous improvement process in place

**Figure 18.7**   CleanRoom implementation checklist.

## Suggested Readings

Balzer, R., Cohen, D., Feather, M., Goldman, N., Swartout, W., and Wile, D. (1983) "Operational Specifications as the Basis for Specification Validation." In D. Ferrari, M. Bolognani, and J. Goguens, eds., *Theory and Practice of Software Technology.* Amsterdam: North-Holland. *This paper describes a formal specification language, GIST, that provides a point of contrast with the OO design techniques described in other references.*

Balzer, R., Goldman, N., and Wile, D. (1982) "Operational Specifications as the Basis for Rapid Prototyping." *ACM Software Engineering Notes,* 7(5): 3–16. *One of the first papers to describe the link between specifications and building a prototype. Note: This paper appears in a Special Issue on Rapid Prototyping (December 1982) which contains other papers of interest as well.*

Basili, V. R., Selby, R. W., and Baker, F. T. (1987) "CleanRoom Software Development: An Empirical Evaluation." *IEEE Transactions on Software Engineering,* 13(9): 1027–1037, New York.

Basili, V. R., and Turner, A. J. (1975) "Iterative Enhancement: A Practical Technique for Software Development." *IEEE Transactions on Software Engineering,* SE-1(4): 390–396, New York. *This paper describes a stepwise refinement technique that is similar to some aspects of CleanRoom technology.*

Biggerstaff, T., and Perlis, A., eds. (1984) Special issues on software reusability. *IEEE Transactions on Software Engineering,* SE-10(5): September, New York. *This special issue presents more than a dozen papers describing different approaches to software reuse—one of the reasons for using OO programming techniques.*

Boehm, B. W., Gray, T. E., and Seewaldt, T. (1984) "Prototyping versus Specifying: A Multi-project Experiment." *IEEE Transactions on Software Engineering,* 10(3): 290–302, New York. *A look at prototyping from the author of Software Engineering Economics.*

Booch, G. (1986) "Object-Oriented Development," *IEEE Transactions on Software Engineering,* SE-12(6): 713–721, New York.

Booch, G. (1991) *Object-Oriented Design with Applications.* Redwood City, CA: Benjamin/Cummings Publishing Co. *A popular OO design book at our lab.*

Budde, R., Kuhlenkamp, K., Mathiassen, L., and Zullighoven, H. (1984) *Approaches to Prototyping.* New York: Springer-Verlag. *This book collects a series of papers that address a variety of prototyping approaches to software development and evolution.*

Coad, P., and Yourdon, E. (1991a) *Object Oriented Analysis.* 2d ed. Englewood Cliffs, NJ: Prentice Hall. *Good book on OO analysis.*

Coad, P., and Yourdon, E. (1991b) *Object Oriented Design.* Englewood Cliffs, NJ: Prentice Hall. *Good book on OO design—somewhat different from Booch.*

Cobb, R. H., and Mills, H. D. (1990), *IEEE Transactions on Software Engineering,* 7(6): 44–54, New York.

Dyer, M. (1992) *The CleanRoom Approach to Quality Software Development.* New York: Wiley. *A how-to book by one of the originators of the CleanRoom approach to software engineering.*

Hekmatpour, S. (1987) "Experience with Evolutionary Prototyping in a Large Software Project." *ACM Software Engineering Notes,* 12(1): 38–41. *Describes three alternative prototyping approaches for evolving software development.*

Hevener, A. R., and Mills, H. D. "Box-Structured Methods for Systems Development with Objects," *IBM Systems Journal,* 32(2): 232–251. *Discusses an object-oriented design methodology.*

Keller, J. (1993) *CleanRoom Software Engineering: Santa Teresa Laboratory Teams' Implementation Results,* Technical Report, IBM Santa Teresa, San Jose, CA. *Documentation of our lab's experience with CleanRoom technology.*

Linger, R. C. (1993) "CleanRoom Software Engineering for Zero-Defect Software," *Proceedings of the 15th International Conference on Software Engineering,* May 17–21, 1993. Baltimore, MD: IEEE Computer Society Press.

Linger, R. C., Mills, H. D., and Witt, B. I. (1979) *Structured Programming: Theory and Practice.* Reading, MA: Addison-Wesley. *One of the earlier technical treatments of structured programming—still useful today.*

Mills, H. D., Dyer, M., and Linger, R. C. (1987) "CleanRoom Software Engineering," *IEEE Transactions on Software Engineering,* 4(5): 19–25, New York.

Musa, J. D., and Everett, W. E. (1990) "Software-Reliability Engineering: Technology for the 1990s," *IEEE Software,* 7(6): 36–43, Los Alamitos, CA.

Neighbors, J. (1984) "The Draco Approach to Constructing Software from Reusable Components." *IEEE Transactions on Software Engineering,* SE-10(5): 564–574, New York. *A technical description of one software reuse scheme that provides a point of contrast with OO schemes.*

Ross, D. T., and Schoman, Jr., K. E. (1977) "Structured Analysis for Requirements Definition," *IEEE Transactions on Software Engineering*, SE-3(1): 6–15, New York. *Outlines a systematic methodology for requirements definition—a precursor to some of the CleanRoom techniques.*

Smith, M. F. (1991) *Software Prototyping: Adoption, Practice, and Management.* London: McGraw-Hill. *A pragmatic look at software prototyping for managers that includes a detailed set of references.*

Taylor, D. A. (1981) *Object Oriented Technology: A Manager's Guide.* Reading, MA: Addison-Wesley. *A short, easy-to-understand, high-level view of object-oriented technology.*

Tracz, W. (1988) "Software Reuse Maxims," *ACM Software Engineering Notes*, 3(4): 28–31. *Of interest to those intrigued by the reuse side of OO technology.*

Wirth, N. (1971) "Program Development by Stepwise Refinement." *Communications of the ACM*, 14(4): 221–227. *An early paper on stepwise refinement which is the grandfather of many object-oriented methods.*

Wood, D. P. and Kang, K. C. (1992) *A Classification and Bibliography of Software Prototyping*, CMU/SEI Technical Report, CMU/SEI-92-TR-13. *An overview, annotated bibliography, and basic road map through the software prototyping literature.*

# 19

# Stage 4: Integration

## Are You in the Integration Stage?

When you've reached the integration stage, quality values are embedded in the culture and day-to-day operations of the organization. In the awareness stage, the quality alarm was sounded. In the coping stage, quick and easy improvements to the existing processes were made. In the management stage, defect prevention, innovation, and teamwork were emphasized. Now, in the integration stage, continuous improvement should be a reflexive response that requires a minimum of prompting from the top of the organization.

The integration stage is the time to expand quality horizons to include suppliers, business partners, customers, and the community at large. It is also a time to push the edge of the innovation envelope, striving to make one's own processes obsolete before the competition does.

The prerequisites for entering the integration stage include success in implementing preventive approaches to quality, successful innovation in the service of quality, and teamwork across various functions in the organization. Groupware technologies and statistical analysis techniques should be solidly deployed in the organization.

Success in these areas should be reflected in a Baldrige self-assessment score above 750. Everyone in the organization should feel proud of being part of a team that produces products and services of unsurpassed quality. The payoff of the quality efforts should be evident in concrete statistics including indicators such as customer satisfaction, defect rates, employee morale, and financial performance.

Table 19.1 shows our lab's Baldrige profile as we neared the threshold of the integration stage. We can say we have just crossed the threshold into the integration stage since we were awarded IBM's gold medal for excellence in quality. One of the requirements for receiving this award is a Baldrige score (as assessed by Baldrige examiners outside the lab) in excess of 750.

**TABLE 19.1   Our Baldrige Profile for the Integration Stage**

| Baldrige area | Indicators |
| --- | --- |
| 1.0 Leadership | Everyone in the organization considered a quality leader |
| 2.0 Information and analysis | Trend data collected and available<br>Data on competitors collected<br>Data analyzed and used to drive process improvements on a regular basis |
| 3.0 Strategic quality planning | Strategic planning process accepted<br>Closed-loop improvement process in place<br>Strategy focused on customers |
| 4.0 Human resource development and management | Ongoing quality education<br>Participation in quality activities seen as business as usual<br>Measurements and incentives for team performance well established |
| 5.0 Management of process quality | Processes documented<br>Process with continuous improvement built in<br>Focus on customer, business partner, and supplier quality<br>Benchmarking widely practiced |
| 6.0 Quality and operational results | Trend data on product quality<br>Trend and competitor data<br>Signs of positive quality impact on operational results |
| 7.0 Customer focus and satisfaction | Trend data on customer satisfaction<br>Data on customer satisfaction with competitive products<br>Customer satisfaction strongly linked to all functions of the business |

## Objectives of the Integration Stage

The challenge for leaders is to continually improve the organization's internal processes and technologies through innovation while at the same time exerting influence beyond the boundaries of the organization.

No matter how perfect a product the organization makes, the law of GIGO (garbage in equals garbage out) still applies. Poor quality on the part of suppliers can produce garbage out. Confused input from customers about what they want or need can produce garbage out. Employees who have not sharpened their skills can produce garbage out.

The process challenge is to establish and share processes that make quality a partnership between the organization and its suppliers and customers. Unless the organization shares its knowledge and helps these partners improve their processes, the highest levels of quality cannot be attained.

The integration stage is about helping customers, suppliers, and the community work together with the organization so that everyone comes out a winner. What this means is that at the integration stage, the organization has become a learning organization. It responds naturally to the external environment in a way that makes its customers more satisfied, its suppliers more cost-effective and responsive, its operations more effective, and its products far more competitive.

Finally, the technological objective is to increase the rate of experimentation and innovation. There is no standing still when it comes to quality. An organization is always either making progress or losing ground. Moreover, unless the rate of innovation is accelerating, the organization stands a good chance of losing ground to competitors who won't settle for a constant rate of improvement.

In terms of Baldrige, Fig. 19.1 lists the areas that we chose to focus on as we neared the threshold of the integration stage.

## Overview of Innovations for the Integration Stage

Table 19.2 summarizes the objectives, innovative approaches, and implementation pitfalls we see at the threshold of the integration stage.

The role of the leader in the integration stage is to inspire innovation and break through the thinking that tries to contain quality solely within organizational boundaries. Since immediate quality levels are good in the integration stage, leaders need to emphasize the expansion of quality techniques and investment in the future. At the same time, the leader in integration has to be willing to get out of the way and let the employees lead. If quality improvement has really become embedded in the culture, improvements should come regardless of whether the leader tries to drive them.

Integration stage leadership innovations include quality reviews for maintaining quality momentum within the organization, quality exchanges as a way of sharing quality knowledge and learning from other companies, and WorkForce 2000—a long-term strategy for educating future workers in the community.

On the process front, the focus is on extending quality processes to include customers and business partners.

Finally, integration stage technologies include extensions of existing tools (e.g., performance mining) and new analysis methods for defects (e.g., orthog-

---

1.3 Public responsibility: Focus on being a better corporate citizen

2.2 Competitive comparisons: Focus on collecting process benchmarks and comparison data

3.2 Quality and performance plan: Focus on formulating and benchmarking long- and short-term goals and plans

4.1 Human resources plan and management: Integrate human resource activities and measurements with business and quality goals

4.5 Employee well-being: Focus on employee morale and a positive work environment

5.4 Supplier quality: Communicate quality standards to suppliers and evaluate their performance on quality criteria

6.2 Company's operational results: Measure and benchmark those who actually make the products

6.4 Supplier's quality results: Measure suppliers on quality and compare them to competitors

7.6 Customer satisfaction comparison: Compare your customer satisfaction results with those of competitors

---

**Figure 19.1** Baldrige focus items for the integration stage.

**TABLE 19.2    Integration Stage Innovations**

| Food group | Objective | Innovative approach | Implementation pitfalls |
|---|---|---|---|
| Leadership | Sustain quality improvement momentum after transformation. | Streamline and include ISO 9000 in continuous improvement reviews. | Settling for results achieved or signaling that the journey is over. |
|  | Find out "What you don't know you don't know." | Quality exchanges and briefings ongoing with other companies. | Fear of sharing, getting arrogant. Failing to seek the best exchange partners. |
|  | Strengthen linkages to the community. | Long-term involvement looking to Work Force 2000. | Making it a public relations function; not focusing on actions that provide value. |
| Process | Further reduce defects and improve customer satisfaction. | Quality partnerships with customers (throughout product life cycle). | Arbitrary customer selection. Mindless attention to only participating customers' input. |
|  | Improve supplier quality processes. | Quality partnerships with vendors and related process initiatives. | Overwhelming partners with bureaucracy. "You're not OK, I'm OK" syndrome. |
| Technology | Find better ways to predict trouble spots in software development process. | Determine trouble spots by using error classification method: orthogonal defect control. | Failing to invest in data-collection infrastructure. Lack of adequate training. |
|  | Improve run-time performance of code. | Use computer-supported team work space for performance mining. | Introducing new defects while correcting old ones. |
|  | Find out where to invest quality dollars. | Record cost of quality activities and develop metrics to estimate Quality ROI. | Mindless use of metrics. Failure to improve metrics. |

onal defect classification) and strategic investment (e.g., quality return on investment).

Each of these leadership, process, and technological innovations is described in more detail in Chaps. 20 to 22.

## Obstacles and Pitfalls

While the most difficult part of previous stages was to remain committed to quality programs without seeing results, the danger in the integration stage lies in letting the results make you complacent. Many Japanese companies have an approach that can be helpful here. In these companies, as soon as a product has broken even, the company itself places a very high priority on making the product obsolete.

This is exactly the opposite of the policy of most U.S. companies, which is to ride the revenue stream of a product as long as possible. Yet the Japanese approach recognizes that if you do not make your own product obsolete, someone else will. Then you will have to spend the money on innovation anyway, but you will be innovating to catch up instead of to dominate the market.

What's true for product development is also true for process improvement activities. We believe that as soon as process improvement or quality innovation has been deployed successfully and has paid for itself, it is time to make a massive push to make that improvement obsolete by inventing something better.

This is *not* continuous improvement in the sense of incremental changes that fine-tune an existing process. We are talking about full-scale, revolutionary innovation! And it's not optional. Because if you aren't innovating in the quality area, someone else is, and before you know it, you'll be behind.

In brief, one major pitfall is to believe the quality journey is over, just because you have attained a certain Baldrige score.

## Signs of Progress

Our experiences both at our own lab and that at IBM's (Baldrige-winning) Rochester site suggest some indicators which are valuable to watch in the integration stage. These signs of progress are listed in Fig. 19.2.

## Our Lab at the Integration Stage

In 1993, our Baldrige score indicated that we had crossed over the threshold of the fourth stage of quality maturity, integration. We feel that the hallmarks of the integration stage are a general acceptance of cross-functional teamwork; integration of customers, suppliers, and the community in the organization's quality efforts, and the propagation of the most effective tools and processes across the organization. An organization in the integration stage should be a learning organization. That is, the philosophy and habits of continuous improvement and innovation should be embedded firmly in the fabric of its culture.

In retrospect, our quality journey so far has been about pushing the scope of our quality efforts in space and time. Along the space dimension, our

---

- Morale is up. People feel they are special.
- Productivity is up.
- Warranty and service costs are dropping.
- Customer satisfaction is up.
- Market share is increasing.
- You are being used as a benchmark with increasing frequency. Companies from other industries want to learn from you.
- Process reengineering takes place without management even knowing.
- Supplier satisfaction is up.
- Managing is fun again.
- A customer perspective pervades the whole organization.
- Innovation is accelerating. Patents, paper publications, conference presentations, and speaking engagements are all up.

**Figure 19.2**  Suggested indicators of progress for the integration stage.

efforts have grown in size. They began with the awareness of a handful of people—the leaders. From there, a vision spread, first to isolated individuals, then to teams, then to cross-functional teams, and now to suppliers, customers, business partners, and the community at large.

Along the time dimension, we have moved from actions that affected only our immediate problems, to proactive actions that prevented future problems, to long-term actions that will ensure quality 10 years down the road.

It has been the leader's job to stretch the organization along these dimensions of space and time. We began the journey by creating a crisis in 1989—before there really was a crisis. Because of our quality vision, the lab has been at the forefront of IBM, consistently profitable, and consistently willing to stretch to reach "unreasonable" goals.

In our vision of the future, the lab must redouble its efforts at innovation. Every employee must be technically vital, and every product area should have several renegade teams working on the next knowledge mining centers and experimenting with radical process improvements. At the same time, we must continue cross-functional communication and teamwork so that the good ideas of one group quickly spread to the other groups.

As customers and suppliers join us in our quality improvement efforts, we expect code quality, revenue, productivity, and customer satisfaction to continue to increase. At the same time, maintenance and service costs must continue to drop.

In 1989, these words sounded hollow, like echoes of wishful thinking. By 1993 we could say that our quality efforts helped us achieve every one of these goals. Our quality program worked. We improved on every one of our critical quality measurements, and we have been recognized as the outstanding lab in IBM, recipient of the company's highest quality award. Now it's time to innovate and make our quality program obsolete.

## Suggested Readings

Brown, A., and Penedo, M. H. (1992) *An Annotated Bibliography on Integration in Software Engineering Environments,* CMU/SEI Special Report, CMU/SEI-92-SR-8. *An annotated bibliography useful to those exploring the technical aspects of integration in software engineering environments.*

Juran, J. M. (1991) "Strategies for World-Class Quality," *Quality Progress,* pp. 81–85, March. *The views of one of the leading quality gurus on how to reach world-class quality levels.*

# 20

# Ensuring Quality for the Future

In a proactive, growing organization, the future lies in expansion—if not in physical size, then at least in competitiveness and in the extent of the organization's vision. For this reason, the leadership innovations of the integration stage are concerned with deepening and broadening the organization's view of quality. The objective is to channel the momentum of past stages into continuous improvement, exchanges with other companies, and community efforts that may have a long-term payoff.

Table 20.1 summarizes our leadership innovations for the integration stage, together with the objectives they help achieve and implementation pitfalls.

Continuous improvement reviews are meant to communicate to the organization that the focus on quality has not gone away. The format is drastically different from that of earlier reviews such as the Excellence Council. The reviews are much more low key and assume that the groups participating in the review will take the leadership role. Whereas Excellence Councils serve mainly to raise awareness and gain buy-in, the continuous improvement

**TABLE 20.1  Stage: Integration / Food Group: Leadership / Themes: World-Class Status; Continuous Improvements; Learning Organization; Emphasis on Strategy**

| Objective | Innovative approach | Pitfalls |
|---|---|---|
| Sustain quality improvement momentum | *Continue improvement reviews:* Begin streamlining review processes Include ISO 9000 | Signal of lack of commitment to improvement Settling for results achieved Not raising the bar |
| Answer categorically: Do you know what you don't know? | *Quality exchanges* with key industry participants Share best practices Membership in key quality organizations | Not exchanging with the best Fear of sharing Getting arrogant |
| Strengthen linkages to the community | *WorkForce 2000 program:* Strengthen linkages with community | Making it a PR function Not focusing on actions that provide value |

reviews serve primarily as a formal mechanisms to report progress and obtain feedback.

Quality exchanges with other companies are an important extension of benchmarking. These exchanges fulfill the responsibility of quality leaders to share what they've learned with others, but the exchanges also help an organization find out what it doesn't know that it doesn't know about quality. Less formal than benchmarking, the exchanges are a good way to form leader-to-leader ties with other companies and to open lines of communication regarding quality issues.

Finally, WorkForce 2000 is illustrative of the long-term thinking and community involvement that typifies world-class companies. While there may be little immediate technical payback from activities that support the community, there is an intangible benefit to morale within the company and to goodwill outside of it. In the long term, we believe programs like WorkForce 2000 will result in a higher-quality workforce, not just because they invest in educating and training members of the local community, but because many top-caliber people worldwide will choose to work for an organization that demonstrates social responsibility as part of its quality value system.

## Innovation 33 (Leadership): Continuous Improvement Reviews

### The objective

The challenge facing our lab in January 1992 was how to deepen our quality efforts at a time when IBM as a company was going through turbulent change. In the midst of layoffs and changes in leadership at every level from the CEO to the general manager, we needed to build on our quality improvement momentum and solidify the programs that were already in place.

On a pragmatic level, we also needed to accelerate compliance with ISO 9000.

The tightrope we walked was to maintain the quality improvement momentum begun by the Excellence Council system without alienating a highly stressed development community. It helped that just about everyone could now speak the language of Baldrige, so we experimented with a new review format. Continuous improvement reviews are a logical extension of the Excellence Council, but with a new name and a much less formal structure.

### An innovative approach

Quality reviews started from the premise that Baldrige had become embedded in the culture and that if the GM asked about quality, he would probably get a Baldrige-style answer whether he asked for it or not. This assumption, which later proved to be correct, freed us to evolve the formal Excellence Council proceedings into a much less formal quality review.

The formality of Excellence Councils phases I to III may have been necessary to demonstrate commitment to quality, but such pomp and circumstance were no longer necessary. In fact, it had become somewhat distracting since most members at the lab found it hard to reconcile the expense with the lay-offs that were happening at IBM for the first time in the company's history.

The function of continuous improvement reviews (also known as IDEAL operations reviews because the first letters of the product organizations involved spell IDEAL) is much the same as that of the earlier Excellence Councils, but the format is much more informal and utilitarian. Figure 20.1 and Table 20.2 show our view of the evolutionary process leading up to these reviews.

With regard to focus, the intent is similar to that of Excellence Council phase III (see Chap. 4), namely, to strengthen deployment and to monitor quality progress. However, instead of strictly following the Baldrige template as in past Excellence Councils, the quality reviews use a reduced set of questions that are targeted at areas needing the most quality improvement.

The format of the reviews is informal, and the presentation teams come from each of the product areas, drawing on cross-functional support as need-ed. The assessors include the general manager, members of the CSE, and other senior managers and technical people at the lab. In other respects, the quality reviews are quite similar to Excellence Council phase III.

So far, the response to quality reviews has been positive, and developers consider them an improvement over the previous Excellence Councils. Interestingly, although there was some concern that Baldrige would be for-gotten if presentations were not required to follow the Baldrige template, this proved not to be the case. Almost all the presentations expressed improve-ment activities in terms of Baldrige terminology anyway. Without our even knowing it, Baldrige had become part of the culture, and now the categories are essentially synonymous with quality.

## Costs, benefits, and risks

The cost of quality reviews is significantly lower than the cost of Excellence Councils. Because presentations are less formal, there is no need for fancy graphics or televised meetings. The emphasis is on clear communication of

**TABLE 20.2    Evolution of Continuous Improvement Reviews**

| | Quality achievement level | | | | |
|---|---|---|---|---|---|
| | Pre-Bronze 1989 | Bronze 1990 | Silver 1991 | Sterling 1992 | Gold 1993 |
| Senior executives | Selling | Coaching | Mentoring | Consulting | Supporting |
| Environment | Skeptical | Aware | Exploration | Acceptance | Way of life |
| Result | Awareness | Learning | Attitude | Behavior | Achievement |
| Program | Business as usual | Middle manage-ment Excellence Council | First-line management Excellence Council | Nonmanage-ment Excellence Council | IDEAL operations review—business as usual |

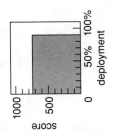

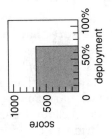

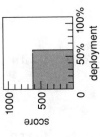

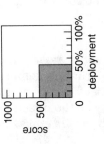

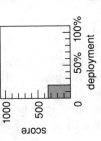

**Figure 20.1** Evolution of IBM's Quality Review System. (*Courtesy of IBM*)

information. Moreover, because many of the processes for gathering data were already in place and because the set of questions was shortened, the amount of work required to gather the data for the reviews was reduced by at least half.

Incorporating ISO 9000 questions into the review added benefit beyond the usual benefits of Excellence Councils. The main benefits of the reviews, however, were to maintain the quality improvement momentum, communicate a results-oriented approach, and demonstrate that the lab has reached a stage where quality improvement is part of the culture. The Excellence Councils pulled the lab through stages of resistance and uncertainty. The reviews serve as checkpoints to make sure that this momentum is not lost and to assess the results of the earlier efforts as they roll in.

The risk with the reviews is that people may misinterpret them as sending a signal that quality is less important. This risk can be minimized by making sure that the general manager participates in the reviews and continues to communicate her or his personal commitment to quality. Also, as the positive results from earlier efforts begin to show up, these must be communicated widely throughout the organization so that people can see that their earlier work has borne fruit.

### Synergy

The quality reviews are synergistic with the Excellence Councils (Chap. 4) and with ISO 9000 (Chap. 10).

### Prerequisites

The total quality management system and vocabulary for talking about quality should be embedded in the culture.

### Implementation advice

The key to a successful quality review lies in making sure that developers take the review seriously. Having senior executive commitment helps. So does choosing the right set of questions to ask, so that the developers gain value when they go to answer the questions. Finally, emphasizing the continuity with prior, more high-profile efforts (such as the Excellence Councils) is important for continuity.

Our GM assessed every presentation and provided feedback, thus demonstrating commitment.

Figure 20.2 illustrates some of the questions that every product area was asked.

Finally, it is important to look for signs that the organization has embedded quality in its culture. If people use the Baldrige vocabulary or speak in terms of quality, that is a good sign. But if you opt for the less formal quality review approach, make sure that it is because the quality culture is self-sustaining, not because you have tired of the struggle to instill quality values.

- What are the customer satisfaction trends for your key products?
- How do your customer satisfaction and dissatisfaction results compare with those of your major competitors by geography (e.g., the United States, Europe, Asia)?
- What are the current levels and trends for the key measures of quality for products, services, support services, and suppliers?
- With particular focus on process control, corrective actions, and quality records, what are your plans for ISO auditability?
- What are your trends regarding employee satisfaction, education, recognition, and team participation?

**Figure 20.2**  Sample questions from continuous improvement reviews.

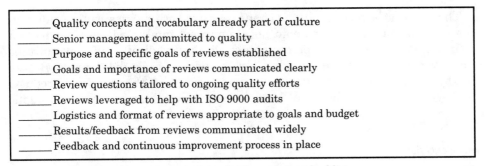

_____ Quality concepts and vocabulary already part of culture
_____ Senior management committed to quality
_____ Purpose and specific goals of reviews established
_____ Goals and importance of reviews communicated clearly
_____ Review questions tailored to ongoing quality efforts
_____ Reviews leveraged to help with ISO 9000 audits
_____ Logistics and format of reviews appropriate to goals and budget
_____ Results/feedback from reviews communicated widely
_____ Feedback and continuous improvement process in place

**Figure 20.3**  Continuous improvement review implementation checklist.

Figure 20.3 presents our implementation checklist for continuous improvement reviews.

## Innovation 34 (Leadership): Quality Exchanges

### The objective

Once you've done just about everything you know to improve the quality of your processes, products, and services, what else is there to do?

The answer is, begin to look for new things that you don't know how to do. But there are two problems. First, sometimes you don't even know what you don't know. Especially at the integration stage, where all the basics have been taken care of, it is easy to miss opportunities for quality improvement, simply because you never thought to look in a certain direction. Second, even if you have an idea of the direction you need to take for improvement, it can take a long time to invent the new quality improvement technology. Our lab developed the quality exchange concept as a way to address both these concerns while providing a public service at the same time.

### An innovative approach

In essence, a _quality exchange_ is a forum that allows two companies, or organizations, to share information about their quality processes, metrics, and innovations. Participants in the exchange discuss common quality challenges and approaches that have been tried.

Sometimes a single exchange is held, hosted by one of the companies. At other times the exchange is part of an ongoing series of information exchanges. For example, our site held a quality exchange with Hewlett-Packard (HP). Representatives from Hewlett-Packard described local programs that were part of the corporate effort to streamline HP's businesses. These included an eight-category process assessment methodology and a 5-year strategy focusing on quality improvement. IBM's representatives described their use of the Malcolm Baldrige template as an assessment tool and outlined IBM's strategy for compliance with international standards such as ISO 9000.

The result of a good quality exchange is that both parties walk away having learned something new about how to improve quality without having had to invent it themselves. When companies with two radically different cultures meet, you can learn things you didn't even know that you didn't know. Best of all, by sharing knowledge about quality improvement, the quality of products and services in the industry at large increases, which in our view is a public service.

### Costs, benefits, and risks

The costs of running a quality exchange program do not have to be large. We have one full-time coordinator for the entire lab, but organizations with less than 1000 people could probably manage with a part-time coordinator. If the partner in the exchange is willing to come to your site, the additional costs are minimal. Typically it amounts to the time required to prepare a presentation for the visitor plus the time of the actual meeting itself.

If travel is involved, things can get more expensive. The number of individuals attending a quality exchange can range from 2 to 50 or more. Travel costs for an active quality exchange program where most of the meetings require airline travel and hotel accommodations could easily total $200,000 a year. To keep travel costs down, we recommend choosing local partners for exchanges if at all possible.

There are other advantages to local exchanges as well. First, they provide an opportunity to discuss quality issues that may arise from location-specific factors. Second, it is easier to prepare for and follow up after the exchange. Finally, local exchanges tend to be more effective than long-distance exchanges because more people (especially executives) are likely to participate if the exchange does not require extended travel.

For example, as the result of one quality exchange, our lab loaned an executive to help a local Silicon Valley firm over a period of weeks. The close proximity of the company to IBM allowed the executive to advise the company while still being available to attend critical meetings at IBM.

The relationship between our lab and Silicon Valley's Council for Continuous Improvement is another example of a successful, ongoing local exchange.

The council has sponsored CEO breakfasts, quality presentations, and networking sessions on a regular basis. As a result, local executives at other companies have participated in reviews of the quality activities at our lab.

Both large and small organizations can benefit from the efficiency inherent in quality exchanges. If the companies that you share with happen to be suppliers or customers, the benefits are even greater.

A quality exchange with a customer demonstrates that you are serious about quality. It also allows you to see which aspects of quality are most critical to your customer. You can use this information to help prioritize your own quality efforts.

Quality exchanges with suppliers also yield benefits beyond the simple sharing of information. One IBM supplier explained that poor quality in one of their $2 parts could have cost millions of dollars had the parts been installed in IBM mainframes. Quality exchanges with this supplier and other suppliers have helped suppliers improve their processes. As supplier quality improves, so does the quality of IBM's products.

One of the discoveries of the quality exchange program was that useful exchanges were possible even across industries and with organizations of diverse types and sizes. For example, our lab has held exchanges with companies in the entertainment business, with the University of California, and with the Japanese Union of Scientists and Engineers. Participating institutions have ranged in size from Exxon to Redwood Design Automation, Inc., a local start-up company with only 25 employees.

The risk that immediately springs to mind is the question of confidential information. It is important that both participants in the exchange sign agreements that neither side will disclose confidential information during the exchange. If, for some reason, confidential information will be disclosed, nondisclosure agreements should be in place so that the confidential information does not travel beyond the party for whom it was intended.

Another risk is that both participants may be at different levels of quality maturity so that the exchange turns into a briefing with one company providing all the value. One way to minimize this risk is to clarify expectations in advance and/or to charge a fee for briefings.

### Synergy

Quality exchanges are synergistic with a number of other programs that reach outside the organization for information including process benchmarking (Chap. 15), educational seminars (Chap. 5), business partner quality processes (Chap. 21), and quality partnership programs (Chap. 21).

### Prerequisites

There are no prerequisites except that both organizations must be at a level of quality maturity where each has something to offer in an exchange.

## Implementation advice

Logistically, the Hewlett-Packard exchange mentioned earlier was easy to set up since both Hewlett-Packard and our lab are located in California's Silicon Valley area. After signing agreements that neither company would disclose information of a confidential nature, teams from the two companies met at IBM. Over the next 2 days, they traded information about programs and processes that could help both companies meet their quality objectives.

Setting up the exchange is relatively easy, but making sure the exchange is effective is more of a challenge. There are four points to keep in mind:

1. Quality exchanges can be used at any stage of quality maturity, but they work best when each organization has achieved some level of proficiency in an area where the partner organization is weak.

2. Before any exchange, make sure both parties define clearly, and agree on, the objectives of the exchange. Create an agenda that describes the specific topics to be shared.

3. During the exchange, foster an atmosphere of openness. Both companies must present honest views of their progress and of areas that need improvement.

4. Establish processes to follow up after the exchange. Follow-up activities should include gathering more information, if necessary, and ensuring that useful information is transmitted to members of the organization who did not participate directly in the exchange.

We also follow every quality exchange immediately with a one-page evaluation form. The feedback on this form helps improve the quality exchange process. For example, one company indicated that it did not have a clear idea of what was expected of it in its presentation. The process was modified to make sure that future participants had clearer information about presentation content.

Finally, here are some questions you might ask to help locate potential partners for quality exchanges:

1. Are your suppliers or customers nearby?

2. How innovative is the neighboring industry?

3. Do cross-company quality organizations exist? For example, in Silicon Valley, the Council for Continuous Improvement qualifies as such an organization.

4. What opportunity is there for quality exchanges with academia? Quality management programs?

Figure 20.4 summarizes our implementation checklist for quality exchanges.

Once the word gets out that you are interested in quality, you'd be surprised at how many other companies come knocking. We've had more than 50 exchanges since the program's inception.

| | |
|---|---|
| _____ | Purpose of and commitment to program clear |
| _____ | Local potential exchange partners identified |
| _____ | Contribution of each partner identified |
| _____ | Goals of the specific exchange clearly communicated |
| _____ | Agreement on logistics and format |
| _____ | Legal issues resolved |
| _____ | Information from exchange disseminated within the organization |
| _____ | Partners contacted after exchange for follow-up |
| _____ | Evaluation and continuous improvement process in place |

**Figure 20.4**  Quality exchange implementation checklist.

## Innovation 35 (Leadership): WorkForce 2000

### The objective

As an organization reaches the later stages of quality maturity, community responsibility and long-term thinking should play an increasing role in quality efforts. On a pragmatic level, the local community may produce future workers for the organization, and it is also the place where most of the current workers live.

The lab wanted to invest in the local community and at the same time accommodate a strategy for ensuring that the laboratory workforce over the next decade would be both diverse and top-caliber. We wanted to ensure that the number of women and minorities would be representative of the local and national populations, and we wanted to foster early relationships with the lab's future workforce.

The challenge was to create a pipeline of programs and processes to produce a continual flow of qualified potential employees. The pipeline would begin outside the organization in the community, but would continue inside the organization. Figure 20.5 illustrates this pipeline concept.

We needed to develop processes and programs to link investment in the community with the future needs of the lab's workforce. To do this, we had to move beyond an isolationist perspective that drew strong distinctions between *us* (inside the organization) and *them* (outside it). From a quality perspective, we couldn't achieve our goals without *them*, so they were really *us*, too. With this realization, the WorkForce 2000 program was born.

### An innovative approach

WorkForce 2000 began as a small task force in 1990 and grew into an established group as our quality maturity increased. By 1991, it consisted of one assigned project manager working with more than 30 volunteers across the lab.

The volunteers were people who, in addition to their regular jobs, felt a strong commitment to the quality of the lab's workforce. Typically, the volun-

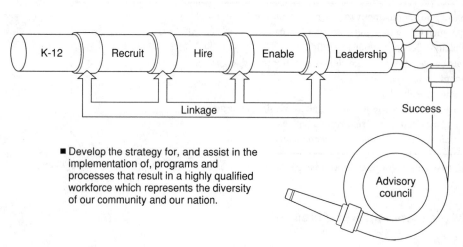

Develop the strategy for, and assist in the implementation of, programs and processes that result in a highly qualified workforce which represents the diversity of our community and our nation.

**Figure 20.5**  The WorkForce 2000 pipeline. (*Courtesy of IBM*)

teers also were concerned with making sure that the lab encouraged and provided opportunities for minorities and women in the community to achieve their potentials.

Working in partnership with our human resources department, people in the WorkForce 2000 program have become involved with a variety of community groups. Activities range from tutoring in high schools, to recruiting at colleges, to working with summer hires in internship programs.

The response from the community has been enthusiastic, as evidenced by a steady stream of thank-you notes from school districts and other community organizations. In our own view, the program has been tremendously successful in creating good relationships with potential future employees. However, perhaps more than any other innovation in this book, WorkForce 2000 represents a long-term investment of time and resources. As the name implies, the harvest of the seeds sown today is not expected until the year 2000.

## Costs, benefits, and risks

The cost of the program is minimal, since more than 90 percent of the workers are volunteers. Even the program manager is a part-time resource.

One of the advantages of the program's low cost is that it makes it easy for management to live with the idea that returns may not be evident for 5 years or more. More immediate advantages include the positive impact that the program has on the volunteers' morale and on the rest of the lab. Team building is another immediate benefit.

Finally, some programs, such as the internship program, provide benefits in the form of low-cost help for activities at the lab. We have worked with many of these interns ourselves, and we are convinced that the program benefits not only the interns (who are usually students) but also IBM.

The risks of the workforce program are minimal. Probably the chief ingredient to success is selection of a dedicated program coordinator with good people skills. Since the program is largely volunteer, there is a minimum of risk to the organization's resources.

## Synergy

WorkForce 2000 is synergistic with process benchmarking and empowerment programs.

## Prerequisites

There are no formal prerequisites for this program. Lots of energy and a heart-felt commitment help.

## Implementation advice

The overall implementation of WorkForce 2000 is summarized in Fig. 20.6, which shows specific programs addressing various stages of the WorkForce 2000 pipeline.

For example, at the K–12 stage, the lab participates in Industry Initiatives for Science and Math Education (IISME) activities. At the recruiting stage, we leverage the National College Recruiting Organization (NCRO). At the hiring stage, we have "golden chits," which are preapproved hiring slots for people with Ph.D. or master's degrees. Finally at the enabling stage, we make opportunities such as "shadowing" senior managers available to fast-track employees. The major subprograms that compose the pipeline are described in more detail below.

At our lab, the WorkForce 2000 program consists of five subprograms: the K–12 program, the college relations program, the summer hire program, the enabling program, and the benchmarking program.

The K–12 program has two distinct but related purposes. First, it aims to strengthen the community's educational infrastructure at the level of kindergarten through 12th grade. Second, it seeks to establish ties with students who may become part of the future hiring pool for the lab.

The K–12 program has "adopted" Santa Teresa High School and is in the process of adopting all schools in the local school district, including eleven elementary schools, two junior high schools, and two high schools. Each of these schools contains a diverse student population representative of the demographics in the surrounding communities.

Over the last 2 years, 50 volunteers from the lab have tutored over 350 high school students. The K–12 program sponsors meetings which help students learn about careers in public service. Two senior managers at the lab have served as "principal for a day" at the high school, and two mathematics and science teachers from the high school were hired for a summer to work at the lab and to learn about the educational needs of industry.

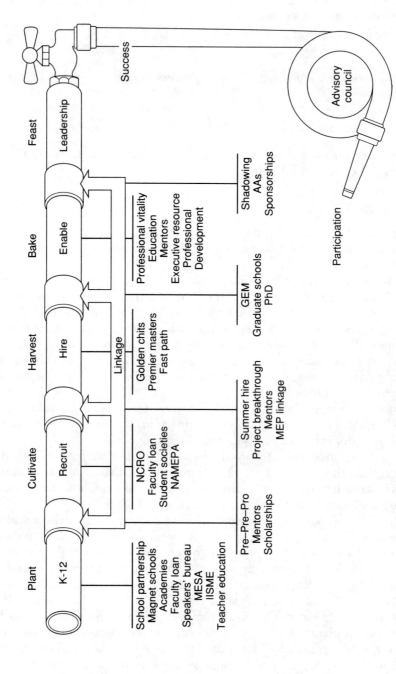

**Figure 20.6** WorkForce 2000: Programs for the pipeline. (*Courtesy of IBM*)

As part of IBM's National Engineering Week, 40 lab employees spoke to 2230 students at 50 schools. A speakers' bureau has since been established. Its mission is to encourage students to further their education in the areas of mathematics and science. The bureau is staffed by 40 volunteers.

Finally, the K–12 program helped with a Technology Fair which raised $8000 for schools to purchase technology for learning. More importantly, this fair, together with a Public Education Fair held in the lab's cafeteria, raised public awareness about IBM's commitment to education.

The college relations program also has two areas of focus. On the recruiting front, the program subcommittee identifies universities with whom we want to establish relationships because of the high caliber of their students. The subcommittee also helps select and train campus recruiters.

A second focus is the interaction between IBM management and deans, faculty, and staff at universities. As with all the subcommittees, the role here is primarily one of consultant to the human resources organization.

The lab currently has an "Adopt-a-College" program with five schools: the University of California at Los Angeles, San Diego, and Berkeley; the University of Southern California; and the University of Washington. A team of eight recruiter-volunteers participates in the program, and they have developed some innovative recruiting software that runs on an IBM laptop computer.

The summer hire program provides an opportunity for students from all walks of life to spend a summer working at the lab on a technical assignment. Student "welcome receptions," roundtable meetings, networking, and mentoring round out the experience for participants. Ten minority students participated in the program in 1991, and twenty were expected to participate in 1992.

The enabling program differs from the previous three programs in that it focuses on the internal community at the lab. It would be foolish to develop the potential of individuals outside the organization without doing the same for our own employees. While the human resources department clearly has the mission for this activity, the enabling subcommittee provides some extra help.

In 1991, for example, this subcommittee developed and distributed "Career Guidelines," a booklet based on interviews with employees at all levels of the lab that clarified what is needed to move up the career ladder.

The "technical vitality" strategy was another effort that helped management become more aware of what was required to ensure that employees kept technically sharp. A mentoring program was also defined to help match employees with mentors who could further their career growth.

The WorkForce 2000 diversity training module explained the changing demographics of the workplace and helped prepare managers for equal opportunity meetings which are held annually.

Finally, the process benchmarking program is responsible for making sure that our human resource development plans are best-of-class. WorkForce 2000 processes have been, or will be, compared with those of Microsoft, Hewlett-Packard, AT&T, and TRW.

_____ Energetic program champion

_____ Purpose and goals of the program clear

_____ Benefits to organization and community understood

_____ Management support, funding, participation

_____ Internal and external publicity

_____ Partnerships established with schools and universities

_____ Volunteers identified

_____ Recognition/celebration of accomplishments

_____ Evaluation and continuous improvement process in place

**Figure 20.7**   WorkForce 2000 implementation checklist.

Probably the most unique aspect of the WorkForce 2000 program is its emphasis on volunteer efforts in the five subprograms. We've found that most employees are concerned about their environment both at work and in the community at large. The genius of the WorkForce 2000 program is that it leverages that concern for the mutual benefit of the employees, the community, and the organization.

Figure 20.7 presents our implementation checklist for WorkForce 2000.

## Suggested Readings

Lillrank, P., and Noriaki, K. (1989) *Continuous Improvement: Quality Control Circles in Japanese Industry.* Ann Arbor, MI: Center for Japanese Studies, University of Michigan. *A good study of the Japanese approach to continuous improvement via quality circles.*

Miller, G. L., and La Rue, L. K. (1992) *The Whats, Whys and Hows of Quality Improvement: A Guidebook for Continuous Improvement.* Milwaukee, WI: ASQC Quality Press. *A contemporary look at continuous improvement methods.*

*Second International Conference on the Software Process: Continuous Software Process Improvement,* February 25–26, 1993, Berlin, Germany. Sponsored by the Rocky Mountain Institute of Software Engineering. Los Alamitos, CA: IEEE Computer Society Press. *A dozen or so technical papers on the topic of continuous software process improvement.*

Shingo, S. (1988) *Non-stock Production: The Shingo System for Continuous Improvement.* Cambridge, MA: Productivity Press. *This book covers many of the principles that launched the surge of interest in continuous improvement.*

For information on quality networking events and exchanges of information at general sessions, contact Council for Continuous Improvement— 1-408 441-7716.

# Quality Knows No Boundaries

The process innovations described here extend the scope of quality efforts to include customers and business partners. Our quality partnership program gathers the insights of customers who use the software after it has been developed. The business partner quality program aims to improve the quality of software and services produced by business partners by sharing expertise and expectations about quality with them. Table 21.1 summarizes these two innovations along with the objectives they help achieve and implementation pitfalls.

These process innovations represent something of a paradigm shift in that they recognize that the boundaries of the organization do not end with the organizational chart. The organization has a dotted-line boundary that includes customers, suppliers, partners, and the community at large. Quality improvement activities ultimately have to transcend organizational boundaries to be successful. The logical consequence of this new view is that processes must be established to promote and ensure quality across organizational boundaries.

**TABLE 21.1  Stage: Integration / Food Group: Process / Themes: Erase External Organizational Boundaries; Include Customers, Suppliers, and Business Partners; Deploy Zero-Defect Initiatives**

| Objective | Innovative approach | Pitfalls |
|---|---|---|
| Reduce level of defects after shipment | *Quality partnership program (QPP):* Customer participation throughout product life-cycle | Arbitrary customer selection in program<br>Mindless attention to only participating customer input<br>Failure to act thoughtfully |
| Increase quality maturity and product quality of suppliers and business partners | *Business partner quality process program:* Develop initiatives to improve suppliers' and business partners' capabilities<br>Share information | "You are not OK, I'm OK" syndrome<br>Overwhelming bureaucracy<br>Failure to learn from each other |

## Innovation 36 (Process): Quality Partnerships with Customers

### The objective

The *quality partnership program* (QPP) was motivated by errors discovered by customers in the field. Although our lab has had a number of different early shipping and beta test programs over the years, these programs were simply not finding enough errors in the field.

As a result, consistently after a product had been announced as generally available, errors would flood in from the field. It was expensive and disruptive to ship programming fixes to all the customers who had purchased the product. Moreover, customers, recognizing that it takes a while for the bugs of a new release to get worked out, might delay their purchases or even choose a competitor's product.

Something had to be done, and in 1990 a task force charted by the highest executive in our line of business recommended a new approach—QPP.

### An innovative approach

The goal of QPP is to get the bugs worked out, with comprehensive customer participation, before the product is shipped widely. This builds a reputation for quality and short-circuits the "I'll wait until the bugs get worked out before I migrate" syndrome. But to figure out why QPP would work where other programs had failed required a detailed analysis of the error history of our software products and of our joint work with customers to date.

The first thing the analysis revealed was that a small proportion of customers were finding a disproportionate share of the bugs. Generally these turned out to be either our largest customers or customers who were simply using the product in more complex ways than most of our other customers.

When we reexamined our past joint work with customers, we realized that their involvement was focused almost exclusively in the very last, or beta test, stage of development. The critical insight was to realize that we had to stop looking at our QPP customers as favored recipients of what we produced who got to peek at the product a few months before everyone else. Instead, QPP customers would be active partners in the development of the product, from design to coding, to development of the test plan, through testing, and finally to early installation and support in their environments.

We realized that if customers were finding errors that our test department wasn't, there was probably something wrong with our test plan and possibly something wrong with our design as well. In QPP, we showed customers internal documents describing designs, early drafts of documentation, and our proposed test plans. This was a revolutionary step for IBM, a company that traditionally had been highly secretive about these matters.

The customers were generally ecstatic. Finally, they had a way to provide input early, at a time when the product could still be changed. Moreover, because they were involved at critical design points along the entire product's development, customers had a better understanding of the quality efforts that were going into creating the product, and this increased their confidence. Customers also got extra attention and support from IBM during the installation and setup of the products in their organizations. Such things as direct access to the product developers and expert assistance in tailoring the product to their needs amounted to getting the services of a free software consultant.

In short, QPP is about bringing customers into the development process, showering them with attention, and making them feel part of the development team. It means giving customers a sense of power and control via unprecedented responsiveness to their needs. It means producing a higher-quality product. And it means working with the users of a product at every critical step of the development process.

As far as our customers are concerned, QPP seems to be working. A manager for Federal Express, a QPP customer for our IMS product, put it this way: "Even more than function or flexibility, Federal Express requires stability. We have an availability goal of 99.7 percent for all on-line systems. With the enhancements provided in [the new release of] IMS and the commitment to quality that has been evident throughout the QPP program, we expect to exceed this goal."

Toronto-Dominion Bank, another QPP customer, put it even more succinctly: "Our experience has been very positive. We believe IBM is listening to us."

As for IBM, if our customers are happy, we're happy.


## Costs, benefits, and risks

QPP is not free. It costs IBM, and it costs the customers in terms of resources that must be devoted to the program to make it work. On IBM's side, because developers, executives, lawyers, and marketing and/or service representatives are all involved, the time cost can be substantial. On the customer's side, the customer must be willing to review documents, to meet with IBM developers, and to struggle with preannouncement versions of the product. To be sure, IBM assists in all this, but the time cost can still be significant.

On the other hand, the benefits of QPP can be significant as well. They include the following:

1. Fewer defects in the field, which translates to substantial dollar savings

2. Happier customers who feel involved and listened to and who get extra support in installing and customizing products

3. Products that address the needs of customers better than if the customers were removed from the development process

Here are some of the comments IBM developers made about QPP in a lab-wide survey:

"Can get early feedback."

"Get involved early on in the development process (during requirements gathering or early design). We implemented the program late, when most of the product testing was already completed, and I think an earlier involvement would have made the program more meaningful."

"We have always gotten much more out of the program than we have put into it. I would like to see more customers and more international customers participate in QPPs."

"The team has found that the selection of the participants is vital to this program's success; i.e., it must be a representative sample of the product's customer set, or else you can end up emphasizing the wrong functions/features in terms of your development effort."

"QPP is a good program in that it involves customers early in the design, test, [and] development cycle of the code."

"There is extra time and support needed, but the quality of the release will definitely improve. It's easier to get more rigorous with this method than by trying to overhaul a test department."

A side benefit is that the program gets people at all levels in IBM and in our customers' companies talking to each other. Executives are made aware of needs and problems that they might otherwise miss. All this adds up to higher quality and increased customer satisfaction.

But QPP is not without risks. The risk of revealing confidential information to customers can be minimized with nondisclosure agreements and careful explanation of what information is sensitive.

Another risk is that individual customers who participate in QPP might have undue influence on the product design to the detriment of our customer set as a whole. This risk reflects the distinction between being customer-driven and market-driven. Our lab tries to be market-driven, so that it can meet the needs of an entire market segment rather than of a few select customers. To avoid conflict on this issue, we made it very clear that the design of products would not be changed unless the change were of benefit to all the product's customers—not just the QPP customers.

Finally, there is the risk of alienating customers if the program is not executed well or if customers see things they don't like. This risk gets at the core issue of confidence in your quality efforts. One reason that we recommend QPP as an activity best suited for the later stages of quality maturity is that, by this stage, your quality really is good enough that customers are more likely to be impressed than turned off.

## Synergy

QPP is synergistic with benchmarking, the defect prevention process, early test involvement, rapid prototyping, and customer satisfaction survey efforts.

## Prerequisites

The organization should have reached a high level of quality maturity and should have good working relationships with its customers.

## Implementation advice

The first step in implementing QPP is to obtain buy-in of senior management in the organization. Because QPP reveals sensitive information to customers, it is important to involve the legal department and to have the executive clout to get the program past the legal barriers.

We grossly underestimated the amount of legal paperwork involved. But if you have several customers, marketing branches, and the development organization involved at several sites, you have a legal nightmare on your hands. One of our QPP managers said, "It was a bit like passing an amendment to the Constitution."

Once you've lined up executive support and given the lawyers some lead time, you need to select customers for participation. At our lab we had far more potential participants than we could handle, so we needed some sort of selection criterion. Because our goal was defect reduction, we chose those customers who had reported the most field defects. We figured that if any of our customers could teach us where we could improve, it would be these customers.

The desirability of objective criteria, such as the number of defects reported, assumes that you have a good defect tracking mechanism. If you don't, you probably are not at a high enough stage of quality maturity to begin QPP.

Because the marketing and service (M&S) groups were included in QPP, another constraint was the availability of M&S to contribute resources to the program. There was at least one case where a customer who was a good candidate for QPP was not selected because the branch servicing the account could not spare anyone to help administer the program. At the lab, we felt strongly that QPP should involve development, M&S, and the customer. The M&S folks had the most contact with the customer already and were able to act as intermediaries and facilitators of communication between developers and customers.

Next, you need to develop a QPP process that clearly specifies the nature and degree of customer involvement. The process should include mechanisms for follow-up to make sure that customers feel their concerns were addressed, to determine the effectiveness of the program, and to identify areas for improvement. Metrics should be kept in order to justify the program's ongoing value.

Finally, it is probably best to begin QPP with a relatively established product of modest size. If you make a mistake while establishing the QPP process, the cost is small. Once QPP is working, you can scale up to larger products.

Figure 21.1 presents our implementation advice for quality partnership programs.

_____ Purpose and goals of program understood
_____ QPP coordinator identified
_____ Products with high field error rates identified
_____ Support and/or commitment from marketing and service groups
_____ Potential customer participants identified
_____ Commitment from customers
_____ Agreement on mechanisms for customer involvement
_____ Legal issues resolved
_____ Program's effectiveness measured and communicated
_____ Feedback and continuous improvement process in place

**Figure 21.1**   QPP implementation checklist.

## Innovation 37 (Process): Business Partner Quality Process

### The objective

The software marketplace is now growing so rapidly that IBM cannot expect to compete in every market segment on its own. Recognizing this, IBM began to pursue partnerships with other companies aggressively in the late 1980s. These companies had technology and market share that IBM did not have. By working with them, IBM hoped to better satisfy its customers and to maintain a large stake in the rapidly expanding software marketplace.

However, from a quality perspective, this new emphasis on partnerships caused some problems. First, we were rapidly increasing the quality levels of our own products at a time when the quality of the new business partners' products was mostly unknown. Second, we had no process in place that would help us understand the quality levels of our partners or help improve them. Finally, a few cases were beginning to emerge in which IBM customers were coming to IBM to express dissatisfaction with IBM's business partners. These business partners were not producing products with the robustness and quality that the customers had come to expect from IBM, yet we had endorsed them. Even worse, we were dependent upon these partners because they provided important pieces of the total solutions that we wanted to offer to our customers.

For example, in one case representatives from Coca Cola came forward and said that they would not do business with us and the company we were partnering with because of dissatisfaction with the level of quality. Although most customers still seemed happy, we felt we needed to address the general issue of business partner quality before it became a major issue. Because of our own investments in quality, we anticipated that the disparity over time between the levels of quality in our own products and those of our business partners would just increase unless something was done.

## An innovative approach

The solution was to develop a quality program in partnership with our business partners. We needed to develop a process that made clear our expectations and required commitments from them, together with a set of checkpoints that would help us understand their level of quality and promote quality improvement. At the same time, we recognized that these companies were very different in culture and size from IBM. What worked for us would not necessarily be best for them. Most of our business partners did not have the same resources to spend on the quality challenges that we did. Moreover, these companies were partners, not supplier vassals. While it was tempting to just mandate levels of quality, this approach really violated the spirit of partnership.

All in all, it was tough to find someone who not only had good analytical skills but also had mastered the art of negotiation and persuasion. We were lucky to have such an individual at the lab. He created our business partner quality process in a matter of a year.

Figure 21.2 shows the vision and goals of the business partner quality program that ultimately led to the process we now use.

Overall, the business partner quality program has been successful in a relatively short time. All software executives at the lab—and at half a dozen other IBM software sites worldwide—now understand the need to have quality expectations from their business partners, consistently, across each and every company. A process now exists for incorporating quality concerns into existing and future relationships with business partners. Finally, the business partners themselves are beginning to address quality in a much more systematic and effective way.

For example, one partner went from completely haphazard and ad hoc quality efforts to a detailed strategy mapped to the Baldrige template in a matter of weeks after attending an IBM Baldrige class. The same partner implemented its own version of a knowledge mining center (Chap. 16) called a "development cocoon." It was so successful that this partner is putting in a second one.

---

**Vision**
- World-class solutions demand world-class partners.

**Goals**
- Continuous improvement
- Superior customer satisfaction
- Defect elimination leading to near-zero defects
- Cycle time reduction
- Measure progress
- Share best quality practices with business partners

---

**Figure 21.2**  Business partner quality program: Vision and goals.

## Costs, benefits, and risks

The program cost the lab 1 person-year plus travel. We dealt with dozens of business partners worldwide. Moreover, some of the business partners dealt with both our lab and other IBM sites worldwide. Depending upon the number of business partners, the number of sites that have dealings with these partners, and the physical proximity of the parties involved, the cost might be significantly less.

As befits a true partnership, the benefits accrue as much to the business partners as they do to IBM. The partners benefit because they have direct access to, and the support of, IBM's tremendous base of quality experience and educational material. They can get all the information contained in this book and more—which provides a terrific competitive advantage for them.

IBM benefits because its partners have higher-quality products and services which reflect well on IBM. It's also possible that the business partners will come up with quality innovations that IBM has not thought of. In this case, a true quality exchange (see Chap. 20) would be possible where both sides get new information.

Last, but certainly not least, the customers benefit because the quality of their solutions increases. They can stop worrying about the quality of software and concentrate on running their businesses, confident that both IBM and its business partners are providing the highest-quality software available. The beauty of the business partner quality program is that, if implemented correctly, it can be a win-win-win situation, for the organization, its partners, and their customers.

The risk is that poor implementation can alienate business partners. As mentioned earlier, we were fortunate to have an excellent manager who not only developed our process but also served as ambassador to other parts of IBM and to business partners. Even so, we had to be careful not to overwhelm smaller business partners with quality programs that might be more appropriate for a larger company like IBM. Sensitivity to the culture and needs of the business partners, a firm determination that quality must be improved, and a willingness to help are the keys to successful implementation without alienation.

## Synergy

Business partner quality efforts are synergistic with quality exchanges, quality partnership programs with customers (see above), and supplier quality efforts. Because a central part of the program involves the sharing of best quality practices, any innovation in this book might become part of the effort.

## Prerequisites

You need to be a leader in quality yourself—or at least have demonstrated unshakable commitment—before you can ask a partner to make the same strong commitment.

There is a good story from India, told by Michael Ray, a professor at Stanford Business School, and coauthor of *The New Paradigm in Business.* The story goes something like this (and if I'm embellishing a little, that's the point of a good story):

An Indian couple have a young son who loves sugar. In fact, the son is addicted to sugar in any form—candy, sugar cane, sugar-coated breakfast cereals, you name it.

Well, the couple is disturbed because the health of their child is deteriorating. So they try everything to get their son to stop eating so much sugar. They try buying healthy foods. It doesn't work. They try psychotherapy in an effort to get him to talk about his addiction. No dice. In desperation they even try getting the kid hooked on video games instead. But even that fails. At last, there is nothing left to do but to go visit the wise man of the village. So even though they are yuppies and don't believe much in mumbo jumbo, they go.

The wise man is sitting on the dirt floor of his hut, chewing on some sugar cane. The couple come in, with their son, and describe the problem. The wise man thinks for a moment and then says, "Bring the boy back to me in exactly two weeks."

Two weeks later, the couple bring the boy. The wise man gets up, walks over to the boy, grabs him firmly by the shoulder, and tells him loudly, "Stop eating too much sugar! Stop eating too much sugar!" He repeats this several times while shaking the boy.

To the surprise of the parents, the boy is cured. They are somewhat puzzled, so they go back to the wise man to ask a question: "If you could cure our son just by shaking him, why did we have to wait two weeks?"

"Ahh," said the wise man. "I needed two weeks because first I had to stop eating too much sugar."

Like the wise man in the story, we need to give up our own poor-quality habits before we can expect our partners to do so. It is a matter of integrity, and it shows.

## Implementation advice

In terms of the infrastructure needed for a business partner quality program, it is important that you build on an established process for managing business partners in the first place. That is, there ought to be a community of people who are responsible for managing the relationship between your organization and the business partners.

In addition, you must ensure that all the executives in your own organization understand and support the need for improving the quality of business partners. If you fail to take this step, executives at the partner company may simply go over your head to avoid what they might see as extra work.

At the same time, it is important to be sensitive to the differences between your partners' and your own organizations. For example, we narrowly avoided the mistake of alienating partners with an overly rigid and structured set of quality improvement expectations which we tried to apply to every partner.

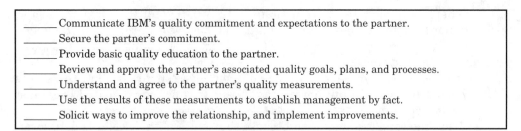

_____ Communicate IBM's quality commitment and expectations to the partner.

_____ Secure the partner's commitment.

_____ Provide basic quality education to the partner.

_____ Review and approve the partner's associated quality goals, plans, and processes.

_____ Understand and agree to the partner's quality measurements.

_____ Use the results of these measurements to establish management by fact.

_____ Solicit ways to improve the relationship, and implement improvements.

**Figure 21.3**  Business partner quality program implementation checklist.

We reasoned that since we were asking our own people to improve their quality 10-fold, we should ask our business partners to do the same.

However, we quickly realized that each partner was at a different stage of quality maturity. Just because we were ready to stretch toward 10-fold improvement, that didn't mean all our partners were. Many were still early in the awareness stage and didn't even have a clear process, let alone the concept of process improvement. We recognized that we would need to work with our partners, regardless of where they were in terms of quality maturity, and help them plan to reach the next stage. And that is what we did.

Finally, it's worth reiterating that one of the best things you can do to help your business partners improve quality is lead by example. It is not necessary to work with all business partners at once. Nor is it necessary or even desirable to force them all to conform to the same standards right away. However, it is crucial that your commitment to quality be highly visible and that you begin to take some steps to help business partners improve.

The logic is inescapable. Unless all aspects of your organization, including suppliers and partners, are world-class, how can your organization be world-class?

The higher the level of quality maturity, the more crucial this realization of interdependence becomes. Ultimate victory can be achieved not through force or compulsion, but only through the cooperative efforts of all the players.

IBM has a general process for selecting and working with new and existing business partners who are known in IBMspeak as international alliance members, or IAMs. Without going into confidential details, we outline seven important process steps in Fig. 21.3.

## Suggested Readings

Gause, D. C., and Weinberg, G. M. (1989) _Exploring Requirements: Quality Before Design._ New York: Dorset House. _A good book that stresses the role of getting customer requirements correctly in order to produce a quality product._

Ray, M., and Rinzler, A. (1993) _The New Paradigm in Business: Emerging Strategies for Leadership and Organizational Change._ New York: Putnam/Tarcher Books. _A fascinating collection of essays that blend humanistic values and emerging trends with business management._

Thayer, R. H., and Dorfman, M. (eds.) (1990) _System and Software Requirements Engineering._ Baltimore, MD: IEEE Computer Society Press.

# Experimental Quality Improvement Technologies

The integration-stage technologies are tools that add rigor to the general thrust of expanding the scope of quality activities. Table 22.1 summarizes these innovations, the objectives they help achieve, and implementation pitfalls.

Performance mining is an application of computer-supported team work spaces to the problem of improving the performance of a product. Orthogonal defect control and quality return on investment (ROI) are intended to provide more detailed information about errors and investment decisions, respectively. Each of these innovations is in the preliminary deployment or pilot stage as of this writing. They reflect the lab's commitment to continued innovation as the driver of future quality improvements.

## Innovation 38 (Tools): Performance Mining

### The objective

Even though computer hardware grows ever cheaper and faster, it still seems to lag behind the programmer's ability to develop software that pushes the

**TABLE 22.1   Stage: Integration / Food Group: Technology / Themes: Deployment of Predictive Methodologies and Development of Methodologies to Increase Customer Value**

| Objective | Innovative approach | Pitfalls |
|---|---|---|
| Improve run-time performance of software | *Performance mining:*<br>Hot-spot analysis<br>Use KMC and cross-functional teams | Improving performance but introducing defects |
| Increase ability to predict progress during development life cycle | *Orthogonal defect control:*<br>Determine progress within life cycle by error classification methodology | Applying without focus on prerequisites: Data collection, analysis, support structure |
| Determine return on investments in quality activities | *Quality ROI:*<br>Record cost and expense of quality actions<br>Develop metrics | Not recognizing the need to constantly improve metrics<br>Mindless use of metrics |

machine to its limits. When that happens, the speed of the software slows and customers get upset.

The lab addressed this problem initially with performance analysis—a way to benchmark the performance of a product. A performance analyst evaluated the product and then provided feedback to the developers. Unfortunately, this approach had problems.

First, the developers responded to the feedback with some statement like one of the following:

"That's the way it was designed."

"There's no time in the schedule to fix the problem."

"I've already improved this as much as possible."

"The algorithm is quite sophisticated and designed for performance."

"Why don't you make some more measurements?"

"Your benchmark is unrealistic."

"Reliability will suffer—good-performing code is tricky."

The scenario was full of defensive situations. The performance analyst was bringing bad news, but looked to the developer for a solution. The developer knew that he did a good job, felt cornered, and wished the performance analyst would go away. Very quickly the scene can degenerate into an adversarial relationship with a wall separating performance analyst and developer.

The problem boils down to teamwork. The analyst may do an excellent job of setting up a controlled environment, running benchmark tests, and analyzing the results; but the analyst doesn't usually understand the intricacies of the code. Therefore she or he is unable to make recommendations about how to fix the problem. The developers, on the other hand, know the code quite well, but are often ignorant about performance concerns.

**An innovative approach**

We addressed the teamwork challenge by leveraging and extending one of the innovations developed earlier—computer-supported team work spaces, known locally as knowledge mining centers. The result was a new innovation which we call *performance mining.*

Performance mining eliminates the "it's your problem" syndrome and encourages teamwork, collaborative effort, and brainstorming to improve performance. Performance mining begins with measurements of the software's performance. The analyst pinpoints areas where the code slows down and schedules time to meet with developers in a knowledge mining center (KMC). Colloquially, this is known as scheduling "time in the mine."

The developers gather with the analyst to examine the code on a large projection screen hooked to a computer. To continue the mining analogy, they are looking to find "gems to remove" or "gems to improve" the code. Changes to the code are made, or new designs/algorithms are quickly prototyped. Then the code is reanalyzed to measure the performance improvement.

Cooperative performance mining efforts seem to result in improvements that individuals could not achieve on their own. Investigation, followed by questioning, enhanced with performance data, and stimulated by discussions results ultimately in better-quality products.

For example, Fig. 22.1 shows the effects of performance mining over a 2-month period on some code from an on-line transaction processing system. In such systems, the time required to initiate and terminate a transaction is critical, to avoid having the system slow down when many transactions are running. As enhancements are made to the code, however, the new code can slow performance. On day 205 (the date where the graph in Fig. 22.1 begins) the developer said to the analyst, "I've done all I can, and the performance is still 160 percent worse than the predecessor product."

The developer thought it would be a "miracle" to get the performance degradation down to 100 percent over the predecessor, but over 2 months the team broke both the 100 percent and the 50 percent barrier. By this time, the developer *knew* we could get down to 0 percent. It was a complete transformation in attitude.

## Costs, benefits, and risks

Assuming you have already invested in knowledge mining centers, the cost of implementing performance mining is minimal. The main cost is the time of the people involved. Typically, it takes the analyst a day to obtain baseline measurements on a product, a day to analyze the measurements, and then a day to prepare for the meeting with developers. However, since some sort of performance meeting would be necessary anyway, we don't think of this really as a new cost.

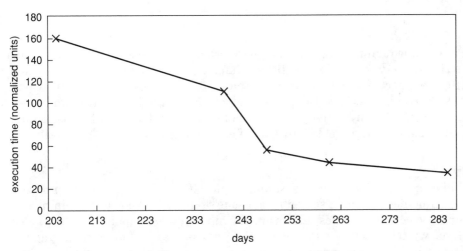

**Figure 22.1**   Performance mining case study results. (*Courtesy of IBM*)

The benefits include reduced cycle time, improved communication, and a better understanding of the product. Together these result in better performance which is a key aspect of quality in the eyes of customers.

Sometimes performance mining enables improvements that are virtually impossible for an individual developer to make due to the complexity of the code. Teams of individuals can make rapid progress when they interact, question, and work toward a common goal.

The educational component of performance mining is also a significant benefit since most computer science curriculums don't emphasize performance.

Finally, there are intangible benefits that come from getting a group of people together in a room, taking on what seems to be an impossible task, and having them realize that incredible breakthroughs really are possible. Team bonding is one of these intangibles, but there is also a change of thinking. When the performance of a product improves before your eyes, right there on the big screen, and when you know that a week ago you thought any improvement was impossible, suddenly anything seems possible. This attitude carries over to other aspects of development.

While performance mining is still relatively new at the lab, the two comments we got on a lab-wide survey were positive:

"Excellent idea that has paid dividends."

"Helped make our code more efficient by showing performance degradations and improvements."

One risk is that you might make product performance worse rather than better. Particularly if you are working late in the development cycle, it becomes riskier to make changes. The solution here is to do performance mining as early in the development cycle as possible. Also it is necessary to acknowledge the risk of losing customers if you *don't* focus on performance improvement.

## Synergy

Performance mining is synergistic with other team development efforts such as rigorous reviews and inspections (Chap. 11), CleanRoom techniques (Chap. 18), the defect prevention process (Chap. 15), early test involvement (Chap. 11), electronic meetings (Chap. 16), and, of course, the knowledge mining center (Chap. 16). Any activity that promotes working together, brainstorming, and focusing on the problem instead of assigning blame will help as well.

## Prerequisites

While in theory performance mining could be done by a couple of programmers huddled around a screen in someone's office, the knowledge mining center's projection facilities and brainstorming support capabilities (e.g., electronic whiteboards) add so much to the process that performance mining just doesn't feel like performance mining unless it takes place in a KMC. So having a KMC is almost a prerequisite.

**Implementation advice**

Performance mining is implemented by five basic steps, illustrated in Fig. 22.2:

1. *Detect the problem.*   Normally this is done by measuring or timing an operation. You may suspect a problem based on knowledge of the design or based on previous experience with similar projects.

2. *Hot-spot analysis.*   Use a tool which will show you (in percent) where time is spent. This tool is valuable because it shows where to concentrate your efforts.

3. *Mine and brainstorm.*   Examine the code, the algorithms, and whatever data structures are necessary. Use a small group of individuals who have the skills to tackle the problem. Typically this requires one or two performance people and one to three developers who can brainstorm together for improvements.

4. *Prototype.*   Create prototypes based on the ideas found during the performance mining session.

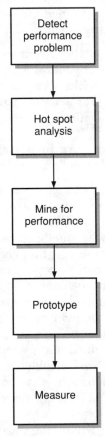

**Figure 22.2**   Five steps to performance mining. (*Courtesy of IBM*)

_____ Purpose of performance mining communicated clearly
_____ "Customers" in development available to participate
_____ Performance mining coordinator identified
_____ Management commitment (funding/resources) obtained
_____ Team agreement to analyze product
_____ Performance problem detected/suspected
_____ Detailed hot-spot analysis
_____ Team brainstorming for solutions
_____ Prototypes of improved code produced
_____ Prototypes evaluated
_____ Measurements communicated to team
_____ Successes publicized
_____ Feedback and continuous improvement process in place

**Figure 22.3**   Performance mining implementation checklist.

5. Measure.   As soon as possible, measure the prototype to determine if more efforts are necessary. This may require returning to step 2 or 3 and beginning the cycle again. Immediate feedback helps motivate the team to keep looking for more improvements.

Marilyn Z. Smith, one of the inventors of performance mining, has spent considerable time extracting general principles of design from numerous performance mining sessions. She likes to draw an analogy between highway systems and code design. For example, she says, "One principle is: Optimize for daily commuters who want to travel as fast as possible. Don't make them take the scenic route...."

In her paper "The Roadmap to Better Performance or Don't Get Lost Taking the Scenic Route," she offers five principles for a faster journey:

1. Keep it simple. When coding, focus on the important parts of the code and avoiding setting unnecessary flags, or doing things "just in case."

2. Concentrate on the Non-Error Path. Many developers have an underlying assumption that software should be user friendly no matter what the user does. While it's true that the program shouldn't crash when a user makes a mistake, most people are not trying to cause errors. So why should we penalize them by doing things needed only in the error case?

Ideally, performance sensitive programs should have two paths, the superhighway—used for most common cases—and the scenic route—for handling errors and not so frequent cases.

3. Delay what you can until it's needed. For example, standard programming practice is to initialize variables before using them. But that doesn't necessarily mean _all_ variables need to be initialized at the start of the program. Items needed only in cases of error don't need to be initialized in the straight-through path.

4. Streamline the code where the most time is spent. This is similar to "keep it simple" but the emphasis is on the small portion of the code where

most of the time is spent. Remember, most of the code is there to support error or unusual situations, and that code is rarely used. The most commonly used routines need to be as efficient as possible.

5. Make frequent performance measurements. Measurements not only track progress but can serve as an impetus to make further improvements.

Figure 22.3 summarizes these implementation steps in a checklist.

## Innovation 39 (Tools): Orthogonal Defect Classification

### The objective

By the time we reached the management stage of quality maturity, we were already collecting good data on the numbers of defects detected for various products in the field. We knew that we needed some way of tracking how well we were doing. Counting the errors that actually affected customers seemed like a logical approach. But as we neared the integration stage, we realized there were a couple of challenges ahead.

The first problem was that our product development cycles often lasted 2 years or more. So it could be that long before developers got feedback on whether their product design and coding efforts were of good quality. Clearly, this lag time was unacceptable.

The response was to focus attention on interim checkpoints, or "in-process measurements." We already gathered data such as "15 people found 500 problems in 2 hours." But was that good or bad? It was hard to tell. Of course, we could compare to baseline data from previous releases—if we had them. But no two releases are the same, and you still end up with only a guesstimate. Moreover, when we confronted developers with poor numbers, we got rationalizations, such as "Oh, we had more reviewers than we usually had" or "Oh, the code wasn't quite ready."

What we needed was a way not only to provide timely feedback to developers, but also to provide feedback that was more meaningful than just "number of defects." Specifically, we wanted some kind of feedback that would tell us where we were having problems in our development process, independent of the idiosyncrasies of a particular release.

Until we solved this problem, we would continue to waste time collecting data that were not used effectively. We would continue to deploy process improvement techniques, such as the defect prevention process (see Chap. 15), to all the development process instead of focusing on "hot spots" that needed the most improvement. We would continue to frustrate developers by throwing numbers at them without giving them enough information to know where to improve the process. And we would continue to trip over the same "rocks" in the development process over and over.

### An innovative approach

We tackled these challenges with an innovation, invented by IBM's Research Division, called *orthogonal defect classification,* or ODC for short.

ODC is based on four key points. First, different types of defects show up at different points in the life cycle. For example, Table 22.2 shows that defects stemming from function issues typically show up during the design, high-level design inspection, function test, and system test stages of our development process. In contrast, defects stemming from interface issues show up during different stages: low-level design, coding, low-level design inspections, and unit test of the code.

The second key point is that it is possible to develop profiles describing the number of defects of each type expected in each stage. Figure 22.4 shows defect signature patterns for four types of defects in four stages of our development process. The figure indicates that in the design stage we can expect to see relatively large numbers of defects associated with function and few defects associated with timing considerations. This makes sense because timing problems typically arise during system test when the product is tested in a simulated customer environment.

Figure 22.4 shows how the number of timing errors climbs over time until it is the most dominant defect type during the system test phase. Meanwhile, function defects steadily drop since the function of the product receives lots of attention early in the development cycle and most of the bugs have been worked out by the time the product gets to system test.

The third key point is realizing that when too many defects of the "wrong" type show up in a particular development stage, something is wrong. For each stage in the process, different types of errors tend to be dominant. If an abnormal number of defects of a certain type appear, that is a sign that something is wrong with the development process.

The fourth key point is that ODC together with root-cause analysis techniques can be used as a diagnostic tool to identify and fix trouble spots in the development process. Contrasting the type of defects occurring with the type that is expected to occur can help diagnose the problem and tell you where the development process needs fixing.

For example, in DB2 we discovered that we did design really well. We did function test really well. But we were falling down on code inspections. We

**TABLE 22.2  Orthogonal Defect Control Postulates That Specific Defects Predominate at Different Stages of Development**

| | Design | Low-level design | Code | High-level DES inspection | Low-level DES inspection | Code inspection | Unit test | Function test | System test |
|---|---|---|---|---|---|---|---|---|---|
| Function | X | | | X | | | | X | X |
| Interface | | X | X | | X | | X | | X |
| Checking | | | X | | | X | X | | X |
| Assignment | | | X | | | X | X | | X |
| Timing | | X | | X | | | | | X |
| Building/packaging | | | | | | | X | | X |
| Documentation | X | | X | | | | X | X | X |
| Data structure | | | X | | | X | X | X | X |

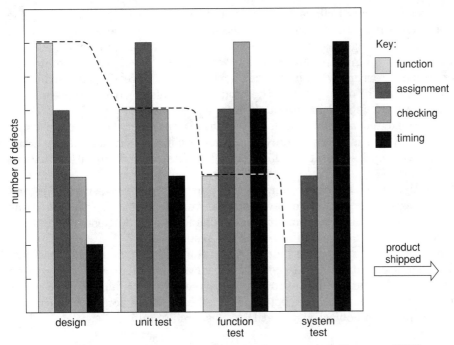

**Figure 22.4** Hypothetical defect distributions by development stage. (*Courtesy of IBM*)

knew we were spending a lot of time in function test, but before ODC we didn't know why.

In fact, the knee-jerk response would have been to say that there was something wrong with our function test process. In reality, it turned out that we were spending so much time in function test because the code inspections—much earlier in the development process—were inadequate. How did we know that? Simple. ODC showed us that the problems detected in function test were not the *types* of errors appropriate to that stage. The errors were really the types of things that should have been caught during code inspections.

The essence of ODC is classification. (The "orthogonal" part simply means that the classification categories don't overlap and are statistically independent of each other.)

Looking at individual defects alone does not provide enough leverage to generalize to future releases. Looking at the numbers of defects alone is too general to be useful. But by looking at categories of defects, we were able to compare the defects with past histories for products and zero in on our problem areas. As long as we were looking at errors in terms of specific bugs, it was very difficult to see a pattern. It was a case of not being able to see the forest (overall pattern) for the trees (the individual errors). As soon as we took the broader classification viewpoint, we were able to perform statistical analyses.

The other important characteristic of orthogonal defect classification is the idea that classification of errors should occur during the development process. We used these categories as in-process measurements which then allowed us to monitor our progress as the product was actually developed. By matching the pattern of errors with historical patterns, we were able to anticipate where errors might occur—*before* the product was released to customers.

Although ODC is still in the pilot stage at our lab, several of our product groups are excited about using it. Our database product, DB2, began using ODC in 1992 and is leading the way. Other products including IMS, dictionary services, and some of our language products have plans to implement ODC.

Currently, the ODC pilot programs are partnerships between our lab and IBM's Research Division. The developers at our lab categorize the errors as they occur in various development stages. The folks at IBM Research analyze the patterns in the errors and interpret the results.

Periodic teleconferences are held in which the researchers provide feedback to the developers about what parts of the development process seem to be going well and what needs improvement. Eventually, our lab plans to do its own analysis. But for the time being, it is helpful to have access to the statistical knowledge and objectivity that IBM Research provides.

### Costs, benefits, and risks

The cost of setting up an ODC program includes the resources required to set up the classification scheme, the cost of the analysis, the cost of meetings, the cost of a program administrator, and the cost of training. These costs will vary depending upon how much existing infrastructure is in place. However, our cost has been small compared to the benefits.

Assuming you are already logging errors in some kind of database, ODC simply involves logging occurrences in specific categories as well. For example, ODC categorizes by (1) defect type, (2) source of the problem, (3) trigger of the problem, and (4) impact on the customer in the field.

We modified our existing data collection tools to allow defect classification. Instead of just recording how many defects occurred in a given stage, we now record what type of defect occurred as well. It takes about 4 minutes per defect to record this additional information.

Once the analysis scheme has been set up (something that was done for us by IBM Research and which is documented in various publications), the cost of the analysis itself is minimal. It amounts to a day or two of effort every few months to run the data through various statistical analyses and prepare feedback for the developers who submitted the raw data for analysis.

The cost of meetings amounts to about 4 hours per month per participant.

Our DB2 ODC program requires a project administrator who runs the program with about one-third of her time. The cost of training developers to classify errors is minimal, amounting to a few hours per developer.

The real cost of ODC lies not in the analysis itself, but in the actions required to improve the development process based on the results of the analysis. Depending upon what needs to be fixed, this can be a very time-consuming job, and quite frankly it is where we have run into the most resistance.

On the positive side, ODC provides an unprecedented level of information about what needs to be fixed. If developers are still not willing to fix the process, you can't really fault ODC.

One of the prime benefits of ODC is that is works with your process. You can see what other companies have done. You can buy tools and try new processes. But there is no substitute for empirical data about your own development process. This technique gives you a powerful way to collect and analyze those data.

Specifically, ODC helps:

1. You fix the current release. If ODC is applied at the start of a release, analysis of errors in the design and coding development phases can help you adjust the test phase to compensate for any soft spots in the code.

2. You warn customers about "soft spots" if it is too late to fix the release.

Even if ODC was started only during the test phases, analysis of errors can help you identify potential trouble spots which QPP (see Chap. 21) customers might look out for.

3. You fix the next release. What you can't fix in this release, you can plan to fix in the next release.

4. You fix your development process. In addition to telling you where to fix the code, ODC tells you what part of your development process needs attention.

5. You raise quality awareness and foster a different way of thinking about errors.

Although still in its pilot phase, ODC has had some small-scale successes. For example, one team had some weak spots, and the tester was getting ready to rerun some tests. ODC provided her with information about which test cases to pick. She knew what the weak spots were.

Another team had some problems with missing function. ODC helped focus efforts on the most critical dozen problems out of 100 errors that had been reported.

Even when the problems can't be fixed in the immediate release (e.g., the problem with code inspections mentioned earlier), ODC still helps you plan where to spend extra resources.

However, since ODC is relatively new, some developers are still awaiting more proof of its effectiveness. Some are optimistic; others point out implementation problems. Here are some comments from a lab-wide survey taken in 1993:

"Haven't used the tool long enough to determine effectiveness, though I do think it is worth trying."

"We are still in the very early stages of usage. It has been interesting so far, but we still haven't had a big payoff. It probably takes 6 to 12 months to start getting good data for analysis."

"We need to use some tool to classify defects so we can learn from past mistakes. Don't expect ODC to be a cure-all or to give immediate value, but rather view it as a potential investment that, given enough data points, may pay dividends for your group."

"We've incorporated some ODC-type questions into our [error data collection] tool so that we collect the right info at the right point....This is more efficient than asking people to go back and do the analysis after the fact. Once again, the pitfall is to collect all of the ODC information and never use it."

"Garbage in, garbage out! There is no consensus on the classification of defects that are found."

"It is imperative that everyone have a common understanding of the meaning of the categories. Otherwise analysis of the results will be meaningless."

These comments highlight one of the major risks of ODC, namely, that the method is only as useful as the classification scheme. If inappropriate categories are chosen or if there is too much variation in how people perform the classification, the data lose their usefulness.

Probably the single most important factor in minimizing these risks is the choice of a competent ODC coordinator. One of the coordinator's responsibilities is to randomly check on the classification process to make sure it is carried out consistently. More training is the solution to the problem of too much variability in classification. To date, we have relied on models developed by research to ensure that the most useful categories are chosen, but presumably categories could be fine-tuned over time.

### Synergy

ODC is synergistic with the defect prevention process, computer-supported team work spaces, the quality partnership program with customers, rigorous design reviews and code inspections, and statistical process control.

### Prerequisites

Orthogonal defect classification requires a database and a method of recording defects. If these two preconditions are already met, implementation is mainly a matter of modifying existing procedures. Otherwise, some additional effort to set up this system will be required.

In addition, the classifiers must be trained since useful feedback depends upon reliable and accurate classification.

Finally, if you are not willing to change, then don't bother with ODC. The data must be translated into action to be effective.

### Implementation advice

Figure 22.5 illustrates the three main steps in the ODC procedure.

In step 1 you identify expected patterns of defects for each phase in your development process. For example, you should know to expect YY percent of the defects to be of type Z during the test stage. IBM's Research Division helped us develop these signature patterns based on data from our lab and other IBM locations. However, any organization that classifies defects and keeps tracks of the numbers of each type occurring at each stage should be able to develop its own customized signature patterns over time.

In step 2 in the overall process, shown in Fig. 22.5, you classify defects as they occur in the development process. Figure 22.6 shows that defects can be classified by a variety of attributes including the type of defect, the source of the defect, what triggered the defect, the environment in which the defect occurred, and the likely impact of the defect. All this information is stored in a database where it can be analyzed by statistical techniques (see Suggested Readings) that search out meaningful patterns.

In step 3, you compare the results of your in-process categorization of defects with the results predicted by your statistical models. If the patterns don't match, it may mean that the code is not mature enough to move on to the next stage of development, or that some part of the development process is out of control. Ideally, specific actions can be taken to correct the problem before the development process continues. If there is no time to fix the process immediately, at least parts of the development process can be flagged for improvement before the next release is developed.

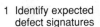

1 Identify expected defect signatures

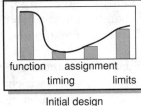

2 Classify actual defects as detected to establish actual in-process signature

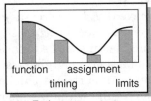

3 Compare actual with expected signatures to assess code maturity and take in-process actions to address findings

**Figure 22.5**  Three steps to ODC. (*Courtesy of IBM*)

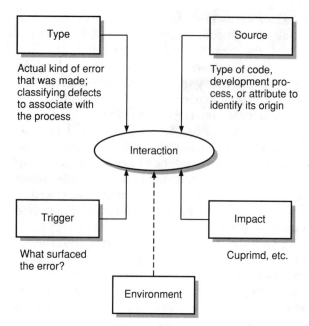

**Figure 22.6**  Categorizing defects by attributes. (*Courtesy of IBM*)

Although following the statistical analysis steps in ODC may provide a technically workable solution, we have pointed out consistently that technology cannot be effective if it is separated from leadership and process. ODC is a case in point.

Perhaps the single most important factor in the success of ODC is the selection of the ODC coordinator. This person needs to be a champion—someone who can gain management support so that the required resources to modify and/or install the tool are available. The coordinator gains the buy-in of developers and must have the skill necessary to help educate and ensure that developers can classify the defects accurately. Finally, the coordinator needs to have good people and meeting skills to facilitate feedback sessions and follow up on the recommendations emerging from the analysis sessions.

Gaining management support is a chicken-or-egg problem: No support without results, and no results without support. Our solution was to convince management to ante up enough resources to buy a small chicken. For example, a small team, 20 people or fewer, can do ODC over the whole life cycle (design, code, test) of a product. This is very cheap, and you get great feedback.

You could do it in one department, but we wanted to go across the whole release because that is what we ship. You could also do the analysis yourself, but we chose to have folks at IBM Research do it because they have a broader, multilab perspective and because they are more objective.

A good coordinator is also aware of the need to push for process change without imposing unnecessary burdens on developers. For example, the classification methodology should be integrated smoothly with the current process for defect data collection. To get buy-in, you can't ask developers to go way out of their way for something of unproven value.

We handled the education and classification problems by creating quick reference cards for classification and by developing our own education courses.

Handling feedback sessions was a more sensitive issue. One problem we had to overcome was a culture where numbers were used without an understanding or deeper concern for what they really meant. As a result, people became fearful of data collection and defect analysis. Simply put, they'd been burned before.

The key is to stay positive and never, never abuse the data that you have. You cannot conduct a witch hunt based on the data you collect and then expect any future cooperation. One thing that helps ODC change the "who do I blame" kind of culture is that ODC tells you what you do well. Most organizations need to emphasize the positive more.

Logistically speaking, it was difficult to communicate immediate feedback to all 200 developers in DB2. The compromise we adopted was to invite a manageable subset of key people to participate in the teleconferences with IBM Research. These people, in turn, disseminated information to people in their departments. We also sent regular status reports to everyone and held special meetings with developers whose areas needed the most work, according to the ODC analyses.

The approach taken in these special meetings was not "this is going to show up in your performance plan." Instead it was "ODC is telling you that you have trouble spots. Now you can stop and own up to them and fix them, or you can keep going. But if you keep going, it is going to cost you more in the long run."

Another potential problem is that in an organization without teamwork, you might have to worry about people using metrics like ODC to lobby for more resources at the expense of other groups. This problem has not cropped up in our pilot projects, primarily because teamwork was already embedded in the culture at the time ODC was adopted.

For example, our DB2 product team members have a strong sense of "if we don't get a quality product out the door, we're all hosed, no matter what group we're in." This attitude may be partly due to innovations like CLIFT and early test involvement (see Chap. 11) which blurred the lines between the development and test departments and promoted cooperation during earlier stages of quality maturity.

In terms of pitfalls, a primary one was misclassification. The feedback is only as good as the classification. In many cases we had to go back and clarify the meaning of various attributes. We also began random sampling of the data before submitting them for analysis, to ensure accurate classification.

The overall process of ODC at our lab follows the implementation checklist outlined in Fig. 22.7.

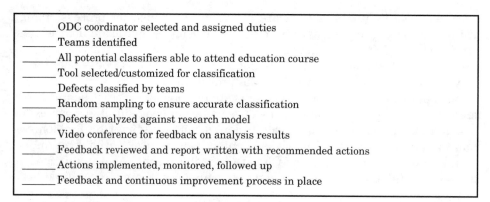

_____ ODC coordinator selected and assigned duties
_____ Teams identified
_____ All potential classifiers able to attend education course
_____ Tool selected/customized for classification
_____ Defects classified by teams
_____ Random sampling to ensure accurate classification
_____ Defects analyzed against research model
_____ Video conference for feedback on analysis results
_____ Feedback reviewed and report written with recommended actions
_____ Actions implemented, monitored, followed up
_____ Feedback and continuous improvement process in place

**Figure 22.7**    ODC implementation checklist.

## Innovation 40 (Tools): Quality Return on Investment

### The objective

As long as there are more projects to invest in than there is money to invest, management and the stockholders will want to know which investments provide the most return. While quality improvement sounds like a nice idea, few investors would be willing to pursue quality unless it also led to making a profit.

At some point, either explicitly or implicitly, those making the investment decisions calculate roughly what they expect the return on their investment in quality will be. Typically this calculation of quality return on investment (Q. ROI) is informal and consists of gut feeling more than anything else.

In theory, it is possible to quantify the ROI for various quality improvement activities. We believe such a quantification, though fraught with risks for misuse and misunderstanding, would nevertheless be useful.

Simply put, an organization cannot afford to adopt an ignorance-is-bliss attitude in a competitive environment. Instead, it must struggle to gain as much information as possible about the effectiveness of its quality efforts, because such information provides a competitive advantage. If this information is quantitative rather than qualitative, so much the better—as long as the methodology for arriving at the numbers is rigorous, repeatable, and well understood.

Notice that we did not require that the methodology yield correct results. In fact, it will probably yield grossly inaccurate results at first. But as long as it is consistent, the inaccuracies can be systematically eliminated until the method provides much more useful information than gut feeling alone.

With these considerations in mind, we ventured somewhat timidly, and with much protesting, into the financial mires of quality ROI. We knew that whatever numbers we came up with at first would be inaccurate, but we also knew we had to take the first step. So we did.

## An innovative approach

We began with a specific objective. We wanted to see if it was really worthwhile to invest in up-front processes because of the savings due to eliminating errors in the field.

So far everyone took this on faith. It made sense. We knew that fixing errors in the field cost a lot of money and that doing a code inspection was much cheaper. All the gurus and books on software engineering advocated investing effort up front. But was it really true? Could we really find the proof at our lab?

To find out, we chose a piece of code that had been developed ahead of schedule. We "dollarized" the defects found in design reviews, code inspections, and test by estimating how much it cost in labor to detect each defect. Next we estimated the dollar savings for every defect that did not show up in the field. Finally, we compared the cost of the errors to the savings to determine whether we actually saved money.

Table 22.3 shows the results of this procedure for one line item of one of our products. We present these data with two caveats: translating defects into dollars is a slippery business, and estimating how many field defects were saved as a result of a design review is probably even more hazardous. However, we could be off by an order of magnitude in our estimates and still reach the conclusion that quality improvement activities more than pay for themselves. Moreover, even if the estimates are consistently inaccurate, by comparing the ROI values to each other, it is possible to see which activities provide the most leverage in quality improvement. For example, it is clear that design reviews with customer involvement are good things to do.

## Costs, benefits, and risks

The analysis shown above was relatively cheap, requiring only the part-time efforts of a member of the finance department and a team leader from development. However, the effectiveness of such analyses depends crucially on collecting good data.

TABLE 22.3  **Quality ROI for One Product Line Item\***

| Defect prevention activity | Estimated ROI, % |
| --- | --- |
| Design review | 600 |
| Review with customers | 2900 |
| Code inspection 1 | 900 |
| Code inspection 2 | 700 |
| Code inspection 3 | 900 |
| Unit test/EC | 500 |
| Rough average ROI of quality activities: | 1100 |

\*Field error cost estimates range from $10,000 to $50,000 each. ROI has been calculated by using the most conservative estimate of $10,000 per field error.

The advantage of an ROI analysis is that it anchors quality to financial considerations and can provide quality advocates with the data they need to influence decision makers. It also helps prioritize quality improvement efforts so that investments are made first where they will have the highest return.

On a lab-wide survey, this relatively new innovation got two comments:

"Helps prioritize where you will spend your quality dollars. Helps reduce [management by] gut feel. Helpful for managers when looking at recognition [issues.]"

"[Similar to] the 'cost of quality'—part of Crosby's quality ethic. It provides a dollar value for 'nonquality' items, the inverse of which is the potential savings from their elimination. A good way to get executive attention."

These comments reflect an appreciation of the benefits of quality ROI, but the risks are also significant. First, quality may be perceived too narrowly, since the benefits of high quality go beyond dollars per defect and include areas which are harder to quantify, such as goodwill and ability to increase market share. How do you put a dollar value on customer satisfaction or the advantages of raising quality awareness at the lab? What about the long-term benefits of improving the quality of the future workforce, investing in technical vitality, or making process documentation efforts? As soon as you talk about quantifying quality, all these objections and a flood of other legitimate concerns appear.

Second, estimates for ROI are likely to have a wide margin of error. For example, in Table 22.3, the number of errors saved is an estimate made before the product was even released. Similarly, the dollar costs for the various activities are estimates. So we are in the uncomfortable situation of calculating numbers which look precise but which may actually contain a large degree of uncertainty.

The discomfort stems not from the calculations themselves. We are quite clear that some information, with known inaccuracies, is better than no information at all. Rather, we are nervous because numbers tend to take on a life of their own. Senior management must recognize the imprecision of the measurements and be willing to view ROI as an indication of a general direction or trend, not as a promise of precise financial returns.

In particular, there are serious risks if management begins to set up incentive or reward systems based on incomplete data. For example, it does no good to reward a development team for a low error rate in test without knowing how thorough the test was. Perhaps the product simply didn't get tested well enough and will fall apart in the field.

## Synergy

Properly used, quality ROI can be synergistic with any of the innovations described in this book. It can help you not only compare investment options but also persuade decision makers to invest resources. Other statistical methods and data collection methods such as error-prone module analysis (Chap. 12), data linkage analysis (Chap. 16), and orthogonal defect classification (see above) can help support quality ROI activities.

### Prerequisites

A prerequisite for quality ROI is a good system for data collection to help determine the cost and number of errors at various stages of development.

### Implementation advice

Obviously the more hard data you have on defect rates and levels, the better. Thus, organizations in the integration stage of quality maturity, which have collected more data, will have an easier time implementing quality ROI than those in earlier stages of maturity. Ironically, integration-stage organizations have already committed to quality improvement, while the awareness- and coping-stage organizations, which could really use an ROI analysis to gain buy-in, are those least equipped to perform a quality ROI analysis.

Having wrestled with this Catch-22 situation ourselves, we can sympathize. Our approach has been to invest in quality improvement on faith at first. We considered quality ROI as a way to help fine-tune our investment decisions. Fundamentally, however, you cannot wait for the results before you begin, or you will never start the journey.

Those who are already firmly committed to quality improvement sometimes feel that any ROI analysis is a waste of time. In the words of one quality advocate,

> We should stop worrying about what happens after you ship the product and you get defects, and we should start managing the front end of the process. Don't haul people into your office to have them explain why they got a PE [an error in a fix after the product has been shipped], haul them into your office to have them tell you how the design is going. You cannot change how many errors that product is going to have once it is shipped, but you can change it at the design phase. You can make a significant impact there.

While we agree with these sentiments, the key point is to realize that quality ROI can and should be used as a tool to monitor and maximize the effectiveness of the "front end of the process." Investment decisions will be made whether good information is available to inform them or not.

Quality ROI is far from being a science. Much progress needs to be made in improving our estimating procedures and in collecting reliable error and cost data. But despite its risks, we feel that quality ROI is a step in the right direction.

Figure 22.8 describes an implementation checklist for quality ROI.

Today, a company is on the leading edge if it does anything systematic to improve its quality. But tomorrow, quality improvement will be accepted practice.

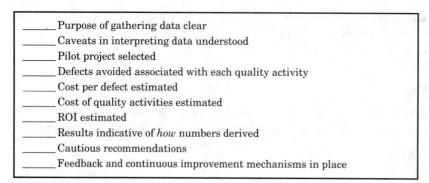

_____ Purpose of gathering data clear
_____ Caveats in interpreting data understood
_____ Pilot project selected
_____ Defects avoided associated with each quality activity
_____ Cost per defect estimated
_____ Cost of quality activities estimated
_____ ROI estimated
_____ Results indicative of _how_ numbers derived
_____ Cautious recommendations
_____ Feedback and continuous improvement mechanisms in place

**Figure 22.8**  Quality ROI implementation checklist.

Today's leaders ask, "Are you improving quality?" But tomorrow's leaders will ask, "Are you improving quality in the most effective ways?" Quality ROI provides the basis for answering this second question and thus gaining a competitive advantage.

## Suggested Readings

Arellanes, R. J., and Smith, M. Z. (1992) _The TEAM Approach to LE/370 Performance Evaluation: Together Everyone Achieves More._ IBM Santa Teresa Working Paper, San Jose, CA, May 14. _Documentation of Santa Teresa's early experimentation with performance mining._

Atkinson, J. H. (1991) _Current Trends in Cost of Quality: Linking the Cost of Quality and Continuous Improvement._ Montvale, NJ: National Association of Accountants. _May be of interest to those trying to estimate quality return on investment._

Bentley, J. (1982) _Writing Efficient Programs._ Englewood Cliffs, NJ: Prentice-Hall. _Description of general rules to achieve efficiency, illustrated with small code fragments, "war stories," and in-depth studies of several important subroutines. Includes considerations on software maintenance, robustness, and development time._

Bentley, J. (1989) _Programming Pearls._ Reading, MA: Addison-Wesley. _A popular little book that contains thirteen essays by a master programmer on how to improve the performance of code._

Bentley, J. (1990) _More Programming Pearls (Confessions of a Coder)._ Reading, MA: Addison-Wesley. _More tips from a top programmer covering a variety of programming topics besides performance improvement._

Chillarege, R., Bhandari, I., Chaar, J., Halliday, M., Moebus, D., Ray, B., and Wong, M. (1992) "Orthogonal Defect Classification—A Concept for In-Process Measurement," _IEEE Transactions on Software Engineering,_ pp. 943–956, November. _This paper explains orthogonal defect control with more rigor and in more detail than we do in this book._

Harrington, H. J. (1987) _Poor-Quality Cost._ New York: M. Dekker; Milwaukee, WI: ASQC Quality Press. _One of the best-known technical looks at what poor quality really costs._

Heldt, J. J. and Costa, D. J. (1988) _Quality Pays: Increasing Profits through Quality Cost Analysis._ Wheaton, IL: Hitchcock Publishing Co. _A management view of the cost of quality._

Kemerer, C. F. (1987) "An Empirical Validation of Software Cost Estimation Models," _Communications of the ACM,_ 30(5): 416–429. _This paper evaluates some of the popular methods for estimating software costs using fifteen real-world cases._

Knuth, D. (1973) _The Art of Computer Programming, Vol. 1._ Reading, MA: Addison-Wesley. _One of the Knuth classics; includes algorithms and their analysis for lists, trees, garbage collection, and dynamic storage allocation._

Smith, M. Z. (1992a) _Mining for Performance._ IBM Santa Teresa Working Paper, San Jose, CA. _Additional documentation of performance mining efforts at IBM Santa Teresa._

Smith, M. Z. (1992b) *The Roadmap to Better Performance or Don't Get Lost Taking the Scenic Route*. IBM Santa Teresa Working Paper, San Jose, CA, September 11. *Good overview of performance mining.*

Van den Bosch, F. J., Ellis, J., Freeman, P., Johnson, L., McClure, C., Robinson, D., Scacchi, W., Sencit, B., van Staa, A., and Tripp, L. (1982) "Evaluating the Implementation of Software Development Life Cycle Methodologies," *ACM Software Engineering Notes,* 7(1): 45–61. *A proposal for quantifying the cost-effectiveness of various software development methods.*

# 23

# Creating Your Own Quality Improvement Program

Reading about quality improvement is one thing. Actually implementing a workable quality improvement program is quite another. In this last chapter we offer a systematic process for creating your own quality improvement program.

The advantage of using this process is that it allows you to tailor a program to the specific needs of your organization. Even if you decide to use innovations not included in this book or to bypass the somewhat technical scoring system described in this chapter, our process overview can help you develop a workable program.

## Overview of How to Do It

Figure 23.1 shows the four essential steps in our process. As the title of the figure implies, we view quality improvement as a continual learning process. We have cycled through the four phases shown in the figure again and again, each time improving our quality a little more.

The learning process is based on the iron triangle, Baldrige assessments, and our four stages of quality maturity. If you are rusty on any of these concepts, you may want to review Chaps. 1 and 2, where they are discussed. The learning process also introduces a new conceptual schema that helps diagnose your quality problems. First we'll go through each phase of the learning process briefly, before considering them in depth.

Phase 1 is the calibration stage. Here you should use the Baldrige criteria (or some other assessment tool) to assess where you are in your quality improvement efforts. If you use Baldrige, you can determine your stage of quality maturity by following the procedures outlined in Chap. 2.

Phase 2 involves diagnosing specific quality-related strengths and weaknesses in your organization. This diagnosis phase uses information about your quality maturity stage as well as a unique procedure that identifies weaknesses in the "food group" areas of the iron triangle: leadership, process,

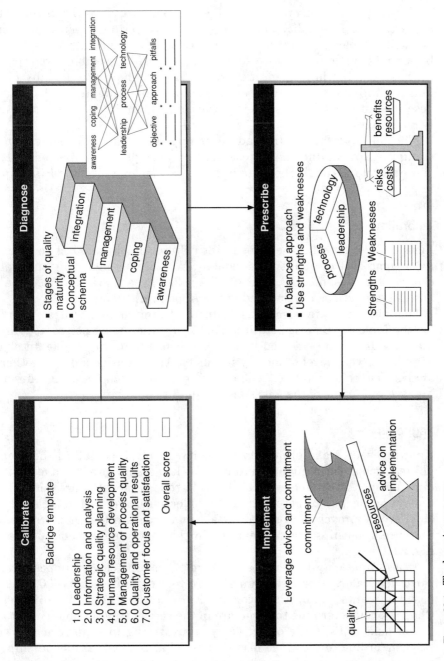

**Figure 23.1**  The learning process.

and technology. By the time you leave phase 2, you should have a list of strengths and weaknesses and a letter grade (A, B, C, D, or F) for each of the food-group areas.

Knowing where you are deficient helps in phase 3, where you actually create a prescription for quality improvement. The prescription takes the form of a portfolio of quality improvement innovations that can be assembled from this book and/or other sources. We describe a process for assembling your portfolio.

Phase 4 is the implementation stage. Here's where you actually put your quality improvement strategy into action. For example, each innovation described in this book has a few paragraphs devoted to specific implementation advice.

Phase 4 is not static. Instead, after implementing some innovations, you should again conduct an assessment of your progress. Periodically, you should cycle through the four phases, as you move upward in a quality improvement spiral.

## Phase 1: Calibration

Figure 23.2 illustrates the steps in the calibration phase. First you must perform some sort of quality assessment. We recommend using the Baldrige criteria for reasons discussed in Chap. 2. Three quick and easy Baldrige assessment options are detailed in the Appendix.

The most accurate form of assessment is to prepare a written application for the Malcolm Baldrige Award. This application need not be actually submitted, but it can be scored by external consultants to provide an objective estimate of your level of quality maturity. The Baldrige score, together with analysis of the qualitative feedback you get from such a scoring, can be used to place you in one of the four stages of quality maturity.

## Phase 2: Diagnosis

Knowing your stage of quality maturity is the first step in the diagnosis phase. Each stage of quality maturity has leadership, process, and technology dimensions. Associated with each food-group dimension are certain objectives, approaches to accomplish the objectives, and pitfalls. Finally each objective, approach, and set of pitfalls may contain one or more elements. These relationships are summarized in the conceptual schema portrayed in Fig. 23.3.

An example may help make these relationships clear. Suppose that you perform a Baldrige assessment and score your organization at 600 out of 1000 possible points. Using this score and qualitative indicators (discussed in Chap. 2), you determine that you are in the coping stage of quality maturity.

You next classify the objectives you are trying to achieve in the coping stage according to the three food groups. That is, there are leadership objectives, process objectives, and technology objectives. Each objective may also have an approach (working or not) and pitfalls associated with implementing

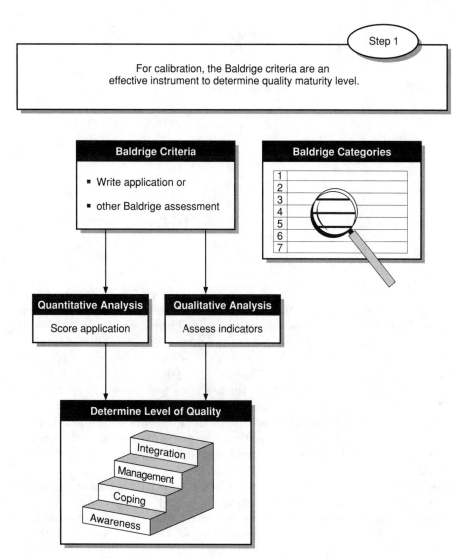

**Figure 23.2**  The calibration process.

this approach. We refer to the triad of objective, approach, and pitfalls as *critical factors* because they are the important factors to consider when an action is proposed to improve performance with respect to one of the three food groups.

Finally, at the most detailed level, an objective may have one or more subparts or objective elements. An approach may have one or more components or approach elements. And there may be more than one pitfall, each of which is considered an element.

This conceptual schema allows us to take an inductive approach to diagnosis. Analyzing the elements tells us which critical factors to focus on.

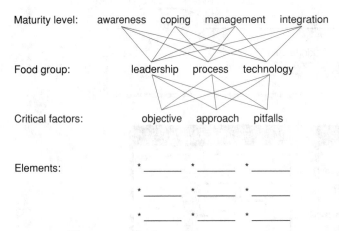

**Figure 23.3**  The conceptual schema.

Analyzing the critical factors tells us what food groups to focus on. And analyzing the food groups helps us create a quality improvement program with the right mix of innovations to move us to the next stage of quality maturity.

As Fig. 23.4 indicates, the analysis at each level in the conceptual schema's hierarchy should result in a score. That is, for each food group we begin by scoring all the elements. Then we use those scores to score every critical factor. Finally, we use those scores to compute an overall score for the food group. The scores of the food groups (and of the elements contained therein) ultimately can help us determine the strengths and weaknesses of the organization. These strengths and weaknesses are what we need to use in the next phase in the learning process—prescription.

However, before we move to the prescription phase, we need to examine the procedure for scoring elements, critical factors, and food groups in greater detail. Figure 23.5 shows the process for scoring elements. For each food group, for each critical factor, for each element, score the element on a three-point scale.

For example, in the case of our lab in the coping stage, we wrestled with the objectives shown in Table 23.1. The first objective had two elements:

1. Line organization assumes responsibility for quality.

2. Promote organizational learning.

Using the scoring system, we ask how important each of these objective elements is. Suppose we say that element 1 is very important and rate it a 3. Element 2 may be only moderately important, so we rate it a 2.

Next we look at the approach. The overall approach is to create a new organization—the Center for Software Excellence. But this overall approach also has two elements:

Given a maturity stage, the purpose of the diagnostic step is to score every food group, every critical factor, and every element.

■ For a given food group:

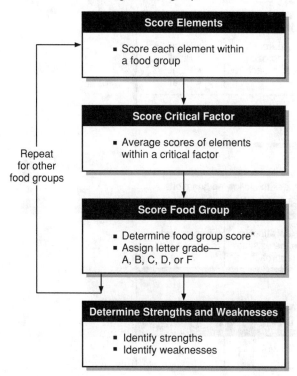

**Figure 23.4**  The diagnosis process. *Algorithm shown in Fig. 23.5.

1. Group acts as a catalyst for quality improvement.

2. Group acts as a repository for knowledge—an experience factory role.

We use the scoring system to rate the effectiveness of each approach element. Let's say that approach element 1 was only moderately successful, rating a score of $\frac{1}{2}$, while approach element 2 had low effectiveness, rating a score of 1.

Finally we rate the severity/applicability of various pitfall elements. In this case there are three pitfall elements:

1. Failure to evolve the group's role

2. Lack of preparation for the inevitable push-back from development

3. Wrong people staffing the group

Scoring of elements, within a food group, is
straightforward by applying the following algorithm.

Recall that for every food group, we have:

| Objective | Approach | Pitfall |
|---|---|---|
| ▪ Objective<br>▪ Objective | ▪ Approach<br>▪ Approach<br>▪ Approach | ▪ Pitfall<br>▪ Pitfall<br>▪ Pitfall<br>▪ Pitfall |
| ⋮ | ⋮ | ⋮ |

To score each element, ask the following questions.

| Objective | Approach | Pitfall |
|---|---|---|
| How important is this objective? | How effective is the existing approach? | To what extent do these pitfalls apply? |

| Very | Med-ium | Low/No | Very | Med-ium | Low | High | Med-ium | Low |
|---|---|---|---|---|---|---|---|---|
| 3 | 2 | 1 | 1/3 | 1/2 | 1 | 3 | 2 | 1 |

**Figure 23.5**  Scoring elements in food groups.

**TABLE 23.1    The Coping Stage**

| Objective | Innovative approach | Implementation pitfalls |
|---|---|---|
| Line organization assumes responsibility for quality<br>Promote organizational learning | *Create a group to act as:*<br>Catalyst for quality improvement<br>Repository for knowledge—an experience factory | Failure to evolve Center for Software Excellence<br>Lack of preparation for push-back<br>Wrong people staffing Center for Software Excellence |
| Get powerful informal shadow organization to buy into quality | Tap into informal organization via a *management council system* | NATO—No action, talk only |

Let's say we rate pitfall elements 1 and 2 as high severity, giving them a score of 3 each. Perhaps we have the right staff, so that pitfall element gets a mild severity rating of 1.

We should repeat this element-scoring procedure for the other objectives, approaches, and pitfalls in the leadership food group, and then for the other food groups. When we have done this, we will have completed our analysis at the element level. The results will be in the form shown in Table 23.2.

Next we compute an overall score for each food group and assign each a letter grade of A, B, C, D, or F. We use the element scores above and the process shown in Fig. 23.6. The scores for the elements within each critical factor are summed. Then an average is computed for each critical factor. These averages are multiplied to produce a score for the food group. The food-group score is then converted to a letter grade by using the grade ranges shown at the bottom of Fig. 23.6.

**TABLE 23.2   Partial Results for Leadership Element Scores**

| Objective elements | Approach elements | Pitfall elements |
|---|---|---|
| **1.** 3 | **1.** ½ | **1.** 3 |
| **2.** 2 | **2.** 1 | **2.** 3 |
| | | **3.** 1 |

To develop a food-group score and a letter grade, apply the following simple process:

- In our example

| | Objective | Approach | Pitfall |
|---|---|---|---|
| | **1.** 3 | **1.** 0.5 | **1.** 3 |
| | **2.** 2 | **2.** 1 | **2.** 3 |
| | | | **3.** 1 |
| Total | 5 | 1.5 | 7 |
| Average | **2.5** | **0.75** | **2.33** |

- Compute average score for each critical factor.
- To determine the food-group scores, multiply the three critical factor scores—2.5 × 0.75 × 2.33 = **4.37.**
- Assign letter grade according to the following:
    A ≤ 0.5   0.5 < B ≤ 1.4   1.4 < C ≤ 3   3 < D ≤ 4.5   4.5 < F
- Repeat for other food groups.   4.37→ D

**Figure 23.6**   Scoring each food group.

Note that if elements shown in Table 23.2 and Fig. 23.6 were the only elements in the leadership food group, that food group would receive a grade of D. This poor grade would reflect the facts that the importance of the objective is high and that serious pitfalls have not been addressed. By addressing the pitfalls, we could upgrade the score to a C. Over time, successful approaches would achieve the important objectives and the grade for the food group would improve further.

The grading system has been designed to approximate a normal distribution. There are 27 possible scoring combinations for an objective-approach-pitfalls triad. Of these 27 combinations, three produce results of A caliber. Seven combinations yield a B, twelve produce C's, two produce D's, and three produce F's. Without enumerating all 27 combinations, Table 23.3 shows more detail about the grade range shown at the bottom of Fig. 23.6.

The final step in the diagnosis phase is to produce a list of strengths and weakness for the organization. For weaknesses, you begin by selecting the low-scoring food group. Within that food group, you identify whether the low score is due primarily to the importance of unrealized objectives, to poor approach effectiveness, or to implementation pitfalls. This determination amounts to picking the worst-scoring critical factor in the food group. Next you pick the weakest element within that critical factor. This process identifies your top-priority weakness.

To fill out the remainder of the weaknesses list, in priority order, you move next to the weakest elements in the other critical factors for the food group. Finally, you repeat this process for the other two food groups.

For example, if we consider the results in Table 23.2 and Fig. 23.6, the unrealized objectives are the most serious problem. The average importance of

**TABLE 23.3   Quality Improvement Grading System**

| (1) | (2) | (3) | Food group score $(1) \times (2) \times (3)$ | Comments | Grade |
|-----|-----|-----|------------------|----------|-------|
| 1 | $\frac{1}{3}$ | 1 | $\frac{1}{3}$ | Have good approach to objective; no pitfalls apply | A |
| 1 | $\frac{1}{2}$ | 1 | $\frac{1}{2}$ | Have adequate approach to objective; no pitfalls apply | |
| 1 | 1 | 1 | 1 | Have inadequate approach to objective; no pitfalls apply | B |
| 2 | $\frac{1}{3}$ | 2 | $\frac{4}{3}$ | Have good approach; objective is important and some pitfalls apply | |
| 2 | $\frac{1}{2}$ | 2 | 2 | Have adequate approach; objective is important and some pitfalls apply | C |
| 3 | $\frac{1}{3}$ | 3 | 3 | Have good approach but one not equal to the importance of the objective; many pitfalls apply | |
| 2 | 1 | 2 | 4 | Have inadequate approach; objective is important and some pitfalls apply | D |
| 3 | $\frac{1}{2}$ | 3 | $\frac{9}{2}$ | Have adequate approach; objective is important and many pitfalls apply | |
| 3 | 1 | 3 | 9 | Hopeless | F |

(Header for first three columns: **Element** spanning (1), (2), (3))

NOTE: The multiplicative nature of scoring ensures that elements (1), (2), and (3) must score well simultaneously to get a high score.

(1) = objective; (2) = approach; (3) = pitfall.

1. Need line organization to take responsibility for quality
2. Lack of preparation for push-back from development
3. Group not acting as a knowledge repository for the organization

**Figure 23.7**  Example of prioritized list of weaknesses.

unrealized objectives is 2.5, or 83 percent of the way toward being absolutely critical ($2.5/3 = 0.83$). The score for the average approach effectiveness is 0.75, or 75 percent of the way to being horrible ($0.75/1 = 0.75$). The average pitfall score is 2.33, which is 78 percent of the way to being horrible ($2.33/3 = 0.78$).

Zooming in on objectives, we see that element 1 (line organization takes responsibility for quality) is the most critical, with a rating of 3. So element 1 becomes the top-priority focus area on the list of weaknesses.

Next we turn to the second worst-scoring critical factor, pitfalls. Within pitfalls, elements 1 and 2 both score equally badly with a 3, so we can choose either one for the weaknesses list. Suppose we choose pitfall 2 (lack of preparation for push-back from development). We add element 2 to our list of weaknesses.

Finally, we turn to the approach elements where element 2 (group should act as a knowledge repository for the organization) is the least effective approach element. We add element 2 to the list of weaknesses.

Figure 23.7 shows how our list of weaknesses would look at this point. We could continue adding to it by repeating the process we just went through for the process and technology food groups.

The procedure for creating a list of strengths is identical to that for creating the list of weaknesses, except that you select the best-scoring elements at each decision point.

## Phase 3: Prescription

The lists of strengths and weaknesses should drive the selection of innovations for your quality improvement program. However, the concept of a balanced portfolio is also important. In the Introduction, we stressed that many quality programs fail because they view quality too narrowly and try to fix the problems with technology or process alone. In reality, technology, process, and leadership are interrelated and a program that neglects any corner of this iron triangle is not sustainable.

Fortunately, it is easy to use our letter grade scoring system to determine whether you have a balanced quality improvement program. Your program is balanced when you pick innovations, rescore, and determine that

1. The letter grade for each food group is the same.
2. The normalized scores for each critical factor are within 25 percent of each other.

Calculating the food-group letter grades is straightforward. Calculating normalized scores just means dividing the average score of the elements in a critical factor by the extreme score possible for that factor. For example, we did this when we wanted to create a list of weaknesses and we had to determine which critical factor was the weakest. In our example with the data from Table 23.2 and Fig. 23.6, we arrived at normalized scores of 83, 75, and 78 percent for the objective, approach, and pitfall elements, respectively. Since these normalized scores are all within 25 percent of each other, there is no balance problem within the leadership food group. The only remaining requirement would be to verify that the technology and process food groups have the same letter grade as the leadership food group.

Figure 23.8 is a flowchart of the process for prescribing specific innovations to address an organization's weaknesses. The first step is to use the weaknesses list to identify weak critical factors. Then scan the innovations in this

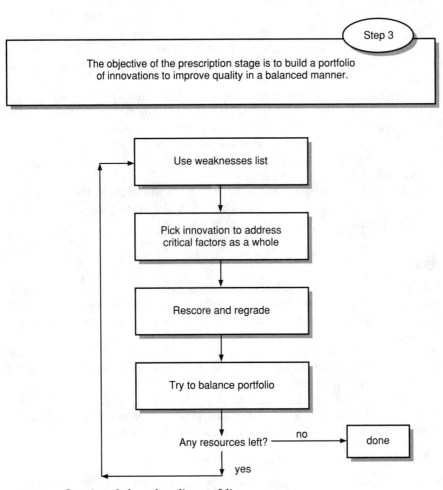

**Figure 23.8** Creating a balanced quality portfolio.

book (and in other sources) for information to help you address them. Tables 1.2 through 1.5 in Chap. 1 may be helpful in this respect. Look for a match between your weak factors and/or elements and the elements described in these tables. You should choose innovations within your resource budget which seem to best address the weaknesses.

After selecting appropriate innovations, you should rescore and regrade the leadership, process, and technology food groups to reflect the anticipated effects of the new innovations.

If you have resources left after addressing weak critical factors, the next goal is to strive for a more balanced portfolio of innovations. This may involve spending additional resources on more innovations. If you run out of resources, you're done. Otherwise return to the weaknesses list, and repeat the process for the next most critical weaknesses.

## Phase 4: Implementation and Continuous Improvement

The last phase is the easiest to describe and the hardest to do. In the implementation phase it's time to "walk the talk."

Begin by reviewing the implementation advice for each of the innovations included in your portfolio. You will probably want to research some of the Suggested Readings listed at the end of the appropriate chapters. Then it's just a matter of taking the plunge and doing it.

Our lab started most innovations—with the exception of lab-wide leadership initiatives—on a pilot basis. Successful innovations were scaled up.

It is critical to continue with periodic assessments (e.g., Baldrige) so that you can measure your rate of progress. Because there is a significant lag between investment in innovation and seeing the fruits of these investments, the assessments are your best in-process indicators that something positive is actually occurring.

The periodic assessments also serve as reminders that the organization must continually improve. New problems continually arise and must be diagnosed and solved on an ongoing basis. The process of quality improvement can seem like an uphill battle much of the time, but results will appear.

Be persistent.

## Concluding Remarks

We began this book by providing a road map (the four stages of maturity) and a compass (the Baldrige template) for a quality improvement journey. We pointed out that improving quality is a long-term project. It takes a lot of effort, but the rewards are proportionally great.

Throughout the book we have provided examples of innovations that helped us move from stage to stage. For each innovation, we discussed the objectives it helped achieve; the costs, benefits, and risks involved; and implementation considerations. In this last chapter, we have described a rigorous method for assembling a portfolio of innovations tailored to an organization's needs.

At various points, we have also tried to provide a flavor of what the atmosphere was like at our lab as we moved from stage to stage. The journey was difficult, but as we reached the third and fourth years, results began to become manifest.

Finally, we want to emphasize that the quality improvement journey is never really over. Quality is not a final destination, but the process of becoming better and better at what you do.

# Appendix

This appendix includes three distinct ways to assess your quality maturity based on the 1994 Malcolm Baldrige Quality Award criteria. Because we have omitted and simplified parts of the Baldrige criteria, these techniques are not a substitute for conducting a rigorous Baldrige assessment using the full criteria available from the National Institute of Standards and Technology or the American Society for Quality Control.

The first assessment method is a pencil-and-paper quiz that uses a simple scoring scheme.

The second method is an on-line version of the same quiz using the computer disk supplied with this book. The on-line version features an automatic scoring algorithm which is more complicated and slightly more precise than the pencil-and-paper version. The on-line version also allows users to change answers to any part of the quiz and to view scores at various levels of detail.

The third method consists of a series of Baldrige score cards. If you are already familiar with Baldrige, this last method provides a quick and easy method of estimating a score.

## Paper-and-Pencil Quality Maturity Assessment

The quality maturity assessment consists of a series of questions for each of the 28 Baldrige items. All the questions are a matter of degree and begin with the words *To what extent....* This phrasing allows you to score each question using the point scale shown in Table A.1.

For each Baldrige item (1.1, 1.2, 1.3, etc.) add the total number of points awarded to the questions and multiply this sum by the item-weighting factor. The result is your estimated Baldrige score for that item. Add your scores on each of the items to get your estimated total Baldrige score. Figure A.1 illustrates this scoring procedure.

**TABLE A.1   Scoring Table**

| If the answer to the question is: | Points awarded |
|---|---|
| To an exceptional degree | 10 |
| To a great degree | 7 |
| To some degree | 5 |
| To a small degree | 2 |
| Not at all | 0 |

You can use the estimated Baldrige score to determine your organization's stage of quality maturity, as explained in Chap. 2.

It is important that you answer *all* questions to obtain an accurate overall score. If you do not know the answer to a question or if it does not seem to apply, award the question the average of the number of points you have awarded to other questions in that category.

For example, you might feel that none of the questions associated with leadership item 1.3 (public responsibility and corporate citizenship) applies to your organization. Don't leave the questions blank. Instead, if you have been awarding 5 points to most of the other leadership questions (e.g., those under items 1.1 and 1.2), you might also award 5 points to each of the questions that you are not sure how to answer.

Note that we include the actual text of each Baldrige item for your reference. The language of the Baldrige criteria makes the implicit assumption that *companies* will be using the criteria, since only companies or large sites

---

1.1 Senior Executive Leadership

Baldrige text: *Describe the senior executives' leadership, personal involvement, and visibility in developing and maintaining an environment for quality excellence.*

Worth: 45 points
Weighting factor: 1.1
*Note:* The thrust here is, Does the leader "talk the quality talk"?

Question 1: To what extent could a person picked randomly from your organization articulate the quality values of the organization?

.
.
.

Question 4: To what extent does the leader of the organization evaluate and improve the effectiveness of his or her quality improvement efforts?

| Score for item 1.1 | | Scoring scale |
|---|---|---|
| Question 1: | 2 | 10 = exceptional degree |
| Question 2: | 5 | 7 = great degree |
| Question 3: | 2 | 5 = some degree |
| Question 4: | 0 | 2 = small degree |
| Total: | $9 \times 1.1 = 9.9 \approx 10$ | 0 = not at all |

*Note:* Round to nearest whole number.

Repeating this procedure for all Baldrige items may yield results something like these:

Estimated score for item 1.1 =   10
Estimated score for item 1.2 =   5
Estimated score for item 1.3 =   8
.
.
.
Estimated score for item 7.6 =   25

Total estimated Baldrige Score: XXX
where XXX = the sum of all estimated item scores

**Figure A.1**  Example of scoring procedure

are allowed to apply for the award. However, we have used the criteria effectively with groups as small as departments of 10 people. Small organizations may want to follow the spirit rather than the letter of the Baldrige criteria. For this reason, we have included notes that often indicate how the criteria might be applied to small organizations.

A final caveat: It is rare that an organization just beginning its quality improvement efforts will score higher than 500 on the Baldrige scale. Unless you had extremely high levels of quality to start with, or unless your quality program is already well under way, expect a score below 500.

**Paper-and-pencil assessment items**

What follows is our quick and easy paper-and-pencil assessment. Note that the descriptive text from the 1994 Baldrige Award criteria is provided for your reference.

### 1.1  Senior executive leadership

*Baldrige text.*  Describe the senior executives' leadership, personal involvement, and visibility in developing and maintaining an environment for quality excellence.

*Worth:* 45 points

*Weighting factor:* 1.1

*Note:* The thrust here is, Does the leader "talk the quality talk"?

*Question 1:* To what extent could a person picked randomly from your organization articulate the quality values of the organization?

*Question 2:* To what extent does the organization take a broad view of quality improvement (e.g., improve customer satisfaction as well as reduce defects)?

*Question 3:* To what extent is the leader of the organization personally involved and committed to quality improvement activities?

*Question 4:* To what extent does the leader of the organization evaluate and improve the effectiveness of her or his quality improvement efforts?

| Score for item 1.1 | | Scoring scale |
|---|---|---|
| Question 1: | _____ | 10 = exceptional degree |
| Question 2: | _____ | 7 = great degree |
| Question 3: | _____ | 5 = some degree |
| Question 4: | _____ | 2 = small degree |
| Total: | _____ × 1.1 = _____ | 0 = not at all |

### 1.2  Management for quality

*Baldrige text.*  Describe how the company's customer focus and quality values are integrated into day-to-day leadership, management, and supervision of all company units.

*Worth:* 25 points

*Weighting factor:* 0.8

*Note:* The thrust here is, Does management "talk the quality talk"?

*Question 1:* To what extent are the plans to fulfill quality values deployed?

*Question 2:* To what extent do individuals know their roles in achieving quality?

*Question 3:* To what extent are you measuring and reviewing quality progress?

| Score for item 1.2 | Scoring scale |
|---|---|
| Question 1: _____ | 10 = exceptional degree |
| Question 2: _____ | 7 = great degree |
| Question 3: _____ | 5 = some degree |
| Total: _____ × 0.8 = _____ | 2 = small degree |
| | 0 = not at all |

## 1.3   Public responsibility and corporate citizenship

*Baldrige text.*   Describe how the company includes its responsibilities to the public in its quality policies and improvement practices. Describe also how the company leads as a corporate citizen in its key communities.

*Worth:* 25 points

*Weighting factor:* 0.8

*Note:* Smaller organizations may want to score these questions using their average score questions in items 1.1 and 1.2. The thrust here is, Does the organization "walk the talk" in public?

*Question 1:* To what extent do the quality values of the organization include corporate citizenship and public responsibility?

*Question 2:* To what extent does the organization promote quality values outside the organization?

*Question 3:* To what extent has the organization demonstrated its quality commitment via concrete programs (e.g., charitable contributions, loan of people to the community)?

| Score for item 1.3 | Scoring scale |
|---|---|
| Question 1: _____ | 10 = exceptional degree |
| Question 2: _____ | 7 = great degree |
| Question 3: _____ | 5 = some degree |
| Total: _____ × 0.8 = _____ | 2 = small degree |
| | 0 = not at all |

### 2.1   Scope and management of quality and performance data and information

*Baldrige text.*   Describe the company's selection and management of data and information used for planning, day-to-day management, and evaluation of quality and operational performance.

*Worth:* 15 points

*Weighting factor:* 0.5

*Note:* The thrust here is, Do you manage by fact?

*Question 1:* To what extent are data collected systematically to run the organization?

*Question 2:* To what extent are the collected data customer-related (e.g., customer satisfaction data, customer profiles, data on number of service calls)?

*Question 3:* To what extent does the organization manage by facts instead of gut feeling?

| Score for item 2.1 | | Scoring scale |
|---|---|---|
| Question 1: _____ | | 10 = exceptional degree |
| Question 2: _____ | | 7 = great degree |
| Question 3: _____ | | 5 = some degree |
| Total: _____ × 0.5 = _____ | | 2 = small degree |
| | | 0 = not at all |

### 2.2   Competitive comparisons and benchmarking

*Baldrige text.*   Describe the company's processes, current sources and scope, and uses of competitive comparisons and benchmarking information and data to support improvement of quality and operational performance.

*Worth:* 20 points

*Weighting factor:* 1.0

*Note:* The thrust here is, Do you collect comparison data?

*Question 1:* To what extent does the organization collect data on competitive products?

*Question 2:* To what extent does the organization benchmark the processes of best-of-class organizations?

| Score for item 2.2 | | Scoring scale |
|---|---|---|
| Question 1: _____ | | 10 = exceptional degree |
| Question 2: _____ | | 7 = great degree |
| Total: _____ × 1.0 = _____ | | 5 = some degree |
| | | 2 = small degree |
| | | 0 = not at all |

### 2.3  Analysis and uses of company-level data

*Baldrige text.*  Describe how data related to quality, customers, and operational performance, together with relevant financial data, are analyzed to support company-level review, action, and planning.

*Worth:* 40 points

*Weighting factor:* 1.0

*Note:* The thrust is, Do you use the data you collect?

*Question 1:* To what extent does the organization analyze customer-related data (e.g., customer satisfaction, customer complaints, customer service metrics)?

*Question 2:* To what extent are the analyses of customer-related data used to take concrete actions (e.g., quality improvements based on customer complaints)?

*Question 3:* To what extent does the organization analyze performance data (e.g., financial performance, defect levels in software, in-process metrics)?

*Question 4:* To what extent is the analysis of performance data used to take concrete actions (e.g., improve the test process based on in-process measurements of the number of errors detected in various stages of product test)?

| Score for item 2.3 | Scoring scale |
|---|---|
| Question 1: _____ | 10 = exceptional degree |
| Question 2: _____ | 7 = great degree |
| Question 3: _____ | 5 = some degree |
| Question 4: _____ | 2 = small degree |
| Total: _____ × 1.0 = _____ | 0 = not at all |

### 3.1  Strategic quality and company performance planning process

*Baldrige text.*  Describe the company's business planning process for the short term (1 to 3 years) and longer term (3 years or more) for customer satisfaction leadership and overall operational performance improvement. Include how this process integrates quality and operational performance requirements and how plans are deployed.

*Worth:* 35 points

*Weighting factor:* 1.2

*Note:* Category 3 asks if you have quality and business plans and if these plans are linked. Small organizations that are not responsible for business planning should answer the questions based on the quality aspects.

*Question 1:* To what extent is the organization's planning process systematic and rigorous?

*Question 2:* To what extent are measures of quality (e.g., defect levels and customer satisfaction) included in the planning process?

*Question 3:* To what extent are the plans actually deployed?

| Score for item 3.1 | | Scoring scale |
|---|---|---|
| Question 1: | _____ | 10 = exceptional degree |
| Question 2: | _____ | 7 = great degree |
| Question 3: | _____ | 5 = some degree |
| Total: | _____ × 1.2 = _____ | 2 = small degree |
| | | 0 = not at all |

## 3.2   Quality and performance plans

*Baldrige text.*   Summarize the company's specific quality and operational performance plans for the short term (1 to 3 years) and the longer term (3 years or more).

*Worth:* 25 points

*Weighting factor:* 0.8

*Note:* Again, if your organization is part of a business, just focus on the quality aspects of these questions.

*Question 1:* To what extent does the organization have specific short- and long-term quality and operational plans (e.g., plans involving defect rates, customer satisfaction levels, productivity, and financial targets)?

*Question 2:* To what extent are these plans deployed?

*Question 3:* To what extent does the organization compare these plans to key competitor and/or industry benchmarks?

| Score for item 3.2 | | Scoring scale |
|---|---|---|
| Question 1: | _____ | 10 = exceptional degree |
| Question 2: | _____ | 7 = great degree |
| Question 3: | _____ | 5 = some degree |
| Total: | _____ × 0.8 = _____ | 2 = small degree |
| | | 0 = not at all |

## 4.1   Human resource planning and management

*Baldrige text.*   Describe how the company's overall human resource management plans and processes are integrated with its overall quality and operational performance plans and how human resource planning and management address fully the needs and development of the entire workforce.

*Worth:* 20 points

*Weighting factor:* 1.0

*Note:* Small organizations should link their (as opposed to the company's) human resource activities to their quality goals.

*Question 1:* To what extent are the organization's human resource activities integrated with its business and quality plans?

*Question 2:* To what extent does the organization collect and use employee data to improve its operations (e.g., satisfaction survey data leading to improvement actions)?

| Score for item 4.1 | | Scoring scale |
| --- | --- | --- |
| Question 1: | _____ | 10 = exceptional degree |
| Question 2: | _____ | 7 = great degree |
| Total: | _____ × 1.0 = _____ | 5 = some degree |
| | | 2 = small degree |
| | | 0 = not at all |

## 4.2   Employee involvement

*Baldrige text.*   Describe how all employees are enabled to contribute effectively to meeting the company's quality and operational performance plans; summarize trends in effectiveness and extent of involvement.

*Worth:* 40 points

*Weighting factor:* 1.0

*Note:* The thrust here is, How much have employees bought into quality and operational plans?

*Question 1:* To what extent have employees bought into quality plans, schedules for products, and the content of product specifications?

*Question 2:* To what extent are the organization's mechanisms for gaining buy-in to quality (e.g., meetings, empowerment activities) effective?

*Question 3:* To what extent do employees participate in creating the organization's quality and operational plans?

*Question 4:* To what extent would most employees agree with the organization's quality plans?

| Score for item 4.2 | | Scoring scale |
| --- | --- | --- |
| Question 1: | _____ | 10 = exceptional degree |
| Question 2: | _____ | 7 = great degree |
| Question 3: | _____ | 5 = some degree |
| Question 4: | _____ | 2 = small degree |
| Total: | _____ × 1.0 = _____ | 0 = not at all |

### 4.3 Employee education and training

*Baldrige text.*    Describe how the company determines quality and related education and training needs for all employees. Show how this determination addresses company plans and supports employee growth. Outline how such education and training are evaluated, and summarize key trends in the effectiveness and extent of education and training.

*Worth:* 40 points

*Weighting factor:* 1.0

*Note:* The thrust is, Do you have good education and quality training? If another organization handles the training for your organization, you might think in terms of the effectiveness of the interface between the two organizations. Or just fill in the average score for other questions in category 4.

*Question 1:* To what extent can you show positive trends with respect to the extent of employee education and training?

*Question 2:* To what extent are the educational efforts and training effective (e.g., is there a correlation between training and key quality or productivity measures such as reduced cycle time, fewer defects, or increased productivity)?

*Question 3:* To what extent does the organization use a rigorous process for determining educational needs?

*Question 4:* To what extent does the organization use data (e.g., satisfaction data for courses) to improve education and training?

| Score for item 4.3 | Scoring scale |
|---|---|
| Question 1: _____ | 10 = exceptional degree |
| Question 2: _____ | 7 = great degree |
| Question 3: _____ | 5 = some degree |
| Question 4: _____ | 2 = small degree |
| Total: _____ × 1.0 = _____ | 0 = not at all |

### 4.4 Employee performance and recognition

*Baldrige text.*    Describe how the company's employee performance, recognition, promotion, compensation, reward, and feedback approaches support the improvement of quality and operational performance.

*Worth:* 25 points

*Weighting factor:* 0.6

*Note:* The thrust is, Is your employee recognition system supportive of quality improvement? Small organizations should answer with respect to recognition efforts within the small organization, not the company at large.

*Question 1:* To what extent are rewards and recognition tied to quality and operational improvement (e.g., is variable compensation tied to quality or performance measures)?

*Question 2:* To what extent are performance evaluation and recognition programs evaluated and updated effectively (e.g., do you use employee surveys, analyze coverage, set milestones and goals, and measure achievement)?

*Question 3:* To what extent does the organization use trend data to evaluate the effectiveness and extent of its recognition system?

*Question 4:* To what extent is the recognition system effective (e.g., is there a correlation between recognition and quality performance and/or evidence of a causal relationship)?

| Score for item 4.4 | Scoring scale |
|---|---|
| Question 1: _____ | 10 = exceptional degree |
| Question 2: _____ | 7 = great degree |
| Question 3: _____ | 5 = some degree |
| Question 4: _____ | 2 = small degree |
| Total: _____ × 0.6 = _____ | 0 = not at all |

## 4.5   Employee well-being and satisfaction

*Baldrige text.*   Describe how the company maintains a work environment conducive to the well-being and growth of all employees; summarize trends in key indicators of well-being and satisfaction.

*Worth:* 25 points

*Weighting factor:* 0.8

*Note:* Small organizations should apply this at a local, not companywide, level.

*Question 1:* To what extent would most employees rate their work environment positively?

*Question 2:* To what extent is employee well-being reflected positively in indicators (e.g., high employee satisfaction, low absenteeism, low turnover, few grievances)?

*Question 3:* To what extent does the organization's work environment compare favorably with appropriate benchmarks?

| Score for item 4.5 | Scoring scale |
|---|---|
| Question 1: _____ | 10 = exceptional degree |
| Question 2: _____ | 7 = great degree |
| Question 3: _____ | 5 = some degree |
| Total: _____ × 0.8 = _____ | 2 = small degree |
| | 0 = not at all |

### 5.1    Design and introduction of quality products and services

*Baldrige text.*  Describe how new and/or modified products and services are designed and introduced and how key production/delivery processes are designed to meet both key product and service quality requirements and company operational performance requirements.

*Worth:* 40 points

*Weighting factor:* 1.0

*Note:* This item is most relevant to organizations directly involved in the design of new products. The thrust: Can you design with quality?

*Question 1:* To what extent is the organization's process for designing products systematic, driven by customer requirements, and quality-conscious?

*Question 2:* To what extent does the organization have a good process for evaluating and reviewing designs (e.g., do you compare designs to product quality requirements, do you check if the designs scale well, are the designs checked against the organization's ability to implement them)?

*Question 3:* To what extent does the organization improve its designs and design process to increase quality and reduce cycle time?

*Question 4:* To what extent do the production, delivery, and service processes meet quality and product service requirements?

|  Score for item 5.1 | Scoring scale |
| --- | --- |
| Question 1: _____ | 10 = exceptional degree |
| Question 2: _____ | 7 = great degree |
| Question 3: _____ | 5 = some degree |
| Question 4: _____ | 2 = small degree |
| Total: _____ × 1.0 = _____ | 0 = not at all |

### 5.2    Process management: Product and service production and delivery processes

*Baldrige text.*  Describe how the company's key product and service production/delivery processes are managed to ensure that design requirements are met and that both quality and operational performance are continuously improved.

*Worth:* 35 points

*Weighting factor:* 1.2

*Note:* The thrust is, Can you build and deliver with quality?

*Question 1:* To what extent does the organization follow a development process (e.g., for code, test, build/integrate, deliver, service)?

*Question 2:* To what degree is the development process monitored (e.g., do you have in-process measurements of the number of errors occurring in early stages of development)?

*Question 3:* To what extent is the development process improved continuously (e.g., do you compare your processes and metrics with those of others)?

| Score for item 5.2 | | Scoring scale |
|---|---|---|
| Question 1: _____ | | 10 = exceptional degree |
| Question 2: _____ | | 7 = great degree |
| Question 3: _____ | | 5 = some degree |
| | | 2 = small degree |
| Total: _____ × 1.2 = _____ | | 0 = not at all |

## 5.3   Process management: Business and support service processes

*Baldrige text.*   Describe how the company's key business and support service processes are designed and managed so that current requirements are met and that quality and operational performance are continuously improved.

*Worth:* 30 points

*Weighting factor:* 1.0

*Note:* The thrust: How well are the business and support functions managed? For small organizations, think of the support tasks or people in the organization.

*Question 1:* To what extent can the support groups (e.g., accounting, pricing, business analysis, planning, education, security, personnel) articulate how they contribute to quality and operational goals and plans?

*Question 2:* To what extent are the business and support processes well designed?

*Question 3:* To what extent are business and support processes measured and improved (e.g., do you know if certain personnel policies have any effect on employee retention, do you take action based on the measurements)?

| Score for item 5.3 | | Scoring scale |
|---|---|---|
| Question 1: _____ | | 10 = exceptional degree |
| Question 2: _____ | | 7 = great degree |
| Question 3: _____ | | 5 = some degree |
| | | 2 = small degree |
| Total: _____ × 1.0 = _____ | | 0 = not at all |

## 5.4   Supplier quality

*Baldrige text.*   Describe how the company assures the quality of materials, components, and services furnished by other businesses. Describe also the company's actions and plans to improve supplier quality.

*Worth:* 20 points

*Weighting factor:* 0.7

*Note:* If your organization has no external suppliers, use the average response to other questions in category 5 here.

*Question 1:* To what extent does the organization define and communicate its quality requirements to key suppliers (e.g., do you have acceptance criteria for vended software, are these in the contract)?

*Question 2:* To what extent do you evaluate and ensure the quality of suppliers (e.g., do you test their products against quality criteria)?

*Question 3:* To what extent do you continuously improve the process for ensuring supplier quality (e.g., have you taken concrete improvement actions recently)?

| Score for item 5.4 | | Scoring scale |
|---|---|---|
| Question 1: _____ | | 10 = exceptional degree |
| Question 2: _____ | | 7 = great degree |
| Question 3: _____ | | 5 = some degree |
| Total: _____ × 0.7 = _____ | | 2 = small degree |
| | | 0 = not at all |

## 5.5  Quality assessment

*Baldrige text.*   Describe how the company assesses the quality and performance of its systems and processes, and the quality of its products and services.

*Worth:* 15 points

*Weighting factor:* 0.8

*Note:* This item applies at the company level. Smaller organizations might use the average of responses to items in 5.1, 5.2, and 5.3. The thrust: How well do you assess the company as a whole—do the pieces fit together well?

*Question 1:* To what extent do you assess the quality and performance of your products (e.g., do you measure them against customer expectations)?

*Question 2:* To what extent do you assess the system that produces the products (e.g., do you benchmark cost ratios or revenue per employee with other companies)?

| Score for item 5.5 | | Scoring scale |
|---|---|---|
| Question 1: _____ | | 10 = exceptional degree |
| Question 2: _____ | | 7 = great degree |
| Total: _____ × 0.8 = _____ | | 5 = some degree |
| | | 2 = small degree |
| | | 0 = not at all |

## 6.1   Product and service quality results

*Baldrige text.*   Summarize trends and current quality levels for key product and service features; compare current levels with those of competitors and/or appropriate benchmarks.

*Worth:* 70 points

*Weighting factor:* 1.4

*Note:* The thrust here: How good are your quality trends and levels for your products?

*Question 1:* To what extent do you have quality measurements for all key products (e.g., number of field defects, reliability and performance ratings, price versus performance measures)?

*Question 2:* To what extent do these measures show positive trends?

*Question 3:* To what extent do you have data comparing your results with those of competitors and/or benchmarks (e.g., survey data, trade articles comparing products)?

*Question 4:* To what extent do your results compare favorably with competitors and benchmarks?

*Question 5:* To what extent have your products won awards or been recognized for excellence—especially in head-to-head competition with competitors?

| Score for item 6.1 | Scoring scale |
|---|---|
| Question 1: _____ | 10 = exceptional degree |
| Question 2: _____ | 7 = great degree |
| Question 3: _____ | 5 = some degree |
| Question 4: _____ | 2 = small degree |
| Question 5: _____ | 0 = not at all |
| Total: _____ × 1.4 = _____ | |

## 6.2   Company operational results

*Baldrige text.*   Summarize trends and levels in overall company operational performance; provide a comparison with competitors and/or appropriate benchmarks.

*Worth:* 50 points

*Weighting factor:* 1.2

*Note:* The thrust here is the measurement of operations—the functions that make the product. Departments and small organizations may not have competitors per se, but probably they could find benchmarks.

*Question 1:* To what extent do key measurements (e.g., development cycle times, asset management, costs, revenue, productivity) have positive levels?

*Question 2:* To what extent do key measurements (e.g., development cycle times, asset management, costs, revenue, productivity) show positive trends?

*Question 3:* To what extent are your key measurements connected to quality and operational performance improvements?

*Question 4:* To what extent do the organization's key measures compare favorably with those of competitors or industry benchmarks?

|  Score for item 6.2  | Scoring scale |
|---|---|
| Question 1: _____ | 10 = exceptional degree |
| Question 2: _____ | 7 = great degree |
| Question 3: _____ | 5 = some degree |
| Question 4: _____ | 2 = small degree |
| Total: _____ × 1.2 = _____ | 0 = not at all |

### 6.3 Business and support service results

*Baldrige text.* Summarize trends and current levels in quality and operational performance improvement for business processes and support services; compare results with competitors' and/or appropriate benchmarks.

*Worth:* 25 points

*Weighting factor:* 1.2

*Note:* This item focuses on support (indirect) organizations.

*Question 1:* To what extent does the support organization manage its costs effectively?

*Question 2:* To what extent can the support organizations show positive satisfaction trends for their internal customers (e.g., low cycle time for getting new hires on board for personnel)?

|  Score for item 6.3  | Scoring scale |
|---|---|
| Question 1: _____ | 10 = exceptional degree |
| Question 2: _____ | 7 = great degree |
| Total: _____ × 1.2 = _____ | 5 = some degree |
|  | 2 = small degree |
|  | 0 = not at all |

### 6.4 Supplier quality results

*Baldrige text.* Summarize trends in quality and current quality levels of suppliers; compare the company's supplier quality with that of competitors and/or with appropriate benchmarks.

*Worth:* 35 points

*Weighting factor:* 1.7

*Note:* These questions refer to suppliers external to the organization.

*Question 1:* To what extent are your suppliers meeting your expectations with regard to quality measures?

*Question 2:* To what extent do the quality levels and trends of your suppliers compare favorably with the quality levels of competitive suppliers or benchmarks?

| Score for item 6.4 | Scoring scale |
|---|---|
| Question 1: _____ | 10 = exceptional degree |
| Question 2: _____ | 7 = great degree |
| Total: _____ × 1.7 = _____ | 5 = some degree |
| | 2 = small degree |
| | 0 = not at all |

### 7.1   Customer expectations: Current and future

*Baldrige text.*   Describe how the company determines near-term and long-term requirements and expectations of customers.

*Worth:* 35 points

*Weighting factor:* 1.2

*Note:* The thrust here is, How well do you determine customer requirements? Customers can be internal customers if the organization has no external customers.

*Question 1:* To what extent do you understand your customer sets (e.g., who you are building the product for, who buys your product, and who you are targeting in the future)?

*Question 2:* To what extent is your knowledge of customers based on hard data (e.g., do you use surveys or gut feeling)?

*Question 3:* To what extent can you be certain that the features and functions that you build actually reflect the needs of customers (e.g. do you have data collection mechanisms, postage-paid survey cards, and a process for using these data)?

| Score for item 7.1 | Scoring scale |
|---|---|
| Question 1: _____ | 10 = exceptional degree |
| Question 2: _____ | 7 = great degree |
| Question 3: _____ | 5 = some degree |
| Total: _____ × 1.2 = _____ | 2 = small degree |
| | 0 = not at all |

## 7.2 Customer relationship management

*Baldrige text.* Describe how the company provides effective management of its interactions and relationships with its customers and uses information gained from customers to improve customer relationship management processes.

*Worth:* 65 points

*Weighting factor:* 0.9

*Note:* The thrust here is, How well do you manage your relationship with your customers? Again, customers can be internal customers if there are no external customers.

*Question 1:* To what extent can members of the organization articulate the key requirements for maintaining and building relationships with customers?

*Question 2:* To what extent do developers have direct contact and interactions with customers?

*Question 3:* To what extent do you have service standards that address your quality goals?

*Question 4:* To what extent would customers rate your organization as customer-friendly (e.g., can they contact you easily via an 800 number)?

*Question 5:* To what extent do you have an effective and systematic process for following up on customer complaints and requests?

*Question 6:* To what extent are the organization's personnel policies geared to improve the quality of interaction with customers (e.g., selection and recognition of friendly and effective customer contact employees)?

*Question 7:* To what extent do you use complaints and feedback to improve (e.g., is the complaint department just there to soothe people or do you really use the feedback you get; are there really improvements)?

| Score for item 7.2 | Scoring scale |
|---|---|
| Question 1: _____ | 10 = exceptional degree |
| Question 2: _____ | 7 = great degree |
| Question 3: _____ | 5 = some degree |
| Question 4: _____ | 2 = small degree |
| Question 5: _____ | 0 = not at all |
| Question 6: _____ | |
| Question 7: _____ | |
| Total: _____ × 0.9 = _____ | |

### 7.3   Commitment to customers

*Baldrige text.*   Describe the company's commitments to customers regarding its products/services and how these commitments are evaluated and improved.

*Worth:* 15 points

*Weighting factor:* 0.5

*Note:* The thrust is, Do you talk the "customer commitment" talk?

*Question 1:* To what extent do you demonstrate customer commitment via concrete policies (e.g., warranties and trade-in policies)?

*Question 2:* To what extent do your customer commitment policies compare favorably with those in the industry and competitors?

*Question 3:* To what extent do you evaluate and improve your customer commitment actions?

| Score for item 7.3 | Scoring scale |
|---|---|
| Question 1: _____ | 10 = exceptional degree |
| Question 2: _____ | 7 = great degree |
| Question 3: _____ | 5 = some degree |
| Total: _____ × 0.5 = _____ | 2 = small degree |
| | 0 = not at all |

### 7.4   Customer satisfaction determination

*Baldrige text.*   Describe how the company determines customer satisfaction, customer repurchase intentions, and customer satisfaction relative to competitors; describe how these determination processes are evaluated and improved.

*Worth:* 30 points

*Weighting factor:* 0.8

*Note:* The thrust is, Do you have a mechanism for determining customer satisfaction? Customers can be both internal and external.

*Question 1:* To what extent do you have a robust system for determining customer satisfaction?

*Question 2:* To what extent are your measurements of customer satisfaction valid (e.g., objective) and effective?

*Question 3:* To what extent are you informed about the customer satisfaction levels of competitors?

*Question 4:* To what extent does the organization continuously improve its mechanisms for determining customer satisfaction (e.g., new survey methods)?

| Score for item 7.4 | | Scoring scale |
|---|---|---|
| Question 1: _____ | | 10 = exceptional degree |
| Question 2: _____ | | 7 = great degree |
| Question 3: _____ | | 5 = some degree |
| Question 4: _____ | | 2 = small degree |
| Total: _____ × 0.8 = _____ | | 0 = not at all |

## 7.5 Customer satisfaction results

*Baldrige text.* Summarize trends in the company's customer satisfaction and trends in key indicators of customer dissatisfaction.

*Worth:* 85 points

*Weighting factor:* 1.7

*Note:* The thrust is, How good is your customer satisfaction? If you don't have external customers, use internal ones.

*Question 1:* To what extent do key indicators (e.g., survey data, customer assessments, awards, customer retention levels) reflect high customer satisfaction?

*Question 2:* To what extent do these same measures show positive customer satisfaction trends over time?

*Question 3:* To what extent do your key dissatisfaction indicators (e.g., complaints, returns, refunds, claims, recalls, litigation) show low levels of dissatisfaction?

*Question 4:* To what extent do these dissatisfaction indicators tend in a beneficial direction over time?

*Question 5:* To what extent do your measures of customer satisfaction and dissatisfaction cover all key products and all key customer groups (e.g., customer types and customer locations)?

| Score for item 7.5 | | Scoring scale |
|---|---|---|
| Question 1: _____ | | 10 = exceptional degree |
| Question 2: _____ | | 7 = great degree |
| Question 3: _____ | | 5 = some degree |
| Question 4: _____ | | 2 = small degree |
| Question 5: _____ | | 0 = not at all |
| Total: _____ × 1.7 = _____ | | |

## 7.6  Customer satisfaction comparison

*Baldrige text.*  Compare the company's customer satisfaction results with those of competitors.

*Worth:* 70 points

*Weighting factor:* 2.3

*Note:* The focus here is, How good is your customer satisfaction compared with the competition?

*Question 1:* To what extent is there evidence that your customer satisfaction levels are higher than those of your competitors (e.g., trade press recognition, awards relating to customer satisfaction, good *Consumer Reports*–style ratings)?

*Question 2:* To what extent are you better than your competitors at gaining new customers (e.g., how does your software license rate growth compare with the competition)?

*Question 3:* To what extent are your key products increasing their market share compared with the competition?

| Score for item 7.6 | | Scoring scale |
|---|---|---|
| Question 1: | _____ | 10 = exceptional degree |
| Question 2: | _____ | 7 = great degree |
| Question 3: | _____ | 5 = some degree |
| Total: | _____ × 2.3 = _____ | 2 = small degree |
| | | 0 = not at all |

Once you have calculated the scores for each item, fill in the score sheet (Table A.2) to compute your organization's overall estimated Baldrige score. This score can then be used with the criteria described in Chap. 2 to determine your organization's stage of quality maturity.

## Quality Maturity Assessment Software

### System requirements

To install and use the quality maturity assessment software included with this book, you must have

1. An IBM (or IBM-compatible) personal computer with a 386 (or higher) microprocessor and an attached mouse
2. Windows version 3.1 or OS/2 version 2.1 installed
3. At least 4 megabytes of free space on the hard disk (C drive)
4. One 3.5-inch A disk drive (1.44 megabytes)
5. 4 megabytes or more of RAM suggested

**TABLE A.2   Assessment Score Sheet**

| Item | Score | Possible points |
|------|-------|-----------------|
| 1.1 Senior executive leadership | _____ | 45 |
| 1.2 Management for quality | _____ | 25 |
| 1.3 Public responsibility | _____ | 25 |
| 2.1 Scope and management of quality data | _____ | 15 |
| 2.2 Competitive comparisons | _____ | 20 |
| 2.3 Analysis and uses of data | _____ | 40 |
| 3.1 Strategic planning | _____ | 35 |
| 3.2 Quality and performance plan | _____ | 25 |
| 4.1 Human resource planning and management | _____ | 20 |
| 4.2 Employee involvement | _____ | 40 |
| 4.3 Employee education | _____ | 40 |
| 4.4 Employee performance | _____ | 25 |
| 4.5 Employee well-being | _____ | 25 |
| 5.1 Design of quality products | _____ | 40 |
| 5.2 Process management: products | _____ | 35 |
| 5.3 Process management: support | _____ | 30 |
| 5.4 Supplier quality | _____ | 20 |
| 5.5 Quality assessment | _____ | 15 |
| 6.1 Product and service quality | _____ | 70 |
| 6.2 Company operational result | _____ | 50 |
| 6.3 Business support results | _____ | 25 |
| 6.4 Supplier quality results | _____ | 35 |
| 7.1 Customer expectations | _____ | 35 |
| 7.2 Customer relationship management | _____ | 65 |
| 7.3 Commitment to customers | _____ | 15 |
| 7.4 Customer satisfaction determination | _____ | 30 |
| 7.5 Customer satisfaction results | _____ | 85 |
| 7.6 Customer satisfaction comparison | _____ | 70 |
| Total estimated Baldrige score: | _____ | out of 1000 |

## Disclaimer

The quality maturity self-assessment software is prototype code written in the SMALLTALK object-oriented programming language. While we have made every effort to produce a quality prototype, we make no warranties or guarantees with regard to the code and offer it for use at your own risk. Specifically, the code was not developed by IBM and has not had the benefit of the rigorous testing and code inspection procedures detailed in this book. (If it did, the expense would force us to sell it as a separate product.)

Because this software is written in a prototyping language, the execution may be slow on some systems—especially during the installation phase. Feel free to get a cup of coffee while the installation is chugging away. Once the installation is complete, the assessment should take less time to complete on-line than it would by using the paper-and-pencil method.

## Overview

We recommend reading the instructions for the paper-and-pencil assessment if you have not already done so. The quality maturity (QM) prototype contains questions that are identical to those in the paper-and-pencil assessment, but the scoring is simpler.

Whereas the pencil-and-paper assessment requires you to assign points (10, 7, 5, 2, or 0) to each question, sum the points, and multiply by a weighting factor, the QM prototype simply asks you to score each question on a scale of 1 to 5. It automatically calculates an estimated score and identifies your stage of quality maturity.

## Installation

1. Bring up Windows 3.1 or the Win-OS/2 screen in the OS/2 2.1 operating system.
2. Insert the QM disk in drive A.
3. Open File Manager.
4. Select the drive A icon.
5. Double-click with the mouse on the file named SETUP.EXE. A message box will appear with the words *Initializing setup*. After 2 or 3 minutes, another message box will appear with a bar graph that shows how the installation is progressing. The total installation procedure initiated by clicking on SETUP.EXE takes about 10 minutes. No input is required from the user during this time, so you can get a cup of coffee. When installation is complete, a window appears with the self-assessment program icon.
6. Double-click on the self-assessment program icon to begin the assessment.

## Taking the assessment

Double-clicking on the self-assessment program icon causes the program to start and the main menu to appear.

Double-click on the menu item Take Quality Maturity Quiz. The first question of the assessment will appear together with a 5-point rating scale.

Type a number from 1 to 5. You may hear a beep or click, which is the program's way of acknowledging your input. Press the Enter or Return key to enter your response, and continue to the next question.

*Note:* If you press Enter without entering a number, the program assumes a default response of 5. Use the Up arrow and Down arrow keys to skip backward or forward in the sequence of questions.

*Hint:* You can go directly to questions for any item in any Baldrige category by clicking on the Category/item pull-down menu at the top of the screen. Clicking and holding the mouse button down on a category will allow you to see the items within the category. Move the mouse so that the desired item is highlighted, and release the mouse button. This will cause questions relating to the desired item to be displayed.

Continue entering responses until questions for all items have been answered (7.6 is the last item!) or until you want to view the results of the assessment.

### Viewing the results

When you have reached the last question for item 7.6, or when you simply want to check your results so far, click once on the View pull-down menu, and then click again on the Results option in this menu.

The Results screen will appear. At the top of the Results screen, the program displays your stage of quality maturity based on your response to questions (e.g., stage: awareness).

The leftmost column of buttons controls the level of detail of the results that are displayed. To see only your total estimated Baldrige score (the default), click on the Total button. To see your score broken down by the seven Baldrige categories, click on the Category button.

To see scores for Baldrige items within a category, click on the category description (in the large central column of boxes). Items that make up that category will appear in the large box below the list of categories.

If you click on the description of a specific item, the questions relating to that item will appear in the lowermost box in the central column. Clicking on the Previous or Next button near the bottom of the screen allows you to scroll through the questions associated with each item.

The last two columns on the Results screen display your score and the opportunity for improvement (total points possible minus your score) at each level of detail. The Opportunity column is particularly useful as a diagnostic aid because it tells at a glance which categories, items, and specific topics need the most improvement.

You can return to the self-assessment quiz at any time to pick up where you left off or to change your answers to particular questions. Just select the View pull-down menu and click on the Quiz option.

### Exiting the program, saving results, and retrieving results

You can exit the program from the Quiz or Results screens by selecting the pull-down menu labeled Exit. Click once on the option Return to main menu. Once you are at the main menu, select Exit program to quit.

From the main menu you can also go to the Quiz screen, go to the Results screen, save results, or retrieve results. Selecting either the Quiz or the Results screen takes you to the screens described above.

To save the results of your assessment—even if they are incomplete—select Save quiz results. A dialogue box will appear. Type in a file name (less than 9 characters) and click on OK to save your results in the file. Click on Cancel instead of OK if you change your mind about saving your results.

To retrieve a Results file that has been previously saved, select Retrieve saved quiz results. A dialogue box will appear, displaying the files that have been previously saved. Select a file and click on OK. The Results screen will appear, displaying the results from the saved file.

*Note:* You can go to the Quiz screen and change or add answers. That is, saving quiz results saves not only the final scores, but also all your answers to individual questions in a form that you can update by using the Quiz screen.

## Caveats

1. The QM prototype requires that users move between program screens (i.e., the Quiz, Results, and Main menu screens) only via the pull-down menus or the main menu. Specifically, do *not* drag screens around the desktop or click on a screen that is behind another screen to bring the first screen to the top. Although the Windows operating system may permit these actions, they are unnecessary and can cause unpredictable results.

2. On systems with gray-scale monitors, you may find it necessary to adjust the colors on your monitor to ensure that all the text (especially the scores on the Results screen) is readable.

## Baldrige Score Cards

The score card assessment technique appears courtesy of Roy Bauer of Competitive Dominance Strategies. The score cards can be used as a quick method to assess one's current quality maturity level against the key elements in the Malcolm Baldrige guidelines. The key elements are not intended to cover all the detail that is contained in the Malcolm Baldrige criteria, but they can help identify the areas that represent company strengths and the areas that need attention (weaknesses).

The seven score cards are illustrated in Figs. A.2 to A.8.

The letters A, D, and R on the right-hand side of each score card indicate approach, deployment, and results.

*Approach:*  Is the process a sound, systematic approach that gives definable, repeatable, predictable results?

*Deployment:*  Does the approach cover a majority of the organization versus just an excellent example in one area of the business?

*Results:*  Are results fact-based? Do they provide trends that demonstrate minimum variability? Can the results be compared to leadership companies to gauge comparative excellence?

The score cards can be used by individuals or preferably by cross-functional teams of assessors. Assess each of the seven categories for strengths and weaknesses. Then rate each category based on the scale indicated at the top of each card. Note that different categories have different scales to reflect the number of points Baldrige allocates to the categories. For example, the scale for leadership ranges up to 9.5, corresponding to the 95 points allocated to leadership in the Malcolm Baldrige criteria.

To obtain an estimate of your Baldrige score:

1. Average the ratings for approach, deployment, and/or results for each score card.

2. Sum the scores of all the cards.

3. Multiply the sum in step 2 by 10 to obtain an estimated Baldrige score.

| Senior executive personal leadership/involvement with customers and quality | | | | | | | | | |
|---|---|---|---|---|---|---|---|---|---|
| 1 | 2 | 3 | 4 | 5 | 6 | 7 | 8 | 9 | 9.5 |
| Good manager | | | Teams roles understood | | Good cross-functional teamwork/participation<br>Sets aggressive goals that encourage excellence | | | Role model<br>Establishes new and innovative initiatives<br>Leadership improvement process in place | | **A** |
| Little involvement<br>Not active<br>Not visible<br>Reacts to situations<br>Minimal public involvement | | | Involved<br>Communicates well up and down the chain<br>Reviews progress<br>Some public involvement | | Good customer focus<br>Plans and reviews<br>Reinforces and coaches<br>Active public involvement | | | Inspires the team<br>Has methods to listen and seek ideas<br>Customer partnership<br>Leadership in public involvement | | **D** |
| Results acceptable | | | Performs to expectations | | Exceeds expectations | | | Leadership results | | **R** |

Strengths:_____    Areas to Focus: _____

_____    _____

_____    _____

Figure A.2   Malcolm Baldrige score card: Leadership.

| Use of data and information (including benchmarking) to drive decisions | | | | | | | | |
|---|---|---|---|---|---|---|---|---|
| 1 | 2 | 3 | 4 | 5 | 6 | 7 | 7.5 | |
| Mostly experiential | | Data sources available and supported by need | | Clearly defined criteria Data used for planning and deployment | | Wide scope and source of data—bench-marked Information improvement process in place | | A |
| Trends lacking | | Reliable and accessible | | Information used regularly Benchmarks available Analysis tools used | | Wide use of analytical tools Historical and future analysis | | D |
| Not actionable data | | Some regular trends | | Actionable information | | Actionable/predictable results | | R |

Strengths:_____    Areas to Focus: _____

**Figure A.3**  Malcolm Baldrige score card: Information.

| How key quality requirements are integrated in the business plan | | | | | |
|---|---|---|---|---|---|
| 1 | 2 | 3 | 4 | 5 | 6 |
| Plans developed within the organization Plan based on history | Plan takes into account other organizations Plan identifies objectives | Plan has cross-functional commitment and involvement Considers industry and market dynamics | | All stakeholders share in planning Considers alternative scenarios Process in place to evaluate and improve | A |
| Little assessment of risk | Plan assesses and calibrates risk | Plan has succinct goals and objectives Plan has short- and long-term considerations | | Plan has succinct goals and objectives and a management system Tactical and strategic plans are integrated | D |

Strengths:_____    Areas to Focus: _____

**Figure A.4**  Malcolm Baldrige score card: Strategic quality planning.

| How the workforce is enabled to develop its full potential to achieve goal(s) | | | | | | | | | | | | | | | |
|---|---|---|---|---|---|---|---|---|---|---|---|---|---|---|---|
| 1 | 2 | 3 | 4 | 5 | 6 | 7 | 8 | 9 | 10 | 11 | 12 | 13 | 14 | 15 | |
| People considered in plans<br>Training requirements considered | | | | People participate in formation of plans<br>Training supports objectives | | | | People goals are set by employee group<br>Training includes development<br>Diversity is considered | | | | Indicators in place to assess health of organization<br>New ways to create cooperation and involvement<br>Systematic H/R improvement process | | | **A** |
| All people assigned tasks | | | | People understand their role and are enabled | | | | Cross-functional team-work activities<br>Environment for idea generation from people | | | | Developmental actions support long-term goals<br>Regular management process exists to monitor employee well-being by groups | | | **D** |
| Morale is average<br>Little evidence of team-work | | | | Morale > average<br>Low turnover, safe environment<br>Some teamwork | | | | High morale<br>Turnover,<br>   safety > average<br>Formal team structure | | | | Leadership morale<br>Recognition and in-volvement indicators | | | **R** |

Strengths:_____    Areas to Focus: _____

_____    _____

**Figure A.5**   Malcolm Baldrige score card: Human resource development and management.

| Systematic processes the company uses to improve operational performance. | | | | | | | | | | | | | |
|---|---|---|---|---|---|---|---|---|---|---|---|---|---|
| 1 | 2 | 3 | 4 | 5 | 6 | 7 | 8 | 9 | 10 | 11 | 12 | 13 | 14 | |
| Considers customer input<br>Documentation exists on the process | | | | Customer/supplier input required<br>Process formally documented | | | | Process is benchmarked<br>Process extends cross-functionally<br>Process contains closed-loop feedback system | | | Process management system is in use<br>Process goals for efficiency and effectiveness are set | | | **A** |
| People's roles not understood well | | | | People's roles defined | | | | People understand internal and external customers | | | Support services and suppliers are involved<br>Leadership bench-marked | | | **D** |
| Process produces vary-ing results | | | | Process produces con-sistent results | | | | Process produces pre-dictable results<br>Process has effective-ness measures | | | Predictable results with improved performance<br>Leads to cycle-time improvement | | | **R** |

Strengths:_____    Areas to Focus: _____

_____    _____

**Figure A.6**   Malcolm Baldrige score card: Management of process quality.

| Company's quality levels and improvement trends | | | | | | | | | | | | | | | | | | |
|---|---|---|---|---|---|---|---|---|---|---|---|---|---|---|---|---|---|---|
| 1 | 2 | 3 | 4 | 5 | 6 | 7 | 8 | 9 | 10 | 11 | 12 | 13 | 14 | 15 | 16 | 17 | 18 | |

| Measurement exists<br>Lacking trends<br>Limited scope<br>Not consistent | Measures show<br>  improved results<br>Trends<br>Product/service scope<br>Importance identified | Measures benchmarked<br>  against industry<br>Trends and goals<br>Product, service, sup-<br>  port scope<br>Criteria for selection<br>  and priority identified | Measures benchmarked<br>  against best practice<br>Trends, goals, and<br>  reduced variability<br>Provides customer value<br>Includes organizations<br>  outside your own,<br>  including suppliers | **A** |
|---|---|---|---|---|

Strengths:_____     Areas to Focus: _____
_____     _____
_____     _____

**Figure A.7**   Malcolm Baldrige score card: Quality and operational results.

**Figure A.8**   Malcolm Baldrige score card: Customer focus and satisfaction.

| Company's understanding of customer needs | | | |
|---|---|---|---|
| 1 | 2 | 3 | 4 |
| Narrow customer defin-<br>  ition<br>Current customer focus<br>  only | Current customer plus<br>  potential customer<br>  focus | All customer groups<br>  defined<br>Future customer needs<br>  identified | Considers industry/<br>  environmental factors<br>Considers new market<br>  potential and/or<br>  growth in existing<br>  markets | **A** |
| Customer needs not<br>  collected | Customer needs<br>  collected | Customer needs col-<br>  lected and analyzed<br>  regularly | Customer needs col-<br>  lected/analyzed/<br>  correlated with other<br>  indicators | **D** |

| Company's relationship with the customer | | | | | | | |
|---|---|---|---|---|---|---|---|
| 1 | 2 | 3 | 4 | 5 | 6 | 7 | 8 |
| No employee-customer<br>  contact standards<br>No service standards | Customer-employee<br>  contact standards<br>  defined<br>Service standards<br>  defined | Employee standards<br>  agreed to by<br>  customers<br>Service standards<br>  agreed to by<br>  customers | Standards reflect indus-<br>  try leadership<br>Partnership of mutual<br>  success with customer | **A** |
| As required response<br>Little follow-up<br>Standard commitment | Based on importance<br>Follow-up as required<br>Commitments better<br>  than competition | Regular contact to build<br>  customer relationship<br>Systematic follow-up<br>Leadership commit-<br>  ments | Actionable follow-up<br>  with improvement to<br>  customer and process<br>Service above/beyond | **D** |

*(Continued)*

| Company's methods for determining customer satisfaction | | | | | | | | | | | | | | | | | | |
|---|---|---|---|---|---|---|---|---|---|---|---|---|---|---|---|---|---|---|
| 1 | 2 | 3 | 4 | 5 | 6 | 7 | 8 | 9 | 10 | 11 | 12 | 13 | 14 | 15 | 16 | 17 | 18 | |
| No competitive data Little trend information | | | | | Systematic customer satisfaction process | | | | | Key information by important groupings Comparisons bench-marked | | | | Broad customer relationship indicators Correlated to other key customer information | | | | **A** |
| Not regularly assessed | | | | | Regular assessment of results and progress | | | | | Regular assessment with follow-up actions | | | | Regular assessment and follow-up results tied to planning system | | | | **D** |
| Results minimal and dated | | | | | Results and trends, no comparisons | | | | | Results reflect improvement trends | | | | Positive trends, with actionable results used for improvement | | | | **R** |

Strengths:_____     Areas to Focus: _____

_____     _____

_____     _____

_____     _____

_____     _____

_____     _____

**Figure A.8** *(Continued)*

## Suggested Readings

Brown, M. G. (1991) *Baldrige Award Winning Quality: How to Interpret the Malcolm Baldrige Award Criteria.* Milwaukee, WI: ASQC Quality Press.

Garvin, D. A. (1991) "How the Baldrige Award Really Works," *Harvard Business Review,* 69(6): 80–93.

Garvin, D. A. (1992) "Does the Baldrige Award Really Work?" *Harvard Business Review,* 70(1): 126–147.

Jones, C. (1991) *Applied Software Measurement: Assuring Productivity and Quality.* New York: McGraw-Hill.

Olson, T. G., Humphrey, W. S., and Kitson, D. H. (1989) *Conducting SEI-Assissted Software Process Assessments,* Software Engineering Institute, CMU/SEI-89-TR-7, DTIC no. ADA219065.

Steeples, M. M. (1993) *The Corporate Guide to the Malcolm Baldrige National Quality Award,* rev. ed. Milwaukee, WI: ASQC Quality Press.

For a free copy of the latest official Malcolm Baldrige Award criteria, contact:

Malcolm Baldrige National Quality Award
National Institute of Standards & Technology
Route 270 and Quince Orchard Road
Administration Building, Room A537
Gaithersburg, MD 20899
(301) 975-2036

For more information about software quality assessments in general, contact:

The I.Q. Company
P.O. Box 554
Santa Cruz, CA 95061-0554

For more information about the Baldrige Score Cards, contact:

Roy Bauer, Founding Partner
Competitive Dominance Strategies
2524 25th Street Northwest
Rochester, MN 55901
(507) 282-5277

# Index

## ABOUT THE AUTHORS

CRAIG A. KAPLAN, formerly a scientist at IBM Santa Teresa Lab, San Jose, California, is the founder of I.Q. Corporation, an education and consulting firm focusing on information technology. He received a B.A. degree in psychology and computer science from the University of California, Santa Cruz, and M.S. and Ph.D. degrees from Carnegie-Mellon University. Kaplan has taught at the University of California, and has written numerous technical papers, articles, and patents. Current projects include developing quality-related software and workshops for Fortune 500 client companies.

RALPH FUJIO CLARK is a program manager with IBM Client/Server Computing Strategy Group. He has served as the senior manager for the Center for Software Excellence at IBM Santa Teresa Lab in San Jose, California, where he led the laboratory's quality initiatives. Clark has wide-ranging experience as an engineer, planner, and strategist. He received a B.S. degree in industrial engineering from Northwestern University and an M.S. degree in operations research from the University of Michigan, Clark has published nine technical reports and has served on the board of directors for the Council for Continuous Improvement in San Jose, California.

VICTOR TANG is director of strategy for client/server computing at IBM, Somers, New York. He received a B.S. degree in electrical engineering and an M.S. degree in mathematics from Purdue University, as well as an M.B.A. from Columbia a University. He has also served as director of strategy and technology at IBM Rochester, director of market analysis at IBM corporate headquarters, and director of planning and quality at IBM Santa Teresa Lab. He has published numerous papers and technical reports and has patents for four inventions. He is also coauthor of *The Silverlake Project*, a book about organizational transformation and general management. He has served as advisor to the United Nations in economic development.

## DISK WARRANTY

This software is protected by both the United States copyright law and international copyright treaty provision. You must treat this software just like a book, except that you may copy it into a computer to be used and you may make archival copies of the software for the sole purpose of backing up our software and protecting your investment from loss.

By saying, "just like a book," McGraw-Hill means, for example, that this software may be used by any number of people and may be freely moved from one computer location to another, so long as there is no possibility of its being used at one location or on one computer while it is being used at another. Just as a book cannot be read by two different people in two different places at the same time, neither can the software be used by two different people in two different places at the same time (unless, of course, McGraw-Hill's copyright is being violated).

## LIMITED WARRANTY

McGraw-Hill warrants the physical diskette(s) enclosed herein to be free of defects in materials and workmanship for a period of sixty days from the purchase date. If McGraw-Hill receives written notification within the warranty period of defects in materials or workmanship, and such notification is determined by McGraw-Hill to be correct, McGraw-Hill will replace the defective diskette(s). Send request to:

Customer Service
TAB/McGraw-Hill
13311 Monterey Avenue
Blue Ridge Summit, PA 17294-0850

The entire and exclusive liability and remedy for breach of this Limited Warranty shall be limited to replacement of defective diskette(s) and shall not include or extend to any claim for or right to cover any other damages, including but not limited to loss of profit, data, or use of the software, or special, incidental, or consequential damages or other similar claims, even if McGraw-Hill has been specifically advised to the possibility of such damages. In no event will McGraw-Hill's liability for any damages to you or any other person ever exceed the lower of suggested list price or actual price paid for the license to use the software, regardless of any form of the claim.

McGRAW-HILL, INC. SPECIFICALLY DISCLAIMS ALL OTHER WARRANTY, EXPRESS OR IMPLIED, INCLUDING BUT NOT LIMITED TO, ANY IMPLIED WARRANTY OR MERCHANTABILITY OR FITNESS FOR A PARTICULAR PURPOSE. Specifically, McGraw-Hill makes no representation or warranty that the software is fit for any particular purpose and any implied warranty of merchantability is limited to the sixty-day duration of the Limited Warranty covering the physical diskette(s) only (and not the software) and is otherwise expressly and specifically disclaimed.

This limited Warranty gives you specific legal rights; you may have others which may vary from state to state. Some states do not allow the exclusion of incidental or consequential damages, or the limitation on how long an implied warranty lasts, so some of the above may not apply to you.